Insurgency and Terrorism in India and Pakistan

INSURGENCY AND TERRORISM IN INDIA AND PAKISTAN

Md. Elyas

MD Publications Pvt Ltd
New Delhi

Published by
MD Publications Pvt Ltd
"MD House", 11, Darya Ganj
New Delhi-110002
Tel. : +91-11-41563325, 41562846
E-mail : contact@mdppl.com
Website : www.mdppl.com

ISBN: 978-81-7533-117-4

PRICE: Rs. 995.00

Published and Printed by **MD Publications Pvt Ltd** at Times Press, 910, Jatwara Street, Darya Ganj, New Delhi.

Contents

PREFACE

An insurgency, or insurrection, is an armed uprising, or revolt against an established civil or political authority. Persons engaging in insurgency are called insurgents, and typically engage in regular or guerrilla combat against the armed forces of the established regime, or conduct sabotage and harassment in the land in order to undermine the government's position as leader.

Insurgent tactics and strategies vary widely, as well as the type of targets insurgents attack. Raids are amongst the most common actions taken by insurgents in a dominated state or province. In addition, insurgents establish ties with other outlaws and double agents to further their goals. Some militants can also be sponsored by competing or enemy state governments. Some elements of an insurgency may use bombs, kidnappings, hostage-taking, hijackings, shootings and other terrorist techniques to target the establishment's power structure and other facilities, often with little regard for civilian casualties or collateral damage. Other elements may restrict their attacks to military objectives and avoid the targeting of civilians. Many times, insurgent groups conduct violent attacks but do not reveal the group's identity or leader. Usually, an individual with iconic and symbolic status throughout the movement becomes its principal leader against the governmental authority. Leaders of differing background from the insurgency movement itself may, at times, take over an insurgency.

Insurgents use a variety of asymmetrical warfare tactics, usually because of the insurgents force's capabilities are unequal to the authority's capabilities. Insurgents' attacks against the authority may take the form of attacks on supply trains and security forces using hidden explosives. These explosive devices, at times made from military-grade materials, are concealed or camouflaged along transport routes and detonated when supply transports or security forces come within distance. Insurgents frequently launch ambushes on military targets, with automatic and antitank weapons. Unarmored targets are commonly targeted. Such attacks are usually broken off before support or reinforcements can be called in.

Insurgency need not require the targeting of non-combatants, although many insurgencies expand the accepted legal definition of combatants to include police and security personnel in addition to the military. Terrorists do not discriminate between combatants and non-combatants, or if they do, they broaden the category of "combatants" so much as to render it meaningless. Defining all members of a nation or ethnic group, plus any citizen of any nation that supports that nation as "combatants" is simply a justification for frightfulness. This book is covering major insurgence, terrorism and Great leaders which become the victims of insurgency. Recently one of the great leaders from Pakistan Benazir Bhutto has assassinated by insurgents or terrorists. This book is beneficial for those dealing with International Politics, Current Affairs and Women Leaders.

Thanks to Mr. Pranav Gupta of **MD Publications Pvt Ltd**, New Delhi, who supported me fully for completing this book.

MD. ELYAS

1

INSURGENCY: DEFINITION AND MEANING

Introduction

American involvement in Vietnam, and its search for a counterinsurgency doctrine, attention must be given to a definition of insurgency. Without a clear understanding of insurgency there is little chance that it can be countered, or more precisely, defeated. With an accurate definition of insurgency in hand, it will hopefully be clear that defeating an insurgency may not always be the appropriate goal, but that becoming the insurgency might be. The desire is to be able to explain the process and existence of insurgency, not simply in political terms, but both as a *method* and as a *type* of war. Insurgency can therefore better be represented as a strategic tool for policymaking. Against this definition and understanding it will be possible to more accurately place irregular warfare events in the American military past and more clearly explore American military thinking in Vietnam.

Numerous writings about irregular warfare found their way into print after 1945, both of an official government nature and of a less formal journalistic nature. When calls for a formal, unconventional war doctrine echoed throughout the country at the beginning of the 1960s, U.S. military leaders, politicians, and academics alike responded with a flurry of effort. These existing studies representing insurgency warfare, however, look primarily at the political and social consequences and do not accurately explain insurgency as a separate facet in war making or as a separate strategic thought. Under these terms, any definition of insurgency war must appear incomplete. Typically the term *insurgency* is intertwined and often confused with other terms. A list of the more prominent transpositions would include the following: *subversion, coup d'etat, terrorism, guerrilla war, revolution,* and even *civil war.* In any number of works related to these subjects, the word *insurgency* might be used as a substitute. It is often alluded to without explanation, or provided as a means to explain individuals that engage in such activities (i.e., *insurgents*). That all of these terms invoke different concepts is clear from the most elementary definitions found in political-military doctrine. Just why the term *insurgency* is blended together with others in so many separate works is not fully understood. It is certain, however, that this careless usage represents a lack of respect for the term's roots.

An English translation of the Latin word *insurgere,* occurred as early as 1765. Many authors found uses for the term in writings ranging from poetry to psychological analysis. Insurgency came to be commonly recognized as having to do with "internal political revolution" perpetrated by a certain group publicly acknowledged as being "nonbelligerent." Along similar lines two centuries later, Jack C. Piano states that an insurgency is "a revolt against an established government not reaching the proportions of a full-scale revolution. Under international law, an insurgency is a rebellion not recognized as a belligerency or civil war." Going further, Roger Scruton notes that *insurgency* is a term used in international law that describes an uprising against a constituted government that falls short of revolution, rebellion, or civil war.

Through many years of continuous refinement and redefinition on the subject of unconventional war, insurgency is still loosely represented as participation in the larger scope of internal political revolution. In many respects, the same could be said for such terms as *guerrilla war, subversion, rebellion,* and *civil war.* In the end, it would appear that all of these terms simply merge with each other, having no significant individual qualities. To appreciate the confusion that surrounds the term *insurgency,* it might be helpful to cite from an array of recent examples.

Official U.S. Army doctrine from the early 1960s best typifies the broad catch-all that the term *insurgency* came to be. One particular manual published by the Army Special Warfare School was intended to train Special Forces advisors en route to Vietnam. Entitled the *Counter-insurgency Planning Guide,* and published in 1963, this manual acted principally as a tactical overview for advisors who needed help in producing operations orders and reports in a variety of unconventional formats not commonly dealt with in previous military experiences. However, the guide contains no definition of insurgency war, implying that the military was not in any hurry to revise its then current understanding of the term outside conventional force application. That the most current military definition is almost no different indicates that perhaps little emphasis has been placed on producing a valid understanding of insurgency. Though the military was apparently void of contention over the issue of insurgency during that critical period, a large international community that was indeed concerned produced a large plethora of works.

A work written in 1964 by David Galula, entitled *Counter-Insurgency Warfare,* received much attention by an American government anxious to understand its then current plight in Southeast Asia. It appeared to be one of the first Western works to establish a hierarchy that attempted to explain insurgency as a separate concept, a part of political revolution and war. Galula lists three stages to this hierarchy: revolution, plot (coup d'etat), and insurgency. These terms embody the elements of "revolutionary war," which Galula explains as an "explosive upheaval, " an accident which might better be explained after the fact. All that can really be ascertained in the early stages of an insurgency is that a revolutionary situation exists. "On the other hand," Galula points out, an insurgency is a protracted struggle conducted methodically, step by step, in order to attain specific intermediate objectives leading finally to the overthrow of the existing order. To be sure, it can no more be predicted than a revolution; in fact, its beginnings are so vague that to determine exactly when an insurgency starts is a difficult legal, political, and historical problem. An insurgency is usually slow to develop and is not an accident, for in an insurgency leaders appear and then the masses are made to move.

Some may take exception with Galula's explanation of the hierarchy, and to some degree with the examples he gives of insurgency war (certainly the experiences in China and Greece after World War II have been labeled everything from revolution to civil war). But, to Galula, "insurgency is civil war." It is never quite clear whether he means that insurgency replaces the notion of civil war, or if he believes that insurgency is a part of a growing discontent that leads to civil war. Although Galula explains in great detail the role of the counterinsurgent against a successful insurgency, he never expands upon the definition of insurgency. Therefore, the reader is left to speculate on just how insurgency differs from a protracted revolutionary war, or, for that matter, how rebellion differs from revolution. Galula, in the end, makes no real distinction between insurgency war and these other concepts, apparently using it in place of the phrase *revolutionary war*.

In 1967, Julian Paget subscribed more closely to the Latin derivative of *insurgency* in his book, *Counter-Insurgency Operations,* stating simply that insurgency describes a kind of armed rebellion against a government. Here, the "rebels have the support or acquiescence of a substantial part of the populace; the methods that they adopt to achieve their aim of overthrowing the Government may include guerrilla warfare, but insurgents may equally well resort to civil disobedience, sabotage or terrorist tactics."

Even ideas that referred to a kind of *pure insurgency* made their way into formal definition. In a work entirely devoted to the subject, Andrew Scott and his coauthors write:

> *The term insurgency in this volume refers to efforts to obtain political goals by an organized and primarily indigenous group (or groups) using protracted, irregular warfare and allied political techniques. This definition excludes sudden coups, short-lived outbreaks of violence, or invasion by non-indigenous guerrilla forces.*

Accordingly, a distinction is drawn between insurgency and irregular warfare. "The term irregular warfare refers only to military activities... insurgency is irregular warfare plus politics."

In their discussion, Scott and his coauthors develop the idea of insurgency around two principal themes: "protracted war strategy" and "indigenous movements"two facets they say are "unexplainable." There is no real way, they assert, of determining just when a conflict becomes protracted, and, in turn, they indicate no specific way to determine how great a degree of outside intervention is compatible with a group being considered primarily indigenous. Yet according to the authors, without these two ingredients, there can be no insurgency. Insurgency is thus reduced to a revolutionary political and social "phenomena."

Prior to the development of the U.S. Army's Low-Intensity Conflict (LIC) Doctrine of the early 1980s, Brigadier Frank Kitson of the British military had written a unique tactical exposition on insurgency war in 1971 entitled *Low Intensity Operations*. He breaks insurgency into two distinct parts. The first part represents pure tactics and is called "The Handling of Information." The second part, entitled "Direction, Units and Equipment, " explains the logistical details needed for effectively countering an insurgency. Although no singular definition is provided for insurgency, Kitson acknowledges that many of his ideas stem from the tactical precepts yielded by Mao Tse-tung.

According to Kitson, as a final phase in the overall scope of revolutionary guerrilla war, armed insurgents come out into the open and fight the forces of the government by conventional methods, but in the earliest stages the war is fought by people who strike at a time and place of their own choosing and then disappear. Sometimes their disappearance is achieved by the physical process of movement into an area of thick cover such as a jungle, and at other times by merging into the population.

Kitson's treatment of the tactical aspects is representative of a time when the term *insurgency* was accepted as a kind of phenomenon, shrouded from Western strategists. These strategists were criticized for operating with fixed beliefs about conventional warfare, and, in the two decades following World War II, were sent scrambling to make sense of this new kind of war for the "atomic age." Ever since the Truman Doctrine, and the idea that "limited war" was not only feasible but necessary, the United States has searched for ways to design just such a limited strategic response to global security concerns.

However, by the mid-1950s the idea of overt military response had not met with great success, particularly on the Asian mainland. The American-led defense of Korea ended in stalemate, and the French debacle at Dien Bien Phu was proof that large conventional military actions were far too costly in men and materiel for the proposed gains. It was believed that for global strategy to succeed in turning away the communist revolutionary tide in Asia, the response needed to be more subtle, more covert, and more focused on the reasons for such apparent sweeping successes by Third World communist nations.

Mao Tse-tung was seen as one who had mastered the phenomenon called insurgency. His rise to power, his establishment of a communist China, and the revolutionary political influence he maintained throughout Asia appeared as testimony. As well, the phenomena of insurgency was seen to be spreading regionally: to Laos, Cambodia, Thailand, Malaya, the Philippines, and Vietnam. It was also spreading globally: to Algeria, Greece, Angola, and Cuba.

Samuel B. Griffith, in the early 1960s, provided the first truly significant Western interpretation of works by the ancient Chinese military and political philosopher Sun Tzu. Mao spoke of, and alluded to, Sun Tzu on numerous occasions throughout his writings. For many strategists and scholars, the study of works like Sun Tzu's was viewed as vital in helping to solve the puzzle of communist uprisings and subversive political successes throughout Asia.

When Mao was discovered, in the early 1960s, to be the preeminent architect of guerrilla strategy, few wanted to see beyond his ambiguous terminology and communist dogma. Such phrases as "controlled terror," "winning over the hearts and minds," and "people's war" were relatively new to modern war vocabulary and caught the imagination of most military and political scholars. It is key to recognize that the majority of those writing on insurgency war during that period, particularly those trying to represent both political and military experiences, pay unabashed homage to Mao Tse-tung by adopting much of his terminology in their own works.

Indeed, Mao's discussions about revolutionary guerrilla war are believed by many to be critical to understanding Western misperceptions about insurgency warfare. However, Mao's works represent to a large and terribly narrow extent, the terminology of the "people's war," not a more eclectic understanding of insurgency. The varying degrees of political indoctrination embodied in all of his writings make it difficult to draw on the underlying strategic value. Therefore, while an explanation of revolutionary guerrilla war using Mao's terminology may be acceptable, using the same terminology to explain the strategic design of insurgency, particularly in its larger context, is not. Douglas Pike refers to several aspects about the Vietnam war which support Mao's ideas of revolutionary guerrilla war. In his important book on the Viet Cong, Pike develops the concept that revolutionary guerrilla war is a unique form of warfare, not to be confused with older concepts such as irregular war, civil war, revolutionary war, rebellion, partisan activity, and so on. He states:

> *Revolutionary guerrilla warfare as practiced in Vietnam was a way of life. Its aim was to establish a totally new social order, thus differing from insurgencies whose objective is either statehood or change of government. It was an important product, revolution from the outside; its stock in trade, the grievance, was often artificially created; its goal of liberation, a deception.*

Thus, it would appear that ideas about guerrilla war embrace a number of factors associated with revolution, and Pike's definition clearly attempts to bridge a gap between old and modern concepts about guerrilla war. Pike, combining these terms in Maoist fashion, is representing what he calls "acknowledged strategy, " superb as an "antidote to modern arms and in harmony with the world's temper, efficiently harnessing social forces already loosened." In answering questions about "limited war" strategy, Pike seeks to divide insurgency into two categories: (1) The political change which is still insurgency and (2) the social upheaval Mao purported to be "revolutionary guerrilla war."

But even when using the term in its most ambiguous sense, one must still ask the question: Does an insurgency have the charismatic power, in the end, to change the social order of things after an established government has fallen? Certainly it does, because that is the fundamental nature of political revolution. By taking this then to extremes, one realizes that if such governments are to fall to insurgent forces, it is because the support and will of the population allows such change to take place, in fact helps it along. Without the support of the people there is no revolutionary intent, therefore no insurgency. Insurgency can, in and of itself, be social upheaval, and can be sponsored internally, externally, or both simultaneously.

It is not so far-fetched to see almost complete social change following quickly on the heels of the defeat of an existing authoritarian regime by an insurgency. Previous examples of insurgency support this claim. An insurgency, even considered in the sense of Pike's "revolutionary guerrilla war," has the capability of turning into a revolution, a civil war, or multiple insurgencies. Careful analysis of sources predating Pike's work that appear allied to his reasoning reveals little which would lead to a dismissal of insurgency as a practical means to prosecute social, as well as authoritarian change. Indeed, insurgencies are grand deceptions, publicly declaring on one hand to be a nonbelligerent movement, while gaining power that could be used to perpetrate political revolution on the other.

In a more concise manner, but similarly to Pike, Chalmers Johnson also addresses the subject of revolutionary guerrilla war:

> *Guerrilla warfare is a form of warfare in the technical sense in which all war involves the use of armed men to annihilate the men and arms of an enemy. The initiation of a revolutionary guerrilla war thus requires that an armed band of men take to the field and launch attacks against a regime's forces.*

The essence of guerrilla strategy is to entrap the status quo forces in the swamp of an overwhelmingly hostile population, and to organize this population to serve a coherent, long-range program of military conquest in which the defending force's strengths are turned to weaknesses.

In similar fashion, Sam Sarkesian defines revolutionary guerrilla warfare as "the forcible attempt by a politically organized group to gain control or change the structure and/or policies of the government, using unconventional warfare integrated with political and social mobilization, resting on the premise that the people are both the targets and the actors."

In both Johnson's and Sarkesian's definitions we see an attempt to correlate the concepts of insurgency and revolutionary guerrilla war. The ideas of a "revolutionary guerrilla war, " and a "people's revolutionary war" cause immediate confusion because of the terms themselves. While revolution may be the end strategic value, guerrilla war is the tactical force that carries the insurgency forth amongst the people. This implies that revolutionary upheaval must be the result of any insurgency. If, however, an insurgency may also exist simply to acquire political recognition within the predominant political and social framework, then its intent would not necessarily be political or social revolution. The phrase "people's revolutionary war" implies revolution from the outset of subversive activity. While an insurgency may eventually focus on political and social revolution, it might in the beginning only focus on political and social inclusion.

That Sarkesian, Johnson, and Pike are all students of Mao Tsetung's works about revolutionary guerrilla war is obvious, as it is with many of those quoted in our preceding examples. But there is no mysticism to Maoist guerrilla philosophy. As W.W. Rostow points out: "It is historically inaccurate and psychologically dangerous to think that created the strategy and tactics of guerrilla war. Guerrilla warfare is not a form of military and psychological magic created by the Communists." It becomes obvious after reviewing works by Mao Tsetung, as well as various secondary sources which analyze doctrinal virtues based on Mao's writings, that he only partially addresses the specific concept of insurgency.

As an antidote to the various misconceptions he saw developing in the mid-1960s, Sir Robert Grainger Ker Thompson observes that, in spite of their "grandiloquent and misleading titles," an insurgency is not a people's revolutionary war. Citing government intelligence figures, Thompson indicates that by 1965 the number of insurgents and their supporters active in South Vietnam never exceeded 1 percent of the total population. With this in mind, he concludes that the insurgency was not qualified to be a people's revolutionary war, but only a "revolutionary form of warfare designed to enable a very small ruthless minority to gain control over the people."

Robert Thompson's practical views about insurgency warfare, particularly from that period, remain the most definitive. Refreshingly, Thompson refrains from mixing terminology, and, although he does not provide a specific definition of insurgency war, his illustrations of insurgency tendencies and peculiarities better explain an important strategic concept that otherwise appears useless.

A first objective must then be to reach a more precise understanding of insurgency without confusing terminology. From this, and in a modern spirit of *insurgere,* comes a working definition and explanation of insurgency war:

> Insurgency *is a political-military conflict waged against a specific faction(s), implementing irregular military actions in support of a unified political outcome, short of revolution and civil war.*

While regular military forces may be employed, irregular operations rooted in political subversion, selective terrorism, and guerrilla operations, play an integral, if not primary, role in the outcome. Political subversion, selective terrorism, and guerrilla operations are then tactics that, when combined, may or may not represent an insurgency.

Insurgency is a strategic political development that implements these tactics as a means to sustain itself until further development can occur. Consequently, an insurgency, as a *type* of war, may lead to and be part of a large conventional conflict, revolution, or civil war. Insurgency, as a *method* of war, implies the attempt to use violence and irregular forms of warfare against a particular faction(s) for the express purpose of political-military gain, which may later lead to inclusion with, or the overthrow of, existing regimes.

The object of insurgency is to force political-social upheaval, in an organized fashion, for the express purpose of validating a cause, and therefore justifying its violent means. Insurgencies do not have the capacity to be a revolution or a civil war, but with staying power and continued support can ignite either.

Therefore, an insurgency is neither revolution nor civil war. As well, there are three major elements identified as tools used in an insurgency: *political subversion, selective terrorism,* and *guerrilla operations*. Any other aspect, political or military, that might be attributed to an insurgency will likely fall under one of these three major tactical elements.

Thompson has stated with consistency that the first phase of an insurgency always begins with subversive activity. He goes so far as to state that "insurgency is a measure both of the success and of the failure of subversion." If the subversion is successful enough to continue the insurgency, but not successful enough to achieve the objective by subversion alone, then the insurgency moves to a second phase: open insurgency or the armed struggle. The second phase consists of the use of guerrilla operations combined with terrorist activities and will typically result in a protracted struggle.

When Thompson spoke about insurgency, he spoke directly about communist insurgency, and thus communist subversion. From his experiences in both war and politics, in Malaya and in Vietnam, one might believe that he was led to this understanding for obvious reasons. And possibly, not unlike many others of the time, Thompson believed that insurgency was a unique tool of the communists, and therefore fashioned to a unique communist design. Many analysts who have since pulled ideas from Thompson have also pulled from him this peculiar error.

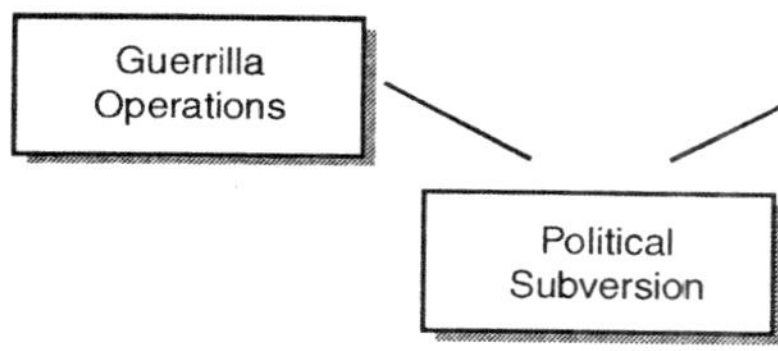

Figure 1.1. Insurgency Model of Tactical Elements.

However, the working definition provided here does not perceive insurgency as being of any particular origin nor specifically fashioned out of any political dogma. Insurgency possesses certain universal qualities that set it apart as a separate strategic concept from revolution and civil war. While revolution is non-indigenous and civil war is indigenous, insurgencies can be either.

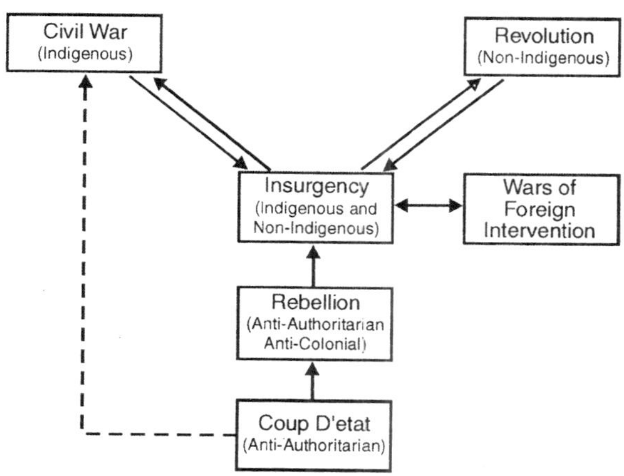

Figure 1.2. Conflict Model.

Typology of Insurgency

The political subversion, selective terrorism, and guerrilla operations are all key elements in an insurgency, political subversion is unquestionably the one element that must exist for the other two elements to have any unified effect. As well, the extent of the political organization of the subversives will likely predict how competent and effective the entire insurgency will turn out to be. The heart of an insurgency is thus the political capability of the subversives, the quality of their organization, and the extent of the roots they set down. To establish a valid insurgency, the subversive organization must acquire the necessary resources and support from both internal and external factions. Just how well this support is managed will determine whether a second phase will be required, or is even possible.

Political subversion attempts to accomplish four specific things: first, to build and test the political infrastructure needed to wage a successful insurgency; second, to generate political clout both internally and externally; third, to support a second phase of open insurgency; and fourth, if it intends to go beyond insurgency war, to plan for government after revolution or civil war is achieved. Those insurgencies resulting in either revolution or civil war represent some of the most skilled and resourceful political organizations. These groups will not appear fanatical in their actions, only ardent in their resolve. While such intent seems "revolutionary" to outsiders, it is purely "evolutionary" to the insurgent. It is this outlook which provide the potential for success, and is the catalyst for all growth.

The crossover to violence is accomplished during the early stages of an insurgency by the use of terrorism. This is the heavy-handed persuasion used by the political subversives as a means of drawing closer attention to their cause; and, when truly selective, it is capable of removing strategic targets that prove to be an obstruction. Indiscriminate terrorism has never been the friend of an insurgent movement. But when implemented correctly and with precision, the results usually favor the subversive political body. Thompson indicates that even in a "preinsurgency" time of murder and terrorism, the "normal processes of law and order will fail to cope with the situation; the police are unable to effect arrests for lack of witnesses, or the crime itself may not even be reported." A strong history and willingness on the part of the subversives to perform vendetta and reprisal killings typically silences the majority of the public.

If the government is internally crippled or substantially unsupported and weak, the insurgency will not need to progress to the second phase. A government of this hobbled nature will succumb to insurgent pressure. It is important to note here that this still does not qualify the insurgency as revolution. While an insurgency may usurp authority if the government falls, assumption of responsibility may not have been the actual intent of the original subversion. The insurgents may get hold of governmental reins before they are actually willing or even capable of successfully governing. These subversives will usually weaken and fall to other factions. Knowing the difference between an actual "revolution" and a failed insurgency may be critical to the foreign policy intentions of an outside government interested in attaining stability in such a country or region. Such misinterpretation could easily lead to false recognition or a false application of force.

A potential merry-go-round of insurgencies can exist under such a state. It is probable that this kind of transfer of power, violent or otherwise, would appear to be a coup d'etat or internal rebellion. But because the subversive activity is seeking change from outside the existing government, it cannot be a coup d'etat. Because the insurgency is more highly organized and seeks long-term objectives through a protracted struggle, it cannot be considered an internal rebellion. But both a coup d'etat and a rebellion differ from an insurgency in a larger sense. While both forms of internal struggle are commonly trying to restore an earlier social and political order, an insurgency commonly seeks to transform power, preempting any attempt to restore old orders.

Revolution and civil war are other matters. Since the object of an insurgency is not necessarily the establishment of a new state the ousting of either external colonial factions or internal civil antagonists the attempt must then be for the subversives to strengthen their cause. This is done through the use of guerrilla operations in the second phase. During this period, selective terrorist activities may heighten, and political subversives will continue to expand their control in populated areas where support will strengthen guerrilla operations. Because the insurgents expect a protracted struggle, a careful search for *base areas* is undertaken.

Two types of base areas exist—one controlled by the guerrillas, the other by the political subversives. The first is the *jungle* base area which provides the guerrillas with sanctuary, supplies, and war materiel in essence, a logistics base for military support. The other base of support comes from the population and is controlled by the insurgent political organization and its terrorist arm. The purpose of these base areas is to sustain recruiting efforts and supply lines for the duration of the protracted struggle.

Insurgent political strength in the rural setting comes from the links maintained with organized *cells* previously established in the large cities and towns. While this *rural* form of operation may be more desirable, another form of insurgency may establish and maintain organized cells within the urban population center. This type of insurgent operation is seen less frequently because of the inherent dangers placed upon movement, concentration, and communication between the subversive cells. No insurgency can successfully grow beyond phase one if it remains solely within an urban environment.

Two specific functions are performed by the subversive insurgent cells. First, they must maintain a continual flow of propaganda, often supported by terrorist activity. This would typically include the assassination of formidable political figures who might turn elements in the population against the insurgency. A second function is to keep the guerrillas supplied with war materiel and technical support not available in the rural setting, and, perhaps most importantly, with intelligence information about government plans, movements, and strengths.

During the subversive phase, much of this planting of base areas is accomplished. Finding these insurgent base areas then becomes a game that the government forces feel obliged to play during the first phase. For the insurgents, success during a second phase depends on how harmoniously its guerrilla operations and its political organization work together. If thorough planning was done by the insurgents, the government may be in for an unwelcome protracted struggle.

The second phase, guerrilla operations, has two stages. During the initial stage the guerrilla units begin operating in conjunction with terrorist units, both in the rural and urban settings. Guerrilla operations in this first stage are diversionary and are employed in consort with terrorist actions in and around government army centers. Often the government confuses the actions of insurgent terrorist with these of guerrilla forces during this period.

When the guerrilla units begin operations on their own in the second stage, they direct their operations specifically at military targets of opportunity. This excludes activity that can be perpetrated by terrorist units, particularly assassinations and the bombing of civilian targets. The guerrilla forces at this second stage are usually engaged in the kind of warfare that they perform best tactics which include hit-and-run, search and destroy, and ambush patrols against government army units.

Strategy on the part of the insurgent guerrilla force becomes evident during this stage. Its intent to exploit the rural villages in a manner that allows them to encircle the cities, its supporters serving the singular purpose of "rendering an as yet undefeated army powerless to save the country." Growing loss of confidence about the government's will rises among the people. A destructive but ineffective military, a surge in inflation and economic disturbance, an overall inability to gain external assistance for internal problems, and an inability to provide capable future governing are all failures that the subversive insurgents hope the common people will begin to perceive as being irreversible within the current government.

Primary and Secondary Insurgency

During the later stage of guerrilla operations, the type of insurgency being conducted against the government can easily be identified. The insurgents must make the decision to follow either a *primary* or a *secondary* course of strategy. Primary insurgency seeks military victory by maintaining pressure through guerrilla operations but avoiding any major set-piece battle with government forces. The intent is to wear down government forces through a protracted conflict that relies upon isolated fights at the guerrillas' own choice of place and time. By keeping the initiative away from the government for an extended period, the hope is that demoralization will establish itself among government officials. With no feasible way in which to win a decisive victory, the government, it is expected, will negotiate a cease-fire with insurgent forces, accepting a "neutralist solution as a means of ending the war."

Secondary insurgency seeks victory by way of changing from isolated, or purely guerrilla operations, to what Mao Tse-tung refers to as a "war of movement." With government forces typically spread throughout the rural setting in a defensive posture, the insurgent forces are able to occupy and move freely among the villages, their direct line of support and communication with the political subversive element. All insurgent forces, spearheaded by guerrilla operations which then take on a conventional military restructuring, unite and concentrate the entire effort on one or a series of government targets. The shock effect, combined with thorough planning and military competence, is expected to send government forces reeling in a continuous state of defense, retreat, and then surrender. Unlike primary insurgency, a secondary strategy looks for the set-piece engagement with government forces, believing that a decisive, more conventional blow can achieve the desired success in a shorter period of time. However, this transition into secondary insurgency is not an easy or readily apparent move for the subversive strategist. Pinpointing the exact moment at which a subversive movement should progress into a secondary phase is perhaps the most difficult part of the transition. Choosing the wrong moment or being poorly prepared could bring disaster.

There are two specific reasons why an insurgent leadership would choose the secondary strategy. First, there may seem to be no other option to the insurgents, thus it would be a last-gasp effort to perhaps ignite the passions of the people to rise and overthrow the government. But this would be premature revolution, and few insurgencies, if any, win by this method. It is probably safe to say that complete revolution is not what the subversives planned for in the beginning, and failing to realize this limitation so late in the game is why disaster looms. Because there is nowhere else to go government forces having grown stronger and the insurgency weaker the inevitable turn is toward desperate strategy. This is a key example of how insurgencies literally self-destruct.

The other reason for choosing this secondary strategy is that it represents the next step in the evolution of the insurgent movement. The idea is that the insurgency grows stronger while its opponents grow weaker. Insurgent leaders find that their military units are in a position to level a decisive blow to government forces, and, with the popular base of support behind them, proceed quickly in that direction. Mao even warned of something called "guerrillaism," an overlong attachment to irregular methods. Successful insurgent leaders realize that undue delay in making that decisive blow can exhaust the popular base of support, therefore extending, unnecessarily, the guerrilla phase. But the opposite error seems historically more common, "as guerrillas succumb to the lure of uniforms, of heavy weapons, of being able to sleep at night, and of conventional, orderly battle."

The transition from an irregular to a regular method of fighting is extremely complicated for the insurgent leadership to make happen in a short period of time. This is one reason why insurgents must take great care in walking that fine line between "guerrillaism" and moving too quickly. But complications are lessened and time is shortened for the insurgents when guerrilla operations can be incorporated into an existing conventional force allied to their cause. This means that the involvement of a foreign military can have the effect of stabilizing a situation which may be out of the insurgents' control or turn the tide toward a favorable insurgent outcome. In relationship to our working definition, it is also why an insurgency can evolve into, or develop from, a larger conventional struggle. Such a struggle may or may not be part of the insurgent cause. Under such circumstances, the insurgent is often caught up in fighting a war it does not want. This is represented in the Conflict Model where insurgencies may coexist with wars of foreign intervention.

Insurgency versus Counterinsurgency

If it were always true that any government with the best intentions of the people in mind was sure to triumph over an insurgent movement, there would be no need to understand the differences between insurgency and countering insurgency. However, as Thompson points out, there are real problems with the very use of the term *counterinsurgency*.

Anyone having any responsibility for dealing with an insurgent movement must know his enemy and what that enemy is attempting to do at all stages. This does not mean that those responsible should be solely concerned with countering the enemy's moves. I dislike for this reason the very term "counter-insurgency." It implies that the insurgents have the initiative, and that it is the government's role merely to react and counter that initiative.

During the subversive phase, signs of an insurgency are not always recognizable to a government, and when problems become evident, the people may be slow to arouse, and government forces may react inappropriately. In this instance, the government runs the risk of either acting too soon appearing repressive because the subversion is little recognized or acting too late. Although much evidence about the subversion is apparent in a late reaction, the government is already in the second phase, or open insurgency of guerrilla war. The trick for any government, then, is to recognize an insurgency during the subversive phase, which will require the least of the military solutions.

In keeping with Thompson's spirit about "counter-insurgency," this study then recognizes that the best counter to any insurgency can only be another insurgency. Because the idea of countering anything conjures up reactionary views, it is best to dispense with the confusion of the term *counterinsurgency* altogether. For a government to maintain authority and thwart an insurgency, that government cannot be countering anything; rather, it must initiate nearly all the political and military moves during the confrontation. The government must be prepared to make the initial moves at a moment's notice. A shrewd, offensive posture must be attained or maintained at all times for the government authority to assume victory. Thus, for a government to stay in power and succeed against a subversive insurgency, it must actually wage a better insurgency than the political subversives themselves. Indeed, a government must possess the "long-term aim" or face the consequences of adopting "short-term ad hoc measures merely as reactions to insurgent initiative or with the limited aim of attempting to defeat the insurgents militarily in the guerrilla phase." Thompson relates five basic principles from which all government measures must evolve:

1. The government must have a clear political aim: to establish and maintain a free, independent and united country which is politically and economically stable and viable.
2. The government must function in accordance with the law.
3. The government must have an overall plan.
4. The government must give priority to defeating the political subversion, not the guerrillas.
5. In the guerrilla phase of an insurgency, a government must secure its base areas first.

There exists no better set of commandments for a government faced with waging an insurgency. As well, the same commandments could be intended for the subversive insurgents. Simply replace *government* with the term *subversive* and one has the same equation: (1) The subversives must have a clear political aim; (2) The subversives must function in accordance with the law (at least according to Mao); (3) The subversives must have an overall plan; (4) The subversives must give priority to defeating the government, not its army; and, (5) the subversives must secure their base areas first.

What exists in the end is nothing more than tried-and-true military theory maintaining the best intentions of Jomini and Clausewitz. Who can get there first with the most? Who has the best intelligence gathering apparatus? Who has the better strategy, resources, and manpower? Who has the support of the people? There should be no question that a government with the proper intent and motivation can swing public support away from any subversive organization. The will to maintain authority, and presumably law and order, as well as superior technology, are usually on the side of the government. When this is the case, there is no acceptable reason for achieving anything short of victory.

The strategic "imbalance of force" between the government and the subversives must be exploited by the government. Weaponry, aircraft, and a navy are all assets that subversives have trouble acquiring. A government usually has a variety of light and heavy weapons at its disposal, an extensive transportation system, an assortment of aircraft and ships patrolling vigilantly, fuel, food, medicines, and some sort of industry that it controls. In addition, a government usually has ties with other nations that readily support its cause. Despite all this capability, a government still faces the one risk of relying too heavily on massive response — too much, too often. An insurgent strategy instead calls for just enough, at just the right time, in just the right place. One is challenged to envision a better concept of balance of force.

There are several strategic considerations for a government regarding balance of force during an insurgency. These include insurgent organization and size, the potential base for popular support, and logistic difficulties. It is likely that all of these elements will be directly affected by the terrain and the dispersement of the population. It is typical that the more rural and dense the terrain, the more sheltered the insurgent forces are. In a successful phase two, sheltering must then take shape outside the urban center. This will in turn aid the insurgents in their quest for a protracted struggle.

In speaking about open insurgency, or phase two of an insurgency, Thompson discusses three specific geographical areas in which insurgent activity takes place. There are first the populated areas within major cities and towns under government control where terrorist activity is the most prevalent. Then there are the rural populated areas where control is disputed between the government and the insurgents and where the guerrilla insurgent forces extend their operations. Finally, there are the more remote, "deep jungle" bases of the insurgent guerrillas, less populated terrain which is also usually difficult to traverse. It is here that the guerrillas place their logistical bases, where they rest, rearm, and plan future operations. In military terms, it is in these base areas where the insurgent guerrillas are most vulnerable to government attack. Terrorist actions, while feared among the general populace, are easily recognized in the urban areas. What is usually the most difficult for government forces to quell are the combined subversive, terrorist, and guerrilla operations that are within that middle geographic area of the rural populated setting.

The great tactical error governments can make is assigning priority to these geographic areas. Often, the government concentrates on the outside and works in, instead of working from the inside out. Remote guerrilla base areas on the outside are not the source of the insurgent problem and therefore should not be the prime consideration for government forces in the beginning of an insurgency. Because the political subversion provides the impetus, it is the subversives that must be stopped. The population within the cities is perhaps the last element to support an insurgency, which is the very reason that the insurgents choose to surround the cities by infiltrating the villages.

It is the middle geographic area, the rural population, where the subversives launch their strongest opposition to the government. The formation of a fair and resourceful constabulary must be the first order of business for any government combating an insurgent movement. The subversion must be stopped at the outset by extending the intelligence gathering arm of the government. Thompson sees this as a "thoroughly methodical approach," one which may appear slow in the beginning but encourages a "steamroller outlook which provides the people with faith in ultimate victory. By preparing for a long haul, the government may achieve victory quicker than expected. By seeking quick military victories in insurgent controlled areas, it will certainly get a long haul for which neither it nor the people may be prepared."

At the beginning of an insurgency, and at some time before the subversive element chooses to instigate a second phase of operations, the military most likely of some regular, conventional structure must be restructured almost wholesale. While some conventional force structure must remain in place to thwart a possible secondary insurgency, substantial training must be done to establish small-unit irregulars that can carry on guerrilla tactics themselves. With a broader range of technical advantages, the government "guerrillas" can presumably be provided with stronger intelligence information than the subversives, better weapons, equipment, supplies, food, pay, and medical treatment, all of which should provide a great morale boost. With air and naval assets, the government units should also have better combat support, and, perhaps the most important element of all, far better mobility. Thompson states:

> *The requirement is for a small, elite, highly disciplined, lightly equipped and aggressive army, with a supporting air force and navy of sufficient capability to make the army highly mobile, so that it can fulfill its proper military role in support of the civil government and in accordance with the five basic principles.*

If a government is aware enough and moves in a positive direction early, it can take the necessary political and military steps to wage a better insurgency than the subversives themselves. However, the strategic and tactical means at hand must not first be put toward the military solution. For a government countering an insurgency, it is the political infrastructure of the insurgents that must be defeated, first and last. Such a strategy is so critical, Thompson cautions, that "even if an armed insurgency is defeated, the political and subversive struggle will go on and can still win." Such a possibility can only be of nightmare proportions for a legitimate government that has expended its resources in an unwise, frivolous manner, extolling little virtue in its understanding of insurgency. Such a nightmare could easily extend to regional alliances, disturb the process of nation-building, and adversely affect desired regional security. This is as much a concern now as it was at the end of the Second World War.

2

Theories of Insurgency

Introduction

The theory of insurgency is ultimately rooted in an underlying theory of society in a vision of the social world that defines the major issues for analysis and the factors that enter into useful explanations. The two approaches that have dominated recent studies of insurgency resource mobilization theory and the various classical formulations have drawn on different visions of society. Resource mobilization theory has drawn its primary inspiration from the conflict theory tradition of Karl Marx and Max Weber. The major issue in this vision of society has been the explanation of social change, especially the transformation of structures of economic and political power. The major explanations of insurgency, then, are cast in terms of social power: structures of dominance that contain antagonistic interests, changes in political power that create opportunities for collective action, the mobilization of resources for sustained challenges, and power struggles that bring about changes in institutional structures. At the heart of this theory is the assumption that insurgency is a ubiquitous form of political action and that it constitutes a set of rational collective actions by excluded groups to advance their interests in the context of a restrictive polity. Instirgencies emerge, develop, and succeed or fail primarily because of changes in structures of social power.

The various formulations of the classical model have drawn on quite different theoretical premises, primarily those of the structural-functionalist tradition rooted in the work of Emile Durkheim and Vilfredo Pareto and the interactionist tradition of early Chicago sociology. The major issue in these theoretical traditions has been the explanation of social order, typically in terms of functional interdependence and the emergence of shared meanings and collective identities. The major explanations of insurgency, then, are cast in terms of the disruption and recreation of a shared normative order and set of collective identities, and processes that lead to the eventual collapse and absorption of these actions. At the heart of this classical model is the assumption that insurgency is of marginal social and political importance and that it constitutes a set of expressive actions generated by short-term disruptions in the moral fabric of society. Insurgencies are important chiefly because of the problem of social Control that they pose to the established sociopolitical order.

Although the clash between these perspectives has created a wideranging debate, the key points have centered on two issues: the processes leading to the generation of sustained insurgency, and the factors shaping the outcome of challenges, especially their success and failtire.

Generation of Insurgency

The sine uqa non of the study of social movements has traditionally been the question of the emergence or generation of-'sustained insurgency. The classical theories have centered on explanations of discontent, arguing that insurgency emerges because of sudden and widespread increases in short-term individual grievances. In most versions, discontents are generated by the pressures or "strains" of rapid social change. These theories have borrowed the rather simple and highly misleading metaphor of a "pressure cooker." The assumption is that discontents mount up like the pressures inside the confined spaces of a pressure cooker, becoming more and more intense until they create an explosion. Although the classical analysts have emphasized different causes of discontent, the general argument has been the same. Rapid social changes impinge on existing social relations, creating "strains" or inconsistencies in the social order. The more rapid and profound these changes, the more severe the "strains" and therefore the greater the intensity and scope of the discontents. As these discontents build up, they overload the normal tension-reduction mechanisims and create explosions of individual aggression.

Insurgency, then, is simply an organized extension of more elementary forms of disorderly action. In mass society theory, for example, the discontents of anomic emerge because of the social dislocations generated by rapid industrialization, wars, and large-scale economic depressions which "uproot" individuals from the intermediary social relations that normally integrate them into larger social structures, thereby making them available for "extremist" politics. Collective behavior theories have provided a more eclectic formulation, identifying a wide variety of social changes-economic crises, wars, mass migrations, the diffusion of new ideas and techniques that create "normative ambiguities" or "problematic situations" in which old norms are suddenly found to be inappropriate, leading to collective searches for new norms and social identities. Similarly relative deprivation and status inconsistency theories have argued that rapid economic developments, urbanization, extensive social mobility, and sudden exposure to the standards of new reference groups create inconsistencies between expectations and satisfactions or cognitive dissonance, both of which create intense and widespread discontents leading to support for social movements. Gusfield captured the general thesis quite well in his classic review for the *Encyclopedia of the Social Sciences* when he argued:

> *A major hypothesis in the field is that social movements are the products of social change. Circumstances arise in which long established relationships are no longer appropriate; the result of this strain between old and new is discontent. One of the sociologist's tasks in analyzing a movement is to identify the social changes that have generated discontent and to specify their relation to the movement.*

This is not the point to argue the merits of particular versions of this classical model. An extensive critical literature already exists pointing out specific empirical and conceptual weaknesses. My concern here is the general assumptions that underlie these classical theories. Each has built on the pressure cooker metaphor, arguing that the intensity and scale of discontent is the central factor in the generation of insurgency. Discontents have been seen as short-term, individual grievances that derive from exogenous social changes such as economic depressions, wars, and natural calamities. Insurgency itself has therefore been seen as a sharp break from the existing social order, as a sudden spontaneous explosion of the outraged masses.

In contrast, the resource mobilization theory of social movements is based on an analysis of social power. Insurgencies emerge and become sustained, not because of sudden and widespread discontents, but because of favorable changes in the structure of social power. The basic image is that of excluded groups organizing and pooling resources in response to increased resources and opportunities. Discontents are seen its indigenous features of social institutions that are ultimately rooted in underlying structural antagonisms rather than transient grievances produced by social dislocations. Insurgencies, then, are direct extensions of ongoing institutional processes rather than explosions produced by fractures in the social order. Although insurgency may initially emerge from spontaneous processes, sustained challenges require concerted organizing and strategic planning, in other words, leaders and social movement organizations. Rather than being a sudden explosion, a sustained insurgency rests on a gradual cumulative process of resource mobilization that typically requires long time periods. As the Tillys have argued, pointing to the long-run effects of industrialization and urbanization on the generation of insurgency during the rebellious century between 1830 and 1930: "instead of short-term generation of strain, followed by protest, we find long-run transformation of power and collective action". Long-standing social antagonisms defined the major actors and issues under contention. Sustained insurgency developed because of favorable changes in power relations, especially increases in the mobilization potential and strategic position of excluded groups, the adoption of effective mobilization strategies and the development of favorable political alignments that altered the collectively perceived costs and rewards of collective action.

What then is the role of discontents? Several analysts have recently argued that discontents are irrelevant because they are structural constants produced by objective social inequalities or the organizing efforts of political entrepreneurs. McCarthy and Zald, for example, have argued that "there is always enough discontent in any society to supply the grass-roots support for a movement" and that entrepreneurs simply manufacture the discontents: "the definition of grievances will expand to meet the funds and support personnel available". Similarly, John Wilson has argued that discontents are a necessary but not sufficient condition "because certain tensions seem to be endemic to society". Speaking specifically of excluded groups, my own previous work has argued that "grievances are relatively constant and pervasive. What changes, giving rise to insurgency, is the amount of social resources available to unorganized but aggrieved groups".

Although discontents are secondary, neither formulation can ultimately stand as a general explanation of insurgency. Discontents are, after all, a question of subjective definitions rather than simple objective deprivations. Excluded groups are always objectively deprived but this does not mean that they will uniformly perceive these conditions as socially unjust and alterable. As Barrington Moore has argued, the development of insurgency requires that subordinants collectively redefine existing conditions as socially unjust and mutable. Elites have to be perceived as responsible, as having violated their social responsibilities. Objectionable conditions have to be seen as alterable. Normally, however, such definitions of social injustice are blocked or cannot be converted into collective images. Past experiences of failed insurgency, elite control of information and socialization processes, disorganization and lack of "free spaces" for creating alternative definitions of reality, and simple psychological adaptation to the state of powerlessness create quiescent attitudes among the excluded towards their objective deprivations. "Given the onus of choice, the powerless internalize their impossible situation and internalize their guilt. The slave often identified with his master and accepted society's estimate of himself as being without worth. The less complete but nonetheless pervasive powerlessness of blacks in America's northern ghettoes has similar effects". The most powerless of the Appalachian mineworkers studied by Gaventa were the most docile and the least likely to label their objective deprivations as injustices. Although theories of social antagonism can show how objective social inequalities lead to structural conflicts of interest and hence the objective potential for insurgency, these conflicts are structural constants and hence cannot explain variations in discontents. Objective social inequalities have to be collectively redefined as the source of social injustices that can be remedied by collective action. In short, the excluded group has to experience a "cognitive liberation" that transforms its collective consciousness.

How does this come about? In the entrepreneurial theory, the transformation of consciousness is simply manufactured by organizers. The greater the resources invested in the organizing campaign, the greater the intensity and scale of the discontents. Like Lenin's classic formulation of class as opposed to trade union consciousness, the transformation is mechanically imported from the outside. But this leaves the link of insurgent consciousness to structural antagonisms problematic, denies spontaneous processes, and treates grievances as simple, linear products of entrepreneurial definition rather than as products of the actual process of social conflict.

A more fruitful theory of discontent begins with the premise that the consciousness of excluded groups is dual or, to use Gramsci term, "contradictory." An insurgent consciousness based on a sense of social injustice coexists alongside a contradictory deferential consciousness that highlights the "fairness" and immutability of the prevailing order. These contradictory belief systems coexist and, because of the dominance of elites and the powerlessness of the excluded, the former becomes private while the latter is public knowledge. The result is the political passivity of the excluded, However, changes in power relations will bring the consciousness of injustice to the fore, making it the dominant and collective definition of reality. In other words, increases in the intensity and scale of discontents are produced by changes in the structure of social power.

A second premise in such a revised theory of discontents is that social conflict is a routine part of social relations. As Ralf Dahrendorf once put it: "social conflict is ubiquitous". Social conflict, however, is not the same as insurgency. Most conflicts are small-scale, isolated acts of insubordination, such as work slow-downs and minor violations of institutional rules, that test the armor of the power structure but, like prepolitical peasant rebellions, do not articulate a clear sense of injustice, much less a coherent set of remedies. Rule and Tilly have appropriately labeled these "testing actions." Since they are randomly distributed, these testing actions continuously explore the protective armor of the power structure. Once chinks are discovered, disruptive actions tend to escalate to fill the open space. Outside cadres are attracted, grass-roots organizers are trained, and excluded groups develop an enhanced sense of their political efficacy, thereby supporting expanded disruptions. In the course of escalating disruptions, the collectively perceived costs and rewards of these actions are gradually transformed. Conditions that were previously perceived as immutable and fair are collectively redefined as mutable and unjust. In short. The key question, then, is identifying the changes in the structure of power that set off the escalation of disruptions and the transformation of the consciousness of the excluded.

Four major aspects of the structure of power shape the generation of insurgency: the mobilization potential of the excluded group; its strategic position in routine institutional processes; the strategies of mobilization adopted by organizers; and opportunities created by the structure of political alignments. The first is essentially a question of the indigenous organizational capacity or readiness of the group as shaped by its resources, its indigenous organization, and the institutional controls of its main antagonists. The second determines the disruptive potential of the group; groups that are functionally important to their antagonists, whose antagonists control resources, and who are lodged in central social institutions have greater strategic leverage. These potentials are put into motion by organizers who, in interaction with spontaneous processes, define strategies of mobilization for the assembly and management of resources. The structure of political alignments is essentially a question of how the relations among politically powerful groups create opportunities for the excluded to organize and act collectively on their interests. Unless there are significant opportunities, a deferential consciousness will remain the dominant definition of social reality. Before specifying the ways in which these factors interact, we need to first look at each separately.

Mobilization Potential. To speak of the potentials of a group is to point to the social structural conditions that shape their capacities prior to actual insurgency, what Coleman has referred to as their "conversion potential." The most important considerations are the indigenous resources of the group, its internal or indigenous organization, and the institutional controls of its main antagonists. In general, the more economically secure the group, the more the indigenous resources and organization and the less the institutional controls, the greater the likelihood of mobilization. As Tilly has argued, resourefull groups ire more readily mobilized and more likely to support preparatory mobilization prior to open contests while deprived groups respond more gradually and in a defensive manner. More directly linked to mobilization campaigns are organizing resources, especially experienced organizers, recognized leaders, and means of communication such as newspapers and meeting facilities. Organizers and leaders are generally grass- roots volunteers drawn from the indigenous community or the fallout of proximate social movements. Motivated by a "missionary impulse", their major role is to coordinate actions and knit together existing groups by creating a sense of solidarity and commitment to an alternative vision of social justice. Generally, organizers are indigenous "opinion leaders", often leaders of social clubs and economic benefit associations. As Lipset found in his study of Saskatchewan socialism, these are typically the earliest and most central recruits. A group endowed with natural leaders or receiving an infusion of outside organizers is more likely to mobilize. In addition, these leaders need means of communications to reach the masses and protected locations for carrying out organizing efforts. To the extent to which the group enjoys "free spaces", the group is more likely to mobilize.

Indigenous organization is probably the most important single factor, providing a communications network for coordinating actions and diffusing an insurgent consciousness, strengthening collective perceptions of efficacy by creating awareness of the number of potential supporters, facilitating collecting redefinitions of conditions as mutable and unjust, and furnishing the context for collective incentives that mitigate the problem of free-riders. As Oberschall has argued, mi organizational base is necessary if isolated ephemeral testing actions such as riots and crowd outbursts are to be transformed into sustained insurgency.

Indigenous organization can be defined simply as the extent to which a category of people sharing some characteristic or interest in common are aware of this interest and linked together by interpersonal bonds or social networks. These networks can have two distinct bases, solidary networks defined by natural groups such as kinship and friendship ties, and membership in formal community organizations such as churches, benefit associations, and social clubs. A social movement organization (or SMO) is, in contrast, a formal association that attempts to interject the interests of excluded groups into centers of Power. Its major task is extending and deepening indigenous organization while harnessing it to the goals of insurgency. Even in advanced phases of insurgency, however, the social movement organization is never coterminous with the movement itself, much less the organization of the group.

The greater the density of indigenous organization, the greater the potential for mobilization. Indigenous organization has two dimensions: inclusiveness or the extent to which social networks link the group together and absorb the time, energies, and social interaction of members, and exclusiveness or the extent to which these networks are isolated from other categories of actors, especially antagonists. Jackson found that the absence of such an indigenous network among property taxpayers in Los Angeles in the late 1950s prevented a tax revolt from emerging despite strong but disorganized interest in tax reforms. Conversely, working class insurgency is critically facilitated by the solidarities forged by community ties and work affiliations. Among nineteenth-century English workers, for example, Foster found that the more extensive and exclusive the local community ties to pubs, fraternal clubs, and extended families, the more likely the development of an insurgent consciousness and collective action. Similarly, the ecological concentration of the working class in separate neighborhoods of large cities has facilitated strikes and union organization. These networks are often the creation of previous movements or political mobilization efforts. Freeman found that the development of inclusive networks among participants in the President's Commission on the Status of Women in the mid-1960s created the basis for launching the National Organization for Women. Likewise, the informal networks among radical women involved in the student movement in the late 1960s created the organizational basis of the radical wing of the women's movement.

Indigenous organization is also decisive in overriding the free-rider problem. As Mancur Olson has argued, individuals rationally pursuing their self-interest will often refrain from collective actions because they stand to gain whether or not they participate. All workers might gain by a union contract, but only those who strike actually pay for this collective benefit. According to Olson, the rational course of action is to free-ride on the contributions of others. Of course, if all individuals acted this rationally, there would be no collective benefits. Thus, according to Olson, organizers of collective action have to provide "selective incentives" such as strike funds and promises of jobs to those, and only those, who pay the costs of collective action. Selective incentives, however, are a weak basis for mobilizing insurgency. Excluded groups lack resources, and although external contributions can help, such sponsors are, as the civil rights movement found, frequently unreliable in the long run. Moreover, as Gamson has pointed out, Olson's narrow self-interest scheme does not explain the contributions of sponsors. Nor does Olson's theory account for the efforts of organizers, unless one adopts the rather implausible explanation that they are pursuing the ephemeral gains of public recognition and career advancement. In most cases, there are more promising avenues for personal advancement.

A more persuasive theory of collective action that links indigenous organization to mobilization has been offered by James Q. Wilson in his discussion of solidary and purposive incentives. Solidary incentives rest on emotional commitments, their receipt on the maintenance of valued social relations. They can be experienced only through the actual process of participating in collective actions, either as the major aim of the action or its direct by-product. These incentives may be selective, such as the special honors and recognition handed out to movement leaders, or collective, such as the exhilaration that comes from participating in demonstrations and marches or collective actions that assert the social respectability of the group as a whole. Purposive incentives differ in deriving from actions that conform to an internalized moral code. In this sense, they are inherently collective, resting on the moral commitments that link the individual to the group. In effect, internalizing a moral code redefines self-interest in terms of collective interest. Significantly, both sets of incentives are ultimately based on indigenous organization. Solidarities and internalized values are largely structured by the social networks of everyday life. In other words, the more cohesive the group in terms of common networks and sentimints, the stronger the indigenous social infrastructure for the operation of these incentives.

These social networks also have to be cooptable to the goals of the movement. Here the critical factor is their exclusiveness and the particular values attached to the networks. Von Eschen, Kirk and Pinard, for example, found that networks defined by membership in conservative political associations such as the Urban League and major political parties discouraged support for civil rights protests while those linked to more liberal associations such as the NAACP and the Americans for Democratic Action facilitated participation. Similarly, Freeman has argued that support for the contemporary women's movement has been structured by women's networks that are linked to a conception of independent female status while the more traditional networks of sororities and women's professional clubs have inhibited support. The more exclusive the networks, the more likely they are to serve as consciousness transforming and mobilizing channels. Foster found that working class communities with extensive cross-class ties experienced little insurgency while exclusive communities were centers of insurgency.

Vertical networks between elites and subordinates are frequently the basis for institutional controls while free spaces provide the basis for mobilization. The most controlled environment is a "total institution" in which the entire lives of subordinants and their networks are envoloped by structures controlled by their antagonists. Free spaces for developing solidarities and alternative definitions of social justice are eliminated. Antagonists develop highly personalized, paternalistic controls over their subordinates and promote intensive competition among them. These ties inculcate a view of the naturalness and justice of the existing order as well as provide informal controls for coopting initial testing actions. Competition blocks in-group solidarity and the transformation of collective consciousness. In contrast, free spaces constructed around sites of autonomous group interaction provide a potent basis for developing alternative definitions of social justice and developing the solidary and cultural bases for mobilization. Poor peasants and tenants are often controlled by intense rivalries and patron-client ties. Conversely, middle peasants who own their own land and live in independent villages possess the open space and solidarities for mounting challenges. Similarly, the paternalistic authority and totalistic controls of slaveowners in the antebellum American South provided virtually complete dominance over their houseservants while fieldhands, especially skilled slaves who worked independently, were less controllable. In the same vein, meritocratic hierarchies promote competition by providing privileges on the purported basis of individual merit while egalitarian rewards create solidarity. White collar workers have generally resisted unionization because of their sense of greater worth and the perks of respectability, clean work and job security, while flat hierarchies among teachers and nurses have encouraged unionization. Similarly, employers have used ethnicity to create rivalries yet ethnic bonds have frequently furnished the basis for unionization.

These institutional controls are, of course, reinforced by direct coercive sanctions. Striking workers are fired, dissident peasants evicted, and slave rebellions crushed with beatings and armed violence. Coercion is generally not used until insurgency has already emerged but, where the memory of repression is direct and fresh, the mere threat often serves as a powerful deterrent. As long as the state monopoly on the means of legitimate violence remains intact, clear and visible signals of support by political elites for the antagonist are often sufficient. The southern cotton plantations during slavery and the tenancy era often resembled armed concentration camps in which plantation owners had virtually unrestricted control over the means of violence and, if challenged, could count on quick, solid backing from local police and courts. In contrast, weakening this state monopoly or even signals of elite indifference often leads to the rapid development of multiple insurgencies.

Strategic Position. All groups, even the most abject and powerless, have some minimum of strategic leverage. At the least they can refuse to cooperate with ongoing institutional processes, supporting "mass defiance" that "violates the traditions and laws to which they ordinarily acquiesce, and flaunt the authorities to whom they ordinarily defer". The strike and the riot are the classic forms, workers withdrawing their labor from production and citizens throwing off their normal civility. Waskow referred to the "creative disorder" of civil rights protests as creating leverage against political authorities and Wilson saw it as the core feature of civil rights protest strategies.

The leverage afforded by mass defiance, however, varies widely. The compliance of some groups with ongoing institutional routines is simply more important than that of others. Moreover, some antagonists control more resources and can therefore more readily make concessions. And some social institutions are more central in the functioning of the larger society, magnifying the significance of disruptions. In general, these conditions reinforce one another. Central institutions control more resources and are more dependent on the cooperation of subordinates. Excluded groups, however, are not generally favored by these considerations. Strikes by skilled workers deprive employers of a critical resource, but those by unskilled menial workers who perform marginal functions have few repercussions. Similarly, protests by the unemployed and welfare recipients have little significance other than temporarily disturbing the tranquility of a few marginal governmental agencies. In the same vein, the antagonists of "poor people's" movements often do not control sufficient resources to make major concessions and are implacably opposed to concessions. Slumlords frequently lack the finances to repair their buildings, and the owners of marginal enterprises cannot pay high wages without bankrupting their firms. As we will see, California growers have determinedly resisted farm worker unions, resorting to extreme measures in their battles against insurgency. Finally, excluded groups are typically embedded in marginal social institutions. Strikes against the large corporations in the core sector of the American economy shake the entire society, but the reverberations of protests against welfare officials, school administrators, and slumlords are largely confined to particular institutions. Of course, these conditions change as institutions decline or become more socially prominent. The industrial enterprise was insignificant in the early nineteenth-century American economy but had become the core of the national economy by the 1930s. Early industrial strikes had little leverage, but the wave of industrial strikes in the 1930s shook the entire sociopolitical order.

Strategies of Mobilization. Although spontaneous processes are often sufficient to initiate insurgency, concerted organizing and deliberate mobilization strategies are necessary to sustain challenges. In fact, in settings where resources are scarce and indigenous networks are weakly developed or only partially cooptable, organizers are often necessary to even initiate challenges because the group is simply too disorganized and dominated by its antagonists. All three of the farm worker movements we will examine were initiated by professional organizers, as were most of the urban social movements of the late 1960s and early 1970s. The major contribution of organizers, however, is sustaining mobilization. As Fainstein and Fainstein found, a formal movement organization with a professional staff, membership lists, and meeting facilities is often necessary to sustain interest during lulls in spontaneous activity. And, as Gamson and Tilly have argued, a formal movement organization increases the combat readiness of a challenge and provides a more flexible tactical repertoire, both of which promise more affective actions and thereby sustained mobilization.

The highly charged debate over the role of social movement organizations has been due in part to the failure to distinguish organizers from formal leaders. Organizers are generally highly committed "grass-roots" supporters receiving little or no pay. Their efforts are focused on knitting together isolated groups, instilling consciousness of social injustices, offering tactical advice, and pushing forward disruptive actions. Formal leaders, in contrast, hold formal positions in social movement organizations and are more concerned with the articulation of formal goals and negotiating relations with institutional elites. Organizers help expand institutional disruptions while leaders articulate goals and negotiate formal institutional access.

In general, social movements with professional or full-time paid organizers are advantaged. Organizing efforts are more sustained and, as Oliver has argued, commitment levels are higher. The rapid growth of the Southern Farmers Alliance in the 1880s, for example, was based on full-time salaried organizers as was the proliferation of industrial strikes in the mid-1930s. Similarly, professional community organizers in the 1960s transformed sporadic testing actions into more sustained challenges against corporations and big city political machines. As Freeman has concluded: "Even in something as seemingly spontaneous as a social movement, the professional is more valuable than the amateur".

The mobilization strategies adopted by these organizers vary widely in their effectiveness. Organizers can tap two constituencies: direct beneficiaries or the group itself, and external or third parties. Although a sustained challenge ultimately depends on indigenous support, external support critical facilitator, especially among deprived groups who lack specialized resources such as organizing facilities, legal advice, and political contacts. In general, a dual strategy that mobilizes both constituencies is more effective.

Studies of group mobilization have repeatedly found that organizers using "bloc" recruitment methods are more successful because they build on the group's indigenous solidarities and culture. As in conventional community organizing, the existing solidary groups of everyday life and their natural leaders are recruited intact and converted into the active cells or structural units of the movement. Conversely, organizers who shun the more solidary groupings, reject prevailing cultural understandings, and insist on their own radical programs will find deaf cars. Similarly, organizers who make use of collective incentives by holding solidary events and inaugurating ideological training programs can override the free-rider problem, while those emphasizing selective material benefits will often receive only transitory support. As we will see, the United Farm Workers generated sustained farm worker support by focusing on existing solidary groups and emphasizing solidarity and consciousness. In contrast, the National Welfare Rights Organization, organizing a roughly similar population, experienced debilitating turn-over rates because it relied on the selective incentive of access to special welfare benefits.

Organizers are also critical to pyramiding resources and actions. By limiting actions to less ambitious but successful projects that fit the capacities of the challenge, insurgencies can use small successes to gradually mobilize support and eventually escalate to more demanding actions. In the mid-1970s, for example, the citizens' organization Massachusetts Fair Share launched an overly ambitious tax referendum campaign that almost exhausted the nascent challenge while ACORN, organizing in a less favorable environment, has successfully pyramided its projects into larger scale contests.

Insurgencies also build off external resources, a point completely neglected in the classic literature. The emergence of the student and antiwar movements of the 1960s depended heavily on the cooptation of the mass media to spread their message and recruit supporters. Similarly, the civil rights and urban movements staged dramatic protests that captured the attention of more powerful groups, "socializing" the conflicts and generating significant external support for the challenges. At the height of the political turmoil of the late 1960s, liberal social service organizations such as the National Council of Churches, the Ford Foundation, and the YMCA became general sponsors of insurgency, supporting the development of a wide array of new challengers.

External support, however, entails significant limits. Bids for support have to be framed in terms of principles accepted by supporters, such as legal due process and equality of opportunity, that can restrict movement goals and actions. The liberal supporters of the civil rights movement, for example, were repelled by the urban riots and the demands for black power and withdrew their support. Similarly, the National Council of Churches refused to support the Movement for Economic justice because of its radical demands for economic redistribution. As Lipsky found in urban rent strikes, external supporters are also often satisfied with quick symbolic victories that provide little basis for a sustained challenge. The receptiveness of potential sponsors also varies widely. Periods of economic prosperity provide slack resources and facilitate rapid growth in the social welfare bureaucracies that house the 11 organizational intellectuals" who are likely sponsors of new challenges. As we will see, the prosperity of the early 1960s was a critical structural facilitator in creating the external support for insurgencies. Probably the most decisive factor, though, is a favorable shift in the structure of political alignments that give potential sponsors more political power and increases their short-term interests in supporting a challenge.

Structure of Political Alignments. The fundamental distinction around which political systems are organized is that between polity insiders or members who possess routine, low-cost access to centers of state power, and polity outsiders or exluded groups who do not. Members have a stake in blocking challenges and maintaining the existing system of polity rules which guarantee their access; excluded groups, in seizing opportunities to mobilize and seeking the transformation of these rules or at least their application to themselves. Polity members will, of course, use their access to block direct challenges, but even members not directly affected by a challenge will generally perceive insurgency as threatening simply because it raises the possibility of a restructuring of access rules and, by acting outside existing channels, violates these rules. This, coupled with the inherent conservatism of the state as an institution fundamentally committed to the maintenance of social order, imparts an intrinsic restrictiveness to political systems. As McAdam has put it, "all social movements pose a threat to existing institutional arrangements in society [because they] raise the spectre of a restructuring of polity membership". The state, then, is institutionally biased against insurgency. Short of a general collapse of state power, political elites will normally move to prevent the development of sustained challenges.

The structure of liberal democratic regimes, however, tempers this bias of the state by allowing routine political realignments that periodically create opportunities for the emergence of challenges. Contrary to most theories of liberal democracy, however, the major basis is not the formal protections on speech and assembly and voting rights enshrined in liberal democratic constitutions. These protections are routinely extended only to polity members. The major factor is realignments inside of the polity, structured largely through the electoral system, that encourage coalitions between polity members and excluded groups and thereby create opportunities for the mobilization of insurgency. In effect, liberal democratic rules rationalize the struggle for political power by converting it into a series of routinized electoral contests between contending factions supported by voting coalitions of polity members. Routine competitive elections insure that political elites have to periodically attend to the views of the groups inside the system. If these groups find that bringing an outsider into the system will bring electoral or other advantages, their sponsorship can create opportunities for mounting a sustained challenge. Political elites may temporarily lift the institutional controls conventionally used to keep the excluded in check and may even sponsor insurgent organizations. Insurgents can then use demonstrations and marches to signal their base of support and promise as an electoral ally. As McAdam has shown, the rise of the civil rights movement was facilitated by several decades of increasing federal protections of black civil rights, especially restrictions on lynchings and denial of voting rights, and increasing infusions of white liberal support for black colleges and churches. Similarly, the development of the movements of the unemployed and industrial workers during the 1930s depended heavily on the support of the Democratic party and middle class liberal reformers. In both cases, political realignments triggered the expansion of new political opportunities.

The scope of these realignments determines the scale and duration of the opportunities. The most dramatic opportunities develop out of generalized realignments and periods of intense struggle among polity members. In closely divided politics in which roughly equal political coalitions compete for governmental power, the solidarity among polity members is reduced and the potential value of outsiders as political allies is increased. The more intense this internal power struggle, the greater the likelihood of generalized sponsorship. Sponsorship can also grow out of more limited realignments. An antagonist loses its political footing and becomes more vulnerable to attack or a single polity member decides to support a challenge. Sponsorship also typically emerges at particular points in the process of realignments. If sponsors are part of a political coalition acquiring increased governmental power, their ability to provide support and their interest in the entry of new groups is greater. The close electoral battles of the early 1930s made the votes of previously marginal white ethnics and blue collar workers a valuable resource, leading Democratic politicians to support the movements of the unemployed and industrial workers. At the same time, increasing dominance by the Democratic party and the declining importance of business confidence as a structural constraint gave political elites more room to support insurgencies. Similarly, as I will argue below, the closely fought electoral battles and the Democratic victories of the early 1960s and the restructuring of peripheral sector capitalist firms created a conducive context for the development of new challenges among blacks and other excluded groups.

The emergence of successful challenges also stimulates new insurgencies. Organizers branch out to new causes. New models of collective action are developed and new resource bases identified, Dramatic successes boost the excluded's sense of political efficacy, and as long as movements do not challenge their allies, reform-oriented political parties and governing coalitions are strengthened. Movement organizers vie for recognition, and as the political pulse escalates, the scope of insurgent demands expands. Polity members become less secure, longstanding coalitions break up, and the entire field of political action becomes more fluid. In such a context, virtually all groups possessing even a modicum of resources and organization will rise up, making their own bids for entry. The successes of the civil rights and student movements in the mid-1960s stimulated challenges from virtually all sides, creating, a period of generalized political turmoil, Insurgencies were launched among groups such as homosexuals and school children who had never previously organized and those, such as the urban underclass, who possessed few resources and little organizational base or strategic position. Of course, such periods of turmoil are rare, precipitated by polity-wide realignments that dramatically restructure the boundaries and rules of the system. Generally, the dynamic of expanding insurgency is halted in the early stages, limiting the changes to the entry of single groups and lesser reforms.

The mobilization potential, strategic position and mobilization strategies of insurgents, and shifting alignments in the polity interact in the development of sustained challenges? In broad terms, each dimension is shaped by long-term structural social changes. Capitalist development brought about urbanization and industrialization which, in turn, increased the organizational strength of the industrial working class and their strategic position in the economy as a whole.In this context, working class organizers gradually perfected strategies of mobilization, developing more effective devices for mobilizing collective action. Simultaneously, the gradual entry of new groups, especially the industrial working class, has democratized liberal democratic states, extending the franchise, legitimating new forms of action and creating broader, more diverse mass based political parties and governing coalitions that have been more willing to support challenges. In other words, long-term structural changes have gradually increased the mobilization potential and strategic position of excluded groups, and these groups have gradually evolved new mobilization strategies and enjoyed increased political opportunities. In the short run, however, the specific changes setting off a challenge can come along any of these four dimensions. Gamson, Fireman and Rytina have provided a convenient way of thinking about the interaction of these factors by offering a "threshold" model of movement emergence. Each factor has to be at minimum threshold point before a sustained challenge will emerge. Within limits, surpluses in some dimensions, such as organizing resources, can compensate for deficiencies in others, such as indigenous organization. Considered independently, the threshold level for each factor is a necessary but not sufficient condition. If all factors reach their threshold, then the necessary and sufficient conditions exist for the development of a sustained challenge.

Outcome of Insurgency

The major goal of insurgency is the interjection of the interests of previously excluded groups into centers of economic and political power. The major criteria for success, then, center on changes in the structure of social power. Social power is, of course, a complex, multidimensional phenomenon. No simple scale or single dimension can capture the full range of changes potentially entailed by insurgent success. Because challenges are defined primarily in terms of specific institutional antagonisms, the primary successes lie in changing the structure of the master or, as Schwartz has called it, "parent" institution that directly molds the lives of the excluded. As Piven and Cloward have argued, "people experience deprivation and oppression within a concrete setting, not as the end product of large and abstract processes. Workers experience the factory, the speeding rhythm of the assembly line, the foreman, the spies and the guards, the owner and the paycheck. They do not experience monopoly capitalism". In order to cement these gains, however, insurgency also has to expand to a broader arena, securing routine access to the polity. Because the state is the primary institution for guaranteeing social claims, the excluded have to secure routine access to the political arena. Otherwise, their antagonists will eventually turn back their newly won rights and gains. A firm independent handle on the ballot box and routine access to legislative chambers and administrative elites are the basic measures.

The structure of social power also has multiple levels or dimensions, setting off different types of insurgent successes. Drawing on the theory of social power outlined by Lukes and Domhoff, we can distinguish three different dimensions of insurgent success. Insurgents can secure policy successes by altering the content of official decisions, such as new Congressional legislation or changes in the investment and hiring policies of corporations. The signal of success lies in tangible gains won in direct and open contests of wills. Insurgents can also score regime successes by altering the processes that routinely define the agenda for decision-making. The principal objective here is transforming the institutional processes that routinely bias decision-making, excluding controversial issues and dissident perspectives from the agenda. Alterations in the channels of elite socialization and recruitment, the articulation of new issues and prespectives, and the introduction of new rules defining legitimate actors and forms of collective action fall into this dimension. A transformation of the issues and perspectives brought to bear in policy-making mark the victories here. Finally, insurgencies can generate distributional successes, redistributing socially valued goods to the advantage of previously excluded groups. Transformations in the distribution of economic resources, alterations in the structure of social prestige, and the decentralization of political power fall into this dimension. The signal mark here is a change in the structural conditions that allow groups to mobilize and realize their interests.

Changes in these three dimensions are, of course, interdependent. Full success comes from altering all three dimensions, while lesser measures begin with policy changes and build toward regime and distributional gains. Although there is no necessary time sequence for these changes, victories generally begin with policy successes and culminate in distributional gains. Successful insurgencies generally have to be contented with partial measures. In general, the more favorable the circumstances and the more powerful the movement, the greater the degree of success.

In the classical literature, the issue of insurgent success has virtually been ignored. Given the tendency to view social movements as apolitical expressive actions, this should be no surprise. Insofar as there has been an argument, it has been about the inevitability of the collapse and eventual failure of social movements. Insofar as success is gauged, it is in terms of the self-defined goals or utopias advanced by charismatic leaders. Gauged by the ideals of utopian beliefs, social movements inevitably fall short. In most classical analyses, social movements are seen as inevitably undergoing an endogenously determined natural development or life cycle leading from unstructured spontaneity to ossification and collapse or institutional accommodation. Political processes are seen as basically irrelevant because, at least in the American polity, power is decentralized, elites are receptive, and the regime is structurally open or, in Gamson terms, "permeable". Because insurgencies are essentially expressive actions, their contribution to actual social change is marginal. Elites, parties, and interest organizations operating within the existing rules of the game are the principal architects of social reforms.

The development and outcome of challenges is far more complex and politically channelled than this classical model has allowed. Insurgencies inevitably decline, but this is often due to successes as well as failures. 'Me classical theories have correctly stressed internal developments such as organizational restructuring and strategic shifts, but as Turner has argued, interactions with authorities, antagonists, supporters, and bystanders are frequently decisive. Political power is centralized and generally the polity is closed, elites supporting antagonists while potential supporters watch quietly on the sidelines. Because of the antagonistic nature of their demands, insurgents have to step outside the rules of the game to create significant leverage. Theodore Lowi captured the situation quite well when he argued: "The proper image of our society has never been a melting pot. In bad times, it is a boiling pot: in good times, it is a tossed salad. For those who are in, this is all very well. But the price has always been paid by those who are out, and when they do get in, they do not always get in through a process of mutual accommodation under a broad umbrella of consensus".

In general, a straightforward continuation of the favorable conditions that lead to the emergence of a sustained challenge creates the most favorable circumstances for its further development and success. Since we have discussed these in detail, they require little further elaboration. What does merit further attention are strategic decisions and the development of further political realignments, especially those creating generalized political turmoil. Action strategies have to maximize the leverage against antagonists while minimizing the challenge's vulnerabelity to social controls. Because there are always multiple targets, insurgents frequently confront conflicting priorities and dilemmas. As for political opportunities, limited realignments created the initial opportunities for mounting the challenge, Dramatic successes typically require further reshuffling inside the polity and the development of generalized political turmoil.

Strategies of Action. In the course of a challenge, the direction becomes increasingly independent of the generating forces, becoming an object for internal debate and explicit deliberations. The social movement organization emerges as the primary arena for these collective decisions, placing organizers and movement leaders in the center of major strategic decisions. The pivotal choices are over alternative organizational structures, the scope of insurgent demands and the tactical repertoire. Challenges have to develop durable organizational structures that increase mobilization levels while minimizing their vulnerability to repression. Insurgents also confront what Ash-Garner has called the "optimizing problem" of choosing whether to pursue marginal incremental gains that are more readily obtained or broader structural changes that will provoke intense opposition and open repression. The basic tactical choice lies between making innovative use of existing institutional procedures and intensified institutional disruptions.

In the course of insurgency, social movements almost invariably move in the direction of greater formalization and centralized control. As Gamson study has shown, clear rules and centralized resource management are major pluses in routinizing the flow of resources, reducing the likelihood of debilitating factional disputes and maximizing general combat readiness. The problem, however, is that these same processes can also strip the challenge of its spontaneity, eating away at the missionary impulse that drives organizers and ties them to the mass base, weakening mass solidarity and commitments to the challenge consciousness, and strengthening tendencies towards oligarchization and cooptation. This is especially true for insurgencies among deprived and severely disorganized groups, because they are less likely to sustain support and leaders often find themselves dependent on external support. The National Welfare Rights Organization and its successor, the Movement for Economic Justice, both experienced these strains. Centralized control anti formalization also make the challenge more vulnerable, creating a single target for repression, and by reducing internal diversity and competition among organizers, temper the missionary impulse. Insurgencies, then, are seemingly caught on the horns of an organizational dilemma, pushed towards increased centralization and formalization and towards decentralized informal structures.

This is not, however, an insoluble dilemma. Lawson has argued that insurgencies with multiple structural levels can enjoy the advantages of both centralized and decentralized structures. A centralized social movement organization operating on a national or polity-wide level can coordinate actions and articulate broad demands yet, by preserving loose links to independent grass-roots locals with their own resources, can retain its spontaneity and diversity. In Lawson's case, the tenant movement in New York has thrown up umbrella-type coordinating organizations that have coordinated political demands and provided technical support while retaining a highly decentralized structure of grassroots locals in specific tenement buildings that conduct mobilization campaigns and organize strikes. Similarly, the loosely structured Leadership Conference on Civil Rights has coordinated national civil rights lobbying while leaving each segment of the movement to pursue its own distinctive programs on a local level. As we will see, a similar rough balance between centripetal and centrifugal forces was also at work in the more successful stages of the United Farm Worker insurgency.

The optimizing problem is less resolvable. As Gamson has argued, insurgencies that restrict their goals to single issues and leave the existing structure of authority uncontested are more likely to secure tangible gains. Those with broader, diffuse goals, especially those that demand the displacement of their antagonists, will provoke intense opposition and repressive controls. Probably the most persuasive tract for cleaving to the conservative side of the optimizing problem is Gelb and Palley analysis of the women's movement. By focusing on incremental, single issue reforms that built on institutionalized conceptions of social justice, the moderate wing of the movement has successfully brought about policy successes in the form of legislation and administrative reforms. Meanwhile, the demands of the radical wing for alternative institutions and new standards of equity have provoked a powerful backlash and elite hostility. This argument for thinking small is limited, however, by what it ignores. Insurgent demands are not fixed, emerging full blown in the initial stages of a challenge. Goals develop out of the process of insurgency, Moreover, demands tend to expand in response to successes and increasing opportunities. In the middle 1960s, the successful attack by the civil rights movement on the Jim

Crow system led to broader demands for solutions to powerlessness and poverty. Instead of Southern white racists, the target became the corporations, the urban political machines, and the secure white middle class. Although radicalization alienated sympathetic polity members and provoked repression, it also temporarily heightened the pressure on the moderates to produce tangible results and softened up elites to accept significant reforms. In the long run, however, radicalization did have debilitating repercussions, destroying the informal consensus and loose coordination that had held the movement together and generating a white backlash that eventually pushed national political alignments in a conservative direction.

Insurgencies also choose between unruly disruptive actions and reliance on existing institutional channels. Unruliness works through negative sanctions that create direct leverage but have the long-term negative effect of alienating targets anti provoking repression. The urban riots of the 1960s created short-term policy gains but alienated white sympathizers who then withdrew support from the civil rights movement and licensed wholesale official repression in many riot-torn cities. Existing channels, in contrast, work through persuasion and positive inducements, thereby creating more durable relations. The problem for insurgents, however, is that their demands and resources generally rule out successes based solely on using existing channels. Persuasion depends on shared values and exchange on the control of valuable resources. Insurgent demands are at odds with the interests of their antagonists, shattering normative agreements. Although positive inducements such as smoother labor relations and voter support are useful, these presuppose that the antagonist has already accepted the challenger as a legitimate bargaining partner. In other words, insurgents have to first secure a degree of access before serious negotiations will be possible. Moreover, insurgents generally have to first use negative measures merely to make their offers of cooperation desirable. Success requires unruliness at some point.

These are not, however, exclusive options. In fact, social movements rarely rely on a single tactical repertoire. The most effective approach has been tactical escalation, beginning with moderate tactics and then escalating towards disruptiveness. As Geschwender found in the Hawaiian land use dispute, the movement's exhaustion of remedies through existing channels created external support for disruptive measures. Challenges that begin with major disruptions are likely to confront devastating repression.

Structure of Political Alignments. The history of U.S. politics is studded with challenges that made a significant beginning only to be destroyed by political repression. The success of insurgencies is even more dependent on favorable political alignments than the generation of challenges. At a minimum, success entails changes in public policies. More durable changes require the development of routine political access. The key questions are the strength of the coalitions forged between insurgents and polity members and the access of this reform coalition to centers of political power.

The stronger the coalition, the more directly polity members become involved in the outcome of actual conflicts. Sponsors often limit their contributions to organizing resources, helping to generate a challenge but leaving its prospects uncertain. Others become more directly involved, providing political protection and openly attacking antagonists. As we will see, farm worker movements have traditionally received meager organizing support and even less political protection. The UFW was distinctive because it received extensive political protection as well as organizing support and, by organizing widely supported boycotts, brought sponsors directly into the fray. Similarly, the civil rights movement received significant organizing support from liberal foundations, church agencies, and labor unions, but only with federal restrictions on the activities of the Ku Klux Klan and the White Citizens Councils and the sustained legal attack by the American Bar Association and the American Civil Liberties Union on southern state governments was it able to organize successful voter registration drives.

The strength of these member-challenger coalitions depends on the bases for support and the reform coalition's position in the broader straggle for political power. Polity members have to perceive a clear and direct advantage to extend sustained support. In liberal demcratic polities, the key consideration is the electoral calculus of bringing new groups into the polity in the context of shifting or unstable electoral alignments and closely contested elections. Reform coalitions coming to power also have more political influence and a larger stake in bringing new groups into the polity. The Democratic party has historically been the major supporter of new groups. In the 1930s, critical Democratic support for the industrial worker movement stemmed from the importance of blue collar votes in the shifting electoral alignments of the early 1930s. Likewise, their electoral victories strengthened their ability to institutionalize the political access of unions. Similarly, black ballots were strategically important in the closely contested elections of the late 1950s and early 1960s, leading to Democratic support for the civil rights movement. As the Democratic party expanded its electoral margin, its ability to institute incorporative social reforms such as the Civil Rights Acts of 1964 anti 1965 increased. The UFW victories stemmed, as we will see, from the same realignments and political coalitions.

The most dramatic insurgent successes flow from generalized realignments that are intertwined with the development of generalized political turmoil. Favorable realignments and insurgent successes spur the development of new challenges. The proliferation of social movements and the spread of institutional disruptions maximize the pressure for further reforms. Electoral coalitions become unpredictable, intensifying party competition for mass loyalties and weakening the hold of entrenched opponents. Sponsors become more optimistic about the prospects for further reforms and step tip their sponsorship. Political elites sponsor the entry of the more powerful insurgencies and institutionalize social reforms that, in part, address their demands. Just as the political realignments and turmoil of the 1930s gave rise to a series of labor and social welfare reforms and the entry of new groups into the polity, we will argue that the successes of the UFW depended on the political realignments and generalized turmoil of the late 1960s and early 1970s.

Conclusion

The resource mobilization theory of social movements offers a distinctive analysis of the generation and outcome of insurgencies. In contrast with the classical theories, it emphasizes the indigenous resources, organization, and strategic position of excluded groups and the creation of political opportunities by political realignments. The images of mass explosions stemming from intense, widespread discontents and inevitable movement collapse have been replaced by those of excluded groups pursuing their collective interests in a restrictive polity. Insurgencies are seen as the major agencies of social change and their success as stemming from effective strategies of mobilization and action and from the political opportunities created by political realignments. The central issues in the study of social movements, then, are questions of power and politics, not the social psychology of grievances and the exotic character of insurgent beliefs.

3

Politics of Insurgency

Overview

The transformation of southern agriculture created a massive black migration to the cities. Excluded from mainstream institutions yet freed from the powerful controls of the plantation owners, the black middle class in these urban ghettoes created a new array of churches, student associations, social clubs, and NAACP chapters. By the late 1950s, this new organizational base provided the context for organizing a sustained challenge against the Jim Crow system. About the same time, a new progressivism emerged among the new middle class created by the expansion of the welfare state and the service economy. Professionally committed to developing solutions to social problems, this economically secure yet marginal segment of the middle class became the general advocate for a wide variety of social reforms advanced in the name of the general public and the excluded.

Both insurgencies were facilitated by the political opportunities created by shifting political alignments. The collapse of McCarthyism led to a leftward shift in electoral alignments and elite coalitions. In a series of closely divided elections, political elites found themselves competing for two new sets of restive voters: the newly urbanized blacks who were no longer wedded to the party of their grandfathers or their plantation masters, and the new middle class that was increasingly non-partisan and interested in ideological visions. By the early 1960s, the Democratic party had emerged as the victor, forging a loose coalition between these new contenders and the New Deal coalition. Democratic victories created new opportunities for insurgency, and after the 1964 electoral sweep, the Democrats were in a position to institutionalize a series of social reforms. Inspired by the civil rights and student successes, a new wave of insurgencies emerged among groups that had previously been unorganize and excluded from routine decision making.

The United Farm Worker challenge was one of the more successful of this new wave of insurgencies. Drawing off the resources and strategic models created by the civil rights and student movements, the UFW organized a mass base of farm worker support and a series of broadly supported boycotts and political campaigns that eventually transformed rural California and gave farm workers a permanent voice in major decisions affecting their lives. The new political alignments weakened their grower antagonists and created opportunities for mobilizing external support on an unprecedented scale.

The UFW confronted obstacles similar to those of other insurgencies among the powerless. The growers were politically entrenched, having built their empire out of organization and political access. Farm worker movements had been routinely destroyed by political repression. The structure of the labor market also weakened the mobilization base for such challenges. Although conditions did improve slightly in the period before the UFW challenge, the farm workers were still structurally powerless. The key factor leading to a sustained challenge that eventually succeeded was the new political alignments that tempered political repression, removed the bracero strikebreaking force, and made it possible to mobilize broad external support. The UFW leadership was also prepared to seize these opportunities, adopting a dual strategy of simultaneously organizing farm workers as well its gaining external support.

A critical element of this dual strategy was an extremely effective organizing approach. A key problem in organizing powerless groups is their lack of solidarity and indigenous leaders. By building a permanent membership association led by professional organizers, the UFW created a sustained basis for organizing efforts. These organizing campaigns were also effectively designed. By emphasizing collective incentives and using bloc recruitment tactics that built on existing solidarities and trained indigenous organizers, the organizers generated a solid base of farm worker support. Although this support was not initially sufficient for effective strikes, it did sustain the challenge against the Teamster attack and pressure the growers to accept unionization. The UFW also tried to adhere to a pyramiding strategy, investing in preparatory efforts and gradually escalating actions in line with capacities. Under the protections of the Agricultural Labor Relations Act, this mobilization strategy eventually paid off in a series of highly effective strikes in the late 1970s.

This experience runs at odds with Piven and Cloward assessment of poor people's insurgencies. They advocate a "cadre organization" that shuns a permanent membership and concentrates exclusively on mobilizing mass defiance. In their view, powerless groups cannot be organized into permanent membership associations. At best, membership organizing diverts energies from mass defiance and, at worst, creates organizational brakes on disruptions. The central problem with this interpretation is that membership associations and mass defiance are not exclusive options. Piven and Cloward are correct that the powerless are an unpromising base for organizing permanent membership associations. In addition to being excluded, they are deprived, disorganized, and often sufficiently marginal that their defiance creates only small institutional disruptions. By this measure, farm workers are an advantaged segment of the American underclass. At least they enjoy a better strategic position than welfare recipients and the unemployed. But, as the UFW demonstrated, the powerless can be organized into permanent associations that provide the basis for mass defiance. The organizing may require infusions of external support, especially salaries for professional organizers and technical assistance such as legal and tactical advice. It may also be the case that the more marginal segments of the powerless lack sufficient leverage to extract significant gains. Sporadic insurgency nurtured by transitory cadres may be all that welfare recipients can mount. But at least for those with a strategic position, a permanent association affords greater promise of a sustained challenge and long-term gains. Piven and Cloward may also be correct that insurgent leaders can blunt insurgency and divert dissidence, but these are strategic choices, not organizational imperatives. Insurgent leaders are sufficiently independent that their strategic decisions can push a challenge towards or away from institutional disruptions. In general, poor people's movements should be able to borrow from the United Farm Worker organizing model.

The UFW also built off the other half of the dual strategy by mobilizing widespread external support. Polity members provided organizing resources, political protection, and external leverage. This support overrode many of the traditional obstacles to organizing farm workers, especially lack of organizing resources and problems in sustaining strikes. Yet, as the experience of most insurgencies testifies, the polity is normally closed. Antagonists use their political access to block challenges, and even polity members without a direct stake generally oppose the entry of new groups because this raises the spectre of a restructuring of polity rules. External support, especially of a sustained character, is rare. The state is an inherently conservative institution. The problem then is how this bias of the state becomes neutralized, polity members rallying to the support of insurgency.

I have argued that the central dynamic is the development of internal political realignments that make the support of new challengers advantageous to polity members. As Tilly has argued, a closely divided polity in which rival governing coalitions battle for control increases the likelihood of such member-challenger coalitions. In liberal democratic regimes, elite realignments are mediated by the currents of electoral politics. Parties court enfranchised voting blocs, attempting to forge broad coalitions on the basis of diverse appeals. Changes or instability in the partisan orientation of these voting blocs, especially those that promise the margin of victory, focus elite attentions on the interests of these swing groups. If electoral contests are close, the advantages of bringing new groups into the polity may more than offset the risks of restructuring the polity. Of course, the excluded group has to constitute a significant potential voting bloc, and the insurgents have to advance demands that are compatible with the interests of other coalition partners. The ascendance of center-left governing coalition also strengthens sponsors, reducing the costs of support and increasing their ability to carry through significant reforms.

These realignments and accompanying reforms may also set off a general wave of insurgencies that creates generalized political turmoil and broader opportunities. Successful challenges excite potential insurgents, provide new models of action, and dislodge resources for groups that had previously been quiescent. Sponsors perceive further gains from supporting new challengers. Entrenched antagonists lose their footing. As the political pulse rate heightens, electoral alignments become less stable. Under pressure from proliferating insurgencies, political elites may grant concessionary reforms and fashion incorporative devices to bring the more moderate insurgents into centers of power. Groups with less mobilization potential rise tip, pressing their own special cause. Although most of these demands will not be met, if only because the proliferation of insurgency also generates backlash effects, the spread of generalized turmoil will increase the short-term opportunities for the more powerful challenges. As these groups scramble aboard, securing a modicum of their demands, new challengers rise up that make even more radical bids. Previous bystanders feel threatened and sponsors withdraw support, bringing the period of turmoil and reform to a close.

This analysis of the politics of insurgency runs at odds with conventional theories of political power. The core issue is the role of the liberal democratic state. Pluralists have erroneously assumed that the liberal democratic state is, to use Gainson term, structurally "permeable." Normally the state is a central agency in the battle against insurgency. Polity members use their access to block challenges, and the excluded are kept out because their interests clash with those on the inside. Yet during exceptional periods of realignment and turmoil, polity members may develop a stake in supporting the entry of new groups. The liberal democratic state temporarily lives up to E. E. Schattschileider vision of it as an "alternative power system" in which the force of organized numbers outweighs institutionalized structures of power. The decentralized structure of the American state also provides an advantage. Scrappy challengers have the opportunity to play on regional divisions, concentrating their efforts in particular locales and using external allies to support their demands. In unitary states, different levels of political authority tend to automatically reinforce one another, but in decentralized federal structures, national levels can be at odds with and neutralize or even counteract local authorities. The UFW played on this cleavage quite effectively, mobilizing national elites against local power structures and then later developing strong political ties in California to consolidate gains.

By the same token, elite and Marxist theories of the state have erroneously assumed that the liberal democratic state is an impregnable fortress that consistently supports the prevailing powers. If reforms occur, they have to be preemptive ones that coopt insurgent leaders while denying genuine benefits to the excluded. This picture, however, is almost as much of a caricature as the pluralist myth of permeability. The polity is normally closed, but political realignments and close divisions can create short-term incentives for polity members to sponsor challenges. The liberal democratic state tempers the bias of the state by creating an electoral arena through which the force of organized numbers can have a decisive say. Although such periods of opportunity are exceptional and insurgents have to delicately balance their demands and unruliness to keep from upsetting such coalitions, these member-challenger coalitions can neutralize the state and generate sufficient leverage to force significant concessions. The liberal democratic state has sufficient potential autonomy from existing structures of social power that it can, at least temporarily, serve as a facilitative agency for the institutionalization of genuine social reforms. The translation of this potentiality into actuality depends, of course, on realignments and the spread of generalized turmoil.

This interpretation also casts light on the relative importance of political opportunities and strategies in bringing about successes and the processes leading to political crisis periods. Political opportunities have to exist for insurgencies to become sustained and eventually succeed. By the same token, not all challengers during a period of increasing opportunity will succeed. The UFW was accompanied by a broad wave of poor people's movements, the majority of which failed. Weak organizing strategies, radical demands, and premature militancy destroyed fragile political coalitions and induced repression. Opportunities without effective strategies are like thoroughbred horses with inexperienced jockeys. Their potentials will be unmatched by successes at the finish line. The processes creating these opportunities are based in political turmoil and the development of political crisis. If my analysis of the crisis of the 1960s is a reliable guide, however, those emphasizing profound societal dislocations such as major economic depressions and war losses have overstated their case. Although structural dislocations may give rise to crisis periods, this is mediated by the impact of these dislocations on political alignments. The key is a series of political realignments that give rise to generalized turmoil.

What then is the prospect for further insurgencies that advance the interests of the powerless and excluded? The social movements of the 1960s left behind a rich legacy of social reforms and new organizational bases for mounting challenges. There is no lack of significant grievances around which new challenges could be organized. The major factor is the lack of significant political opportunities. The dominance of centerright governments since the mid 1970s has raised the costs of insurgency and discouraged sponsorship. The continued decomposition of political parties and their electoral supports, especially for the Democratic party, have further eroded the chief mechanism through which political realignments have traditionally been structured. By these calculations, the prospects for another period of political turmoil appear dim. Yet the UFW experience does offer a promising model for mobilizing the powerless. If new realignments should again create opportunities for challenges, the UFW experience provides a fertile set of lessons for successful insurgency.

4

Typology of Insurgency

Introduction

The analysis of insurgency can proceed, however the main types of insurgency must be distinguished. The basis for the distinction used here is the character of the counterinsurgents, and when this standard is applied, three types of insurgency emerge: civil insurgency, anticolonial insurgency, and insurgency against an invading or occupying army. Each of these types has characteristic features.

Types of Insurgency

Civil Insurgency

If the counterinsurgents are an autonomous, indigenous government or an indigenous ruling elite, the insurgency is classified as a civil insurgency since both the insurgents and the counterinsurgents are indigenous.

Anticolonial Insurgency

An insurgency is termed anticolonial if the insurgents are drawn from the controlled country and if their efforts are directed against an outside or colonial power that controls the country's decision-making processes.

Sometimes only a fine line can be drawn between military administration by an occupying army and the governing of a colonial territory. Usually, however, the invading or occupying army will lack the status inside an occupied country that may be enjoyed by a colonial region. During an anticolonial insurgency, the colonial power may even be able to recruit troops from the nationals of the country that is being dominated. An invading force would normally have little success in this direction. In addition, the methods of control used by a colonial regime will be primarily political rather than military. The military forces that the colonial power maintains are there for garrison purposes and not for conducting major military operations.

Insurgency against an Invading or Occupying Army

The third type of insurgency is that against an invading or occupying army. Most instances falling in this category are readily identifiable. Prime examples are the efforts of the French, Russian, and Yugoslav partisans against the German forces during the Second World War. This type of insurgency involves the conduct of irregular warfare in areas occupied by an invader. It may be conducted in conjunction with a regular army or by itself after the regular army has been defeated or withdrawn. Unlike the other two types of insurgency, it is not antigovemmental. Indeed, the government of the country invaded may be directing the insurgents or working with them while in hiding or in exile. It is internal war only in the sense that it is being fought within the country's boundaries by an irregular citizen army. In substance, the struggle is really between the forces or peoples of two separate nations.

In a colonial situation, as noted above, the colonial power exercises control largely by political means. In the case of military occupation, however, primary reliance is placed upon military means. If a territory were to be shifted from occupation status to colonial status, this change would be effected by diminishing the role of military instruments of control and increasing the role of civil instruments of control.

Genesis of Insurgency

In order to understand the genesis of insurgency one must consider the setting in which it takes place, the preconditions for insurgency, and the initiating event.

Preconditions

The setting of a potential insurgency includes many situational factors. These situational factors may (or may not) satisfy the preconditions of insurgency. Four preconditions for insurgency must be satisfied to some degree before an insurgency can be initiated:

1. Hostility to the controlling political or military power
2. The existence of a discontented elite willing to provide organization and leadership
3. A relatively widespread acknowledgment of the necessity for the use of nonlegitimate or violent means to achieve political goals or to obtain redress
4. The capacity to conduct insurgent conflict

These preconditions need not invariably be satisfied in the same way. Indeed it is likely that they will be satisfied in quite different ways depending upon the type insurgency involved.

Preconditions: Civil Insurgency

Numerous situational factors may help satisfy preconditions for a civil insurgency.

A. low level (or low sense) of political participation leading to a low level of support for the regime in power

B. discontent with the quality of life under the present regime

C. discontent with the policies of the present regime

D. existence of isolated and alienated elites which are denied access to the instruments of legitimate political power and which can arouse latent hostility and provide leadership and organization to the discontented

E. ban on normal political opposition which might have the effect of forcing the discontented to express their dissatisfaction by illegitimate or violent action

F. inadequacy of communications channels between the regime and the masses

G. widely felt inequality in the distribution of important values in the society

H. lack of a tradition disapproving of the use of violence or of illegitimate means to achieve political goals or redress grievances

I. existence of racial, ethnic, linguistic, or class segments of the population that are excluded from the political processes of the society

J. existence of groups ready to capitalize on anti-regime sentiments and to channel discontent into action

K. emergence of an attractive ideology incompatible with the existing social or political system

Factors such as these can combine to create the preconditions for insurgency. External factors could have some influence, but in civil insurgencies internal conditions are likely to play the dominant role. While nationalism provides the momentum for colonial and antioccupation insurgencies, social, economic, and ideologic cleavages provide the drive in civil conflict.

Preconditions: Anticolonial Insurgency

It is difficult for a colonial nation, even an enlightened colonial nation, to avoid taking actions which will lay the groundwork for insurgency. Hostility to foreigners, which is likely to be produced under the best of circumstances, is almost certain to be increased if the foreigners occupy a dominant position in a country. Formal subordination to foreign rule helps to create the preconditions for insurgency. It unites people and provides a focus for nationalist sentiment. The charge of economic exploitation by the colonial country is likely to be effective in stirring men to action. The doctrine of national self-determination is always at hand and can provide whatever theoretical justification is needed for a nationalist movement. Those situational factors, mentioned in the previous section, that help create the preconditions for civil insurgency may also contribute to the development of insurgency against a colonial power.In the case of anticolonial insurgency, local elites are usually quick to volunteer to lead the struggle against the colonial nation. Among these may be nationals the colonial power has educated in the mother country. To be sure, individual nationals may be co-opted by the colonial power and serve as a brake on the development of insurgent sentiment.

Preconditions: Insurgency against an Invading or Occupying Army

One of the preconditions for insurgency is hostility toward the controlling regime. This precondition is almost automatically satisfied in the case of a foreign invasion or military occupation. The same is true of the need for a discontented elite willing to provide organization and leadership to the insurgent movement. The third precondition, a readiness to use force, is also customarily satisfied when a nation is invaded.The difficulty is likely to center around the fourth precondition, the capacity to conduct insurgent conflict. The factors that contribute to the capacity to resist would include the following.

A. absence of complete population control by the invader
B. will to resist
C. belief in the feasibility of resistance
D. leadership and organization
E. sources of supply

Precipitating Event

It does not follow that if the preconditions for insurgency are satisfied insurgency will instantly erupt. The conflict must await a precipitating event. Figure 4.1 may be helpful in indicating the relationships among situational factors, preconditions, initiating event, and insurgency.

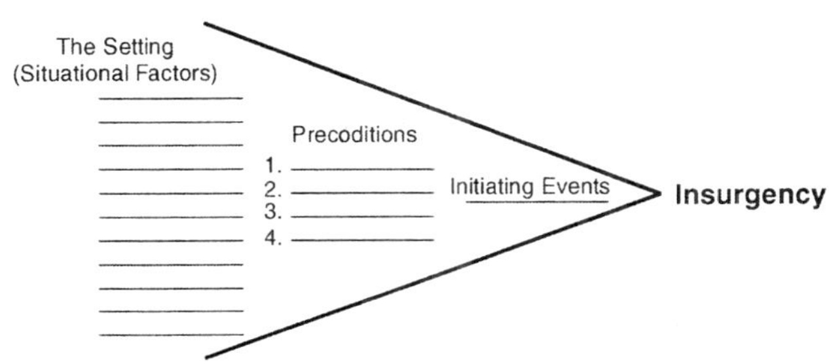

Figure 4.1

An initiating event takes place within the setting and is of such a nature that it serves to mobilize the energies of the discontented and to direct them toward violent action. Its impact is psychological rather than purely physical, and the impact need not follow immediately upon the event. The event may have little intrinsic significance but may be seized upon at some point by an elite or organization and may be given a special significance. A listing of possible initiating events would include the following.

A. an event which acquires symbolic significance such as an economic or social disaster, a particularly antagonizing action by the regime, or a heroic act of defiance by an individual rebel

B. an event that forces action, such as an invasion by a foreign power

C. the emergence of a charismatic leader

D. the perception of a tactical, or strategic advantage by a revolutionary elite

E. the decision by a revolutionary elite to issue a call to arms

F. the influence of foreign agents or propaganda

The more ripe the time, the greater is the range of events from which the initiating event can be drawn. If the situation is explosive (which is to say some or all of the preconditions have been satisfied to a high degree), almost any event may serve as an initiating event. The ripeness of time may also produce a flood of events in a short period of time so that it would be difficult to point to a single event as the act that precipitated the struggle. In such a situation it may be more helpful to think of a series of acts as precipitants.

Objectives of Insurgent Movements

Any discussion of the objectives of insurgent movements must distinguish between formal objectives and informal, unannounced objectives. Followers may be exhorted in terms of one set of objectives, and actual planning may move forward in terms of a quite different set. Informal objectives, that are likely to deal with questions of political tactics and personal advantage, are important for the leadership even if they tend not to be suitable for exploitation and the winning of broad support.

Tito's formal objective was driving the Germans out of Yugoslavia, but his informal objectives included the acquisition of political power by the Communist party and himself once the Germans departed. This meant the Chetnik movement had to be discredited and destroyed since it was a potential competitor for power. The formal objective of the French resistance was the defeat of the Germans. Informally, however, each of the major factions sought to strengthen its political position and to weaken that of the opposition in preparation for the postwar showdown.

Objectives: Civil Insurgency

The formal objectives of an insurgency might be arranged along a continuum. At one end would be minimum objectives such as minor reforms. At the other end would be an objective such as the complete reorganization of society. Between the extremes would be objectives such as achievement of significant reforms, participation in the government, control of the government, overthrow of the government, and modification of the entire political system.

During the course of an insurgency objectives are likely to evolve. Typically the demands of the insurgents escalate as the struggle begins, as blood is spilled, as relations become embittered, and as the insurgents devote more thought to the reasons for their discontent. Later, if victory is not achieved, the insurgents may be forced to reduce their demands in order to settle the conflict. Extreme demands may be excellent for morale but they may also prolong conflict.

Objectives: Anticolonial Insurgency

The major an complaints of those trying to organize an anticolonial insurgency are, customarily, inadequate participation in decision-making, economic exploitation, and denial of selfdetermination. These complaints may be restated by the discontented in terms of positive objectives: expropriation of foreign holdings in the country, ouster of all foreign nationals, independence, and establishment of a noncolonial governing system.

Objectives: Antioccupation Insurgency

The primary objective in an insurgency against an invading army is the expulsion of the enemy from the country. There may be secondary objectives such as institution of a new political regime, once the enemy has departed, or achievement of significant social reforms.

Basic Input Factors

Input factors common to the three kinds of insurgency are examined in chapter IV. Here, however, the aim is simply to note the way in which the role of these inputs may vary depending on the type of insurgency involved.

Leadership and Organization

Leadership in a civil insurgency may come from an established political or economic elite or from a class whose members feel that they have been cut off from the exercise of political power. Some of the leadership in a civil insurgency may come from outside the country. Such outside assistance may be either voluntary on the part of the individuals concerned or may be part of a governmental program.

Leadership in an anticolonial insurgency may come from any of the sources mentioned above, but it is more likely to come from the educated and propertied classes in this instance than it is in the case of civil insurgency. However, leadership in an insurgency against an invading or occupying army is a somewhat different matter. The insurgency is likely to be sponsored by the legitimate government in exile. Regular army officers may play a prominent role as Red Army officers did in the Soviet Union after the German invasion in 1942. Leadership may come from the same sources as in an anticolonial insurgency or a civil insurgency, but it is more likely to be exerted by those elites that would exercise legitimate power if the country were not occupied by a foreign army. If the insurgency is being underwritten by an allied government interested in continuing the struggle against the invader, leadership will be offered by foreign officers. This was the case with the British in Norway and the Americans in the Philippines during World War II.

Logistic Support

During a civil insurgency the insurgents are apt to have difficulty obtaining weapons and supplies because the various sources for this material may be inadequate.

1. *Theft or seizure*. Theft cannot provide a continuous flow of supplies and the volume of supplies from this source is also

likely to be small. During the early stages of a movement seizure will probably be risky. Later on, of course, seizure may become a vitally important source of supply.

2. *Domestic purchase.* The government is usually able to cut-off or sharply reduce the flow of weapons and supplies purchased from sources within the country. Because of the government's control of roads and railroads, the insurgent usually finds it difficult to move large quantities of material internally.
3. *Foreign purchase.* The insurgents are likely to suffer from a shortage of funds and will therefore find it difficult to buy needed quantities of weapons and supplies from abroad. In addition, there is the problem of smuggling the supplies into the country, given the government's control of port facilities and roads, and of distributing them.
4. Provided by a friendly foreign power. A foreign power may be willing to provide weapons and supplies. This will ease the financial burden on the insurgents but the problem of smuggling the supplies into the country and distributing them will remain. In addition, there may be a political price tag associated with this support, such as the acceptance of advisors and guidance from the foreign power.

An anticolonial insurgency is likely to be faced with similar supply problems because the colonial government will be able to control the internal transportation system if it wishes to do so. There are several features of the situation that may be more favorable, however. First, if there is widespread opposition to the colonial power, the insurgents may be able to move supplies with less fear of informers than would be experienced in the case of a civil insurgency. Second, if the wealthier segments of the society are supporting the insurgency, the financial problem may be eased to some extent.

In the case of an insurgency against an invading army or an occupying force, the supply problem will be somewhat different. Weapons may be available from regular soldiers who refused to put down their arms when the army surrendered or broke up. If there is a government in exile, it may be able to provide supplies, and a friendly power would be another possible source of supply. Internal movement of supplies will remain difficult, however, if the country is under actual occupation.

Manpower and Population Utilization

The most important factor determining manpower practices and population utilization practices in the three different types of insurgency is the prevailing distribution of attitudes in the population. This distribution, in turn, is influenced by the experiences the population has undergone. If a country has suffered a foreign invasion, the population is likely to be easily reached by the appeals of insurgents. The predisposition to resist will be there, and the insurgent leadership need only activate latent feelings and channel the resulting action.

Insurgents can usually take advantage of predispositions produced by a colonial experience. Nevertheless, as Thomas Jefferson noted in the Declaration of Independence,"...all experience hath shewn, that mankind are more disposed to suffer, while evils are sufferable, than to right themselves by abolishing the forms to which they are accustomed." If colonial rule has been longstanding, apathy may be widespread. However, such rule will also have provided grounds for complaints and dissatisfaction. If the insurgent leaders can combine these concrete complaints with a strong nationalist appeal, they are likely to have a solvent capable of removing apathy and disinterest.

In the case of a civil insurgency, on the other hand, the insurgent is usually denied a clear-cut nationalist appeal. The call to drive out the invader or to resist the colonial oppressor crosses all sections of the population and therefore can elicit society-wide support. During a civil insurgency, however, a society will be split rather than unified by the appeals made to it. The disadvantaged may be set against the advantaged, the disenfranchised against the franchised, race against race, minority against majority.

Intelligence

Each of the three types of insurgent movements requires intelligence. There appear to be differences in the nature of the intelligence requirements for each type movement, the sources from which intelligence would characteristically come, and the intelligence-gathering techniques that each would use. Since limited data is available, however, generalization will not be attempted.

Strategy and Tactics

A variety of strategies and tactics are available to the antagonists in an insurgent conflict. Which of the available strategies will be selected will depend upon the type insurgency involved and the particular circumstances surrounding that insurgency. Nevertheless, certain types of strategy are likely to be associated with certain kinds of insurgency.

Strategy and Tactics: Civil Insurgency

In this type insurgency, the insurgent faces an indigenous governing structure. Unless the members of the government choose to flee the country, they have no choice but to resist. From the point of view of the counterinsurgent leaders, resistance cannot cost more than defeat, therefore they will resist to the end. Harassment of the government, in the hope that it will give up the struggle, will probably not be a winning strategy for the insurgents.

Each side may feel somewhat restricted in the coercive measures that it can use against the populace. The use of severe measures may lead to a loss of popular support and a consequent weakening of the insurgency. This matter is discussed in a later chapter.

Strategy and Tactics: Anticolonial Insurgency

Insurgents fighting a colonial power will seek to raise the cost to that power of retaining the colony. The cost will be measured in money, lives, loss of international good will, and loss of political support at home. At some point, the insurgents hope, the colonial power will conclude that the colony is not worth the cost of keeping it. The war of the Viet Minh against the French in Indo China was won at Dien Bien Phu and in Paris. The French army did not lose the war in Algeria, but the French nation conclude that the benefits from keeping Algeria a part of France not compensate for the cost of doing so.

Pursuit of military victory is a possible Strategy for the insurgent. In view of the probable disparity in military strength between insurgent and counterinsurgents, however, a strategy aimed at the opponent's will to resist may be more realistic than one aimed at direct military victory.

An anticolonial insurgency may also incorporate diplomatic elements into its overall strategy. It is usually not very difficult for an insurgent movement to muster diplomatic support from nation that are anticolonial in orientation.

Strategy and Tactics: Insurgency Against an Invading or Occupying Army

The strategic options open to insurgents in this case are somewhat restricted. If there is an indigenous army still in the field or if an allied army continues to fight, the insurgents may be able to make a significant contribution. They may be able to harass the enemy's supply lines and communications lines and, by so doing, force the enemy to divert substantial numbers of troops from combat to population control. The resistance in Yugoslavia is commonly said to have tied down thirty-five German divisions. If a conventional army no longer remained in the field to fight the invaders, however, the effectiveness of the insurgents might be problematic. If the bulk of the German troops had not been tied up fighting conventional forces, they would probably have been able to deal with the Yugoslav partisans. It is difficult to imagine the Germans being driven out of France or the Netherlands by the resistance. The troops of the invading army are probably prepared to be ruthless, and this is an advantage to them. All chance for gaining popular support was probably dashed by the invasion, and therefore they have little left to lose and will feel free to use harsh measures against the populace.

Internationalization of Insurgency

Each state, colony, or territory is a part of the international system. That being the case, national politics cannot exist in a vacuum. To some extent at least domestic politics are open to the gaze of foreigners and to intervention by foreigners. It is rare for an insurgency to remain untouched by foreign influence.Insurgencies involving colonial or occupying powers are internationalized by definition. That is, the struggle is not between elements that are primarily indigenous. In civil insurgencies intervention may take any number of forms diplomatic intervention, direct participation by a foreign power (or powers) in the conflict, or covert participation.The logic that leads to internationalization of an insurgent conflict can be seen in the following example. An insurgency develops in country X for a variety of reasons related to internal conditions. The insurgents, hard-pressed by the government forces and badly in need of supplies, approach country Y for assistance. Country Y might consider assisting the insurgents for any of a number of reasons.

A. It is opposed to the government of X, and supporting the insurgents offers an economical, low-risk means of embarrassing that government.

B. It is opposed to another country (Z) that supports the government of X, and it sees support for the insurgents as a way to embarrass Z.

C. It is inclined to support the insurgents for ideological reasons.

D. If the insurgents were to be victorious in country X and owed their victory to Y's support, the government of Y might be influential in X and would have won the friendship of the new government of X.

Therefore the government of Y decides to offer large-scale support to the insurgent movement. This support begins to endanger the position of the government of country X. That government, therefore, turns to country Z and seeks its support. For reasons similar to those of government Y; the government of Z offers its support to X. The conflict is now thoroughly internationalized with Y supporting the insurgents and Z supporting the government. The nature and level of the support may be such that the entire nature of the insurgency is altered, and the conflict may even become one that is primarily between the intervening nations.

Summary

It is apparent that characteristics of one type of insurgency may not be found in the other two types. Caution should therefore be exercised in drawing conclusions on the basis of an examination of one type and assuming that these conclusions will hold for the other types as well.

5

MODEL OF INSURGENCY AND COUNTERINSURGENCY

Introduction

This chapter offers a general model for the analysis of insurgent-counterinsurgent conflict. The over-all model consists of several elements: an operational model and a model of the control system of each of the antagonists. These elements are related to each other as shown in Figure 5.1.

Information about the course of the conflict flows from the operational model to the control systems of both sides. The control systems process this information, in keeping with their impressions and attitudes, and generate decisions which in turn influence action in the operational model. It should be remembered throughout the subsequent discussion that the elements of the model are analytic constructs and do not necessarily possess physical analogs. To demonstrate the working of the entire model the discussion will first describe the operational model in isolation, then the control system model, and, finally, the process of the conflict itself.

Operational Model

Several preliminary points should be made about the operational model at the outset. First, it possesses symmetry since the key elements and the basic mechanisms that it depicts are identical for both the insurgents and the counterinsurgents. Profound differences appear at a lower level of generality, however. Both sides have capabilities, but the nature and magnitude of those capabilities will slow wide variation. Both sides make judgments about strategy and tactics, but the strategic and tactical decisions will be very different.

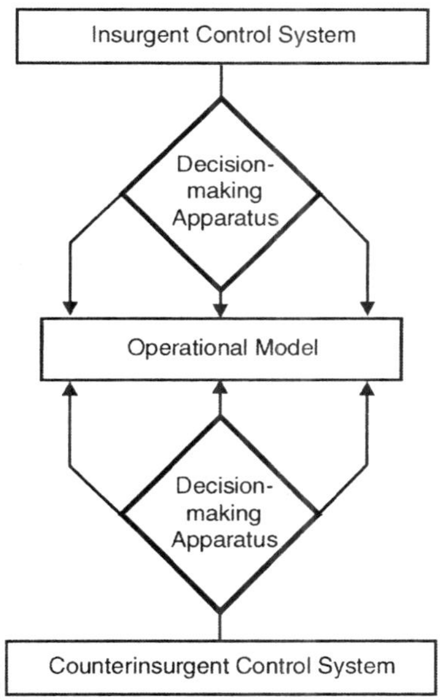

Figure 5.1. Insurgent Control Model.

Second, everything beyond the outer boundary of the system is a part of the international environment. The participants in the domestic struggle may be able to influence to some extent the way in which that environment impinges upon the struggle, but they will not be able to control it. Inputs from the external environment may be vague and indirect, such as a U.N. resolution eliciting a popular response within the nation. Conversely, they may be more direct, such as the provision of weapons or troops to one side or the other. The graphic model places the decision gate on such inputs outside the boundaries of the system, indicating that the crucial decisions with regard to them are made by external actors rather than by the indigenous antagonists.

Third, through the model flow physical resources and psychological responses. A flow is deemed to be physical if it has an obvious material component (weapons, supplies, men). A flow is deemed to be psychological if it is nonmaterial and has to do with morale, ideology, and the loyalties of individuals and groups. Many actions related to insurgency will, of course, produce both physical flows and psychological responses.

Arena of Conflict

The discussion of the operational model can usefully begin with the arena of conflict, the hub of the model. In the arena of conflict insurgents and counterinsurgents interact, and their competing efforts collide. This arena can be thought of as a "black box" which receives the inputs of both the insurgents and the counterinsurgents. These inputs reflect the capabilities of the antagonists and are deployed in accordance with their respective strategies and tactics (G1). In addition, there are inputs from the environment and those that are products of chance. These inputs are processed within the box (A) and emerge as outputs (IV and V)—the results of what has taken place in the arena of conflict. These outputs may have both physical and psychological manifestations.

It demonstrates the dynamic features of the model and the central nature of the arena of conflict. In essence the elements complete the loop between inputs to and outputs from the arena (A) and demonstrate the interconnected nature of the model within the boundaries of the system. This makes it clear that inputs into the arena (A) are processed there to produce outputs which in turn effect the nature of subsequent rounds of inputs. Thus the model depicts a dynamic, cyclic round of action in which what has gone before effects what is yet to come.

Inputs into the Arena of Conflict

More specifically, there are four types of inputs into the arena of conflict: (1) situational factors (I); (2) chance (II); (3) insurgent capabilities (physical and psychological) III (I); (4) counterinsurgent capabilities (physical and psychological) III (CI).

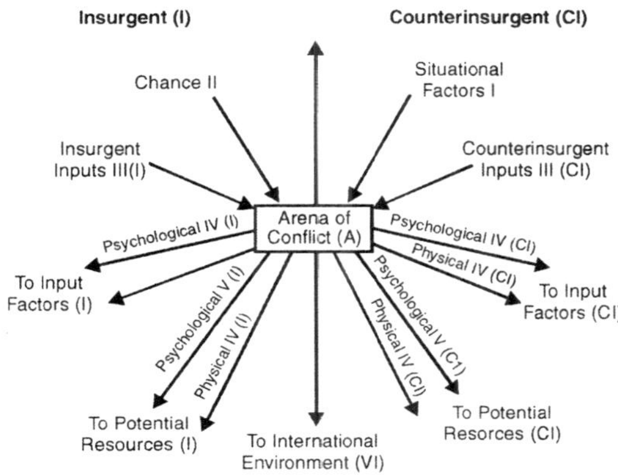

Figure 5.2. Types of Inputs.

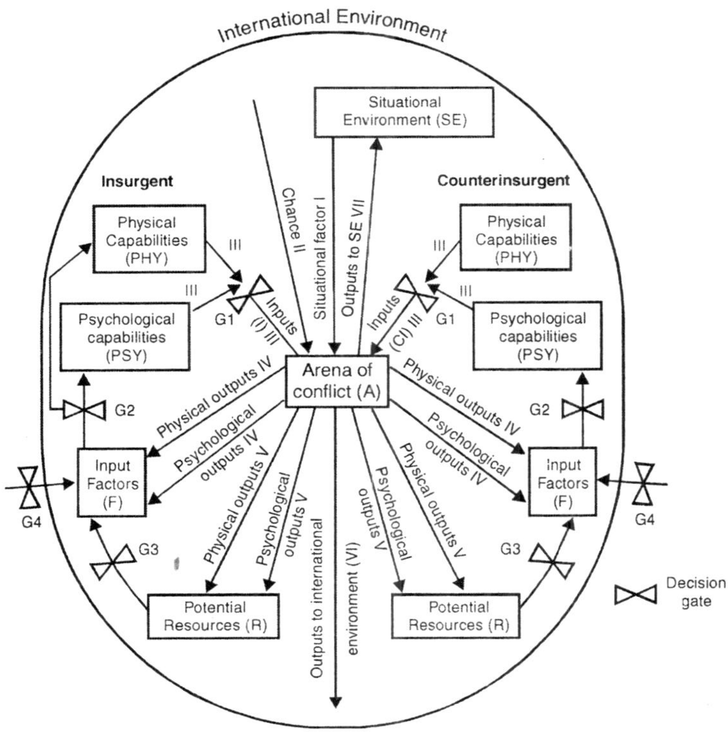

Figure 5.3. Model of Insurgent and Counterinsurgent.

The situational environment (SE), consists of both political and physical factors. The term *political factors* refers to the situational variables which differentiate civil, anticolonial, and antioccupation insurgencies. Inputs, outputs and decision-making (control) patterns will all be influenced by the nature of the insurgent-counterinsurgent relationship. Through their influerce on the objectives, resources, and vulnerabilities of the parties to the conflict, these variables lead to major differences in strategy and tactics, resource utilization, leadership recruitment, and other inputs.

The physical aspects of the situational environment consist primarily of terrain and climate. These inputs are fixed since they may have a profound influence on the nature of the conflict but do not respond readily to human efforts at control. For example, it would no doubt have benefited the Algerian rebels if they could have had a jungle available for concealment, but there was no way that they could manufacture one. Weather also falls into this category. The monsoon season creates problems for counterinsurgent forces dependent on air power, but those forces are incapable of altering the monsoons. The model does show a feedback loop to the situational environment (VII), however, to indicate that change is at least occasionally possible. Efforts at defoliation in Vietnam provide an example.

Chance is indicated as an input into the arena of conflict because it is present to some extent in almost all human activities. One might refer to it alternatively as luck, a random factor, noise, or the will of the gods. Examples of chance in warfare are numerous. During a routine police raid in Manila, the government forces chanced to round up most of the Huk leadership. Before the battle of Antietam General McClellan chanced upon a copy of Robert E. Lee's battle plans.

The capabilities of the insurgent and the counterinsurgent generate the capacity of each to operate in the arena of conflict. What are the main types of input into the arena coming from each participant? First, as noted above, each side can take actions generating physical flows and psychological responses. Second, each side is trying to alter the balance of capabilities in its favor. Doing this will require "constructive" actions aimed at increasing its own capabilities and "destructive" actions aimed at reducing the capabilities of the opponent. For convenience, therefore, actions might be classified in accordance with the simple fourcell matrix depicted below.

A given action may, of course, fit into more than a single category. A successful action against enemy troops, for example, might also undermine enemy morale. This example makes it clear that a physical action an attack in this case can alter both physical (PHY) and psychological (PSY) capabilities. It is also evident that a psychological operation, such as a propaganda campaign, can also alter both physical and psychological capabilities.

Similar actions may have a dissimilar impact upon capabilities depending upon the type of insurgency involved. For example, population control measures aimed at reducing insurgent capabilities, such as the resettling of local populations in Vietnam and Algeria or mass imprisonment of males in areas occupied by Germany in World War II, would have more serious feedback consequences for an indigenous counterinsurgent who needs popular support than for a colonial power or an occupying army that will have already written off the possibility of popular support. Similarly, insurgent use of terror will be less likely to produce adverse popular reaction when aimed at colonial or occupation forces than when aimed at the forces of an indigenous counterinsurgent.

There may be a marked disproportion in the quantity of inputs fed into the area of conflict from the two antagonists, but this fact should not obscure the similarity of the process in each case. Each side will try to a alter the relative balance of capabilities in its favor and each side will have some capacity to do so.

Outputs from the Conflict Arena

The interaction of the insurgents and the counterinsurgents in the arena of conflict generates various results or outputs. These outputs will be shaped by the the interplay of all the elements feeding into the arena of conflict: chance (II), situational factors (I), the capabilites of each side (III), the way in which the capabilities are employed (G1), and the interaction and conflict that take place in the arena (A).

Outputs from the conflict arena take the form of influences of a physical or a psychological nature. These influences may affect the basic input factors (F) of either side or the potential resources (R) of either side. In addition, some of the outputs from the arena of conflict will feed back into the international environment (VI).

	Constructive Actions	Destructive Actions
Actions producing physical results	Increasing manpower, weaponry, etc.	Killing enemy troops destroying enemy supplies.
Actio9ns producing psychological results	Improving morale, improving loyality of population, etc.	Understanding morale of enemy troops, trying to alienate population from enemy etc.

Potential Resources

The term *potential resource* (R) is used to refer to a resource over which one of the contestants has a degree of control and may be able to utilize at a later date. This may be a resource a contestant has chosen not to try to use, such as a manpower resource which the government has not exploited. It may be a resource which a contestant has not learned how to use or determined whether it is worth the effort necessary to employ it.

Actions can be taken by a participant to increase the potential resources available to him or to diminish those available to the enemy. These actions may be designed to generate a flow of physical resources or of psychological responses. Figure 5.3 indicates that the box representing potential resources (R) is connected to that representing input factors (F) by a decision gate (G3). The gate signifies that a decision is required before potential resources (R) can be mobilized and transformed into input factors (F) and fed into the arena of conflict as physical (PHY) or psychological capabilities (PSY).

Basic Input Factors

Six input factors (F) must be available to each side if it is to carry on the struggle: manpower, population utilization, intelligence, leadership, organization, and logistics. The input factors differ from potential resources in that they are already mobilized for use.

The basic input factors may be fed from three sources: from the arena of conflict (A), from the pool of potential resources (R), and from the international environment. The first of these is usually the most important. Since these input factors provide the basis for a participant's capabilities, efforts to alter the balance of capabilities are naturally directed toward them. For example, when the British forces in Malaya sought to cut off the Malayan guerillas from their food supplies, they were striking at the insurgents' logistical input factor, the point at which they considered the insurgents to be most vulnerable. The leaders of the insurgent movement, which will be typically weaker than government in its military capabilities, will strike at those basic inputs where the government is weakest, such as, perhaps, intelligence.

Physical and Psychological Capabilities

Basic input factors are not the same thing as capabilities. The input factors (F) are the raw material, so to speak, from which capabilities (PHY and PSY) are manufactured. Before the manufacturing process can get under way, however, decisions have to be made concerning the kinds of capabilities to be produced and the desired amount of each. The decision gate (G2) shown on the graphic model indicates the necessity for decisions on these matters.

When decisions are made they are implemented by varying the mix of basic inputs. The basic input factors can be blended in a wide variety of ways to produce different mixes of capabilities. For example, if the counterinsurgent leadership decided to increase sharply its capability for civic action, it would have to alter the blend of input factors (F) (manpower, logistics, leadership) that had previously been designed to produce a maximum combat potential.

Strategy and Tactics

The extent of the capabilities available to each side and the way that those capabilities are utilized in the arena of conflict will usually determine the victor in the struggle between insurgent and counterinsurgent. Capabilities do not employ themselves automatically in the conflict arena however. There are likely to be many ways in which a given set of capabilities *can be* employed, and decisions have to be made concerning the way that they *will be* employed.

It will be seen in the graphic presentation of the model that capabilities flow into the conflict arena through a decision gate (G1). This gate signifies the necessity of making decisions on the employment of capabilities in the arena. These decisions are governed by decision-makers' perceptions of the respective capabilities of the two sides and their tactical and strategic objectives. Each side will make continuing strategic and tactical decisions concerning the employment of its capabilities in the arena of conflict in pursuit of its goals.

With the flow of capabilities into the arena of conflict, as modified by each side's selection and employment of strategy and tactics, the loop has been completed, and the discussion of the operational model is back to the point at which it began.

Cycle of the Model

Having completed a discussion of the elements in the operational model, it might help to clarify the working of the model to trace an example through an entire cycle.

A preliminary caveat is in order. Thus far the discussion of the model has ignored the element of time. The flows that have been depicted do take time, however. In some cases, lags will be of great significance. Today's potential resources (R) are not necessarily tomorrow's capabilities (PHY or PSY). It is one thing to decide to mobilize thousands of civilians into an army and quite another thing to actually do it. In addition, there is usually noise and confusion in the channels through which the flows move. Events may occur with no one being sure what they are or what they mean. Combatants on both sides may leave a battlefield demoralized from mutual perceptions of defeat or buoyed by the belief that they had been victorious. In short, while the flows depicted in the model represent the basic processes at work, it would be naïve to expect that developments in an actual conflict would be so rapid, clear-cut, and certain.

A description of the cycle might begin at the point where inputs enter the arena of conflict (A). We shall trace a typical insurgent operation the ambush of a counterinsurgent convoy. First, the insurgent employs some of his capabilities, for example, a company of hardened guerrillas. Their plan (G1) is to attack the convoy at a certain point of the road. The counterinsurgent, too, has capabilities employed in this operation the men and equipment of his convoy. They also plan to move from point A to point B, taking precautions against ambush. The situational environment (SE) plays a role too. Perhaps it is raining, thus hampering the counterinsurgent's air support, and the terrain is heavily wooded and rough. This creates a variety of good ambush sites (I). However the counterinsurgent has modified the environment somewhat (VII) by clearing a swath on both sides of the road, making ambush more difficult. Chance (II) may intrude. A guerrilla accidentally steps on a mine, thus revealing the ambush, or an accompanying counterinsurgent armored vehicle turns back due to mechanical failure. Whatever the precise situation, the stage is now set. We enter the arena of conflict (A) as the first shot is fired. Perhaps the insurgents are completely successful and destroy the convoy and its complement of soldiers. Perhaps the counterinsurgents are prepared and deal the insurgents a sharp reversal. Whatever the precise nature of the conflict, certain results emerge from the conflict arena. Some results of an insurgent victory might be the following.

A. an improvement in insurgent morale (a psychological developmental output.

B. The capture of useful weapons (a physical developmental output)

C. the destruction of counter-insurgent material (a physical destructive output

D. a deterioration in counter-insurgent morale (a psychological destructive output

The results may be reversed. Or there may be a mixed bag of pluses and minuses for each side. At any rate, results flow from the action, and they have an impact upon the basic input factors for both sides. Potential resources (R) of the antagonists may also be affected. The ability or inability of the counterinsurgents, to keep the road open may greatly affect the status of areas along the road. With the road closed, the insurgents may take over a previously contested region and thereby increase their potential resources [V (I)]. Or, if the road is opened, the counterinsurgents may be able to control a greater area than had previously been possible.

Each antagonist may also seek to use the outcome of the recent action to modify the relative balance of capabilities. The insurgents may exploit the newly won territory [R (I)] to increase basic input factors such as more troops and better intelligence. The counterinsurgents, if victorious, might take the occasion to bring in more troops and increase the security of the area.

The results of the action may affect potential resources (R) and will probably affect the basic input factors (F). This means that physical (PHY) and psychological (PSY) capabilities will also be affected. In addition, the strategy and tactics (GI) adhered to by both sides may be altered. The insurgents may decide to place greater emphasis upon ambushes and may decide to try to close the road altogether. The counterinsurgent commander may place greater reliance on armored escorts or may be moved to organize a search and destroy the mission directed against the insurgents. We are now back to our starting point, having completed a military action and having traced some of its possible ramifications through the system.

Control Systems

The control systems of the insurgents and the counterinsurgents are symmetrical. However what occurs in equivalent boxes on the two sides may be different, and the relative weight of the various factors in determining decisions may be thoroughly asymmetrical. Asymmetry in the evaluation of factors may also be associated with the type of insurgency involved. The control system of the counterinsurgent may be a colonial power, a national government faced with overthrow, or a military command occupying conquered territory while responsible to its home government. The varying circumstances of these different control systems will inevitably lead to differences in objectives, motivation, and determination, the stakes involved, and the time and attention devoted to the struggle. The control system of each antagonist is depicted in the figure below. Perhaps the best way to begin an analysis of this schematic diagram of a control system is to think of the entire system as a "black box" and to ask what constitutes inputs into the system and what emerges as outputs. On the input side, we find primarily perceptions of the course of the conflict. These perceptions may be relatively accurate in some cases, but, as perceptions, they are always bound to introduce some element of distortion. The actual events in the field are filtered through a perceptual screen and the antagonists act on the basis of these filtered results. The out of the control system is a continuing set of decisions concerning strategy and tactics (G1), the desired blend of, input factors (G2), and whether and how potential resources ought to be utilized (G3). The control system as a whole, therefore, is a means for converting a stream of perceptions concerning the conflict into a stream of relevant decisions concerning present and future behavior.

Relative Capabilities Analysis

The first step toward the formulation of strategic plans for the conflict by either side is the analysis of the relative capabilities (RA) of the two sides. This analysis must concern itself not only with present capabilities but probable lines of future development. There are three main elements which are relevant to this analysis.

A. the assessment of one's own capabilities, including other capability requirements, basic input factors, and potential resources (C)

B. the opposition's capabilities, basic input factors, and potential resources (EC)

C. an estimate of the enemy's will and determination (ED)

Each of these elements is subject to a substantial degree of error in measurement. When the three are taken together, it is not surprising that the analysis of relative capabilities (RA) often falls wide of the mark. Nevertheless the relative capabilities analysis does represent the more rational part of the decision process. It is the point at which each antagonist determines the nature of the situation that it faces.

The views of either side concerning the stakes (ST) in question are derived from one's perception of the relationship of one's own goals (G) to the goals of the opponent (EG). The stakes for a participant may be thought of as the gains that he would derive from victory relative to the losses that would be associated with defeat.

The counterinsurgent will define his stakes primarily in terms of what defeat will mean since victory will probably involve little more than the continuance of the status quo. If the insurgent is perceived as seeking limited reforms or simply a role in the government, the stakes for which the counterinsurgents are playing are less than if the insurgents planned to turn the government out of office and execute its leading figures. Similarly, an indigenous regime will be more agitated about the overthrow of the existing political and social system than a colonial power will be about the loss of a distant territory.

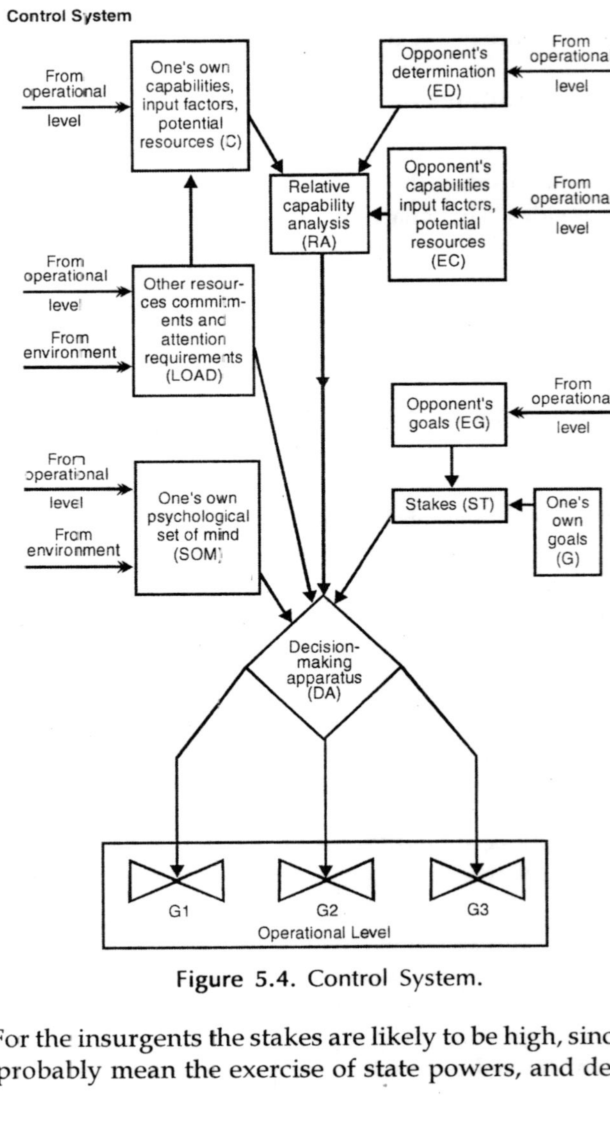

Figure 5.4. Control System.

For the insurgents the stakes are likely to be high, since victory will probably mean the exercise of state powers, and defeat may mean death. The counterinsurgent leadership should be aware that they can alter the stakes for the insurgents by their own actions. For example, if they promise to execute all the leading insurgents, then the threatened insurgents will be prepared to pay virtually any price for victory. On the other hand, if the government offers amnesty to the insurgent leaders, some of them may be induced to surrender when the situation becomes difficult.

Psychological Set

The truly rational decision maker would not be governed by passion or emotion in making decisions, but all ordinary mortals are prey to the influence of nonrational psychological factors. For example, if a foe is deeply hated, decisions concerning behavior toward that foe are likely to incorporate a nonrational element. The fact that sacrifices may already have been made in a struggle is also likely to introduce a nonrational element. It may lead to a solemn resolve that those who have died shall not have died in vain. To be sure, the sacrifices of one side in every war are likely to be in vain since someone must lose the war. This consideration is akin to the economists' *sunk-cost fallacy*. The personal characteristics of leaders including determination, flexibility, willingness to compromise—also contribute to the psychological set (SOM) of the participants.

Decision-Making Apparatus

Each participant in the struggle seeks to alter the balance of capabilities in its favor in order to achieve its ultimate objectives. The factors influencing the way this is to be done are four: the relative capabilities analysis, the stakes involved in the struggle, the psychological set of the decision makers, and the over-all load on the administrative organization.

The actual decisions are generated at this stage by the decision-making apparatus (DA). This is the mechanism-and it may be organized many ways which produces the decision that activates the three decision gates of the operational model (G1, G2, G3). Here decisions will be made concerning when and how potential resources are to be converted into basic input factors (G3), the particular way in which the basic input factors are to be blended to produce capabilities (G2), and the tactics and strategy to be used in deploying capabilities in the arena of conflict (G1).

For maximum efficiency the decision-making process should coordinate all three types of decisions in accordance with an overall strategic plan. As a practical matter, however, these different types of decisions are often not fully co-ordinated. The men concerned with strategy and tactics may emphasize population control and suppression while those concerned with building increased psychological capabilities may be emphasizing good relations with the populace. A second difficulty is the existence of time lags and noise in the channels that pass the decisions of the top authorities down to lower levels. Orders may be delayed, never received, misinterpreted, or ignored.

A third problem involves administrative load. Decision making occurs in an environment in which matters other than the military struggle are usually competing for the attention of the decision maker. The insurgent leader, for example, may have to deal with the collection of taxes, the maintenance of order, and the provision of food in areas the movement controls. Counterinsurgent leaders are likely to be burdened far more. They must normally deal with the full range of problems confronting an ongoing government. For a colonial power, the conduct of war against an insurgent may comprise a small part of the total decision-making load. A government conducting a large war may be able to give little attention to suppressing partisan insurgents in occupied areas. For example, German occupation forces in Yugoslavia were often hampered in combating partisans because of the low priority given to their efforts and the resulting difficulty in getting an appropriate allocation of resources. A control system's control will often, therefore be less than perfect. Nonetheless, it will strive, if rational, to alter the capabilities balance in a favorable direction.

Cycle of a Control System

To trace the working of a control system, it might be useful to return to the earlier example of an insurgent ambush and note the response of the counterinsurgent control system to the results of that action. Reports on the action would provide a basis for assessing its effects on the counterinsurgent's capabilities, basic input factors, and potential resources (C). If the action ended in a defeat for the counterinsurgents, it might produce the following results.

A. Loss of men and material would reduce the basic input factors—manpower and logistics.

B. Inability of the counterinsurgents to cope with this type attack might lead to a sharp scaling down in estimates of the physical capabilities of the counterinsurgents.

C. Defeat might lower the morale of the survivors, thus lowering the psychological capabilities of the counterinsurgents.

D. Defeat might cause the counterinsurgents forces to appear less formidable to the populace and hence reduce their psychological capability.

For the insurgent, on the other hand, there would be numerous pluses. The capabilities balance has been altered as a consequence of the action, and the counterinsurgent is likely to conclude that he must do something to restore the situation and to alter the new capabilities balance in his favor (RA). Perhaps, after their triumph, the insurgents began to loot and burn the homes of government supporters in the region near where the action took place. This new development would indicate that the insurgent's goals (EG) have escalated and that reconciliation has become less likely. Furthermore, the attack in territory that had hitherto been quiet may indicate to the counterinsurgent that he cannot allow the insurgents to roam freely in this area but must either drive them, out or destroy them. The stakes have been raised, inhibitions have been thrown off, and the psychology of the decision makers (SOM) has been altered.

Now the counterinsurgent generates his plans for altering the capabilities balance. At the strategic and tactical gate (G1), he decides the lost territory must not go uncontested. Hence, helicopter assaults are ordered on various villages to inhibit insurgent exploitation. Since the action has revealed inadequacies in the counterinsurgent's capability mix, decisions are made to improve the mobility and aggressiveness of the troops (G2). Further, since the escalation of the conflict demonstrated the seriousness of the situation, new taxes are levied and more troops mustered into the army as the counterinsurgent girds for the next round (G3).The working of the counterinsurgency control system has now been traced through a complete cycle. The process would be similar if the working of the insurgent control system were examined. It must be emphasized again that the information fed into a control system is filtered through a perceptual screen and is also likely to be distorted by lags, noise, and sometimes outright deception (e.g., junior officer falsifying combat outcomes).

Escalation

Escalation means an increase in the magnitude and virulence of the conflict. To have escalation, at least one side must decide either to utilize its existent capabilities more intensively or to acquire and employ greater capabilities.

Motivations for Escalation

Given the ability, the insurgent leaders might escalate for several reasons.

A. They may believe the present level of conflict is so low it holds no promise of victory.

B. They may conclude, as a result of a relative capabilities analysis, that they can stand the strain of escalation better than the counterinsurgents can. If the counterinsurgents are trying to maintain a multiple of insurgent strength, say eight or nine to one, a net addition of one unit to insurgent strength would force the counterinsurgents to add eight or nine units.

C. The insurgents might conclude that if they escalated the conflict the total potential resources available to the counterinsurgents would soon be committed, and the ratio of insurgent to counterinsurgent forces could not fail to improve.

D. After examining the goals and stakes of the opponent the insurgents might conclude that they should escalate further since the counterinsurgents would be unwilling to (for example, if the counterinsurgents represented a colonial or occupying power) and hence would have to make concessions or sue for peace.

E. The insurgents might increase the level of their activity because counterinsurgent escalation left them no alternative.

In other circumstances the insurgents might be wise to avoid escalation or even to seek to de-escalate the conflict. For example, the leaders of a movement might be well advised to operate at a sufficiently low level of activity during the early stage of their movement to avoid drawing a full-scale counterinsurgent effort from the government. Such an effort might be fatal to the movement. If the movement were operating at a high level of activity and was nevertheless slowly being crushed, the leaders might wish to consider a sharp reduction in the level of effort in the hope of encouraging a corresponding reduction in effort by the counterinsurgents.

Guevara advised revolutionaries to adjust the level of insurgent activities to keep it slightly below the all-out response threshold of the counterinsurgent. It may be difficult for the insurgent to locate this threshold, but an approximation is probably better than nothing. The insurgent should be aware that the location of this threshold may shift during the course of a protracted conflict. As a movement grows, however, a time may come when Guevara's advice can no longer be followed. If it is to continue growing, it must inevitably precipitate an all-out response from the counterinsurgent.

The counterinsurgents may also have reasons for wanting to escalate the conflict. In the early stages of an insurgency, the movement is likely to be very vulnerable: leaders are still learning their jobs; training and logistics arrangements are likely to be poor; manpower may be inadequate; and the flow of intelligence is also likely to be inadequate. It would be a rational course of action for the counterinsurgent to overreact to the insurgency and to crush it at the outset. However, the very vulnerability of the movement causes its threat to appear minimal, and the response of the counterinsurgent is therefore likely to be minimal. Furthermore, when a government is faced by a civil insurgency, it is usually loathe to acknowledge that a serious threat really exists and will incline in the direction of under reacting rather than overreacting.

There are good reasons for each side to consider escalation a desirable strategy. Tracing the escalation of an insurgency through the entire model serves a twofold purpose: exploration of the phenomenon of escalation and demonstration of the efficacy of our model for describing the complex interrelationships of insurgent situations.

Process of Escalation: An Example

The working of the operational model and the control system model will be illustrated by the use of an example, an example of escalation. A number of flows move through these models simultaneously, but for purposes of exposition the process has been simplified. To have a point of entry into the model, it will be assumed arbitrarily that the insurgents have decided upon a significant escalation of effort. The consequences of this action will be traced until a cycle has been completed.

The insurgent control system has decided to increase the level of its operations in a province close to the counterinsurgent capital city. Three types of interrelated decisions have to be made concurrently. One type decision (G2) concerns the input factors necessary for the escalation. If there is to be an escalation of effort, it will require increases in certain inputs: manpower, logistical support, and intelligence. Significant changes in leadership and population utilization policies are also planned. A new mix of input factors is designed to provide for the increased capabilities needed.

A second type decision (G3) concerns the mobilization of potential resources. If inputs are to be increased to generate greater capabilities, mobilization of additional potential resources is required. Therefore, it is decided to broaden the recruitment effort, expand the training program, develop new sources of supply, and to improve the insurgent intelligence gathering apparatus in the province.

The third type decision (G1) involves strategy and tactics. The insurgent leaders decide to marshall what troops they can to make surprise attacks on government troops in their barracks in a number of towns. At the very least, the insurgents believe, their successes will humiliate the government and have an impact upon public opinion, and their successes might set in motion a chain of events leading to the government's downfall.

The insurgent plan begins to be executed. The physical and psychological capabilities of the insurgents, applied in accordance with their decisions on strategy and tactics, become inputs into the arena of conflict. The counterinsurgent input (III-CI) consists of military garrisons in several major towns plus various unimaginative policies with regard to the population. As noted earlier, situational factors comprise one of the inputs into the arena of conflict. The terrain in the province is wooded, which is to the advantage of the insurgents. A fairly elaborate system of roads, however, is advantageous to the counterinsurgents. A final input into the arena of conflict is chance. Chance plays a role in the unfolding of events in the arena of conflict because the commanding officer of the government forces in the province proves to be a singularly inept individual. Several months earlier he personally assured the president that the insurgents were no more than a handful of bandits and posed no real security threat. When reports of a planned attack came to him, he rejected them out of hand.

The insurgent attacks were well planned, and tactical surprise was complete. The attacks were simultaneous, followed the same pattern, and were made at night. Barracks were set afire, and soldiers were machine-gunned as they tried to flee the burning buildings. By dawn organized government forces had ceased to exist in the province. For the time, at least, the insurgents controlled the province. They proceeded to imprison some government officials and execute others. The insurgent organization, that had operated clandestinely to this point, came into the open and began to function in a limited way as the *de facto* government of the province. A large-scale propaganda program was instituted to persuade the populace of the villages and towns to give their allegiance to the insurgents.

Insurgent inputs into the arena of conflict interact with the other inputs and result in certain outputs. Some of these outputs affect the insurgents themselves and others affect the counterinsurgents. On the constructive side, the potential resources available to the insurgents increase sharply as the insurgents begin to exercise control over the province. The constructive psychological output from the arena of conflict takes the form of improved morale among the insurgents and the improved standing of the insurgent movement among villagers and townspeople. The only destructive psychological output derives from the bitterness of a portion of the populace because of the damage to their homes and farms as a consequence of the fighting. There is a destructive physical output because of casualties suffered and equipment lost.

A number of destructive physical outputs from the arena of conflict affect the government. Garrison forces (an input factor for the counterinsurgents) have been destroyed. The government has lost control of the food production in the province, and this is a serious matter since the capital city is dependent to an extent upon those foodstuffs. Loss of control of the province also reduced the opportunity for recruitment of young men into the armed forces. The destructive psychological outputs for the counterinsurgents are scarcely less important. The prestige of the government and of the military forces suffered greatly. The populace was exposed to the arguments of the insurgents over an extended period of time, and many appear ready to co-operate with the insurgents either from fear or from conviction.

On the balance, the outputs from the arena of conflict following the insurgent escalation are highly favorable to the insurgents. The counter-insurgent control system receives information about events in the province and evaluates that information. A new relative capability analysis (RA) is made. The counterinsurgent control system perceives that the government's capabilities, its basic inputs, and its potential resources have all been adversely affected. It also perceives the gains of the insurgents (EC). In much the same way that the capabilities of the insurgents had previously been underestimated, they now tend to be exaggerated. Once again the raw information received by the control system is fairly accurate, but the system introduces a significant element of perceptual distortions (SOM).

The government reassesses the determination of the insurgents (ED) and finds it greater than anticipated. It also begins to perceive, in a different way, the stakes involved (ST). The opponents' goal (EG) is now correctly perceived to be the overthrow of the government. As a consequence of events in the province and the control system's analysis of those events, the government now concludes: (1) that it is not dealing with bandit gangs but with an organized and growing insurgency; (2) that the insurgent movement is determined and well led; and (8) that its capabilities are far greater than had been realized.

Until the attack on the province, the insurgent offensive remained below the threshold at which the government would perceive itself as threatened. Now that threshold has been passed, and the government's reaction is one of alarm. In the past the government had been content to react locally and on a small scale to what it regarded as relatively inconsequential acts of banditry. Now its goal with regard to the insurgency becomes more comprehensive, namely, destruction of the movement.

Decisions are made to give effect to this new goal. Potential resources are examined, and it is decided to make a sharp increase in the number of men conscripted. Aid is sought, and received, from a foreign country, thus constituting an input (G4) from the international environment. The mix of basic input factors is altered to give a different output. Strategy and tactics are modified in the light of the new situation. Changes are made in the leadership of the military forces, and the commanding officer in the province is retired in favor of a younger and more aggressive officer. A decision is made to alter the stakes for the individual insurgent, and it is announced that all insurgents who are captured will be executed in the field. The president also announces that the properties of those who collaborate with the insurgents are subject to confiscation. In short, the counterinsurgent control system responds to insurgent escalation of the conflict by organizing a pronounced counterinsurgent escalation.

These actions provide a new counterinsurgent input into the arena of conflict. A series of attacks are mounted on towns held by the insurgents. These inputs generate a new series of physical outputs. The towns are recaptured by the government forces with relative ease, substantial quantities of insurgents' weapons and supplies are seized, and several prominent insurgent leaders lose their lives in the fighting. The psychological outputs are also important. The insurgent movement ceases to look like the wave of the future to many villagers, and they adopt a more cautious attitude toward collaboration with the insurgents. The government's threat of property confiscation is taken very seriously. Within the insurgent movement morale drops, the desertion rate rises, and the flow of new recruits into the movement almost ceases.

The insurgent control system perceives and evaluates the physical and psychological outputs from the arena of conflict. After considerable soul searching, the insurgent leaders acknowledge that the attack on the province was premature and ill conceived. They acknowledge that this action has aroused the government and that their own forces are not yet capable of engaging government units in the field. They decide to return to hit-and-run tactics, albeit on a larger scale than previously, and to build for the future. They console themselves with the thought that they have demonstrated the vulnerability of the government forces and have put their movement on the map.

Appropriate orders are given by the insurgent control system, and the actions that are taken in consequence provide a series of new insurgent inputs into the arena of conflict. Since this example of escalation began with a series of insurgent inputs, the cycle that was to be examined has now been completed.

6

Perspectives of Insurgency

Introduction

The setting in which an insurgency occurs is likely to have a great impact upon its nature and its outcome. It is helpful to think of this setting in terms of four situational factors: (1) the physical and demographic environment; (2) the strength of the counterinsurgent and the nature of his challenge; (3) the role of traditions, expectations, and attitudes; and (4) the impact of the international environment. In addition, the context in which insurgent conflict takes place is shaped by the fact that insurgency may exhibit some of the characteristics of limited war and by problems associated with the termination of insurgent conflict.

Physical and Demographic Environment

The physical and the demographic features of a country affect the nature and the locus of insurgent military activity. Since he is weak by conventional military standards, the insurgent needs access to a base area or sanctuary which is relatively secure from attack by the counterinsurgent. Ideally, such a region would contain rugged, thickly forested mountains or swamps, an adequate water supply, and either land suitable for farming or proximity to an isolated agricultural district. In addition, it should be large, separated from major population centers, and close to the border of a nation sympathetic with the rebels. The importance of one terrain element, vegetation, can be seen by contrasting the French experience in Algeria with the American experience in Vietnam. Using a few planes, simple electrified barriers, and surveillance devices, the French were able to patrol a large area and to cut off a substantial portion of the supplies to the FLN coming from Tunisia and Morocco.

In Vietnam, the Americans, making extensive use of a variety of sophisticated aircraft and a variety of advanced technical devices, were never able to interdict the movement of supplies along the Ho Chi Minh Trail even though the area involved was far smaller than that in Algeria. Vegetation explains much of the difference. The French were standing watch on an area that was near desert while the Americans were dealing with a densely forested area.

Terrain facilities the conduct of some operations and militates against others. Military operations should be undertaken in the daytime only when a rugged, relatively inaccessible refuge is available nearby. Since the guerrillas will typically be operating in small groups, they cannot afford prolonged encounters with the superior manpower and firepower of the enemy. Guevara minimizes the danger of encirclement, since the guerrillas can escape individually after nightfall. However, it is imperative that they be able to fade away into a secure area before the counterinsurgent can relocate them the following day. This requirement places a range limitation upon the operations of the insurgents. An urban insurgency, such as that in Cyprus or Warsaw, is less dependent upon surrounding terrain. The mountains of Cyprus did however provide a refuge for the leaders and an area for staging minor harassing operations.

The density of the population and its composition are factors to be considered in the formulation of insurgent strategies. If the population is highly concentrated, the incumbent regime may be able to insulate the populace from a rural-based insurgent movement. This would deny manpower, intelligence, and logistic support to the rebels. If the population is distributed in a fairly uniform way, on the other hand, it will be almost impossible for the counterinsurgent to protect continuously both the populace and vital installations. The insurgent will find it easier to penetrate the population and to extract needed resources from it.

Climate is another ecological factor. The late David Galula has noted that a mild climate is most favorable from the insurgent standpoint since it permits continuous operations without posing grave problems of equipment maintenance and survival. "Contrary to the general belief, harsh climates favor the counterinsurgent forces, which have, as a rule, better logistical and operational facilities. This will be especially favorable if the counterinsurgent soldier is a native and, therefore, accustomed to the rigors of the climate. The rainy season in Indochina hampered the Vietminh more than it did the French. Winter in Algeria brought FLN activity almost to a standstill." Galula performed a service by puncturing the long-held notion that climatic extremes are always an advantage for the insurgent. In doing so, however, he passed over the diversity of effects that various climatic conditions may have on different opponents. When air support, including both tactical bombing and troop airlifts, is vital to counterinsurgent operations, monsoon rains may be a severe handicap to the counterinsurgent. Cold weather, on the other hand, may create greater difficulties for the insurgent than for the counterinsurgent since the former lives in rude conditions.

Nature and Strength of the Counter Insurgent Challenge

The broad political objective of an insurgency will usually be to utilize the population and its resources to make the capability balance more favorable. The strategy to be used in achieving this objective will normally vary with the type of insurgency involved. In the case of an invading army, the strategy may call for building popular support on the base of traditional loyalties and inducing the populace not to co-operate with the invader. If the counterinsurgent is a colonial overlord, the strategy may be to arouse nationalistic fervor, to control the populace, and to demonstrate to the imperialist power that attempts to retain the colony will not be worth the cost involved. When an indigenous regime is in power, however, the political strategy is likely to involve attempts to undermine the legitimacy of the government, to foster a sense of frustration and exploitation in target groups, and to persuade the populace that insurgent rule would be both more efficient and more just.

The military capabilities of the counterinsurgent will normally have a great influence on the strategy and tactics used by the insurgent. The latter will seek to avoid the counterinsurgent's strengths while exploiting his vulnerabilities. For example, if the counterinsurgent can call upon tactical air support, this has implications for the behavior of the insurgent. Concealment must be nearby, and actions must be terminated quickly. The opponent's mobility is also an important factor. Airmobile units, such as those used by the Americans in South Vietnam and the French in Algeria, can rapidly encircle a guerrilla unit. If the counterinsurgents initiate a maneuver early in the day, they may be able to close the ring and annihilate the insurgents before nightfall. If the guerrillas can hold out until darkness, they will attempt to escape individually through the encirclement. As mentioned earlier, counterinsurgent possession of such an air transport capability places a definite range limitation upon insurgent operations, they cannot safely travel further from a secure area than the distance of a night march.

The mobility provided by land transport vehicles must also be taken into account. Whether cross-country motorized transport, such as that accorded by armored personnel carriers APC's), or road-bound vehicles alone are at the disposal of the counterinsurgents is a key consideration in tactical planning. Counterinsurgent naval forces may have a role to play in the interdiction of supplies and recruits being delivered to the insurgents by sea. If this is the case, their effectiveness is a factor in strategic planning since the level of insurgent operations is a function of the availability of resources.

The capabilities of the counterinsurgent are determined not only by the equipment available, but also by the quantities of all of the basic input factors at his disposal. The level of operations of the conterinsurgent is governed both by the availability of resources and by his willingness to make the maximum use of them. Therefore, the resource level of the counterinsurgent at any given time is an important factor in determining the operational options open to the insurgent.

Traditions, Expectations and Attitudes

A third situational factor involves the distribution of political, social, economic, cultural, and religious attitudes among the population and the intensity with which various attitudes are held. In conventional conflict, the principal task of the psychological warfare arm is to reduce the enemy's effectiveness by demoralizing his troops. Psychological warfare during an insurgent conflict will not ignore enemy troops, but the principal target will be the population of the country. The insurgent will try to elicit supportive or neutral behavior from the populace. Psychological warfare techniques, in conjunction with the exercise of physical control over people, will also help the insurgents to extract needed resources from the populace.

The existence of cleavages and antagonisms within the society ethnic, religious, social, economic, political is to the advantage of the insurgent. While the government must attempt to mediate differences and to calm inflamed tempers, the insurgents will try to exacerbate frictions and make use of internal tensions. They will be eager to contrast the lot of the disadvantaged with that of the well-to-do or to argue that the government is systematically persecuting a political, ethnic, or religious minority. The Catholic-Buddhist schism in South Vietnam, for example, played a key role in the downfall of the Diem Government in 1963 and illustrates the disruptive potential of such cleavages.

An important attitudinal factor affecting the insurgent's choice of population utilization strategies is the degree of social mobilization in the target society. Social mobilization refers to "the pressures that cause populations to form political communities in other words, the changes that cause people of towns, villages, and regions to knit together into new political orders which transcend these areas as their inhabitants realize that their mutual interests extend beyond daily contacts." If only local and regional allegiances are salient for the populace, the introduction of a disorienting influence (such as a foreign invasion) may provide an opportunity for the insurgents to develop a whole new set of social relationships in the strife-torn society. This is precisely what the Chinese Communists did against the Japanese invaders in World War II and the Yugoslav Partisans did against the Germans, as Chalmers Johnson has demonstrated. The effort to politicize a provincially oriented peasantry is also characteristic (despite the absence of a newly injected disruption from abroad) of the Malayan, Cuban, Algerian, Philippine, Viet Minh and Viet Cong insurgencies. All have taken place in countries where a widespread sense of national identity was lacking.

The attitudes held by the populace with regard to violence will normally influence the strategies and tactics chosen by the insurgents. As J. K. Zawodny has suggested, it makes a difference whether the local people are Quakers or Catholic Poles when it comes to the use of violence against civilians or the provoking of reprisals by the enemy.

International Environment

A final situational consideration in the formulation of insurgent strategy relates to the international environment. An insurgent movement may be concerned with foreign affairs for a number of reasons. First, the leaders of an insurgency may want a privileged sanctuary, a base area in an adjoining country with which the counterinsurgent is not at war. The insurgencies in Greece and Algeria demonstrate the importance of such a sanctuary. When hard-pressed, the Communist insurgents in Greece were able to withdraw across the border into Yugoslavia. Tito's closing of this border, following his split with Stalin, denied sanctuary to the insurgents, and they were defeated in 1949.

The insurgents may also be interested in the international realm because of their need for weapons and supplies from abroad. As the weaker party in the conflict, the insurgents must strive to improve the relative balance of resources, and this means seeking resources that may be available in the international environment. Few modern insurgencies have come to power without substantial aid from abroad, and many have come to power with it.

Unless the prospects of an insurgent movement are reasonably good, a foreign government may see no reason to provide it with aid and jeopardize relations with the incumbent government.

To establish its prospects an insurgent movement may try to achieve a striking victory or take some important symbolic act such as creating a *de facto* government in a liberated area. The insurgents must bear in mind, however, that outside assistance is not always an unmixed blessing. An insurgent movement may find that its acceptance of outside support is being exploited by the incumbent regime to arouse patriotic sentiment against it. The counterinsurgents can argue that the insurgents are tools of a foreign power. A second danger is that the country offering aid may use its assistance to acquire influence over the insurgent movement. The insurgents may cease to be their own masters and may become virtual tools of the outside power. "If the domestic ally has become dwarfed in terms of autonomous capabilities by the preponderance of outside power, the outcome of the internal war-cum-intervention may be the loss of effective sovereignty and the emergence of another puppet or satellite regime."

An insurgent movement may also be interested in diplomatic recognition as well as foreign aid. This may be the recognition of foreign governments or recognition by international organizations. The existence of international organizations and regional organizations may come to have a substantial influence upon the success of insurgencies. They provide a forum in which the insurgent may have an opportunity to argue his case before a world audience, and regional groupings, such as the Arab League and the OAU, may provide an institutional framework through which foreign assistance to insurgents (or counterinsurgents) may be channeled.

The insurgents may wish to impair the image of the incumbent regime abroad and damage its international relations. They may hope to deny legitimacy to that regime and to acquire it for the insurgency. This might have important implications in terms of diplomatic recognition and cutting off aid to the government in power.

Trying to influence public and governmental opinion abroad, the insurgents must operate within a given climate of international opinion. If the incumbent regime is a colonial power, it will operate at a considerable disadvantage in the contest for world opinion. As George Modelski has noted, "In recent years, near-universal acceptance has been gained for the view that colonialism is a thing of the past, that all colonial territories ought to be granted independence, and that colonial wars are therefore justified." Insurgencies against colonial regimes will receive a sympathetic hearing in many countries and international organizations.

If the incumbent regime is indigenous, the insurgent movement may seek to label it as neocolonial. The incumbent regime may find itself characterized as barbarous, repressive, and exploitative and may be accused of committing atrocities and genocide. It will not be easy for the foreign press to assess the truth of these charges, and some journals, for ideological reasons, may be inclined to accept them at face value.

Insurgency as Limited Conflict

In the aftermath of the Korean War, military analysts began to understand that nations could engage in war on a limited basis and that this type of conflict was likely to become common in a world that feared nuclear war but had not eliminated violence as a means for settling disputes. In the late 1950's and early 1960's the concept of limited war began to receive attention and to be subjected to systematic analysis. The concept of limited war is closely related to that of insurgency, and therefore much of the analysis that is applicable to the former proves also to be applicable to the latter. In the literature on limited war the antagonists are nation states. The logic of limited conflict, however, is not confined to nation-states at war but can be applied to many kinds of conflict such as political campaigns, parent-child relationships, labor-management disputes, and street fights. Limited war is a special case within the far broader category of limited conflict that may also include certain kinds of insurgency. In the same way that analysts have, until recently, tended to assume that modern warfare is always an all-out activity, so too they have tended to assume that insurgent conflict is always waged at full throttle. This need not be the case.

At the outset, however, it is important to distinguish between civil insurgencies on the one hand and anticolonial insurgencies and those against an invading army on the other. The stakes are different in the two cases, as has been noted on several occasions. Because the stakes tend to be higher in civil insurgency, the conflict is usually fought more nearly at the capacity of the adversaries. The only restraints observed may be those imposed by the capabilities of the contestants, the dictates of politico-military strategy, or cherished cultural traditions. Agreements, tacit or explicit, are likely to be short lived, and the insurgent will be careful not to deny himself advantages that inhere in the special nature of insurgent conflict. The discussion below, therefore, will apply to civil insurgencies less often than to the other two types.

Just as warfare between nations can be carried on at different levels of activity, so can insurgent conflict. Just as international war can be prosecuted under a variety of constraints and rules of the game, so can insurgent warfare. An insurgency may be limited with respect to geography, level of effort, types of targets hit, weapons used, combat techniques used, and objectives pursued. The restraint may be symmetrical or asymmetrical. That is, it may be practiced by one or both of the antagonists. The restraint would be asymmetrical, for example, if a counterinsurgent force were devoting a limited proportion of its energies to combatting an insurgent force that was delivering its utmost effort.

The rhetoric and pretensions of insurgent conflict may make it difficult for either the insurgent or the counterinsurgent to acknowledge that he is practicing restraint. The counterinsurgent wants to assure supporters that the struggle against the criminals, bandits, and traitors who are the enemy is being prosecuted in a whole-hearted way and without letup. A discussion of the degree of vigor that should be used against an insurgent would undermine the image of stern resolution which the counterinsurgent is probably trying to convey. For reasons of morale and ideology, the insurgent usually finds it useful to portray the counterinsurgent as a ruthless oppressor of the people. Having done so, it is then difficult to justify anything short of an all-out, unrelenting struggle.

It is often helpful to distinguish between the formal, announced goals of an insurgent movement and the operational goals revealed by the behavior of the leaders and of the movement. As suggested above, the rhetorical objective of the movement may be to attack the enemy in an unrelenting way while the operational objective may be more modest. Another reason the formal goals and the operational goals may be different is that the leaders of an insurgency may have a set of secondary, unannounced goals that modify the movement's official goals.

A discussion of limited insurgent conflict raises a number of interesting questions. When will a contestant want to escalate a conflict and when will he want to de-escalate it? What keeps a limited insurgent conflict limited? Under what circumstances would such a limitation prove unstable? When might the insurgent and the counterinsurgent have a common interest in co-ordinating their behavior to a degree? Each side might conclude that its interest would not be advanced by escalation and might therefore want to avoid it. The insurgent and the counterinsurgent need not necessarily have the same reason for pursuing a restrained policy. The insurgent might be playing for time or awaiting some favorable political development while the counterinsurgent might believe that the existing level of conflict would soon exhaust the enemy.

The contestants may also have a common interest in developing certain rules to govern the conduct of the conflict. It might serve the interest of both sides if it were mutually understood that no one is to use torture, that there are to be no attempts at assassinating the leaders of the other side, that fighting will cease during religious holidays, and that there is to be a moratorium on serious conflict during the winter months.

If the antagonists have a common interest in agreeing on a level at which the conflict shall be prosecuted and on certain rules of the game, how are they to achieve this co-ordination under circumstances in which communication is severely limited. Thomas C. Schelling has posed the issue: "The problem is to develop a modus vivendi when one or both parties either cannot or will not negotiate explicitly or when neither would trust the other with respect to any agreement explicitly reached." His answer to the problem is, of course, that enemies can engage in tacit bargaining. "The study of tacit bargaining—bargaining in which communication is incomplete or impossible assumes importance, therefore, in connection with limited war, or, for that matter, with limited competition, jurisdictional maneuvers, jockeying in a traffic jam, or getting along with a neighbor that one does not speak to." Agreement can emerge in a conflict situation without explicit negotiation. That holds true for insurgent conflict as well as for conflict between warring nations. Both the insurgent and the counterinsurgent might become aware of the element of restraint in a particular situation, and each might want to preserve that restraint. In such a situation a tacit bargain can be struck if each combatant exhibits restraint. By his restraint, each is saying to the other, "I do not plan to do anything untoward, and will not, unless you force me to." Seasonal lulls in insurgent conflict and reductions in activity during religious holidays have sometimes emerged from tacit bargains. Tacit agreements have sometimes emerged, and remained stable for a time, concerning the geographical limits of the struggle. The counterinsurgent may refrain from going into the hills after the insurgent, and the insurgent in turn may refrain from attacking towns or army barracks and embarrassing the counterinsurgent. In this way the hills may belong to the insurgent and the towns to the counterinsurgent, and the struggle between the antagonists will revolve around the road system and the attempt to move personnel and supplies.

A tacit rule may emerge, may be observed for a time, and then may begin to be ignored by one or both antagonists. It is in the nature of a tacit rule that it will usually be observed only as long as each side believes it to be in its interest to observe it. To be sure, one side might continue to observe a particular rule even though it was disadvantageous to do so in order not to endanger the observance by the other wise of the entire structure of rules that might exist. On the whole, however, the stability of a rule is governed by the immediate interests and capabilities of the antagonists. A tacit rule is a special kind of rule. Since it is unwritten and has not been formally agreed to, the antagonists will feel no pressure to adhere to it because of the general principle that rules must be obeyed. It is not that kind of rule. If the insurgent perceives that the counterinsurgent has been so weakened politically and militarily that he cannot respond to an escalation of the conflict with a sharp counter escalation, the insurgent would feel free to ignore the tacit agreement that has stabilized the level of effort and to increase the pressure against the counterinsurgent.

Termination of Insurgent Conflict

This volume has discussed the origins of insurgency and its dynamics, but little has been said about how insurgent conflict might be ended. Such conflict can be terminated either through negotiated settlement or through victory for one side and defeat for the other. There are variations of each of these types, of course. For example, an insurgent movement may dissolve without suffering a decisive defeat and without surrendering formally.

A negotiated settlement requires dialogue between the leaders of the opposing sides. The dialogue can be carried on face to face, in writing, or through intermediaries. It can also be carried on in the press by means of a series of unilaterial announcements, ultimatums, and responses. This last method would allow the leaders to negotiate without making an explicit acknowledgement that they were negotiating. Indeed, in the early stages of feeling out one another, they might not be fully aware that they were, in fact, negotiating.

The course of the negotiations, when started, will be influenced by the communications process involved and by several other factors. It will be influenced by the objectives of each side. Leaders may have to learn to distinguish between the objectives they proclaim in their rhetoric and the gains they would actually be willing to settle for. The negotiations will also be influenced by the normal drift of objectives. The initial objectives of an insurgent movement may be modest and reformist in nature, but these may gradually be replaced by more ambitious goals as the struggle continues and as the criticism of the counterinsurgent becomes more through going and the struggle generates increased bitterness. The negotiations will also be influenced by the success, or lack of success, that each side is enjoying in the field. Success in the field will normally lead to an expansion of goals and a hardening of a bargaining position while reverses will lead to the reverse. In addition, the negotiations will be influenced by the stakes involved and by the way each side conceives its future prospects.

Initially each side will be loathe to consider a negotiated settlement. Formal negotiation is likely to be incompatible with the rhetoric that each engages in and with its statement of objectives. Prolonged conflict and stalemate, however, may lead the antagonists to be more receptive to the idea of a negotiated settlement. This would be particularly the case if the insurgent leaders had important secondary objectives that might be jeopardized by prolonged fighting. Each side may begin to sense that it will have to settle for something less than the total surrender of the enemy and the complete achievement of its own objectives. The counterinsurgent may begin to wonder whether the costs of continuing the struggle might not outweigh those of instituting some of the reforms demanded by the insurgent. The insurgent, in turn, might be willing to give up some of his more extreme demands in return for concessions on other points and a promise of amnesty.

Since the stakes are normally higher in civil insurgencies than in other insurgencies, termination of the conflict may present special problems. The interests of the adversaries are more likely to be defined in zero-sum terms, and there will be less room for negotiation and bargaining. In any settlement, the terms finally agreed upon will be the result of a bargaining process. Bargaining does not necessarily cease simply because the two parties are at war with one another.

War is always a bargaining process, one in which threats and proposals, counterproposals and counter threats, offers and assurances, concessions and demonstrations, take the form of actions rather than words, or actions accompanied by words. It is in the wars that we have come to call "limited wars" that the bargaining appears most vividly and is conducted most consciously. The critical targets in such a war are in the mind of the enemy as much as on the battlefield; the state of the enemy's expectations is as important as the state of his troops; the threat of violence in reserve is more important than the commitment of force in the field.

Even if one side were slowly defeating the other, a bargaining relationship might still exist. The negotiation would then be over the terms of the surrender. If the counterinsurgents believed that they were winning, their spokesmen might say to the insurgents, "You are going to be defeated sooner or later. The longer you resist the greater will be the damage inflicted upon you. Since it is costly for us to have to continue inflicting this damage, it is in the interest of *both* of us that you should surrender, and the sooner the better." The insurgent might respond to this line of argument by asking what concessions the counterinsurgent was prepared to make to obtain this surrender. Despite the fact that the insurgent might have some bargaining power even in defeat, his position would, of course, be clearly the weaker of the two. An aroused antagonist might choose to make no concessions whatever except amnesty for those who deserted the insurgents or surrendered.

This discussion has assumed that both antagonists are capable of rational analysis of their own interests and can examine as sensitive a topic as surrender with a degree of detachment. In some cases, such as a bitter civil insurgency or a prolonged and bitter anti colonial insurgency, this assumption may not be valid. The insurgent, even if he is losing, may pledge to fight to the end despite the readiness of the counterinsurgent to negotiate. The counterinsurgent, in winning, may be implacable. Instead of promising amnesty he may demand unconditional surrender and look forward to the moment when the last of the insurgents are in his power and helpless. If the insurgent had been almost ready to discuss surrender, the demand for unconditional surrender might strengthen his will to resist and prolong the struggle.

All insurgent movements proclaim a common goal victory. The operational meaning of victory is subject to great variation, however. Victory may mean one thing to one set of leaders and something quite different to another set. One set, while proclaiming victory as its objective, may be prepared to settle for less than the other set. Unless the concept of victory is given a more specific content by the use of mediating concepts, it may actually mislead the insurgent or the counterinsurgents. Success in insurgent conflict should not be defined in narrowly military terms. As the term is normally used, victory for one antagonist is presumed to imply the defeat of the other. In a military struggle, this suggests that victory can be won only if the enemy is defeated militarily. In an insurgent conflict, however, the struggle may be won without a victory that is signaled by the military defeat of the enemy, and a decisive military engagement may not result in the termination of the conflict.

Insurgent victory, for example, may not hinge on the military defeat of the enemy but upon the enemy's analysis of the cost of prolonging the struggle. In the case of Algeria and again in the case of Cyprus the struggle went on and on, and the costs casualties, material losses, domestic political costs, diplomatic costs, costs in world opinion, cost of having troops tied down and unavailable for other uses continued to mount. As the cumulative costs of the struggle became greater the counterinsurgent leaders began to wonder if those costs did not outweigh any benefits that could reasonably be expected from continuing the struggle. Finally, they concluded that the costs were unacceptable and, at the conference table, agreed to relinquish that which the insurgents had never been able to wrest from them in the field.

The insurgent will probably not be able to locate with accuracy the point at which the costs of prolonging the struggle will be deemed unacceptable by the counterinsurgents. Its location will vary with the type of insurgency involved and with the stage of a given insurgency. In an age of anticolonialism, colonial regimes have sometimes proved easily discouraged. In the case of a domestic insurgency, the counterinsurgent leaders are probably prepared to fight to the bitter end since defeat means death or exile. By raising the costs of the conflict, however, the insurgents may be able to set forces in motion which may lead to the overthrow of the incumbent regime.

In his propaganda the insurgent may want to emphasize the pursuit of victory, but in his planning he will be better advised to focus upon the objective of raising the costs of the struggle to the enemy. The concept of victory, by itself, has little operational significance, but the cost concept is easy to understand and may provide a day-by-day guide that shows the way to ultimate success for the movement. Insurgent leaders, both in headquarters and in field units, can examine proposed alternative courses of action in terms of the relative costs of each to the counterinsurgent and the insurgent.

The existence of emotional fervor or strong hatred can alter the cost picture because of the impact it has on the morale and determination of the antagonists. The insurgent will to resist may be nourished by hatred of a social class and attendant exploitation or by a passionate nationalist hatred of a foreign oppressor. The counterinsurgent may lack such energizing motivation. In the case of the Algerian insurgency, for example, the French were a long way from home and knew they were not fighting for the survival of France. In view of this motivational asymmetry, it is not surprising that the French finally succumbed to exhaustion and despair. The costs of the struggle continued to mount, and neither the interests of France nor the motivation of the French forces dictated its prolongation.

Stated generally, the problem facing the counterinsurgent is how to subdue an enemy that hates him implacably. A central objective in most warfare is the destruction of the enemy's will to resist. This is normally accomplished by inflicting military defeats upon the enemy in the field. What is one to do, however, if defeat does not weaken his will but leaves it unchanged or even strengthens it? If emotional fervor is great enough, a defeat may not be accepted as a defeat. An insurgent unit may be defeated and dispersed, but, instead of surrendering, the survivors disappear into the hills and vow revenge. Despite heavy losses the leaders of the movement may vow to fight until the counterinsurgents are dead or driven from the land. Eventually the counterinsurgent must begin to wonder how important his military victories are and how he is to terminate the conflict. In the case of the Algerian, Cypriot, Palestinian, and Tunisian insurgencies, the insurgents did not win their wars in the traditional military sense, and the counterinsurgents were not defeated; they simply despaired of ever winning. They despaired of ever being able to govern on the basis of willing co-operation from the local residents.

If the insurgent refuses to surrender despite defeats, this reduces the options open to the counterinsurgent for terminating the conflict. A negotiated settlement is eliminated, and he may have to consider waging a virtual war of extermination. The physical cost and, more importantly, the political cost of waging such a war may be prohibitive. If that is the case, the counterinsurgent may then have to consider giving up the fight himself. If one cannot defeat an enemy, one may ultimately be defeated.

7

The Counterinsurgent

Introduction

In conventional warfare, the principles of strategy and tactics apply equally well to both antagonists. In insurgent warfare, on the other hand, the course of action that the insurgent tries to pursue with regard to the counterinsurgent is quite different from that which the counterinsurgent tries to pursue with regard to the insurgent. The difference in strategy and tactics is grounded in the disparity between the resources of the counterinsurgent and those of the insurgent. The counterinsurgent will typically have a distinct advantage in such things as manpower, firepower, airpower, transport, communications, and apparatus for population utilization. Because the strategic and tactical principles of insurgent warfare are different from those of conventional warfare, each side has much to learn. One must learn to fight a stronger foe; the other must learn to fight a foe who is weaker and who therefore wants to change the rules of the game. Each must learn to conduct a struggle that is both military and political, a struggle in which the contours of public attitudes and behavior may be as important as terrain contours and in which major victories may be won without either side firing a shot.

There is little room for tactical and strategic dogmatism in insurgent warfare, and the advantage lies with the side that learns quickly and adapts more easily. For the counterinsurgent there is no one "best" strategy or tactic. There is not even any one mix of strategies and tactics that is invariably best. Which mix is best depends upon the total situation, including the resources and behavior of the insurgent, the resources and strategic situation of the counterinsurgent, and the general situation with regard to the populace. For example, the strategic hamlet plan, which held the key to victory in Malaya, proved ineffective in Vietnam.

Situational Factors

The physical and demographic features of a country are not as critical for the counterinsurgent as they are to the insurgent, but they do have an impact upon counterinsurgent strategy and tactics. Because he is weaker, the insurgent must try to conduct his activities in areas and under conditions that neutralize the counterinsurgent's generally superior strength and technology. Even under conditions in which he can use surprise, speed, and elusiveness his advantage may be slight and temporary. The counterinsurgent, because he is stronger, can operate under a wider variety of environmental conditions. Terrain, vegetation, and climate may create problems for him and neutralize some of his capabilities, but only rarely will survival be dependent upon them. For example, the use of aircraft in Kenya allowed the British to spot and attack Mau Mau detachments from the air. The survival of the Mau Mau was at stake but not the survival of the British units.

One reason the physical and demographic features of a country are important to the counterinsurgent is because this will determine the number, size, and location of the areas favorable to guerrilla operations. If the areas favorable to insurgent operations are few, small, and isolated, counterinsurgent forces may try to eliminate the insurgents in a given area by sealing off the area and starving the insurgents into submission. The process would be repeated in one area after another. On the other hand, if terrain and other conditions allowed it, the security forces might enter an area and attempt to hunt down the insurgents. An example of this type of effort was seen in Bolivia in 1968 when army units, aided by Indians, hunted down and eliminated the entire insurgent force. It was in a climactic engagement during this campaign that Che Guevara lost his life.

If the areas favorable to insurgent operations are numerous and difficult to isolate, a different approach may be employed. Some military units might be used to harass the insurgents in these areas while other units might be employed in security and population control activities. At the same time, political and economic reforms might be introduced to blunt insurgent appeal to the populace. This pattern would be similar to the one used successfully in Malaya.

Physical and demographic features may influence counterinsurgent strategy, but they are not the only influences on strategy, and they may not even be the most important influences. If the counterinsurgent possesses an advanced technology, terrain features may be less important than would otherwise be the case. For example, aircraft may increase his reconnaissance, attack, and airlift capabilities and reduce the significance of mountainous areas. Radar and other electronic devices can markedly improve his surveillance ability. It is hard to imagine a modern T. E. Lawrence operating in the desert against an enemy equipped with modern aircraft. To be sure, the counterinsurgent may become overly dependent on his advanced equipment and may not be able to liberate himself from it. Apparently the French in Indo China became excessively dependent on mobile armored units and oriented most of their thinking toward operations with such units. As the French became road-bound, the Viet Minh forces were able to move through the countryside and to control it. They could strike against units moving along the roads or against isolated strongholds and then fall back, knowing the French had little taste for non mechanized pursuit.

The Insurgent

A factor that shapes the environment in which the counterinsurgent operates is, of course, the insurgency itself. The record indicates that one of the most difficult tasks which an incumbent regime faces is to recognize that an insurgency exists and that it is a real threat. Until the counterinsurgent regime recognizes that its existence is being threatened, it is likely to find it difficult to develop the sense of urgency that is required if the challenge is to be met effectively. The activities of a new insurgency are likely to be on a small scale, and the incumbent regime may be inclined to treat these activities as isolated phenomena which can be ignored or dealt with by normal police activity. The government may fear that it will lose face if it acknowledges that its citizens have taken arms against it or that it will simply call attention to the movement and encourage it by organizing to control it.

When the counterinsurgent leadership recognizes that the movement must be taken seriously, its initial reaction is likely to be to make a military response. This response will probably take the form of an attempt to use the armed forces in a conventional way. The army is equipped for conventional combat, and officers and men have been trained for it and only for it. A substantial reorientation is usually necessary before an army can respond effectively to an insurgent challenge. Officers must learn to ask new questions: Who is our enemy? What are his objectives? What strategy is he utilizing? What tactical mix is he utilizing? What are his vulnerabilities and how may we best strike against him? This reorientation is difficult and time consuming at best; at worst, it may prove impossible. The slowness of the counterinsurgent in recognizing the challenge and in adjusting to it may be one of the greatest advantages that the insurgent possesses.

A second element in a counterinsurgent response may be a heavy emphasis upon repression. A government that finds it difficult to strike directly at the guerrilla may attempt to strike at him indirectly by utilizing control measures and a counter terror. This may, of course, be counterproductive. When Batista's regime in Cuba relied on repression and terror, it antagonized many who had previously been indifferent to it, and it drove a number of young men into the hills for refuge. Some of these young men subsequently fought for Castro.

Counterinsurgent regimes have found it difficult to understand that the insurgent challenge is a politico-military one and that it requires a political response as well as a military response. They tend to conceive of the problem as essentially one of maintaining law and order and are slow to consider the introduction of basic social, political, and economic reforms.

Traditions and Expectations

Sometimes incumbent regimes do seek to introduce reforms. The government of Magsaysay in the Philippines introduced land reform and other reforms. In Bolivia land reform was also introduced. This path is often a difficult one, however. The government may well be caught in a squeeze between the demands of citizens for a greater share in the resources of the country and the competing demands of powerful groups in the country whose support the government needs if it is to stay in power. Various technical problems may also impede land reform. In the central highlands of South Vietnam, for example, competitive claims to land ownership were advanced by Vietnamese, Montagnards, Chinese, and French.

In the case of invasion and a resulting insurgency, a somewhat similar situation may exist with regard to land reform. The invasion may have made substantial demands on the resources of the invader, and combating the insurgency places further demands on his resources. The immediate interest of the invader, therefore, may lie not in instituting reforms desired by the populace but in finding ways to draw the maximum amount of resources out of the country. Japanese policy in China from 1940 to 1945 illustrates this point. Initial attempts at economic reform soon gave way to harsh punitive measures.

The resources available to a government are apt to be great compared with those available to the insurgent, yet a government almost always feels that its resources are inadequate and are stretched to the breaking point. It feels that it is the focal point for competing demands that cannot all be satisfied. Furthermore, as is obvious, the government must also carry on the normal functions of government. That confers certain advantages, but it also carries disadvantages with it in the form of demands on its limited supply of skills, energies, and resources. If the government does not continue to perform such governmental functions as protection of the populace, it will lose support. The insurgents charge that the government is incompetent to do its job properly and then seek to demonstrate the truth of their charge by making the government's job impossible.

One of the situational factors that serves as a constraint on the counterinsurgent is the image that the regime has within the country. The insurgent movement can create an image and a reputation that it hopes will contribute to the achievement of its goals. The incumbent regime is not in a position to radically alter its image, however. It must live with the image that it has earned. This may be a negative factor (the French in Indo China, the Batista government in Cuba) or a positive factor (the British in Malaya). Whether negative or positive, the image and reputation of the counterinsurgent will have a great impact upon the ability of the incumbent regime to utilize the population and resources of the country. For example, a government such as Batista's, which had the reputation of being autocratic, harsh, and unresponsive, could not gain much from the institution of limited social or economic reforms. The government that waits for an insurgency to develop before taking an interest in reform may have waited too long. The options open to it may have contracted, and the actions that might once have been sufficient to forestall trouble may now appear inadequate and insincere.

International Environment

Insurgent movements are often highly dependent upon outside support. An appropriate counterinsurgent strategy, therefore, is that of trying to cut off the insurgent from the international environment and to thwart his efforts to get support from it. Sometimes, however, the counterinsurgent may not give sufficient weight to this consideration. During the rise of the Castro movement in Cuba, a series of articles on Castro and his movement appeared in United States newspapers such as the *New York Times*. This publicity played an important part in shaping the way the international environment came to view the Batista regime and its insurgent opponents. In this case, it was Batista who was isolated and cut off from outside support.

To accomplish his aim of isolating the insurgent, the counterinsurgent may rely upon diplomacy, propaganda, control of communications and travel, and military operations. Since the insurgency must normally have some reasonable prospect of victory before it can gain support from abroad, the counterinsurgent will seek to demonstrate that the movement is small and weak with no prospect of victory. It will also seek to present the insurgency in an unfavorable light, perhaps as a group of self-seeking bandits or fugitives from justice. In addition to trying to prevent the insurgent from gaining assistance from the international environment the incumbent regime may seek help for itself. If the counterinsurgent receives foreign support, he may encounter the same problem faced by the insurgent—that of maintaining autonomy. Conflicts in Southeast Asia have demonstrated how domestic insurgencies can became internationalized. In such cases one or both parties may closed freedom of action.

Capabilities and Basic Inputs

Leadership is a vitally important input factor in any insurgency, and the names of charismatic insurgent leaders come to mind easily—Mao Tse-tung, Castro, Guevara, Ho Chi Minh, Tito, T. E. Lawrence. This does not mean that leadership is less important to the counterinsurgent than to the insurgent. It may suggest, however, that insurgency, because it is dramatic, tends to attract the dramatic personality. The kind of leadership called for by insurgency is different from that demanded by counterinsurgency. The same array of qualities appears to be needed, but the various qualities are needed in different proportions. It is vitally important that the insurgent leader be able to raise the spirits of his men and generate faith and confidence when the situation looks dark. The counterinsurgent leader, on the other hand, functions as the head of a government and can manage with little in the way of charisma. It is important that the insurgent leader have administrative abilities, for he must create an organization and see to its operation. For the counterinsurgent leader, however, this quality is absolutely essential. He must oversee the functioning of an army, supervise a large nonmilitary administrative apparatus, supervise the development and utilization of the resources of a nation, and adjust the competing demands of groups within the country. Magsaysay was greatly aided in his campaign against the Huks by his ability to develop a series of programs utilizing a wide range of governmental capabilities.

The administrative machine that the counterinsurgent leader inherits is usually one that was formed by evolution and circumstance. It is likely to be cumbersome and inefficient yet very hard to change. Key positions may be held by unqualified appointees who are more interested in prestige and personal gain than in accomplishing assigned tasks. His personnel needs may exceed the number of skilled and dedicated technicians and civil servants available. The counterinsurgent leader, if he understands his problems, may lament that his responsibilities exceed the capabilities of the organization that he commands.

A political capacity must go hand in hand with managerial capabilities. Governments in countries in which insurgencies are occurring are often unstable, and the head of the government must build and maintain political support as a prerequisite to undertaking social, political, or economic reforms or a vigorous counterinsurgent program. In most cases, while reforms may benefit some, they will hurt others. The reforms that the counterinsurgent leader may wish to institute are likely to be costly to his supporters. His problem, therefore, assuming that he wishes to institute reforms, is how to do it without eroding the basis of his own support. In short, while the resources that are at the disposal of the government may be great in theory, in fact those resources may only be available if the leader is determined and politically skilled.

Effective population utilization is important to both the insurgent and the counterinsurgent. Each side must utilize the population effectively if essential needs are to be met. The insurgent, for example, needs to draw recruits from the population. The counterinsurgent also needs manpower for its forces and must seek to cut off the flow of manpower to the insurgents. The counterinsurgent has a recruiting advantage denied to the insurgent, for the government can introduce conscription. In liberated areas that it controls, the insurgent can do virtually the same, of course.

The government has a marked advantage when it comes to the logistic input. The government may feel that its resources are inadequate to meet the demands made upon them, but its plight will almost never be as serious as that of the insurgent. The government can tax, appropriate, borrow, and it can receive aid from abroad. Furthermore, it has less of a problem transporting material. It can use trucks, trains, planes, and carts openly and subject only to the danger of ambush. If it receives military aid from abroad, ocean-going ships can tie up in its harbors and unload hundreds of tons of equipment. The insurgent leadership, on the other hang, may have to devote an inordinate amount of time arranging the smuggling of small quantities of arms into the country. The insurgent must worry about acquiring resources, and the counterinsurgent must worry about managing the resources he has. Management not only includes getting resources of the right kind to the right place at the right time, it also means denying those resources to the enemy. This is no small task. The counterinsurgent sometimes supplies both himself and his opponent.

Counterinsurgent Strategy and Tactics

The main objective of counterinsurgent leaders will usually be the retention of political power. What they will do with their power if they stay in office is another question. They may want to maintain the social, political, and economic *status quo*, or they may want to preside over a program of gradual and moderate change.

They would like to retain power at the least possible cost, but if it is necessary they will be prepared to pay a very high cost. Their interest in holding down the cost of retaining power does not reflect an abstract concern for cost efficiency but their concern with staying in office. The more costly the struggle against the insurgency, the greater are the resource demands that the counterinsurgent leader must make on elements within the society that have supported him.

When designing a program to counter the insurgent movement, the counterinsurgent leadership should focus on the basic input factors of the insurgents (i.e., leadership, organization, population utilization, manpower, intelligence, and logistics). It should see if there are ways of reducing the supply of each input to the insurgents or increasing its cost. If the supply of a given input is already a problem for the insurgent, the counterinsurgent should do what it can to further aggravate the problem.

Magsaysay's anti-Huk campaign in the Philippines is illustrative. To undermine insurgent leadership and create uncertainty within the movement, he established a system of financial rewards for information leading to the capture of key insurgent leaders. To reduce popular support for the insurgency, he encouraged his soldiers to make friends with the people wherever possible, ordering them to repair roads and bridges, build schoolhouses, provide medicines and medical help, and mix with the people on a friendly basis. To reduce the manpower input, he offered amnesty to the insurgents and gave land and homes to those who defected and were willing to be relocated. To reduce the flow of intelligence to the insurgents, he made it clear that severe action would be taken against those who informed against the government. To reduce the flow of weapons to the insurgents, he established a monetary reward for serviceable unlicensed weapons which were turned in.

If the insurgency is deriving significant support outside the country, the counterinsurgent may try to interfere with this support. These efforts may take the form of improved border patrols so material cannot reach the insurgent and so the insurgent cannot make use of privileged sanctuary in a neighboring country. They may take the form of diplomatic actions aimed at denying the insurgent material and funds from a neighboring country or training and sanctuary in that country.

To decide which strategy or tactic to employ, the counterinsurgent must take several things into account: (1) whether he possesses the capabilities needed to employ the strategy or tactic; (2) whether its use fits into his over-all political, military, and psychological objectives; and (3) what benefits are to be realized from its use in relation to the cost of its use. It is often easy to tell if the first condition is met but more difficult to tell if the second condition is satisfied. The use of a particular strategy or tactic might not fit the over-all objectives of the counterinsurgent. The destruction of a village, for example, might wipe out a few insurgents but be counterproductive psychologically and politically.

The third question is often still harder to answer with confidence. Any course of action that the counterinsurgent considers will have certain benefits and costs associated with it. Costs include any and all disadvantages that will result from the use of the strategy or tactic under consideration. They may be economic, political, psychological, or military and are likely to be difficult to estimate with any precision. In addition, for planning purposes, the counterinsurgent will want to be able to compare the costs and benefits of competing strategic and tactical proposals.

The remainder of the chapter will examine some of the courses of action open to the counterinsurgent. The figure shows on next page suggests the relationship to one another of goals, objectives, targets and tactics.

Psychological Activities

The counterinsurgent may undertake psychological operations aimed at the population in general and at particular targets such as the armed services and those who support the insurgents. The objective of a given operation will vary depending upon the specific target but will probably fall into one or the other of the following broad categories: continuation of favorable behavior; adoption of favorable behavior; temporary deterrence of unfavorable behavior; discontinuance of unfavorable behavior. The various techniques that are used contribute, in one way or another, to the processes of coercion, persuasion, and conditioning.

Goal	Objectives	Targets	Tactice
		Population	Destroy Ins. Pol. Org. Psych. Opns. Public Relations Military Civic Action Pop. & Res. Control Pol. & Econ. Reforms
Retain Power	Alter capabilities (i.e., increase those of counter-insurgent and decrease those of insurgent)	Insurgent Organisation	Defeat Ins. Forces Undermine Ins. Morale Deny Base Areas Deny Resources Amnest Programs Intel./Counterintel.
		International	Sympathetic World Opin. Diplomatic Support
		Audience	Material Support
			Military Support

The counterinsurgent will have control of such media as exist in the country and will be able to mobilize them to some extent in support of his efforts. The availability of the media, however, may lead him to rely upon them unduly. In developing nations the effectiveness of the mass media is limited, and governmental concentration upon them may involve neglect of face-to-face communication. The insurgent, in turn, may place heavy reliance upon face-to-face communication since the media are not available to him. This has been the pattern in Vietnam. Sometimes, of course, the counterinsurgent may make intensive use of face-to-face contact as the French did for a time in Algeria.

The incumbent regime will normally try to picture the insurgency in an unfavorable light. It may try to portray the insurgent leaders as bandits, as terrorists, or as dupes of a foreign power. If this effort is successful the insurgents may find themselves isolated from the people, and they may also find that the recruitment rate is dropping and the desertion rate climbing. If the counterinsurgent can weaken or remove the insurgent's will to fight, his task will be much eased. In designing a program to achieve this end, an amnesty program can play an important part. When the insurgent movement is enjoying success, few insurgents may take advantage of the opportunity to return peacefully to their homes. On the other hand, when the weather is bad, when the insurgents are being harried by counterinsurgent troops, when the movement has suffered defeats, and when victory seems almost hopeless, the opportunity to return to the comforts of home and family may begin to appear attractive. If, at that time, the incumbent regime can take actions to show that it means to right political and social wrongs, it may be able to defeat the insurgent movement from below. The individual insurgent, making his own personal calculation of cost and benefits, may conclude that the benefits of continued participation are outweighed by the risks and discomforts. The killing of insurgents is not the only way to defeat an insurgent movement.

Civic Action

After an incumbent regime has been struggling against an insurgent movement for a time it usually becomes clear to that regime that its relations with the populace are a matter of critical importance. In any campaign by the government to broaden its base of popular support, the army is likely to play a prominent role. The behavior of the army can have a great influence on the way that the incumbent regime will be perceived by the people. This is understandable since the army is a symbol of government that the people often contact. A government's effort to improve its relations with the people can be easily undermined if the army behaves in a harsh and arrogant way.

If the army and its resources are used properly, it can be an important factor in improving relations between government and people. Its officers and men can show compassion for the people while engaging in combat near villages and can be careful and helpful. In addition, when not engaged in combat activities, troops can be used on projects needed by local communities—building schools, giving medical care, teaching children, and adults to read, improving the water supply. In some cases the net benefits from the civic action programs of the army may be greater than from its counterguerrilla activities. One of the decisions that the counterinsurgent leadership must make concerns the proportion in which the army's energies will be devoted to civic action programs and counterguerrilla activities. Valuable as civic action programs are, however, the people also look to the military to provide security. The diversion of troops to civic action projects when insurgent military activity constituted a serious threat to the people might well be counterproductive. Civic action programs can best be employed in areas where enemy activity is low.

Population and Resource Control Programs

A population and resources control program seeks to deny to the insurgent the human and material resources needed to continue the insurgency. The design features of such a program will depend upon the sources of guerrilla support. If the insurgent is receiving substantial support from external sources, one of the aims of the program will be to seal the border and prohibit movement of goods or personnel from the border to internal areas. If the main sources of supply are indigenous, the program will aim at controlling the movement of persons and resources within the country.

The counterinsurgency effort in Malaya offers an example of a successful population and resources control program. Family pictures were taken, and families were spot checked from time to time. All members of a family had to be accounted for. Identification cards were issued and checked frequently. In some villages central eating facilities were established and identification cards were required for entrance to meals. Production and distribution of food was carefully controlled to prevent it from falling into the hands of the insurgents. Curfews were established. Travel was curtailed and carefully controlled. Strangers in a village were easily noticed and observed. The strategic hamlet program was used in conjunction with clear-and-hold operations in the hope that the two together would gradually destroy the insurgent command system. "This has two simultaneous effects; first, it forces the insurgent units to fight to support their infrastructure at the point at which government forces are at their most concentrated and strongest, thereby automatically increasing the contact-and-kill ratio; and, second, it reduces their sources of supplies and new recruits. The reason for the success which will be gained from this type of operation is that the government forces are fighting in the *same element* and for the same purpose (control of the population) as the insurgent forces."

The administration of a population and resources control program of this kind is very burdensome, and its cost is very great. Furthermore, it is likely to be extremely inconvenient for the people and force a remodeling of their lives. The counterinsurgent will need to consider carefully whether the potential gains from such a program will outweigh potential costs. If such a program is to be instituted, it must be embarked upon in a whole-hearted way. A half-hearted program might be sufficient to antagonize the populace without being energetic enough to interdict the flow of resources to the insurgent. In such a situation, the program would be clearly counterproductive. The loss of popular support might well be accompanied by an increased flow of intelligence and recruits to the insurgent movement.

Since these programs, when successful, eliminate the village as a base for guerrilla support, insurgents are strongly opposed to them. In Vietnam the insurgents tried to discredit the resettlement centers as concentration camps and argued that they were meant to deny land ownership to the small farmer. "The strategic hamlet was portrayed as a technique for depriving farmers of land (the land on which the village was built) or as a means of swindling farmers out of good land in exchange for bad. Cadres asserted that the GVN represented the rich landlords and pursued a false land reform scheme; that GVN land taxes were unreasonable; that the ' U.S.-Diem clique' confiscated millions of hectares of the best rice land for military purposes such as building military bases,"

Military and Related Activities

An insurgency is a politico-military phenomenon. If the counterinsurgent centers his attention exclusively on the military aspects or the political aspects of the problem he is likely to be defeated. To be effective, the counterinsurgent must wage political and military campaigns simultaneously. These campaigns must be closely co-ordinated. If the boundaries of military districts are drawn on the basis of terrain and do not take political realities into consideration, the opportunity for unco-ordinated action will be great. In Vietnam, for example, the military undertook a "search and clear" operation in an area just before harvest time. To protect the people while the area was being cleared, they were relocated in refugee centers in another area. By the time the military operation was completed, the crops had rotted in the field and the efforts at political consolidation in the area had been nullified.

The counterinsurgent must establish his political and military goals, but he must understand that the strategy and tactics appropriate to one area may be inappropriate in another. In one part of a country, companies and battalions may engage in tactics that are very nearly conventional. In another section small units may be relied upon. These units may operate over wide areas, concentrating on raids, ambushes, reconnaissance, and political action.

The counterinsurgent, with limited forces, must try to defend vital installations, protect the population, protect his lines of communications, and carry the fight to the insurgent in the latter's sanctuary areas. He must determine how each of these tasks is to be performed and what proportion of available energies and resources should be devoted to each to maximize results. He must decide which insurgent initiatives to respond to and what actions to initiate to carry the fight to the insurgent. Because of his fixed obligations, it is not usually possible for the counterinsurgent to seize and maintain the military initiative unless his troops outnumber those of the insurgent in a ratio of fifteen to one or more. Much depends, of course, on the quality and training of the troops, available firepower, the quality of the intelligence being used, and the mobility of the troops. For both military and psychological reasons it is important that the government forces be able to react quickly when the insurgent strikes. This quick reaction capability may be achieved by the use of motor vehicles, helicopters, or rapid movement on foot across country. To be effective, mobility must also be combined with an efficient high-speed communications system.

The counterinsurgent leadership will be interested in attacking the insurgent control system and in defending its own control system. Sometimes force will be used for these purposes. The counterinsurgent control system is visible to the insurgent and relatively easy to strike at, but the reverse is not equally true. The insurgent's control system operates underground. Its leaders are wanted men. Outlawing the insurgent organization may discourage young men from joining it and make it harder for the organization to function, but it will rarely destroy it.

The most effective weapon to use against the insurgent control network is intelligence. Intelligence may come from defectors, prisoners of war, agents working within guerrilla units, and sympathetic members of the population. The last mentioned source is dependent upon the establishment of a communications system which will transmit information efficiently without revealing its source and making individuals vulnerable to reprisal. An example of such an arrangement is the census grievance system in South Vietnam. A trusted member of the community is hired by the government to listen to the grievances of the local inhabitants. Individuals talk to this official privately, and it is hard for insurgent observers to know which individuals are providing intelligence and which are not.

The insurgent movement may attempt to use violence and intimidation against the counterinsurgent control system, as in Vietnam. The counterinsurgent apparatus must try to defend itself physically against these attacks if possible, and it may also try to use political techniques in its defense. It may try to overcome corruption in its ranks or simply silence those who suggest that there is corruption. It may try to improve the economic situation or silence that situation. It may follow the path of reform in the hope of psychologically isolating insurgent terrorists, or it may institute elaborate control measures in an effort to apprehend them.

8

VIOLENCE BY SMALL GROUPS

Introduction

In all feudal types of societies there have always been individuals and small groups who were driven by hunger and humiliation to commit acts of violence in such a way as to amount to turning things upside down. These acts were almost invariably designated as 'crime' by the rulers of such societies. For instance, many of the offences prescribed for punishment (*danòdòa*) in the Smròti texts constituted crime in so far as they were reversals of the existing codes of deference. Even after the British introduced relatively more modern legal institutions in the subcontinent, political arrangements at the village level were allowed in many cases to continue as of old, so that the local elite went on exercising with impunity their traditional right to discipline members of the lower classes and castes for using the language, dress, transport and other status symbols of their social superiors. For a Chamar to speak like a Rajput, for a Bareia to sport a turban like a Patidar, for a Balahi to ride a horse through a Bundela village, for a peasant not to leave his cot and stand up at the sight of his landlord were all regarded as acts of inversion and severely punished. By the same token, in eighteenthcentury England where 'game was a special currency of class based on the solid standard of landed wealth', poaching was, in the eyes of the landed aristocracy, 'not only stealing a peculiarly valuable kind of social capital' but 'also debasing its coinage'. For it allowed the lower classes to share with the gentry such food and sport as were considered to be the exclusive symbols of privileged status. Consequently the landed aristocracy which was still strong enough to swing the 'rule of law' in line with its own interests, found it necessary to use its authority in order to save the food of the gods from desecration by the underdogs: the draconic Black Act of 1723 was enacted, on the pretext of an emergency, as a legislation aimed equally against the 'ancient offence' of poaching and the 'displacement of authority' caused by it.

While those in control of the instruments of punishment tend thus to act upon a definition of crime broad enough to permit a defence not only of the material basis of their power but also of their prestige, the more audacious of the outlaws in India and elsewhere have been known, conversely, to add insult to injury in their defiance of authority. Shibeyshani, a notorious dacoit of Nadia at the turn of the nineteenth century, when surprised by a villager and challenged to identify himself, answered back, 'Your father' an euphemism, in Indian usage, for 'You bastard!' Apprehended, he was made to pay for his robbery compounded by the crime of abusing his upper-caste landlord captor a serious breach in the code of verbal deference. He had his forearms chopped off and bled to death.

However, it was not in all cases that the inversion effected by crime involved such a crude and frontal assault on codes of deference. Some of the more powerful criminals are known to have brought this about by the knightly device of dealing with the forces of law and order as noble enemies. Sultana, the legendary bandit of Uttar Pradesh, combined a cool disregard for the authorities with humour, hospitality and even chivalry to impose the rhetoric of a combat between equals on a campaign launched by a Special Dacoity Police Force set up for the purpose of destroying him and his gang. He was eventually caught and hanged. Corbett who was one of the small group that planned and led the police war against him, concludes his account of Sultana's career with a remarkable tribute.

Society demands protection against criminals, and Sultana was a criminal. He was tried under the law of the land, found guilty and executed. Nevertheless, I cannot withhold a great measure of admiration for the little man who set at nought the might of the Government for three long years, and who by his brave demeanour won the respect of those who guarded him in the condemned cell. I could have wished that justice had not demanded that Sultana be exhibited in manacles and leg-irons, and exposed to ridicule from those who trembled at the mere mention of his name while he was at liberty. I could also have wished that he had been given a more lenient sentence, for no other reason than that he had been branded a criminal at birth, and had not had a fair chance; that when power was in his hands he had not oppressed the poor; that when I tracked him to the banyan tree he spared my life and the lives of my friends. And finally, that he went to his meeting with Fredy [Young, the commander of the Special Dacoity Police Force] not armed with a knife or a revolver, but with a water melon in his hands.

Nothing could speak more eloquently of the inversive function of crime than these words. The criminal had in this instance so fully achieved the ultimate objective of rebellion, so thoroughly had he turned things upside down that in the eyes of the custodians of order he was transfigured from an outlaw into a hero and his record remembered no longer as one of offences against the law but that or valour and humanity.

An inversive function of this kind is common to peasant insurgency and certain (though not all) classes of crime. But these two types of violence are clearly distinguished in one important respect. Unlike crime peasant rebellions are necessarily and invariably public and communal events. To generalize, the criminal may be said to stand in the same relation to the insurgent as does what is conspiratorial (or secretive) to what is public, (or open), or what is individualistic (or small-group) to what is communal (or mass) in character. In other words, crime and insurgency derive from two very different codes of violence.

The distinction between the two codes is not always easily perceived by observers at the initial stages of a peasant uprising. Used to reading all signs of violence against society under 'normal' conditions as crime, they are inclined at first to read the same set of signs in a violence that has already switched from one code to another. Since the passage from crime to rebellion is not fully comprehended yet, there is a tendency-almost universal on the part of the authorities at the outbreak of an insurrection to interpret the increased intensity and incidence of violence in quantitative terms alone by attributing it to the secret design of a small number of malefactors rather than the initiative of individual offenders against the law. Insurgency is thus mistaken for that larger type of crime which is produced by conspiracy.

Conspiracy theories figure prominently in the official response to many Indian peasant uprisings. The conspirators are in most of these cases suspected to be members of one or the other rural elite group on the simple assumption that the peasant has no initiative of his own and is a mere instrument of his master. At least one notorious tyrant is known to have escaped the full measure of legal punishment by manipulating precisely such elitist assumptions. Deby Sinha whose oppressions as a revenue farmer of the East India Company goaded the peasantry of northern Bengal into revolt in 1783, argued in self-defence 'that it was the intention of the Zemindars to keep back their revenue for this year and that they had instigated therefore the ryots to rise'. He got away lightly. How keen and predisposed officialdom could be to try and attribute a plot to an event of this kind may be seen from a report written by one of them about his own part in the military action which finally led to Titu Mir's defeat and the fall of his rebel stockade on 19 November 1831. 'On the 20th Instant', he recalled, 'I repaired to the Stockade in order to search for Papers which might have been useful to Government to develop a Plot, if any such existed.'

'To develop a Plot' was also the instinctive response of some of the leading officials to the Kol rebellion of 1831-2. They saw in it the hand of the local chief. The maharaja of Chota Nagpur, wrote one of them, 'may have considered the summary expulsion of the Mahajuns and the destruction of their houses, papers, and effects, the most convenient way of squaring all accounts with them, to many of whom he is understood to be much indebted'. However, a fairly thorough investigation carried out by the government produced no direct evidence of any such elite involvement, although Nagvamsi sympathy (as against conspiracy) for the Kols as the enemy of their enemies-the suds could not be doubted. The outbreak of the Santal rebellion in July 1855 illustrates again how the regime often tended to reach out for a conspiracy theory at the drop of an arrow. Reports received by the Calcutta authorities from their men on the spot during the first fortnight of the hool hinted darkly and rather hysterically at invisible strings pulled by hidden hands. Since it was 'evidently a planned and concerted thing' and appeared to be 'long meditated and well organized', and 'as the Sontals [were] generally the most timid people in the world and dreadfully afraid of the Police', it followed 'that all this was at the instigation of some one else', that 'they [had] been put up to this'. Even the name of an identifiable conspirator emerged at one point. Meer Abbas Ali, a former Amir of Sind, was suspected of being at the root of all the trouble. But as an official enquiry was soon to establish, it was his passion for sport rather than rebellion that had made him recruit, in the spring of 1855, a large number of Santal as jungle-beaters from the region affected soon afterwards by the uprising.

To mistake rebellion for crime in the characteristic form of a conspiracy theory is not a matter of mental habit alone. The conceptual inertia that refuses to acknowledge, at first sight, the altered figure of violence, feeds on the sharp increase in criminal activity which often inaugurates a peasant revolt. Quantity again plays a trick on quality. A sudden rise in the incidence of rural violence has been known to herald some of the most massive uprisings in India. The link between the Santal hool and the come wave that preceded it was obvious enough to be noticed by the Lieutenant-Governor of Bengal in his minute of 19 October 1855 three months *after* the outbreak. 'I see no reason to doubt', he wrote, 'that the present disturbance had an *intimate connection* with the so-called Dacoities of 1854 or rather that these Dacoitics were *in fact the commencement of the present insurrection.*' We have a clear recognition here of the passage from crime to rebellion, an insight on the part of the peasant's enemies into a process by which violence switched codes. The insight, alas from the official point of view, did not come soon enough. For the process had indeed been building up since 1852 when in one single year dacoities increased by 89 and 58 per cent respectively in Birbhum and Bankura, two districts which were both to be caught up in the insurrection soon afterwards. In Bhagalpur, the other district to burn in 1855, as many as 12 gang dacoities had been committed in the previous year and led to 123 arrests and 74 convictions. 'The occurrence of so many robberies in quick succession within a jurisdiction where such acts of violence had for many years been quite unknown, excited surprise & alarm': these words taken from the Bhagalpur Police Report for 1854 show, incidentally, how difficult it can be for the contemporary observer to identify violence as it transits obscurely through the grey overlap between codes. Too close to the actual events, the Police Commissioner did not have the advantage of hindsight that was to illuminate the Lieutenant-Governor's understanding of crime as the precursor of rebellion.

A somewhat similar pattern of 'preliminary disturbances' could be seen in the jacqueries of Poona and Ahmadnagar districts of Maharashtra twenty years later. The actual outbreak of the riots there in 1875 was preceded by a spate of rural violence during the previous year. Directed invariably against Marwari moneylenders this ranged from what the Deccan Riots Commission called 'social outlawry' and 'petty annoyance' to dacoities committed by the Koli outlaws in the hills of the western districts of Poona and Nagar. The parallelism between these Indian experiences and the English agricultural labourers' movement of 1830 known popularly as 'Swing' is close enough to merit some mention here. Hobsbawm has shown how in one particular county, Norfolk, crime increased by at least 30 per cent during the six years ending in 1830, how in the twenty-two counties comprising nearly the entire domain of the Swing movement there was a spectacular rise in crime in 1829 on the eve of the outbreak, and how the incidence of poaching, the most defiant of all rural crimes, 'rose particularly steeply in the years immediately preceding the rising of 1830'.

Statistics such as these usually indicate a lowering threshold of the peasant's tolerance towards the conditions of his existence. Poverty has a way of compelling recognition from all Indian governments if only as a law and order problem. The British had to take notice of it from the earliest days of the Raj. A district official in Bengal observed how in the spring of 1771 even the honest elements among the tenantry were being driven by hunger to take to banditry: 'Numbers of ryots who have hitherto borne the first of characters among their neighbours, pursue this last resource to procure themselves a subsistence.' The great Bengal famine which followed added dramatically to the number of starving villagers as well as of the banditti. Again, in 1792, another local administrator mentioned 'the last year's scarcity' among the causes that had 'increased the Number of Robberies' in his district. The remaining one and a half centuries of colonial rule followed by more than three decades of government under a successor regime have made little significant change in this causal connection between starvation and violence in the countryside. The account of the restless life and bullet-ridden death of Banjara Singh, as given by a leading police officer of independent India and published with a foreword by the country's Home Minister, is therefore still and integral and authentic part of contemporary history.

Banjara Singh was a shepherd boy who grew up to be the leader of a formidable band of dacoits in the Chambal region. His father was a poor peasant turned poorer when he pawned half of his small plot of land, sold his flock of sheep and took a loan from the sahukar all in order to pay for his daughter's wedding. Then he died. And as we learn from the testimony of his adversary and biographer:

The turning pint in Banjara Singh's life was the death of his father. He disposed off the field to fulfil his duties as a devoted son in connection with the last rites of the dead. The *sahukar* turned up to press his demand for the payment of loan. Banjara Singh had no money to give. The *sahukar* remonstrated with abuses. The young man at first kept quit but later retaliated by uttering abuses in reply. At this, the *sahukar* hit Banjara Singh with his stick. At the first touch of the stick, Banjara was wild and assaulted him with his lathi. The *sahukar* fled. That night Banjara Singh decided to leave his dilapidated house and his semi-deserted village.

Many an outlaw's career begins in almost identical circumstances all over rural India. There are regions of chronic poverty like Banjara Singh's own district where for hundreds of years peasant youths have been slipping out of desolate villages and starvation and bonded labour in order to take to dacoity as a profession. There are demographic masses branded by colonial legislation as 'criminal tribes' (a stigma nominally removed since 1952 but still intact in social practice) for whom the very fact of having been thus classified has made crime the only means left for livelihood. The Lodhas are one such group of the rural poor in western Bengal. A forest people they used to earn their living, traditionally, as hunter, trappers and gatherers of food and fuel from the jungle. But the jungle, their provider, was taken away from them by the zamindar and the sarkar as land hunger and rising birth rates combined to turn more and more of the woodlands of Midnapur into paddy fields and villages. Cut off thus from their principal source of subsistence the Lodhas had, by the turn of the century, adopted robbery and theft as almost a second profession. And then, in 1916, the law stepped in to fasten on them a new identity by naming them officially as a 'criminal tribe'.

The Lodhas had taken to crime rather than agriculture because there was nothing for them in agriculture to take to. They had very little land of their own. A study of landholding by a hundred families in five Midnapur villages showed that an average Lodha family of 4.8 members owned 0.65 acre of land, that is, 0.134 acre per head. Of the families surveyed 57 per cent were landless, 20 per cent owned less than one acre, and 17 per cent more than one acre but less than four. No wonder that the Lodha peasant starves most of the time. 'A few families were found in the course of the enquiry to have no grain of rice for 7 or 8 days at a stretch, and they depended wholly on wild tubers for their food.' Again, in one of the villages 'a good number of families were found to starve or remain without any food for the whole day. This is a common phenomenon in the life of a Lodha here. Even the children are kept starving. Sometimes they are found to collect some edible small or big fruits and leaves to tide over the period of starvation. One woman was found by the writer to swallow a morsel of soil in crushing hunger.' What crime, if any, this particular woman was eventually driven to, we shall never know. But the author of the melancholy monograph from which these facts have been taken does tell us of another woman who was arrested and convicted. She was a widow with four children and the only way she could feed them was by stealing food or articles sold or exchanged for food. Children too had to provide for themselves by similar means. A ten-year old girl was arrested by the police for theft: she had been 'starving for two days and was tempted to lift [a] brass cup with a view to selling it in the market for a little cash by which she could procure some food to eat'.

Hobsbawm has noticed the distinction made by the English rural labourer of 1830 between two classes of crime committed as an escape from poverty. The labourer 'could seek a relief from poverty in crime in the simple theft of potatoes or turnips which constituted the bulk of the offences which he would himself regard as criminal, and in poaching or smuggling, which he would not'. Hunger has forced the Lodhas of Midnapur to do away with such fine moral distinctions. Parents have to feed their families, and if crime is the only means of access to articles of common consumption, the morality lies with the criminal. Far from being censured for offences against the law, a Lodha punished by the court would often be regarded by his kin as above reproach. 'In a few cases', to quote again from the account mentioned above, 'the wives of the criminals defended their husbands as innocent and spotless in character. They strongly asserted that they knew nothing wrong about their husbands.' Impoverished bread-winners do indeed figure prominently in Lodha crime statistics. In a sample of 180 of them listed as criminals it was found out that 82.2 per cent had no land at all, 12.2 per cent owned one acre or less and 5.6 per cent two acres or more, while 9.4 per cent of the same population belonged to small families of 1 to 3 members each, 46.7 per cent to medium-sized families of 4 to 6 members each, 31.1 per cent to large families of 7 to 9 members and 12.8 per cent to very large families of more than 10 members each. Thus the great majority of Lodha criminals are those who have the largest number of mouths to feed and the least resources. What makes the connection between hunger and crime quite explicit is that it is the practice of Lodha dacoits to carry off from the houses they raid everything they can lay their hands on and exchange it as quickly as possible for food; any foodstuff that can be readily consumed, they consume on the spot during a raid.

Offences of this nature committed in a desperate search for food are not limited to the Lodhas of Midnapur alone. There is nothing in this that is specific to their culture or the region where they belong. Such defiance of the law arises from a common and ubiquitous tradition of resistance to poverty which, at least during the colonial period, received an acknowledgement from the authorities themselves. This was typically expressed in the words of the Police Report of 1852 for the Lower Provinces stating how the number of dacoities in Birbhum district had suddenly increased by about one hundred per cent since the previous year as the direct result of distress following a severe drought:

There appears a considerable increase in the offence of Dacoitee; but bearing in mind that this is one of the districts in which the people suffered most from the want of rain in 1851 and that the nature of the country affords great facility for the perpetration of this offence and the escape of the offenders, such a result might have been expected.

The identification of scarcity as a cause of crime occurs in the administrative literature relating to many other parts of the subcontinent as well. In some districts of Uttar Pradesh, for instance, the authorities saw in dacoity 'the form of crime to which the Bundela Rajput always reverts when pressed by hard times'. The connection between famine conditions in this province and the rise in the incidence of crime during the years of drought and scarcity in the late 1860s was documented by Frederick Henvey. 'In times of famine it is usual to expect an increase in the number of crimes against property', he wrote and went on to show how taking 1867 as the index year the percentage increase for 1868 and 1869 was respectively 175 and 214 in dacoity, 158 and 185 in robbery, 124 and 170 in lurking house-trespass, and 118 and 171 in theft (other than that of cattle).

For the south, too, David Arnold has demonstrated in his excellent study of this subject how drought, dearth and high prices constituted 'the most readily identifiable factor in the incidence of dacoity' in the Madras Presidency in the late nineteenth and early twentieth centuries. The correlation was indeed so clear that the authorities came to rely on it as 'a true index to the state of distress' a sort of local barometer of the prevailing degree of deprivation and 'the Inspector-General of Police invariably prefaced his annual report on crime with a summary of the year's rainfall and gain prices'. Again, in the west country hunger often turned peasant in dacoit as witnessed thus by a young Indian civilian in charge of relief operations in Gujarat devastated by a famine at the turn of the century:

I had set up camp for a few days on the outskirts of a small village some miles away from the nearest railway. Provisions used to be sent up for me by train from the district headquarters. One day it so happened that the entire supply (amounting in fact to eight loaves of bread) was looted on its way to my camp. The police blew up the incident out of all proportions. After three days, five Kolis, all skin and bone, were sent up on charges of dacoity for trial at my own court! 'We had nothing to eat for three days in a row', they said without any show of repentance whatsoever. 'Our bellies were burning with hunger. Should we have come across all that food and not eaten it?' Indeed, how were they to let all that food go? But how could I let them go without punishment either? So I worked a bit on the evidence provided by the police and defined the offence as a case of theft rather than dacoity. Then I sentenced them to imprisonment for a day and a fine of half a rupee per head. This was the verdict which I entered in the court records, but felt so embarrassed about the whole business that I said to them, 'Now go away. You are free. Don't steal again.' The fine I paid out of my own pocket.

There is more to this anecdote than a parallelism between the various instances of starvation crime discussed above. It helps to define the ambivalence of the deed on which the young and evidently sympathetic officer was asked to sit in judgment. Was it an offence to be interpreted and punished according to the Indian Penal Code or was it to be justified by a code of social morality that provides for a minimum subsistence as an overriding right? A form of violence against property was obviously switching codes when it was brought before the court and obliged the young officer to produce half an answer to that question in terms of one code and half in another.

The resistance of the rural poor is bound to create dilemmas of this sort for the rulers in any society with a large peasant population, although not all guardians of law and order may turn out to be as conscience-stricken as the young civilian of Gujarat. The mysterious King John's band of 'well-disciplined social rebels' known popularly as the Blacks rode through a part of England in 1723 'administering folk justice' to the evil gentry and inevitably precipitated a lot of 'freelance actions' by poachers, smugglers, etc. with whom they had nothing directly to do. But, as E. P. Thompson observes, 'all of these actions were, of course, seen by the authorities, within one common blur, as outrages by the Blacks'. This blur represents classification by a familiar and convenient code. It was obviously convenient for those in power to make no distinction between the activities of the Blacks and others and to lump both kinds of violence as crime a code which they knew how to handle.

Significantly, however, the peasant's own perception of violence, too, can be and often is characterized by 'blurring' with the difference that with him it operates in reverse. While his foes landlords, moneylenders and officials would tend to lump all forms of defiance of the law as crime, the peasant would tend to lump them together as perfectly justifiable even honourable acts of social protest. Both points of view are governed by *atidecœa* in so far as they both read the signs of one kind of violence into another. But they do so in opposite directions and thereby produce, under conditions of extreme polarization, a categorical conflict so broad and generalized as to amount to a clash between two incompatible theories. Mao Tse-tung's reflections on the antonyms 'terrible' and 'fine' used as contradictory descriptions of the Hunan uprising of 1927 help us to understand the emergence of such mutually hostile theoretical perspectives as the outcome of a peasant revolt.

The fact is that the great masses have risen to fulfil their historic mission [he says in the *Human Report*] and that the forces of rural democracy have risen to overthrow the forces of rural feudalism. It is not'terrible'at all. It is anything but 'terrible'. 'It's terrible!' is obviously a theory for combating the rise of the peasants in the interests of the landlords; it is obviously a theory of the landlord class for preserving the old order of feudalism and obstructing the establishment of the new order of democracy, it is obviously a counterrevolutionary theory. If your revolutionary viewpoint is firmly established and if you have been to the villages and looked around, you will undoubtedly feel thrilled as never before. Countless thousands of the enslaved the peasants are striking down the enemies who battened on their flesh. What the peasants are doing is absolutely right; what they are doing is fine! 'It's fine!' is the theory of the peasants and of all other revolutionaries.

There must indeed be two different and contradictory ways of looking at the violence of peasant rebellions the rebel's and his enemy's, giving rise to two different and irreconcilable ways of interpreting and generalizing the experience of that violence two theories. But even before antagonism in rural society reaches the point of insurrection, elements of the alternative theory already constitute a part of the peasant's perception of the conflict between himself and his foes. These are expressed most commonly in his attitude to certain acts of disregard for the law, especially those committed in response to unbearable degrees of economic deprivation or social humiliation. The Italian woman from Piana dei Greci who during the peasant rising of 1893 justified the admission of petty criminals to the Fascio on the ground that 'if they have stolen a bit of grain they have only done so out of poverty', expressed what is indeed an almost universal tolerance of starvation crimes in all peasant societies. It is again this sort of a linkage between smuggling and poverty that made many rural communities in eighteenthcentury Sussex rally not merely to the support but even in defence of 'plebeian gangs' of smugglers, for 'to the common people they were certainly not seen as criminals'. The way the poor villager's 'resentments of decades' allowed the legendary 'King John' of the Blacks to play Robin Hood in Hampshire and 'sheltered him and his band', has been assigned a classic guerilla status: 'His supporters seemed to be able to disappear as easily into the folds of popular concealment as did the Vietcong.' This is how Sultana, *'India's Robin Hood'*, too, managed to evade the law for a very long time. For 'having known what it was to be poor, really poor he never robbed a pice from a poor man, never refused an appeal for charity'. Consequently, says Corbett, 'his intelligence staff numbered hundreds'. This could be said also of Banjara Singh the bandit who 'ravaged the tract between Jamuna and Chambal rivers and beyond with ruthlessness to the rich and with benevolence to the poor'. He too, proved to be a most elusive quarry for the police. For, according to the officer who eventually cornered and killed him, he relied for his strength 'on the support of the many the many who inhabited the mudhouses on the willingness of the people to aid his struggle against the rich and his vendetta against the Police'.

The peasant appears thus to be ready to put up with and often positively approve of a wide variety of crimes induced by poverty. These may be big or small ranging from petty larceny involving a brass tumbler pilfered by a hungry Lodha child or a handful of grain by a Sicilian pauper to the more spectacular and massive acts of defiance by a band like King John's or Sultana's. Since E. J. Hobsbawm's pioneering formulation of the concept of 'social banditry' an attempt is being increasingly made by historians to distinguish between such offences in terms of the differences in their social content. Sussex smugglers, it has been said, 'were often the rebels of the countryside' who resembled 'social bandits' in the sense that they 'were not regarded as simple criminals by public opinion', although in certain other respects they did not conform to Hobsbawm's categories. E. P. Thompson defines the Blacks the 'armed foresters' of eighteenth-century England as an intermediate type between 'social bandits' and 'agrarian rebels' sharing 'something of both characters' but identical with neither. But whatever the point of the spectrum to which one assigns an activity of this kind, it has as its core an element of class conflict.

Whether this is more or less evident in any particular instance is of course a function of its relative entropy. Sporadic acts of defiance of this genre are unlikely to have their class character noticed by the rural population. In other words, they fail as signals which transmit poorly because of channel noise or ambiguity or a combination of both. And like all other messages rural crime too requires an adequate level of redundancy or a duplication of the coding system for its class content together with the rest of its meaning to come through clearly enough to make sense. This would explain why it was easy for the Deccan Riots Commission to characterize the events it had been set up to investigate as 'a disturbance arising out of the relations of the agricultural and moneylending classes'. The incidence of criminal offences committed against moneylenders during the previous thirty years in general and the last five in particular was high enough to make the class character of the jacqueries of 1875 obvious not only to the agrarian population but also to officialdom. They conformed to a clearly recognizable pattern. There were far too many incidents of the same kind involving the same class of offenders and the same class of victims to leave anyone in doubt as to who in rural society was trying to settle scores with whom.

As early as 1845 a large body of Bhils led by Raghu Bhangria had spread terror among the Marwari sahukars by chopping off their ears and noses and plundering their property. Bands of Kolis of the hills between Poona and Thana districts had from time to time murdered, mutilated and robbed moneylenders. Two of the latter were assassinated in broad daylight and in full view of the public during 1852 in widely separated parts of the Bombay Presidency and this was cited by an official as evidence of tolerance, if not approval, of violence against usurers among the rural poor. And the statistics of crime committed against moneylenders during this period in seven districts of the Bombay Presidcncy 14 murders, 16 dacoities and robberies, 34 thefts, 8 arsons, 39 cases of hurt and wounding and so on adding up to a total of 170 offences in the five and a half years preceding the riots of 1875, an annual rate of about 31 cases leave nothing unsaid about the focus of the peasant debtor's hostility towards his class enemies. Concentration such as this generates a sort of synonymy which helps to disperse at least some of the ambiguity of this particular type of rural crime. The diversity of violence addressed to one single group of the population murder, arson, robbery, assault, etc. all directed against moneylenders has the effect of underscoring not only the wickedness of the objects of such violence but also the morality of the latter as a measure of just retribution in the eyes of the less delinquent members of the agrarian community. There is in this perception the beginnings of the peasants' sense of themselves as a social mass defined not only by a common grievance but also by the possibility of obtaining redress through militant and collective action the beginnings, if no more than that, of a recognition of their identity as a class-for-itself.

It is precisely the combination of a high frequency of occurrence and a duplication of the coding system that makes the class character of the more powerful and massive peasant uprisings so explicit explicit at least to the rural masses. For an insurrection incorporates crime such as what has been discussed above and abolishes it thus as a form of social protest: an optimal defiance of authority, it subsumes all other acts of defiance of lesser magnitude by providing them with a total and new context. This is the context of a class war that is, a struggle in which opposing classes consciously allow force to decide between irreconcilable aims. And just as 'meaning is controlled by the use of language in situations', crime in the new's social context comes to signify an integral part of a comprehensive system of defiance a *parole* in a new *langue*: in short, it changes codes.

This code-switching is seldom overlooked by the peasantry. Tolerant, by tradition, towards crimes of indigence as a necessary aberration rather than as a positive virtue, they now see in rebellion the operations of a *rite depassage* turning criminals into insurgents. This is an experience shared by many agrarian societies. Poor peasants driven to crime by feudal oppression in China rallied to the banner of the hero of *The Water Margin* in his revolt against the Emperor. Some notorious 'bad characters' turned out to be important local leaders of the peasant war in Germany in the sixteenth century. Rudé has noticed how the Swing movement of agricultural labourers in parts of southeastern England was on some occasions led by smugglers 'a natural group of "activists" in this part of the world'. The outlaw has indeed some advantages over others in leading an insurrection: he is less bound by deference to the authorities with whom he has already been at war for some time; and of course he has already acquired a certain amount of expertise in the techniques of defiance. This is why on the outbreak of a revolt existing bands of brigands could be better suited to act as its 'shocktroops', as Hobsbawm puts it. A Russian experience he cites in support of this view illustrates at the same time and very elegantly indeed the formal acknowledgement by the peasantry of the criminal's transformation into the insurgent. Two men who had taken to brigandage after being expelled from an Ukrainian village community as criminals were readmitted to it when they emerged as the leaders of a local uprising in 1905.

The history of India under British rule is not wanting in instances of those who had once broken the law as individuals or members of small criminal bands and did it all over again on a larger scale as initiators and organizers of rural revolt. There is a reference to a certain Siddoo Sitooba, described as an 'old offender', leading the riots against a moneylender of the village of Pimpalgaon during the anti-usury struggles in Maharashtra in 1875. What particular offence made the Deputy Superintendent of Police of Poona district attach that stigma to Sitooba's name we do not know. But we have on record a curious detail of Titu Mir's career to show how radical the shift from crime to insurgency could be. He was apparently a professional wrestler who, according to a knowledgeable official, 'became a servant to any Zemindar who desired to create Disturbances or to exact from their Ryotts'. Convicted for 'his Service in an affray which took place in the Nuddeah District' he was in prison for some time before going on a pilgrimage to Mecca from where he returned as a disciple of Syed Ahmed and a reformer. When he eventually shot into fame as a leader of the Barasat bidroha he was still mentioned in official correspondence as 'a released convict'. A mercenary who used to hire himself out as an instrument of landlord tyranny against the peasantry had obviously turned his own consciousness upside down a genuine case of *fanshen* in order to serve as an instrument of popular violence against landlords.

The trajectory of peasant consciousness was not in all instances characterized by such a dramatic change of direction. More often than not it was a matter of robber turned rebel. Two of the principal dacoits of the Kajirhat area were mentioned by Goodlad among the organizers of the dhing of 1783. Again, one knows of Merhai Singh, 'a dacoit who formerly was tried for theft, &c. and was imprisoned in Agra Jail but at the outbreak [of the Mutiny] escaped and [had] ever since been causing a great deal of trouble'. By the time he was captured by De Kantzow in the vicinity of Pawayan and sent back to Agra in the summer of 1859, he was described in the Anglo-Indian press as yet 'another rebel leader' brought to justice. None of their exploits however testifies more fully to such a transformation than the carrers of two Santal bandits. The hool, as we have seen, was preceded by a spate of gang robberies. That these were the acts of famished men driven to desperation was obvious even to the authorities. 'In many of the cases entered as Dacoities', wrote the police chief of the province, 'nothing but articles of food were carried off, and the prisoners averred that their sole object was to procure food. Many committed offences against property for the purpose of being put in jail and thus escaping from starvation.' Yet this did not stop the law from dealing most severely with them. The details that we have for a small sample of 42 of such 'dacoits' convicted in Bhagalpur show that 13 of them were sentenced to 16 years each of hard labour in irons and the rest to 10 years each of hard labour also in irons the terms to be spent, for both categories, in externment away from their home districts. And their age distribution 85.7 per cent in the 25-40 group-makes it clear how hunger and the hand of colonial justice combined to hit the community in the guts, first by turning its most mature male adults into criminals and then by cutting them off from their families. Among these 'dacoits' there were, in 1854, two men, Kewala Paramanik of Sindree and Domon Majhi of Hatbanda, who were both to figure prominently in the rebellion. The former, described after his capture as 'the person who was principally concerned in the Sonthal dacoities of last year & who then evaded apprehension', emerged in 1855 as a principal leader of the hool. An exceptionally capable organizer by all accounts he had managed to avoid official attention for most of the time during the rebellion until in fact his arrest towards the very end of the pacification campaign when the government realized that the man in their custody (who, meanwhile, had assumed a pseudonym) was indeed 'one of the chief instigators & planners of the present insurrection. He apparently was one of those who had masterminded the two key moves the communal hunt at Buro Koondee and the march to Hazaribagh in the spring of 1855 which mobilized the Santals and made them ready for the uprising. Then he led the hool in its western sector. Domon Majhi, too, surfaces in the records of the counter-insurgency campaign, but as Domon Daroga. The new designation indicates a change of his role from village head to rebel captain a change mediated by brigandage and acknowledged both by the Santal high command and the masses who called all their second-ranking war-leaders 'Darogas' that is, captains of the rank-and-file 'Sipahis'. He was certainly close enough to Kanhu to be trusted, together with Kewala, for the dangerous and at that particular juncture, politically crucial mission of executing the traitor who had betrayed Sido to the authorities. An intrepid fighter, his death made some people very happy indeed. 'I rejoice in the death of this man,' wrote a gleeful official on receiving Domon's severed head from a collaborator: 'his death will be a blow to the insurgents.'

The transformation of robbers into rebels made sense to the Santals. Most of the dacoities of 1854 had been committed against the Bengali moneylenders regarded by the peasantry of Damin-i-Koh as their most vicious oppressors. The officials too knew this to be true, as one can see from the Bhagalpur judge's reference in a letter written in the spring of 1855 to 'the fact of some dacoities having occurred at the close of that year which were attributed to the Santals' discontent with the Bengallee Muhajuns'. Thus even as crimes these contained, from the peasant's point of view, an element of moral justification in so far as they represented a desperate attempt by the poor to relieve hunger at the expense of their over-fed exploiters. Yet the law had singled out the Santal for punishment while the mahajan was not merely spared but positively pampered by the police and the courts. The leaders of the hool registered their protest against such iniquity in all their statements. 'I have often complained [about] this to Pontet', said Sido about the way the Damin-i-Koh official of that name had dealt with him, 'but he never listened, I gave him petitions at Burrisuagore, Barhet, Gutcharree, but he will not listen. I also petitioned him at Rajmehal. He only said you have eaten first from the Mahajuns "banchut Sala" now you come to complain "Sala banchut".' It was the use of such double standards which was one of the most important causes of the uprising. Even a myopic officialdom came to see this for itself, albeit rather late in the day, as it was alerted to the rumour which spread soon after the outbreak to the effect that 'avenging the punishment inflicted on their comrades concerned in last year's Dacoities' was the purpose for which the rebels had taken up arms. 'Those Dacoities were committed on the Bengallee Mahajuns who had oppressed them; and they complained that their comrades had been punished, while nothing had been done to the Mahajuns whose exactions had compelled them to take the law into their own hands.' It was easy therefore for the Santals to regard the rebellion as a collective bid for social justice already initiated in a small, if rather aberrant, way by the dacoities of the previous year. The hool provided a context in which that limited and somewhat tainted violence of 1854 was transformed into a purer, generalized and just war, cleansing and transforming the previous year's agents too in the process.

There was of course no immediate recognition of this process on the part of the authorities. During the earlier phase of the uprising the official point of view tended to cling on the whole to the familiar penal code, although there was a shade of difference between those in remote control and those on the spot. To the administrators one remove away from the village the Santals were 'rebel dacoits' an ambiguous expression in which the adjective, though by no means an acknowledgement of a just cause, signifies at least a grudging acceptance of the exceptional nature of this particular 'crime' as an open and collective act of defiance. Their subordinates, however, were far too close to the event and far too tied to routine to notice any difference. Hunter has commented on this combination of insensitivity and inertia among the men on the spot. Some of them, he points out, had reported much progress in the material conditions of the people and a corresponding decline in crime only a few months ago, so that 'it took time for men who had written in this strain in February to realize that their district was the seat of rebellion in July'. Besides, they failed to grasp, at the initial stages at least, that the violence which had just erupted was, despite some apparent similarities, quite different in character from gang robbery so familiar to them.

Night attacks on houses by bands of from five to fifty men had always been common in Bengal, and it *was a difficult matter to pronounce the exact line at which such enterprises cease to be civil offences and become overt insurrection.* A single example will suffice. 'The whole inquiry only tends to prove', wrote the magistrate of Beerbhoom, with regard to the sacking of a Bengali hamlet, 'that it was one of those occurrences common in Bengal, when the Dacoits were bold, adventurous, and determined, the Bengali a coward and helpless, and the village watchmen all absent from their posts.' It is possible that in this individual case the magistrate may have been right in his conjecture, but in many similar cases there can be no doubt that *he mistook rebellion for robbery.*

The Birbhum Magistrate was not the only one of local officers to mistake rebellion for robbery. To Mahesh Lal Datta, the daroga of Dighee, too, the sullen mass of peasants around him on that July morning looked like dacoits. For twenty years he had grown up with crime (or what he broadly understood to be so) in that area and dealt with it as a chore according to his not too refined notion of law and order. Blinkered by routine he had not noticed the change that had come over the Santals he thought he knew so well, and ended up by paying for this with his life. What happened at that flash point when Sido drew his sword and inaugurated the hool by slaying Mahesh Daroga, is not clear in all respects. As with many other flash points, here too the historian must content himself with an impression which has most of the detail bleached out by overexposure. Yet the residual outline pieced together from the recollections of one of the protagonists is clear enough to suggest that a clash between the peasants' view of themselves as rebels and a daroga's insistence on dealing with them as criminals is what triggered off the insurrection.

For years it had been Mahesh Daroga's practice to accept bribes from the mahajans in order to harass, arrest and send up the Santals to the nearest district headquarters for detention and trial on false charges of dacoity. He did this so indiscriminately that even the more affluent Santals had turned against him. One of them whose prosperity had made him so much or an object of the mahajans' envy (presumably because it was not easy for them to exploit him) and the daroga's oppression that after being manhandled by the latter he swore: 'We shall see how much twine could the Daroga procure so as to fasten all the peaceful Santals whom the wicked Daroga wanted to be sent up.'

The twine with which the innocent peasants of Damin-i-Koh would have their hands tied behind their backs as they were marched under police escort to Bhagalpur on false charges of house-breaking and robbery, had apparently come to be regarded as a hated symbol of official justice. Indeed, the expression 'cart loads of rope' occurs several times in Kanhu's statements. According to him, a man from the police station had called at his house on 6 July 1855 to have a look at a gathering of the Santal chiefs there and 'went away saying he would return the next day with the Darogah and a hundred men with two cart loads of rope to bind them'. He proved true to his word, for, as Kanhu's narrative, taking both the versions together, goes on to say:

The next morning it was proposed to go out to Shikar. Kanoo, Seedoo, many Manjees and others, amounting to 40 or 50 went out for this purpose, armed as usual for a Shikar. On their way they met the Darogah of Burro, Mohesh Lal, with two Sepoys of the Police and several Mohajuns and two cart loads of rope, and asked where going, replied to Shikar, but the Darogah said, they were intending Dacoitee and were complained against by the Mohajuns accompanying. The Mahajuns complained to Buiro Darogah that Seedoo & Kanoo were collecting men to commit a dacoitee. The Mehajuns gave him 100 Rs to come & catch us. I said why have you come he said that the 'Moiras have come to complain that you are collecting men for a dacoitce'. I said prove it, if I have committed a theft or Dacoitee said the Mohajura must be fined 5 rupee each for false complaint. The Mahajuns said, 'If it costs us 1000 Rs to your 5, we will do that to get you imprisoned' saw the cart loads of rope and told the Darogah he had prejudged them, else why the ropes for binding them. An altercation ensued. The Mahajuns began to tie Seedoo my brother. Then I drew my sword. Then they left off tying my brother & I cut Manick Modie's head off & Seedoo killed the Darogah & my army killed 5 men.

Mahesh Daroga was thus a martyr to his own incomprehension. He could not understand that by refusing to submit to starvation or seek relief in gang robbery, the Santals had transformed themselves into rebels and their consciousness changed codes. This is why the 'cart loads of rope', a punitive message meant to intimidate dacoits and meaningful only in terms of the old penal code, failed to frighten those who had just constituted themselves into an 'army' and were about to declare war against the Raj itself. Those first fatal cuts at Panchkathia were clearly the outcome of a dialogue in which neither of the interlocutors understood the other's language.

Such miscognition was characteristic of a good deal of the official response to the peasant uprisings of the period of the Mutiny too. This is more than amply documented by the reports we have from the district administrators of the time on the disturbances in Uttar Pradesh in 1857-8. What emerges from this vast body of literature is a perception impaled on a single stereotype of rural violence. Unable to distinguish between rebellion and dacoity it tended to classify all 'rebels' as 'dacoits', as if the two words meant the same thing. 'Large bordes of *dacoits* from Rampore and the Moradabad District filled the Bhabur villages of lower Kota', wrote the Commissioner of Kumaun; 'I could not offer any efficient resistance, and the *rebels* having in a few days plundered the villages, the country was left a desert.' Or, take the following extracts from the 'narrative of events' written by R. M. Edwards, Officiating Magistrate of Muzaffarnagar, on the eve of the insurrection there:

> *On the 15th of May 1857 or following day information was received that the* people of the neighbouring villages *were collecting in great numbers round the city and proposed attacking and plundering it. On this the Cotewal and the Duffadar of sowars went with a party of district sowars, attacked and completely dispersed the* dacoits *bringing in some 15 or 20 prisoners.*

In the absence of a jail [destroyed by the insurgents the previous day] *these dacoits* were ordered to be flogged and released. The prisoners were caught *with arms in their hands in open resistance to Government authority* and should one and all have been hung on the spot.

Quite clearly Edwards was confronted with a rising of the rural population around the town of Muzaffarnagar. Indeed he came close to acknowledging this to be so when he referred to the participants as villagers 'with arms in their hands in open resistance to Government authority'. However, the habit of identifying any serious violence in the countryside as dacoity won out in the end and an all too familiar term taken from the lexicon of the thana and the *faujdari adalat* was made to describe a very different order of disturbances.

The local leaders of these *émeutes* too were often branded by the same name. They emerged in large numbers in the rural areas as the mutiny of the sepoys in the nearby garrisons detonated pent-up anger against moneylenders, landlords, officials and a host of village tyrants. The jacqucries which thus broke out were led by men with grassroot connections. Inevitably, there were among them a handful of professional dacoits who were tempted to join in the violence only by the prospect of loot or were, as discussed above, re-integrated into the agrarian community by the very force and mass of an insurrection. But it is clear even from the government's own information that the great majority of them were not criminals. More often than not they were members of some of the local subaltern groups and had come to acquire a degree of authority as a result of dislocations in the existing power structure. Or, they belonged to big landed families, and took up arms in order to grab more land, gain a following and settle old scores with rivals or with the sarkar itself if they had any particular grievance against the latter over lost privileges. Whatever their status they were able to mobilize the peasantry in a manner and on a scale quite clearly distinct from dacoity. Yet the distinction was not always grasped by the district and subdivisional authorities. The trauma of these sudden explosions drove them to stigmatize their protagonists indiscriminately as dacoits.

For some fairly representative samples of such 'blurring' one could turn to the contemporary accounts of the disturbances which occurred in Etawah district in 1858. Here the authorities had much difficulty in coping with the activities of Benkut Singh. He led a large force of sepoys and armed peasants against the government, clashed with and killed some members of a party headed by Alan Hume, the Magistrate, and sacked a place called Ajitmal. A local leader of considerable standing he was, according to Hume's own estimate, 'assisted by the entire population of the villages of Shahpore, Rajpoorah, Ramnugger and Ayanah'. When the magistrate led a raid into one of these villages, he found it 'entirely deserted, even by women and children', and again, when he and his men were about to withdraw after burning down an insubordinate village, 'the sepoys [i.e. mutineers] and a large force of armed villagers issued' from another. The figure sketched by these details taken from official sources is unmistakably that of a popular leader whose following was large enough to enable him to engage a superior enemy in the classic steps of a guerilla war. And yet with all this evidence before him the Magistrate spoke about Benkut Singh as a dacoit leader and a rebel almost in the same breath in two consecutive paragraphs of his 'narrative'.

There were some other Etawah leaders too for whom the two appellations were used interchangeably in much the same way. One of them, Ganga Singh, claimed to have been 'appointed Nazim of Etawah'. He led 'a well organized attack', though with no success, on the government's forces in an attempt to recover Nimree, 'one of the chief rebel strongholds on the Jumna-Chumbul Doab'. His name is often mentioned together with Niranjan Singh's and Roop Singh's in contemporary accounts. Members of well-established landed families in the district they could hardly be confounded with professional criminals. The former was the Raja of Chakarnagar and the latter an uncle of the minor Raja of Bhurry. Together they put up the most enduring resistance to British rule in this region during the period of the Mutiny and were recognized by the authorities as having 'maintained the only remaining hostile force in the Etawah District' as late as September 1858. Niranjan Singh eluded the law for a long time before he was finally captured in May 1861. By then, three years after the end of the great rebellion, even the semi-official *Friend of India* had regained enough of its sense of perspective to acknowledge him as the rebel who had 'assumed independent authority and seized the revenue of the district in 1857'. In the official reports of 1858, however, he remains classified as a dacoit leader.

Roop Singh was perhaps the most formidable of all the Etawah insurgents the British had to deal with. He appears to have been the rallying point for many other rebel bands in the region including those led by Benkut Singh, Ganga Singh, Peetam Singh and Niranjan Singh, and for a time there was a ground-swell of support for him from the mass of armed peasants and soldiers on their way back home from mutinous garrisons. By October 1857 he had gathered about a thousand men and was reported to have 'commenced, at the request of the mutineers, a bridge at Sheregurh' to enable the latter to cross the Jamuna. Dalalnagar pargana in the Auraiya tahsil fell to him. His stronghold, a mud fort at Ayanah which 'promised to be of very great strength', according to Hume, and was 'the terror of the neighbourhood', as the colonialist press put it, went on defying the British until April 1858. There could indeed be no doubt about the terror exercised by Roop Singh and his men against those who continued actively to collaborate with the Raj in that part of Uttar Pradesh. As a correspondent from Etawah wrote to the *Bengal Hurkaru and India Gazette* on 9 June 1858:

> *The Ajeetmul Thannadar was attacked by a party of Burhee rebels as he was passing the rebel village Bowain, on the Jumna; he and his party escaped. but two of his Burkundazes who were lagging behind were seized, disarmed and murdered at the village, and their heads carried off to Roop Singh at Burhee.*

Mr Lance immediately proceeded but before Bowain was reached the rebels had recrossed the Jumna and were comfortably settled in their stronghold, the Burhee fort. For a somewhat different version of the incident see ibid.: 792.

The rebel occupation of the fort at Burhi continued for some time to cause much anxiety to the British. Located at the confluence of the Chambal and the Jamuna it commanded the passage of the river and was thus a source of much strategic advantage to whichever party held it. Eventually, in September 1858, it was reduced and in fact blown up in a carefully planned and combined operation of the local troops and the Madras Sapper. Dislodged from his stronghold Roop Singh retreated with his followers and some of the allied bands to the ravines on the Gwalior bank of the Chambal. In this traditional sanctuary for fugitives from the law his support among the people was still large enough to make the British authorities warn the local zamindars who had sheltered him and his men that 'if repeated, their conduct would be punishable'. They also made a representation to the Gwalior Darbar 'with a view to obtaining its consent to a suggestion by the Magistrate of Etawah that he should have authority in effect to punish at his discretion certain villages of the ravines of the Chumbul and Kowaree in Gwalior which had harboured or abetted Roop Singh and other rebel plunderers mostly natives of Etawah'. The British and the Gwalior State governments planned a joint expedition 'to sweep the ill-affected portion of the Gwalior Territory', and a detachment made up of European and Darbar troops was sent out at one point to stop him from joining forces with Man Singh. The last that we hear of him from the records is that a police party led by a Lieutenant Forbes surprised him at a village called Manikpur near Baiswarah on the Chambal, but he gave them the slip.

Nothing more is known about him. However, it should be clear even from this brief sketch based entirely on official sources that there was hardly anything either in Roop Singh's background or in his career during those stormy years to justify characterizing him as a common bandit. Scion of a landed family he emerged as the focal point for rebel mobilization in an entire region a sort of Kunwar Singh of Etawah district. Even after the initial reverses in his battle against the Raj, even in the period of his retreat into the Chambal ravines he seems to have secured and retained a base among the peasantry strong enough to protect him against the counterinsurgency operations mounted jointly by the colonial and princely armies. There is no evidence at all to show that he ever lost any of this popular support and was forced thereby into a life of crime. Yet the words 'dacoit' and 'rebel' were used almost interchangeably to describe him in the official statements of the time a fact which goes again to demonstrate how slow the administration could be in its response to the radically changed character of rural violence in conditions of insurgency.

A certain degree of cognitive failure of this kind was of course inevitable during agrarian disturbances under the Raj. It represented that inertia which made it difficult for an alien and authoritarian regime to grasp promptly enough the meaning of a quick change of temper among the habitually docile mass of peasantry. For that stagnant, semi-feudal social order derived its stability from a firm and traditional if tacit agreement between the rulers and the ruled on a mutually acceptable code of dominance and subordination. Any abrupt and extensive deviation of the subaltern masses from this code was bound to take the authorities by surprise, and the almost unavoidable delay on their part in adjusting themselves to a switch of this order had often to be dearly paid for. Indeed it was thus that, as mentioned above, Mahesh Lal Datta, *daroga*, found himself trapped between two codes, one that was known but moribund and the other emergent, hence unfamiliar, and triggered off that fatal explosion by trying to decipher a message put out in the new language of rebellion in terms of the old one of criminality. Yet his incomprehension is not difficult to explain. It resulted from his failure to read correctly the sign of a change in Santal consciousness at a moment when this change was actually taking place that critical split-second when a mistake of this sort could not but cause a collision.

Historians however have been known to make the same mistake with less justification and get away with it. It is still very common for many of them to let their source material, almost invariably of an administrative nature, command their view of peasant revolts both in fact and judgement. The reliance on official evidence cannot be helped in most cases because of the absence or inadequacy of information of any other kind. But for a modern scholar to vitiate his work with the subjectivity of the guardians of law and order is to renounce the advantage he has over any contemporary witness of an event-that is, the advantage of looking at it as a past and the corrective influence this has on the bias generated by instantaneous reaction. Colonialist historiography of course abounds in exercises of this kind, but that is hardly surprising in view of the intimate connection that existed between writing history and running the Raj. What is curious is the continuing imitation of this idiom in post-colonial India. Thus, in a study of the Pabna disturbances of 1873, published a hundred years after he event, the historian's voice has been allowed to merge with that of the local sub-divisional officer as he speaks of the 'bad characters' and 'the criminal sections who took advantage of the excitement'. This agrees with the colonialist claim so lucidly formulated by William Hunter at the time when he said that by these struggles 'the rural population have proved themselves quick to appreciate and to act upon the rights which English rule secures to rich and poor and are conducting before our eyes an agrarian revolution by due course of law. Any act of lawlessness, therefore, has to be explained away as an aberration caused by 'the bad characters who had evidently joined them [the peasantly] for their own gains and induced them in many instances to go far beyond their original intentions'. And to buttress this view the author quotes from a contemporary periodical which stigmatizes all cases of violence during this movement as 'the acts of a number of professional clubmen and thieves joined by the more foolish and ignorant villagers'. An echo of the regime's concern at any critique of high landlordism turning into a 'critique by arms' on the part of the rural masses, this was precisely what had alarmed a district officer years ago when he observed how Titu Mir's forces brought about 'the voluntary junctions of the Dacoyts and bad Characters of the Country to their ranks'.

Why do 'foolish and ignorant villagers' who are usually so peaceful and averse to crime and often preyed upon at other times by clubmen, dacoits and 'bad Characters of the Country' join the latter on such occassion? Because a powerful and sustained class struggle like the resistance of the Barasat Pabna peasantry tends to invest the disparate attacks on property and person with new meanings and rephrase them as a part of a general discourse of rebellion. Consequently, each of these acts acquires an ambivalence: wired at the same time to two different codes the code of individualistic or small-group deviance from the law where it originates and that of collective social defiance which adopts it it bears the twin signs of a birth-mark and a becoming. It is precisely this duplex character which permits it to be interpreted one way or the other depending on the interpreter's point of view. A *daroga* or a historian who thinks like a *daroga* would be inclined to interpret it in terms of its past and condemn it. On the contrary, a rebel or a historian who adopts the rebel point of view would tend to seize on its present signification as the highest form of social protest and justify it.

9

TERRITORIALITY IN INSURGENCY

Introduction

Trotsky gave voice to a common exasperation in this respect when he commented on the failure of the Russian revolution of 1905 to generalize itself in the countryside. 'Local cretinism is history's curse on all peasant riots', he wrote. Even Mao Tse-tung who took on the whole a more positive view of peasant militancy found peasant 'localism' a serious impediment to party-building in the Hunan-Kiangsi border area in 1928, that critical year of retreat and regrouping in the career of the Chinese revolution. Ten years later, at the beginning of the war of resistance against Japan, he was still unhappy about the existence of localism in peasant guerilla units and guerilla bases 'which are frequently preoccupied with Local consideration to the neglect of the general interest'.

These observation link both these leaders directly to a historiographical tradition going back to Engels. The Latter in his famous work on the German Peasant War of 1525 dwells again and again on this particular limitation and shows how the want of co-operation between the armed peasantry of neighbouring regions led often to their defeat. Words and imageries signifying the peasant's inability to rise above local considerations abound in his text. 'The mass of the peasants never overstepped the baoundaries of local relations and local outlook.' They were 'confined to their local horizon'. Indeed, what 'ruined the Peasant War' was, according to him, their 'stubborn provincialism' and 'appaling narrow-mindedness', qualities which he described as 'always inevitable among the peasant masses'.

What is this consciousness which is so bitterly denounced by revolutionaries as a limiting factor of peasant insurgency? It is made up, in its Indian form, of a sense of belonging to a common lineage as well as to a common habitat an intersection of two primordial referents which, for the purpose of the present discussion, we shall call *terrotoriality*. The relation between its two components, consaguinity and contiguity, was the subject of an argument among scholars for a long time. Maine, and following him Morgan, had attributed to the former a sort of historical precedence abd structural primacy until R. H. Lowie Demolished this theory to prove that 'the two principles ... however antithetical, are not of necessary mutually exclusive'. He showed that in the historically earlier social formations 'both the bilateral (family) and the unilateral (clan, sib, moiety) unit are rooted in a local as well as a consanguine factor'. Our use of the concept of territoriality in this chapter and elsewhere in this work agrees with his conclusion that 'the two types of union'-by blood tie and local bond 'are in reality intertwined' In this we conform to the practice of Indian sociology, especially in the field of village studies where the nation, if not the temr itself, often occurs in descriptions of unity and discord. What we intend to do however is to try and extend its application to the series of larger and more intense, hence qualitatively different, rural conflicts which rocked the subcontinent under the Raj from time to time.

With the exception of the uprisings triggered off by the Mutiny (to which we shall turn later on in this chapter) the most extensive disturbances of this type until 1900 were those caused by tribal peasant revolts. Even these were *on the whole* local in character a fact which appears to have impressed many observers close to those events. The Birsaite ulgulan ranged over an area of 400 square miles, yet in retrospect the *General Administration Report of Chotanagpur Division for 1899-1900* could describe it as no more than a 'localised affair'. In much the same vein the Lieutenant-Governor of Bengal commented on the hool as it was still sweeping irresistibly through Damini-Koh: 'I do not see reason to believe that the rising is any but a local one'; and again, 'Every thing that has been heard confirms me in the conviction that this rising is merely local.' Dalton, too, in his account of the Kol insurrection of 1832, noticed a tendency on the part of the rebels not to operate beyond their immediate neighbourhoods. 'It does not appear that the Kols in their work of destruction moved far from their own homesteads', he wrote.

In each of these instances the range of the rebellion was contingent on a whole set of material conditions relating to the economic life of the populations concerned, the terrain on which they fought, their strength in arms and men as against that of their foes and so on. The force and combination of these factors differed from one local event to another and gave each of them its particular character. What was common to them all, however, was the manner in which the rebels' view of the enemy as an alien provided the domain of an uprising with its subjective determinations. These latter were made up of two categories of concepts denoting ethnic space and physical space, each of which again had a negative and positive aspect depending on the whether it sought to define the domain in terms of the otherness of the alien or in those of the self-identity of the insurgent themselves.

Hostility towards 'foriegners' which was such a prominent feature of the rebellions mentioned above, antedates them by a considerable length of time. In the Chota Nagpur plateau it was perhaps as old as the last quarter of the seventeenth century when the jagirdari system was first introduced there. In Damin-i-Koh, too, thanks to the intrusion of Hindu lanlords and moneylenders into what was originality designed as a Santal sanctuary, it had at least two full decades to mature before the outbreak of the hool In the event the term *diku*, used generically in the local tribal languages to describe anyone belonging to 'non-tribal' out-groups', came to acquire a meaning which indicated at the same time both the ethnic and the class aspects of the exploitation of the peasantry for these regions. The semantic range assigned to this lexeme in Hoffmann *Encyclopaedia Mundarica* and Bödding *Santal Dictionary* clearly brings this out. *Diku* in these works stands for 'a Hindu', 'a Hindu lanlord', '*Hindi* or *Sadani*', 'a Hindu or Bengali of the better class', etc., and *diku-n* 'to become the landlord of a village'. It has also been noticed that in at least one language of the Mundari group *di* means 'that' and the plural *diku* 'those', a telling deixis which leaves little room for doubt about the speaker's insistence on his own separate identity.

Linguistic evidence such as this was recorded by missionaries and adminnistrators at a time when the memory of some of these tribal insurrections was still quite vivid. Yet nearly sixty-seven years after the last of these great revolts and twenty years after the end of the Raj the pejorative associations of the term were found to be still quite firmly embedded in popular mentality among the adivasis of Chota Nagpur. A survey conducted by a group of sociologists in this area in 1967 showed that it had not only retained its dual function of signifying the nonautochthones (such as Hindus Musalmans, Europeans, Marwaris, Biharis, Bengalis, etc.) and class enemies (such as rural capitalists, banias, moneylenders, rajas, zamindars and landlords' servants), but had acquired for itself a new and expressive moral connotation. Diku, said many of the Munda, Oraon and Ho informants, deriving, ironically enough, from an alien etymology, meant for them 'trouble-makers' (*dik dik karnewale*). The stereotype which was thus established was backed by a host of other words, phrases, imageries and adages to emphasize the malevolence, avarice, meanness and generally the negative qualities of the outsider. Looter, deceiver, exploiter such were the epithets predicated on him. He was unreliable and fearsome. His eyes (*diku med*) were like those of a dog, for he fawned on his master for small favours and snarled at all others to keep them away. He was unfriendly: he would not recognize his own neighbour. 'A *deko* friend a thorn tree; they prick': so ran a Santal proverb. When a Munda oppressed another, he was said to be *dikuing*. And if he set himself up as a zamindar and lived off rents extracted from other Mundas, he was regarded as *dikuized*.

No wonder then that the diku figured as a major target of violence when the time came for the tribal peoples of Damin-iKoh and Chota Nagpur to settle scores with traders, moneylenders, landlords and their staff. This was indeed so conspicuous a feature of these insurrections that their essentially anti-colonial character was often overlooked by some observers who regarded these as nothing but a conflict between some of the exploiting and exploited sections of the Indian population itself. Yet the very error of this perception was itself an authentic register of their impact on contemporaries if only because it has a lot to tell us about the way these uprisings *looked* at the time (as different from what they *were*). For there could be no mistake about the fact that resentment against the alien intruders was what provided, for each of these massive explosions, the spark that ignited the fuse. Bindrai, the Kol leader, spoke for all tribal insurgents of the nineteenth century when he explained why his people had taken to arms in 1832:

> *The Pathans had taken our Hoormut and the Sing our Sisters and the Koour, Harnath Sah had forcibly deprived us of our Estates of Twelve Villages which he had given to the Sing. Our Lives we considered of no Value, and being of one Caste and Brethren, it was agreed upon that we should commence to cut, plunder, murder and eat. It is with this resolution that we have been murdering and plundering those who have deprived us of both honour & homes.*

The selective violence of that rebellion measured up to the bitterness and anger of these words. In villages where the tribal people and the dikus lived together as neighbours, it was oil the latter that the Kols concentrated their attack. To the local representatives of the Raj this looked clearly like a movement aimed at the expulsion of the diku. 'The whole of the Moondas and Coles', they said in a report on the progress of the insurrection, 'have taken up arms against the respectable inhabitants of the country, burnt and plundered their houses and property, and expelled them.' Their superiors in the Calcutta Council too acknowledged that the 'extermination or expulsion of every inhabitant of the Country, who came under the designation of Foreigner' was what the rebels wanted, although, more aware than their subordinates of the overall implications of the uprising, they mentioned 'the utter annihilation of the Government' as its other objective.

Even the violence of the Santal hool which made no distinction between the sarkar and the diku and focused on both with equal intensity from the very outset, was considered by some observers as exclusively directed against the latter in its early stages. This can be clearly seen, for instance, in the demiofficial account, "'The Sonthal Rebellion'", published in the *Calcutta Review* of 1856 and regarded as one of the most important sources of information about that event. There is much internal evidence to show that its author had access to the reports received by the Bengal Government about the uprising and its initial thrust in Damin-i-Koh, all of which spoke emphatically of the rebels' hostility both towards the government and towards zamindars and mahajans. He had also read or been told about the *parwana* issued by Sido and Kanhu on the eve of the hool. It accused the dikus as well as the sahibs of 'sins' committed against the Santals, announced the end of the Raj ('the Thacoor has ordered me saying that the country is not the Sahibs') and asked the white men to retire to the order side of the Ganges failing which, it said, there would be war: 'The Sahibs and the white Soldiers will fight. The Thacoor himself will fight. Therefore you Sahibs and Soldiers [will] fight the Thacoor himself." One could hardly mistake this as anything but a clear declaration of belligerence addressed both to the colonial authorities and their protégés, the native exploiters of the tribal peasantry. Yet the author of the *Calcutta Review* article read in this text nothing but the Santals' determination 'to banish the traders and zamindars and all rich Bengalces from their country' and to commit 'the instant slaughter of all the muhajuns, of the Darogahs'. The *parwana,* he wrote, 'expressly disclaimed all intentions against the government', an error echoed a decade later by William Hunter when he wrote that even on 7 July 1855, the day the hool broke out at Bhagnadihi, the Santals 'do not seem to have contemplated armed opposition to the Government'.

What generated such optic illusion it is difficult to say. Perhaps a degree of official complacency made many nineteenthcentury administrators look away when confronted with the evidence of failure in the machine they were given to run with a sense of historic mission. For the Raj had by this time come to believe firmly in its role as protector and benefactor of the peasantry, so that whenever a jacquerie occurred it was comfortable for the authorities to look upon it simply as a revolt of the underdog against his native oppressor rather than against the colonial government. Whatever the reason, the blind spot which had thus developed inspired a false historiography dedicated to absolving the regime of any responsibility for making the life of the tribal peoples too miserable to bear. Its filiation was by no means limited to the school of British administrator-historians like Hunter. Indian scholars such as S. C. Roy too ignored the anti-colonialist content of these uprisings and helped to perpetuate the myth that they were nothing but demonstrations of ethnic antagonism. Suresh Singh is right in joining issue with the latter on this point and insisting on the predominantly political and anti-colonialist character of the Birsaite ulgulan. Yet as he himself points out, even this, perhaps the least racially oriented of all the great tribal rebellions of the nineteenth century, was marked by 'an under-current of hostility against *Dikus*' particularly in its earlier and preparatory phase.

Going by Hoffman's testimony it is clear that the malevolence of the *diku* already been codified by this time in such imageries as snakes (*bing*), witches (*najom*) and tigers (*kula*) in Mundari usage. It was to be expected therefore that sentiments of fear and hatred such as these would be used to power any violent mobilization of the masses in this region. Indeed it is not difficult to locate this as an important element in Birsaite agitation on the eve of the ulgulan. The Munda leader's parable of stones and clods related during his visit to the Chutia temple in 1898 provides an example. He pointed to a structure of stone topped by clods of earth to serve as a crude stove of the kind often used in the country for cooking outdoors. and apparently made his followers believe that the stones and clods changed places before their very eyes, just as Mundas and dikus, he told them, were bound to do one day. Again, at an important assembly of the tribe at Dombari hill the following year he unfurled a two-coloured flag with its white symblozing the purity of the Munda and red the exploitation by the diku and prophesied that 'there was going to be a fight with the *dikus*, the ground would be as red as the red flag with their blood'.

Thus the domain of the rebellion defined itself negatively by exclusion of the diku just as the tribe defined itself in terms of the otherness of the alien. But the parallelism extends even further. There are many ideas relating to *ethnos* used by a tribe positively to assert its own identity. One of these, the notion of an ethnic space, occurs in all the tribal revolts discussed above. In each of them the domain of insurgency was considered to be as large as the tribe itself, a *coincidence* emphasized in all those preparatory acts of ritual solidarity, ceremonial gathering and herontic consultation as well as in the tendency of that violence, once it broke out, to permeate the entire tribal diaspora. The Santal insurrection was hardly a fortnight old when the authorities were alerted to the contact it had already established 'with the numerous population of the same tribe which inhabit[ed] the districts of Pachete, Manbhoom, Singbhoom and other districts south of the Grand Trunk Road', and feared 'that the insurrection might spread from Beerbhoom to those districts which [were] the original site of the Sonthal tribe'. In this respect Major

Sutherland's perceptive comment on the Kol disturbances of 1832 could apply to the whole genre. One of the officials most knowledgeable about Chota Nagpur and the first amongst them to examine the nature of that event, he wrote:

The insurrection had no limit but that which it found in the class of people by which it was instigated. Had the Country between Chota Nagpoor and Calcutta on the one hand and Benares on the other been inhabited by Dânger Coles, the insurrection would have spread to those places. The Coles are one large family which can unite for any purpose good or bad. It is perhaps fortunate for us that they are not more extensive, and that there are not many such families in India.

The tribe, in other words, was not merely the initiator of the rebellion but was its site as well. Its consciousness of itself as a body of insurgents was thus indistinguishable from its recognition of its ethnic self. 'The tribe remained the boundary for man, in relation to himself as well as to outsiders': this observation made by Engels about the Iroquois was true of the Indian adivasis, too, not merely when they lived in peace with themselves and the Raj, but even more so when they took up arms both as a positive and a negative affirmation of their ethnicity.

Corresponding to ethnic space there was also their notion of physical space which figured prominently in every tribal rebellion and constituted an important element of its territoriality. Its function was to enable the insurgents to assert their own identity in terms of what they claimed to be their homeland. As with the category of *ethnos*, antagonism towards the diku provided it with its negative determination. It had its roots in the undoubted fact of the expropriation of the adivasis. 'They have taken away from us our trees, fishes, lands and jagirs', said Singrai, the Kol. The massive alienation of tribal lands to outsiders in the years preceding the insurrection which he led, testified to the truth of his indictment and was indeed officially acknowledged as one of its primary causes: 'We have reason to believe that lands were taken by the Rajah and the Jageerdars from Coles or Raoteeas and given to Farmers for an increase of Revenue, and it is easy to understand that the ousted parties would try by all means to recover their lands.' This was confirmed by a well-informed administrator who, commenting on the event seven years later, ascribed it to 'no one cause so much as the dispossession of the Moondas and Mankies who are the Bhoonears of Sonepoor of their lands'.

These dispossession *bhumihars* were among the more active participants in the Bhumij rebellion and the Sardar agitation which formed the most important links between the revolt of the Kol and that of the Birsaites at the end of the century. Bindrai, one of the mankis responsible for inspiring the Kol to rise in arms, joined forces with Ganganarayan in the Bhumij rebellion in 1833, while from 1858 onward the 'class of uprooted *bhumihars*' constituted, according to Singh, 'the core of the Sardar movement'. Both represented the uneasy response of the tribal peasantry of Chota Nagpur to the combined impact of the *diku* and the colonial government on an agrarian order which was the very basis of their livelihood as well as of their way of life. The protracted campaign of the Sardars was in fact called *mulkui larai*, meaning, literally, the fight for the land. Spread over a period of forty years the larai exceeded the purely economic objective it had assigned itself in the initial stages, and what was originally conceived as a struggle for land assumed, by a series of transformation, the character of a struggle for a homeland. When, therefore, the hour struck for he ulgulan, the ritual chants of the Mundas rang with lament for a lost primordial *disum*. Here are some stanzas from Suresh Singh's translation:

> *The land given to us in the beginning [of Creation] by Singbonga was snatched away by our enemies We shall assemble in large numbers with weapons in our hands The new sun of religion was born, the hill and valley were lit up The zamindars harassed and put us to trouble*
>
> *Birsa Bhagwan is our leader . . . We shall not be afraid of the monkeys We shall not leave the zamindars, moneylenders and shopkeepers [alone] They occupied our land We shall not give up our khutkatti rights From leopards and snakes we reclaimed our land The happy land was seized by them*
>
> *O Birsa, our land is afloat Our country drifts away . . . The big enemy, the sahebs donning the hat Seized our land.*

But the notion of an 'original home' was more than a mere zero sign of rebel consciousness. Neither the Kols nor the Mundas resigned themselves to mourning an absence. Territoriality expressed as a sense of physical space had also a positive side to it. In the insurrection of the Kols this was indicated by the fact of their 'never having attempted to cross the Subarnareeka [Subarnarekha] River (which at that season is nearly dry) into the adjacent Pergunnahs of

Patcoom and Seldah of the Jungle Mehals, which while those Pergunnahs presented every temptation to plunder from the opulence of the many Inhabitants, were wholly unprotected and could not, it appears, at that time have offered any resistance'. Obviously for them that river was the frontier by which the realm of insurgency defined itself a sort of geopolitical sign of the aims of the uprising, similar to what the Ganges was to be for the Santal hool later on in the century.

This positive spatial aspect of territoriality was even more clearly emphasized in the ulgulan. The recovery of the lost homeland of the tribe (*ekasi piri tirasi badi*, to mention it by its picturesque name) was a central aim of Birsa's campaign, and he educated his people for this task by ceremonial visits to their ancestral sites and his emphasis on recovering the tribal 'records of rights'. The idea was obviously powerful enough to be incorporated into their religion. Some Birsaite hymns like the one cited below bear witness to this:

> *O Lord, Chutia Garh was our ancestral place. The Lord [Birsa] on his return from Jagarnathpur took brothers and sisters to Chutia Temple. He went there to bring the records of rights, manners and customs for us to support our ancestral rights which had been taken away by the enemy. Now we shall worship the Tulsi plant. We shall live according to the religion in our lands and spread it all over.*

What had begun thus as a simple declaration of spiritual faith absorbed in the course of the ulgulan some of the anxieties generated by that conflict. '*O Dharati Aba*', they chanted then, 'help us today/ With your strength turn bullets to water/ Let all enemies fall prostrate/ *O Dharati Aba*, ours is the land, ours the country.'

The adivasi view of the otherness of the *diku* in spatial terms was an element of the territoriality of the hool too. The selfdifferentiation of the autochthones in this particular respect is perhaps more clearly enunciated in the *Mare Hapram Ko Reak Katha* than in any other recorded tribal tradition. Its account of the early history of the Santals sets them apart from the dikus by their residence in clearly demarcated areas even when there was no hostility between them: 'They settled in the more open parts, we in the hills and the jungles.' But that was a long time ago when they lived together in peace in the legendary land of Champa. Since then however their relation had been one of Continuous antagonism. Wherever the tribe settled down in the course of their restless wanderings they invariably clashed with the 'others', that is, Hindus and Musalmans. They lost Champa to the former who followed close on their heels into the plains (*tandi desh*) and ousted them from there. The Santals pushed on still further but only to come into contact with the Musalmans (*Turuks*) and flee in fear. 'We moved on and on like caterpillars.' In the 'Shikar country', they cleared the king's jungles and acquired some villages for themselves. 'But the Hindus chased us away even from there and seized our lands and settlements.' Eventually they came down to the plains again, and were 'driven by Hindu oppression and hunger' to cross the Ajay and spread over the hilly tracts to the north and east up to the Ganges. 'We had to fight many a battle with the dekos', says the *Reak Katha*; 'and we are not reconciled to them even today. Wherever we clear up some land for a settlement, the dekos come and grab it.' Inevitably, therefore, this grievous sense of loss formed a part of the complex motivation for the uprising of 1855. As a Santal folk song has it:

Sido, why are you bathed in blood?
Kanhu, why do you cry Hul, Hul*?*
For our people we have bathed in blood
For the trader thieves
Have robbed us of our land.

However, in the hool, no less than it was in the ulgulan, the fight for land merged in the general struggle for a homeland. According to Dalton, the region between the Ganges and the Kasai was regarded by the Santals as their 'fatherland'. Sherwill mentioned Monghyr as its westernmost point. This was confirmed by yet another officer who wrote about their plan to march 'via Bhaugulpore to Monghyr to take possession of the Fort, which they affirmed to be the western boundary of a Kingdom once their own'. Whatever its precise geographical boundaries (as a country of the mind it didn't *need* any) its presence as an ideological factor in their rebellion was obvious. Even before it actually broke out, 'mysterious allusions' were often made to a certain Morgo Raja of the Pareshnath hills who, it was believed, would set up 'an independent kingdom of the south country, meaning the original country of the Sonthal tribe'. And in the third week of July 1855 when the hool was still going strong, the colonial authorities were alarmed at the prospect 'that the insurrection may spread from Beerbhoom to those districts which are the original site of the Sonthal tribe'. The insurgents themselves referred to the Ganges as a frontier of this 'original site'. In the parwana issued by Sido and Kanhu on the eve of the insurrection, they asked the Europeans to retire to the other side of that river. 'If you are satisfied with the Thacoor then you must go to the other side of the Ganges', they advised. This, according to the *Reak Katha*, was to apply to all other outsiders as well. One of the elders whose testimony is recorded there, mentions that 'the Ganges was regarded as our frontier at the time of the rebellion' and the dikus would have been driven beyond it but for the intervention of the sahibs on their behalf. Old man Jugia's reminiscences, too, confirmed this. ' Sido and Kanhu then commanded', he said, 'we shall slay all the rajas and mahajans, and chase away all other Hindus beyond the Ganges; we shall then rule ourselves.' The insurrection was thus a consciously defined space for them.

A correlate of the category of space was a sense of time. As such, this also entered into the subjective determination of territoriality as one of its elements and helped a tribal rebellion to define its domain in terms of the insurgents' relation to the diku. Expressed in its most generalized form as a contrasted pair of times (*then/now*), a good past negated by a bad present, its function was to endow the struggle against the alien with the mission of recovering the past as a future.

The traditions of the Santals are overlaid with nostalgia. Collected as folklore fifty years after the hool, some of these refer to a state of grace from which they are believed to have fallen by sinning against God. Others, recorded closer to the event, in 1871, are informed by a more secular vision. They look back to an age of relatively greater affluence and purer ethical conduct. The decline since then is said to have been caused by factors of two different kinds-those which are internal to the tribe itself and those for which the responsibility lies with the dikus. 'Times have degenerated now': the Santals no longer observe the customary norms of deference due from women to men, from daughters to mothers, sons to fathers, and the youth to the elders; the majhis have lost their ancient authority; disputes, so rare in the past, are common even among affines; there is no longer that peace and accord with which people used to live together in former times; the high standards of sexual morality once based on religion and maintained by the fear of reprisal and communal sanctions have given way to seduction and promiscuity; industry which in the past made the people produce what they needed for their own immediate consumption has disappeared and sloth taken over; and so on. As against these there are some other symptoms of moral and material decline attributable directly to the intrusion of the dikus into Santal life. Some of these are vices acquired by the Santals when they came into contact with the aliens. Specified in the *Reak Katha* these are as follows:

Begging: 'Formerly there were no beggars. The few who go around begging in the villages nowadays have learnt to do so from the dikus. This is generally disliked. Nor is this necessary. For whoever is willing to work can find enough subsistence within the village.'

Stealing: 'Formerly the Hor Hapans (Santals) never stole. But nowadays they have learnt to do even this in emulation of the dikus.'

Quarrelling: The Santals often fight among themselves over land and quarrels break out over the use of boundaries between fields. 'These two forms of dispute have now spread all over our land, thanks to the example set by the *deko hapans* (Hindus). There were no such disputes in the past.' It is the dikus 'who are making us fight between ourselves and grab each other's properties. Where they are, there's no amity. Had the 'deko pusis" not been there amongst us, we the Santals would have been better off morally.'

Lying: 'From the very beginning until the other day we the Santals didn't know how to tell a lie; we said only what we saw with our own eyes, whether this concerned our enemies or our own brethren. Since the advent of the sahebs some of our people have been hanged to death only because they owned up to the truth. It was not customary with us to produce the witnesses one after the other before our own tribunals; they were all presented together and made to face each other. And yet no one would commit perjury. But the Santals have now learnt the language of intrigue from the dikus and like them are selling off their life and honour for a tumbler of country liquor.'

The dikus, however, were held responsible not merely for the moral corruption of the Santals but also for the loss of their material prosperity. The intrusion of the moneylender and trader in the economic life of the tribe was recorded in its tradition as a watershed dividing a happy past and a poor present. The phenomenon was integrated into the legends of its early wanderings and assigned a place in popular imagination by many a hostile proverb and imagery. 'Formerly no one borrowed from the mahajans', said Kaloyan, the wise old man of the race, in his ancestral account, 'nor indeed were there any mahajans around. It was only in Shikar country that they latchedd on to us for the first time. Since then until this very day we have been in their clutches and they are tearing away at us like vultures. As the saying goes: "The Hindu *sahukar* will chew up even the dry bones of the aged and the decrepit." As a matter of fact it was their extortion which put us on the run again from Shikar as well. However, at the beginning they were not so unscrupulous about charging interests but their oppression increased as time passed. We, too, on our part have to take some of the blame. People fall into the mahajans' clutches without considering the pros and cons of what they are doing [while transacting with them].'

A sense of time expressed in terms of a *then/now* distinction may be said to have been implicit in the Santal hool if for no other reason than that it was a determined and concious attempt to end the tyranny of the diku. However, it would be reading too much into the evidence to say that the termination of an unbearable present was regarded by the rebels as the means of recovering the past. We know that the establishment of some kind of a political kingdom was a part of their stated aims, and that the parwana issued by their leaders had, indeed, announced the advent of 'the region of Truth' and "True justice'. But it would be rash to suggest that this rather hazy vision of the shape of things to come was to any significant degree invested with the qualities of an idealized past. By contrast, the temporal component was more fully developed in the Birsaite ulgulan. Its spatial objective, the purloined *disum,* was assigned a place in time not only as a memorable past but also as a desirable future in the Munda imagination. The domain of rebellion extended thus in both directions from the subject's locus in an embattled present.

A tendency to look back in time had featured in the Sardar agitation too, but it was only under Birsa's leadership that the distinction between past and present came to acquire a decisive ideological function. Codified in the form of the antinomy Satjug/ Kaljug, it derived at the same time from the Hindu myth of the four epochs (*yugas*: *Satya, Treta, Dvapara, Kali*) and Judaeo-Christian millenarism, imbibed respectively from the Vaishnava contacts of his early youth and his schooling at a missionary institution as a child. Whatever its origin, the opposition between the two *jugs* figured most prominently in the religious discourses and rituals by which he prepared his tribe for the uprising of 1899-1900.

In the Birsaite homiletics the difference between the past and the present conditions of the Mundas is represented as a contrast between conditions characteristic of Satjug and Kaljug. The comparison ranges over all the salient aspects of material and spiritual life. In Satjug the Mundas were directly ruled by Niranjan, the creator of the universe. In Kaljug they are ruled by Queen Mandodari, the spouse of the mythical demon-king and archetypal evil, Ravana. The contrast between life under divine rule and subjection under the Raj presided over by Queen Victoria could not be more clearly stated.

Land constituted the material basis of the blissful life of the Mundas in Satjug. Their ancestors cleared the jungle and made the land habitable for man. They lived in harmony with nature and with the wild beasts around them. They set up colonies, controlled floods, excavated wells and tanks and learnt the use of natural springs for the supply of fresh water. They introduced agriculture and made the earth ready to bear the grains and fruits they needed. In Kaljug the Mundas have been expropriated of this land which once belonged to them. They have been robbed by zamindars and mahajans who have made their way in their midst like 'a substance smooth like oil' and ruined them. In general, the natural economy of their Golden Age has been replaced by a money economy, industry and commerce, their freedom and self-sufficiency by the tyranny and exploitation of the dikus. As a result they have nothing left of their ancient prosperity. In Satjug they used to gather seven harvests from each sowing; in Kaljug they have only one harvest per sowing. In that happy ancestral past they used to eat their meals out of gold and silver dishes. Now they starve to death. In the old days no one died of disease. Now it is common to suffer from and die of illness. Gone is the time when there was no sorrow on earth.

This decline in material well-being corresponds to it moral degeneration. Thanks to the dikus, Munda society has been penetrated by alien influences. The prevalent of *karam* and *paika* dances is symtomatic or a general and widespread corruption of their race in Kaljug. A high standard of social and spirirtual morality was characteristic of their culture in Satjug. The Mundas in those days would commit no violence against their kinsmen. Sexual morality was strictly observed and unlike the dikus, men would not exceed the socially prescribed degree of joking with women. Spiritually, Satjug was characterized by an emphasis on religious faith and ritual observance. The rules of purity were taken seriously. No one would eat or drink before taking his bath. Alcohol was forbidden. People wore the sacred thread on their person and the sanctified themselves by sandal paste marks. They prayed and made ritual offerings at their ancestral temple. they turned away from anti-gods (Asur) and worshipped the sacred *tulsi* plant twice every day. All this has disappeared from Munda life in Kaljug.

This contrast between the two jugs was used by Birsa to encourage his people not only to reject their inglorious present but also to fight for a better future and Satjug was his blueprint for that future. He prophesied the end of Kaljug in chiliastic terms; "O men, beware! This world will not end like this it will end in great misery. I will turn deep waters into outlets. I crush the hills.' And the reign of the enemies of the Mundas was to be 'destroyed in a violent conflict'. All 'the Romans, Germans, British, Rajas and Zamindras, Satans and devil's would be driven away from the land. 'The Zamindras are now very happy and they laugh at us. But their allotted period, their time-limit is over.' The land was to regain its former purity when washed with the sacrificial blood of 'a white goat', that is, the white men. The Mundas would then march to Delhi, occupy the 'throne', and 'rule in the land'. Eventually, 'when they win back our kingdom, they will make merry and their happiness will never end'. This was to be the beginning of yet another Satjug, a recapitulation of the original: 'And the cultivation of only one field will do for us. The people will not take land even if it is tied to their neck. There will be no war in the land. All will be done in accordance with religion. Just as our ancestors ruled according to their religion, so shall we reign.'

The coming end of Kaljug and advent of Satjug was a theme on which Birsa played again and again in his sermons at mass congregations and parables told to smaller groups of disciples. At Thakurdura, for instance, he looked into a dried up well and 'exclaimed that Satjug had arrived and Kaljug was on its way out'. The termination of the bad present was ritually enacted at some of the larger gatherings of his people on the eve of the ulgulan. A contemporary account of the Birsaite assembly at Dombari in February 1898 offers us a glimpse of this picturesque ceremony:

> *. . . to perform the last rites of the enemies an artificial grove was improvised on Dombari hill. And they cut a banyan tree in the name of the Queen and observed the Holi festival. They placed the earthen lamps all over the tree and pitched a red and white flag near it. Then they danced the* Karma *dance of Kaljug. They chopped it from one side. A red flag was pitched on one side a white flag on the other. For the faithful, all the Birsaites, an artificial enclosure was built and the white flag pitched. All customs and manners, dance, garland, bangle, flowery finger ring and flower comb of Kaljug were prohibited and given up. And he put them [his enemies] to death. He danced on the dancing ground to the accompaniment of drum beats and declared that the Empire of the British Queen had come to an end. They proclaimed that in the name of the Queen they would shoot arrows at her effigy. They set the plantain tree on fire and cut it down and did away with it in her name.*

It was thus that the wicked epoch and its institutionalized form, the Raj, were symbolically destroyed to make way for a return to Satjug and Munda rule.

The Hindu festival of Holi celebrated by burning the effigy of Holika, the she-demon, to mark the end of the old year and usher in the new, was its ritual equivalent. And since the function of mime is to make a wish come true, the ulgulan when it came darkening the sky with arrows and dotting the land with columns of fire, was to be the actualization as it was in the fantasy of a Satjug, it was nevertheless a step forward in the direction of a *real* future. In that future the Mundas were not destined to walk on earth as twenty-one foot tall giants like the fabled supermen of the Golden Age dreamed up by Birsa. However, thanks to this dream they gained immensely in stature as rebels fighting for a life free from the domination of foreign and native oppressors.

It will be wrong to deduce from what has been said above that territoriality was characteristic of the outlook and uprisings of the tribal peasantry along. On the contrary, this was an element of consciousness common to all of the rural populations including Hindus and Muslims and deeply ingrained in their view of society, politics and culture secular as well as religious. The growth and consolidation of a colonial empire with its centralized bureaucracy, army and legal system, its institutions to purvey a western-style education, its railways, roads and postal communication, and above all the emergence of an all-India market economy did much to undermine the force of territoriality. Yet the habit of thinking and acting on a small local scale, continued throughout the colonial period and partition of politics on a sub-continental scale was still to take some time fully to develop.

It is generally believed that the *Pax Britannica* contributed much to the reinforcement of casteism at the expense of territoriality. Yet in a curiously paradoxical way it was this very process which guaranteed the survival of the latter and most caste populations, including, as Dumont points out, even the widely distributed Brahman castes of Uttar Pradesh, tended to concentrate in a few districts as their respective foci. For territoriality, though by no means identical with caste consciousness, was still for a long time to count as one of its basic components. Miller's observation about the system of territorial segmentation in Malabar as 'a necessary correlate of a rigid caste system' could be said to apply to all of India, for everywhere, as in Malabar, it was the function of these small local units to promote intercaste relations and sustain the caste hierarchy at the village level. They represented the villager's notion of the size and spread of his own subcaste a correspondence so direct, indeed, that in many cases a subcaste was known by the name of its locality. The range of affinal links of a village subcaste group was yet another instance of such correspondence. Described by Mayer as a 'subcaste's region' it acted, among other things, as a catchment area for marital transactions involving its members. Pocock's study of such transactions among the Patidar of Gujarat shows how until recently the territorial factor used to be a determining influence on marriage alliances concluded by the members of an *ekada*. And one may cite linguistic usages such as *parasamparke bhai* ('neighbourhood-related brother'), *gramsamparke kaka* ('villagerelated father's younger brother'), etc., in Bengali as further evidence of the link between kinship and locality. Altogether it is difficult not to accept Mayer's observation that at 'the level of the effective caste group and subcaste group we step down to purely local relationships'.

Caste, of course, is pre-eminently Hindu and casteism alien to canonical Islam. Yet in the local societies where Hindus and

Muslims live together the latter, too, are assigned ranks, rights and obligations in what amounts virtually to caste terms. This, according to Imtiaz Ahmad, involves them in an actual recognition of caste distinctions and its rationalization in religious terms. No wonder, then, that the divisions within Muslim society too are partly conditioned and the relations between them governed by territoriality. Thus, the Muslim Meos of Rajasthan and Haryana parallel the Bengali practice mentioned above in attributing an imaginary kinship to fellow villagers: 'The entire community is visualized as an extended family and members of each generation born in the village are believed to be like siblings, unless, of course, they are actually closely related in a different way.' A study of a local Muslim population in a West Bengal district has shown how it regards itself as an aggregate of ethnic communities called *jats* (meaning castes in colloquial Bengali) with a single jat living on its own in each of the ten villages out of a group of thirteen and two living together in each of the remaining three villages, but with one jat vastly outnumbering the other in every case even there. A clear pattern of territorial segmentation has been noticed among the Muslims of south India too. In Malabar the division between the father-right and mother-right Moplahs who 'usually form two different compartments', corresponds, in spite of a certain overlap, to fairly distinct regional concentrations the former in the interior of South Malabar and the latter in the coastal regions of North and South Malabar and Mangalore. In Tamil Nadu the four subdivisions of the Muslim community 'appear to be distributed within territorially distinct parts of the state' with Kayalars and Marakayars located primarily along the Coromandel coast and Labbais and Rawthers in the interior. The division between the last two groups again corresponds to that between a predominantly southern and a northern cluster. With all four endogamy and territorial terms. Very much the same pattern holds for Uttar Pradesh where local Sheikh Siddique groups (which for all practical purposes act as subcastes) assert their identity positively in terms of endogamy and common habitation within a particular circle of villages and negatively by refusing to acknowledge by intermarriage of otherwise the rest of the Sheikh Siddiques in that neighbourhood as members of their own caste. Finally, it may be in order to mention that over 60 per cent of Meo marriage alliances in a Rajasthan village were found to have been contracted within a radius of twenty miles and over 90 per cent within a radius of thirty miles clearly a case of 'kinship enforced by propinquity' (to quote Lowie's happy phrase) and a close parallel to the Patidar practice cited above.

Territoriality thus is no less essential to the Hindu and Muslim way of thinking and acting in society than it is to that of the tribal peasantry. Indeed, this is what links even the local administrative units, such as the village and the *nâd* as Srinivas says of Coorg, to 'the sentiments of the people'. Such sentiments permeate all levels of the superstructure. In politics these can be traced back to a period of about a thousand years beginning with the later Vedic age when petty kingdoms were slowly evolving out of local tribal settlements *grâmas* amalgamating into *râshtòras* and tribal chiefs transforming themselves into kings, a process ritualized, for instance, in the picturesque Hiranòya-garbha ('Golden Womb') ceremony which, conducted by Brahman priests, helped the chieftains of the *âtòavika* tribes to be 'reborn' into another caste or even into a caste for the first time. 'Royal prerogative', writes Kosambi of the earlier part of this period, was still 'seriously restricted by tribal custom and tribal law' and territoriality, that hallmark of tribal polity, was made explicit by such punishments as ostracism that is, by actually cutting off the territorial bond between an offender and his local community or as the term *aparuddha* implies, by pronouncing him to be a person denied the right of access. Subsequently as castes began to emerge 'the essentials of tribal society were retained in this transition, namely endogamy' and 'expulsion from *jâti* remained the most potent and dreaded punishment, as expulsion from the *gens* or tribe had been earlier'. Vestiges of such correspondence between politics and territoriality are still to be found both in the authority of the local caste panchayats and in such expressions of rural justice as the temporary banishment of a man beyond the village boundary in order to punish him for the highly polluting offence of causing the death of a cow.

In many parts of colonial India the village boundary was and perhaps is even today a particularly sacred mark of territoriality. A host of godlings and rituals were its ubiquitous symbols. Srinivas mentions a 'familiar deity in Telugu and Tamil villages' whose name, Ellamma, literally means 'boundary-mother'. Poleramma and Kalamman were two other boundary goddesses listed by Whitehead in his account of the village gods of south India. He also describes the worship of the boundary stone, *ellai-kal*, which 'is very commonly regarded as a habitation of a local deity, and might be called a shrine or symbol with equal propriety'. In one such village near Puddukkottai he found an elaborate ceremony involving as many as nine boundary stones. The central Indian village studied by Mayer, too, had a number of shrines of this kind-three of them devoted to Adyapal Maharaj, the lord of the southern, western and eastern gates of the village, two to Bisesa Maharaj and Udeyrao Maharaj, deities who presided over its northern and south-eastern borders respectively and one to Chira, a holy stone that divided the village from a neighbouring hamlet. And in Coorg the nâd-boundary was the ritual site for the customary 'plantain honour' done to a groom on his way to the bride's village as well as for offerings made on the outbreak of an epidemic to Mariamma, the goddess of pestilence.

Suffused thus with religiosity the territorial sentiment itself tended to be spiritualized to some extent. In Coorg, for inc stance, 'it was common for deities to be identified with their *n?ds*' and consequently, for chauvinism with religion. 'A patriot', says Srinivas, 'was also a devotee.' Raiding and defending temples, 'the most sensitive part of a n?d', victories and defeats in such encounters and deeds of great daring on such occasions were the stuff of which the folklore of local patriotism and the legendary reputation of individual heroes was made. At the hour of the birth of a hero in a *nâd*, it was believed, the tower of the most important temple in its rival nâd would crack.

However, local solidarity was not made up merely of feuding over temples even in Coorg. The closing up of ranks by all villagers irrespective of caste in the face of a natural calamity befalling any one *okka*, the ritual mourning by all of bereavement in any single household, the village dance which concluded the harvest festival, the communal hunt which followed and the terminal feast, literally called 'village harmony', on the occasion of certain festivals,were all highly formalized expressions of a territorial tie which was no less secular than religious. In Malabar, too, Miller found this tie to be very strong indeed:

'The *desam* was the locus of nearly all intercaste relations from the lower (non-military) Nayar subcastes downwards.' So was the 'village region' in Malwa. A correlate of the subcaste's region but less obviously articulated in institutional terms, it was a significant element of the villager's idea of himself as a member of a local community. As Mayer defined it:

> *This region is never made manifest, for the village as such never invites guests or acts as a body in this way. Nevertheless the village region to some extent exists because villagers do think of an area in which they are at home,* where people are not felt to be strangers. *In the same way as a subcaste member coming from a distance is not admitted until he can claim some connection with 'recognized' relatives, so* villagers see the people outside their region as strangers, *with different customs, different ways of speech, etc.*

It is important to notice how the villager's self-identity in terms of his own region was negatively defined. If solidarity was one axis of territoriality, exclusion was another, and the latter had many determinations depending on the context in which it functioned. It could take the form, as it did in Malabar, of denying immigrant astrologers or barbers a *desam avakasam*-that is, the right to practise their traditional occupation in a desani without the approval of the family which had the hereditary privilege to render these services in that particular area. Or it could find expression in a tragic dilemma like that of the Coorg physician, Kunge, dramatized customarily at harvest festivals. He was split between his sense of duty to attend to a severely wounded man from a friendly nâd and his obligation to heed his mother's injunction not to do so on the ground that the man belonged to a village traditionally hostile to her native nâd and the wound had been received during a feud between the two. The mother prevailed and the warrior died testifying to the fact that a non-tribal villager's hatred of an 'outsider' could fully match a Santal's or a Munda's antagonism towards a diku.

One such outburst of hatred, historic rather than legendary, was witnessed in the Deccan riots of 1875. Moneylenders were the invariable targets of these jacqueries of the Kunbi peasantry. Their attempt, in all cases, to seize and destroy the bonds, decrees and other related documents held by their creditors, their willingness to spare the latter any further violence once the incriminating papers were obtained and resort to physical assault only if the bonds were not surrendered, leave no doubt about the precise character of the riots as a conflict between moneyed capitalists and the agriculturists exploited by them through usurious transactions. Yet this conflict was so overdetermined by territoriality that it was, for the peasant, no less a resistance to 'foreigners' than a struggle against oppressors.

The great majority of the moneylenders vanis, as they were locally known were, indeed, not natives of Maharashtra. They had migrated from Gujarat and Rajasthan and settled in the Kunbi villages of Ahmadnagar and Poona districts. The power of their purse made them indispensable to the local peasant economy without, however, assimilating them into the local society. 'Their insistence on maintaining intact all affinal and ritual ties with their native provinces, their aggressive techniques of money-making and above all their indifference to local sentiment had done nothing over the decades centuries in the case of the older immigrant families to endear them to the Kunbis even during Maratha rule. What, however, had been until then a state of uneasy symbiosis broke down altogether under the combined impact of the ryotwari system and the judicial procedure introduced by the British. It helped the vani to enmesh the peasant even further in usury and displace at the same time the village community and the traditional elite who under the old regime mediated between the state and the cultivator as well as between the latter and his creditor. No wonder then that within two decades of British rule the moneylenders came to be regard not merely as ruthless exploiters of the peasantry but also as elements who stood clearly outside the local tradition and subverted it. This image was not made up of peasant prejudice alone. In official statements, too, they could be represented as 'chiefly foreigners, different in religion from their clients, entirely out of sympathy with them, and accustomed to retire with their profits after a sufficiently long course of business to their homes in Rajputana'. As for the Kunbis themselves the idea of the vani as an outsider appears to have been a directive principle of their violence in 1875. It was aimed almost exclusively at moneylenders, but within that class it discriminated carefully between the 'indigenous' and the 'alien', as the Deccan Riots Commission observed:

> *The Marwari and Gujur sowkars were almost exclusively the victims of the riots, and in villages where sowkars of the Brahmin and other castes shared the money lending business with Marwaris it was usual to find that the latter only were molested.*

A negatively defined territoriality was thus as basic to Maratha peasant insurgency as it was to the tribal uprisings above. However, there is some evidence to suggest that the territorial tie operated among the Kunbis not merely as a measure of exclusion. They also appear to have used it, as did the Santals and the Mundas, to promote solidarity between neighbouring villages against their common foe. A letter sent by the inhabitants of Kallas in the summer of 1875 to those of Akola reproaching them for not joining in the campaign of excommunication against Marwaris 'who are deemed as excluded from the community of this village', appealed for cooperation, 'for the good of all of us . . . *as we consider Kallas and Akola as one village*.' One wonders if in sending out this appeal the Kunbis of Taluka Indapur were drawing consciously on a tradition of Maratha peasant militancy based on coterritoriality. For the latter is known to have played an important part in popular resistance to fiscal surveys in Khandesh in 1852. This movement derived its strength from the solidarity of the Pajna and Tilole Kunbis who lived in the Savda and Yaval regions of that district. As the officials most concerned with this event wrote at the time, 'The fact of all the chief men of the Pajnee and Teelolee castes to which the mass of the cultivators in the Yawul and Sowda districts belong, being residents of the villages of Sowda Mahal, accounts for the agitation having originated and attained its greatest development there.'

Nothing brings out more clearly the role of territoriality as a positive factor of rebel mobilization among the non-tribal peasantry than the massive jacqueries triggered off by the Mutiny. What made insubordination within the army particularly dangerous for the Raj was its linkage with peasant violence especially in large areas of what is now known as Uttar Pradesh and Madhya Pradesh. Here the insurrection of the sepoys boiled over and spread beyond barracks, cantonments and sadar stations into the sorrounding countryside to acquire innumerable local bases for its articulation. These figure in many accounts of the rebellion as an acknowledgement of its territoriality by those who had the most to lose from it. As many as sixty-two villages were name by Qazi Kamaluddin, Munshi Lachhman Sarup and Shivabans Rai Vakil, three pillars of Sikandarabad society in their statements describing the sack of that town by the populace from its immediate neighbourhood. The colonial authorities, too, were keen on tracing the agrarian violence to its local roots. Many amongst them were completely taken aback by the outbreak of these jacqueries and their force and extent. H. D. Robertson, Assistant Magistrate of Saharanpur, who had toured the tranquil countryside around Deoband an official business in April 1857 wrote thus in utter astonishments at what he saw there on his return six weeks later: 'Troops might mutiny, but hardly realize this rapid changes among peaceful villagers.' His words echoed the sentiments of those who functioned at the lowest levels of the administration close to the villages. And it is their response to the sudden rise in the local temperature that summer which explains more than anything else why their narratives of the Mutiny exude such a strong sense of place.

A most authentic source of our information of what happened in the rural districts of northern and central India in those days, these local reports and despatches bristle with place- names-the names of parganas and mauzas, particles of geography caught in a beam of history. An extract from a Collector's report on the disturbances in a Rohilkhand district may serve to illustrate this. 'When the mutineers came to Budaon from Bareilly', he wrote, 'the inhabitants of Surai Jullundri, Surai Miran, Naee Surai and Surai Nahr Khan and mohulla Brahempoor all mohullas in the city of Budaon, and those of Nugla Shurkee, Rusoolpoor and of other adjoining villages united with them in plundering the furniture and property in the bungalows of the European officers and residents in the station . . . The villagers of Nugla Shurkee also in unison with the residents of the Brahempoor, Puttialee Surai and Naee Surai mohullas of Budaon, plundered and destroyed the records of the Moonsiffees as also those of the Kotwalee. On the news of the outbreak at the Sudder Station becoming known in the pergunnahs of the district disturbances broke out in every direction.' And he went on to list forty-five inhabitants of thirty-four villages in ten parganas as 'individuals and villages [that] would appear to have been conspicuous in their own respective localities.'

But perhaps the most impressive tribute paid by the Raj to the territoriality of that rebellion was to pick out its rural sites as the focus of the counter-insurgency campaigns of 1857-8. These were military forays in which fire was as important an instrument of pacification as the sword a pattern common to all British attempts to deal with the peasant wars of nineteenthcentury India. Small mobile segments of what remained of the colonial army, often reinforced by all adult white men in a given area, penetrated into the countryside in Uttar Pradesh, just as they had done in Bihar and western Bengal two years earlier to suppress the Santal hool, and as on that occasion crowned most of the punitive raids on villages with exemplary acts of arson, execution and arrest. The activities of R. Spankie, Magistrate of Saharanpur, were fairly representative in this respect and deserve therefore to be recalled in some detail. This is how he described these in an official letter to the Commissioner of Meerut Division:

> *Some signal example was necessary. All the Europeans of the place accompanied me with the district sowars and twenty men of the 29th, with a view to disperse the assembly. The villagers would not meet us, and scattered, deserting their villages, three of which were burnt a number of prisoners were captured and brought into Saharanporc.*

I determined on the 22nd May to march to the village of Gurhow some7 miles from the station. I found it deserted. I went on to Nagul, three miles further, and thence to a round of villages on the right; they were all deserted. I managed however to find the Lumberdars of mauza Kunkuri and Phoraur. These men had refused to pay their revenue. I brought them into Saharanpore.

On the 23rd May I visited several villages on the Deobund Road and off it. On this occasion I was also accompanied by several gentlemen of the station. I burnt one village.

On the 30th May I went down towards Munglour accompanied by Messrs. Trench, Plowden and Edwards, and by Captain Garstin. We were joined at midnight at a given point by Mr. Robertson and Captain Wyld. Our intention was to attack the village of Manuckpore we found the village all but deserted. It was burnt, and we captured a few prisoners.

On the 3rd of June the Goorkhas under Major Bagot arrived. On the same evening I took a portion of the Groorkhas and some of the 4th Light Cavalry to attack and disperse a body of Goojurs. The Cavalry pursued them for some distance. A few men were cut up, and some prisoners were made. Two villages were burnt. In this affair I was joined by Mr. Brownlow and most of the residents, and of course by my own officers.

A report on some of the auxiliary operations carried out in the same district by another officer, W. C. Plowden, fills in some of the details of this campaign how on 21 May 1857 he and his troops punished the village Chowree by flogging its headmen and destroying their houses and how two days later they raided the village Tarpah in order to sieze Bukshee, a rebel leader. 'But though Bukshee remained at large, the object of our expedition was in a measure attained. The village of Tarpah was burnt to the ground. The headmen were secured and a quantity of cattle was captured.' A year later, almost to the day, the village of Chit Baragaon, the principal seat of the Kausik Rajputs in Ghazipur district, which had provided a strong local base for Kunwar Singh, was given the same summary treatment. When the army attacked it after some hesitation 'the village was so strong' it was found to be empty. 'Two of the notorious ringleaders were, however, fortunately caught lurking in the neighbouring ravines and immediately tied and executed; their houses and those of the other ringleaders were levelled to the ground.' Soon afterwards Brigadier Douglas's force reached Gahmar in the same district in pursuit of Amar Singh only to find him gone; so he 'burnt it, the villagers having openly sided with the rebels'.

What the pacification campaign sought to achieve thus by taking on the offending villages one by one was to cope with the concrete articulation of the rebellion, for territoriality as the intersection of geographical and social space was indeed what constituted this concreteness. The jacqueries of 1857-8 were strictly local affairs: they operated within discrete local vicinages and had their social bases in local units with clearly recognized boundaries.

To take up the first of these two aspects, the domain of each jacquerie coincided with the domain of the peasants' relationship with their local enemies official as well as non-official. More often than not the villagers would turn on the nearest seat of government as the foremost and immediate object of their attack. In their eyes, a sadar station the Anglo-Indian term for district headquarters stood for sarkar itself. Situated usually in a small town its official buildings housed the court, the treasury, the police station, the jail and so on, and were the visible symbols of an authority which the peasants regarded with fear rather than affection at the best of times. Now that this authority had weakened and become vulnerable a mutiny in a local garrison was often believed to be the signal of the end of the Raj country literally invaded town to settle scores with tax collectors, court officials, policemen and not the least, those sinister files which ruined the cultivator by expensive and unintelligible legal processes.

Sadar stations therefore ranked high on the list of casualties in all accounts of the rebellion in the northern provinces. Mathura provided a typical case. Here a detachment of native infantry mutinied in the afternoon of 30 May 1857. They killed a European officer, set fire to the administrative buildings, destroyed the public records, plundered the treasury, released all prisoners and then marched out of the town in the direction of Delhi. 'This state of things continued until the afternoon of the 21st May when the inhabitants of the surrounding villages made an inroad into the Sudder Station and plundered all the inhabited bungalows of the entire property belonging to the residents and from those which were not occupied they removed the doors and *chowkuts*, including those of the Government buildings; a few of the bungalows have also been burnt down by the insurgents.' Elsewhere in that district the people of Nohjhil and their neighbours pillaged a tax collector's office and destroyed all documents they found there. At Raya too the police station with all its records was burnt down by the villagers. Similarly, the demolition of the Bulandshahr district headquarters was the combined work of the Gujars from the surrounding countryside and the inhabitants of that town: they burnt down the dak bungalow and other official residences, destroyed all government buildings and their records, carried off or consigned to fire whatever property fell into their hands and released all prisoners.

At Badaun, again, the pillage of the bungalows belonging to the Europeans, the attacks on administrative offices and the police station and destruction of records were carried out by villagers fro the immediate neighbourhood backed by the townspeople. In Bunelkhand the peasants from the surrounding villages poured into Jhansi, broke open the jail, liberated the detainees and set fire to all the bungalows. At Muzaffarnagar, too, some of the bungalows were burnt down, kacharis destroyed, the jail barracks demolished and all their doors, shutters and iron rails carried off by the raiders who lived within an easy distance of the town. The pattern was the same everywhere. It repeated itself so often that one could hardly disagree with the Officiating Magistrate of the last named district when he observed: 'The burning of the cutcherries at Moozuffurnugger is not a solitary instance, on the contrary we see that throughout this rebellion the first thing the "*budmashes*" have done in getting a footing in a station has been to burn the Government offices.'

Not merely government offices, but all that represented the Raj either directly or by association in any particular area-railways and railway stations as in Ghazipur and Allahabad, indigo and opium factories owned by white planters in Jaunpur and Ghazipur, bungalows as a clearly distinguished form of European residence everywhere, dispensaries and colleges run by the government as at Badaun and even charitable asylums set up by Christian effort, in fact 'every building however large or however insignificant with which we are connected' was, as a District Magistrate wrote viewing the carnage around him in July 1857, 'burnt down and demolished with as much ill-will as our public offices'. Clearly no local representation of the authority of the Raj was safe from insurgent attack.

The other relationship which helped to determine the territoriality of this particular violence was the antagonism between peasants and moneylenders. The latter are described in all contemporary accounts as those who, apart from the government, were hurt most by the rural insurrection. 'I need scarcely say that the great feature in the rebellion here has been the universal ousting of all bankers, Buniyas, Marwarees, etc. from landed property in the district, by whatever means they acquired it, whether at auction, by private sale or otherwise.' This observation by the Collector and Magistrate of Hamirpur could apply equally well to almost any other part of the NorthWestern Provinces. Indeed, Spankie, the officer in charge of Saharanpur, was so greatly impressed by this phenomenon that to him it appeared 'as if the disturbances in the commencement were less directed against Government than against particular people and castes', that is, against banias and marwaris. His idea that the uprisings developed in two stages first against the mahajans and then against the regime might have been true of particular instances, but there were innumerable occasions when the peasants attacked both these adversaries simultaneously or in reverse order.

In most cases, however, the insurgents made no attempt to distinguish between them, for in their own experience, the two were inseparably linked. What needs to be emphasized here is its local dimension. In the eyes of the common villager the mufassil towns symbolized the alliance between sarkar and sahukar. The coexistence there of administrative buildings and bania wards the coexistence of kachari and *haveli* was its topographical expression; the interplay between legal processes and usurious transactions its function. By focusing his violence on a sadar station or a township endowed with a tahsildari office the peasant registered his response to the local character of this symbiosis. Robertson, Assistant Magistrate of Saharanpur, showed a clear grasp of this aspect of insurgent mentality when he explained: 'The creditors of the poorer class of cultivators invariably inhabit the larger towns, so the these towns naturally enough became a point of attack when the civil power was paralysed.' What he saw in that district fully confirmed this. For the raiders came in a large body from villages around Nakur, the headquarters of the pargana of that name, burnt down its police station and tahsil offices, and tore up and scattered all records including mahajans' bonds and accounts.

Again, the sack of Deoband where the bankers and banias had been living in constant fear of 'invasion from without and sedition from within', was the work of Pandar Rajputs and Gujars, all of whom belonged to the pargana of which that town was the principal administrative centre. As Strikes has noticed, all eight of the most offending villages selected by Robertson for his two punitive expeditions in this region 'stood close to the Kali Nadi or its tributaries north and cast of Deoband and within a 4 to 5 miles radius'. The district headquarters of Muzaffarnagar too fell to the wrath of its surrounding countryside. 'Here as in other parts of the country', wrote its Officiating Magistrate, 'the Buneahs and Mahajans were in the been majority of case the victims and fearfully have many of them been made to suffer for their previous rapacity and avarice.' And here, as elsewhere, the villagers 'burnt the Government offices so that all the transactions of sale and mortgage of property of Mahajans and other papers might be destroyed', thus demonstrating yet again their understanding and dislike of the complicity between moneylenders and government at the local level.

The territoriality of these uprisings of 1857-8 derived also from their ethnic character. All contemporaries testify to this phenomenon. To some extent, of course, it is the very language of the current system of classification which made them do so. For in the nineteenth century it was customary with both native and foreign observers to conceptualize Indian society in ethnic-primarily caste terms. Yet this taxonomic bias was itself an index of the social organization which inspired it that is, the tendency of large populations belonging to the same caste to congregate in contiguous areas and perpetuate this territorial arrangement by ritual and kinship. It is common therefore for the Mutiny records to describe the peasant rebellions of the time as the revolt of particular ethnic masses of the Rajputs, the Mewatis, the Gujars and so on.

To start off with the Rajputs and a fairly transparent case of territoriality relating to the most prominent of its ethnic constituents, the rebellion in Bundelkhand was reported as the work of the eponymous Rajput sept, regarded by Crooke as 'almost entirely' confined to that part of the country. A caste with a strong sense of attachment to their traditional habitattheir prohibitions against marriage included 'residence among foreign peoples' they were active in vast numbers in the Jhansi area. A rebel camp of over 20,000 men at Mhow was, according to British army intelligence, made up entirely of Bundelas. Again, it was the 'fighting horsemen and kinsmen' of the Bundela gentry of Gohand in Hamirpur who were said to be responsible for the serious and prolonged disturbances in that district. In Azamgarh the uprising was led by the Palwars who were very numerous there and belonged to the same *gotra*. Their challenge to the Raj was serious enough to make its end appear imminent in the eyes of the common people of the area: 'When at Azamgarh the battle raged between the British troops and the Palwars, many illiterate persons gathered and awaited the result; if the Palwars became victorious they also would join the Palwars.'

In the adjoining district of Jaunpur it was yet another hostile concentration of Rajputs those of the Rajkumar sept who constituted a threat to British power on this highly sensitive border of Awadh. The rebellion in Bhadohi, noticed below, came to be identified with the Monas, the most numerous and powerful caste of that pargana in Mirzapur district. The revolt headed by Shazada Firoz Shah in September 1857 at Mandsore in Malwa was based largely on the support of the local Mewatis who constituted nearly half of the insurgent army. LieutenantColonel Durand recognized this as an advantage of some significance in his enemy's favour. 'It must be remembered', he wrote surveying the military situation from his camp at Mhow, 'that this Shazada has selected his point Mundisore judiciously enough, for that neighbourhood abounds with turbulent Mewatees.'

It was the Gujars who were the main force behind the series of jacqueries that convulsed the north-western districts of Uttar Pradesh. In Saharanpur the 'hard-core areas' of the rebellion were the western part of Deoband pargana, eastern Rampur, a small sector of Nagal and all of the parganas of Nakur and Gangoh, forming what Stokes calls 'the Gujar heartland'. According to him, 'Here solid clan settlement provided a powerful framework of organisation for revolt. Of particular importance was the cluster of 52 villages in Gangoh and Laknauti held by the Batar subdivision (*gotra*) of Gujars.' In Meerut, too, they set the country afire. 'The Goojurs throughout this district are in open rebellion', reported the Magistrate on 28 June 1857. Some five thousand of them of by Shah Mal of Bijroul sacked the township of Baraut, looted a bazaar at Baghpat, and tried to wreck a strategic bridge on the Hindan river in order to cut off military access to that region. They elected Kadam Singh of Parichhatgarh as their raja 'in furtherance of the plan of establishing a Goojur Government'. And their raids on the prosperous and loyalist Jat villages who 'almost invariably behaved nobly in the support of law and order', helped to emphasize by contrast the specifically Gujar character of the uprising. In Bulandshahr again the principal area of the insurrection coincided with that of the compact Gujar settlements in Dadri and Sikandarabad parganas, described officially as 'the most turbulent part of the district inhabited principally by Goojurs'. The latter rose in arms as soon as they heard of the events in Delhi and Meerut and 'at once commenced plundering in all directions, burning Dak Bungalows and destroying the Telegraph'. The attack on the district headquarters of Bulandshahr and the pillage of the township of Sikandarabad were mainly the work of peasants of this particular caste from the surrounding villages a classic case of country encircling the cities.

Most though by no means all of the villages from which the masses of armed peasantry issued from time to time to harry the nearest towns were single-caste settlements. In each of these nearly all the population, barring females acquired by marriage, claimed descent from a common patrilineage, consanguinal or mythical, and regarded themselves as members of the same clan or gotra. This belief in a shared ancestry made the village assert itself positively by acting as a solidarity unit and negatively by operating an elaborate code of discrimination against aliens. Habib cites a late seventeenth-century case to show that it was rare and indeed risky, judging by the given instance-for a Rajput to take up residence in a Jat village. His remarks on the caste composition of the typical north Indian village during Aurangzeb's rule applied to conditions in the eighteenfifties as well:

> *Although any number of castes existed among the peasants in general, peasants of a village probably belonged most often to the same caste. This is true of many villages today. In Central Doab, for example, villages are often distinguished according as they contain Thakurs, Jats, Ahirs, Gujars or other castes of peasants. One can conjecture that this was still more the case when the ties of castes were much stronger. The peasants of a village were most often members not only of the same caste, but also of the same division or subdivision of that caste. They claimed the same ancestry and so belonged to the same bhaiyachara, brotherhood or fraternity. This fraternity by invoking ties of blood, bound the peasants in a unity far stronger than could have been expected among mere neighbours.*

These village-based primordial ties were the principal means of rebel mobilization, mauza by mauza, throughout northern and central India in 1857. Brought about by the peasants on their own initiative or by their landlord masters, its motivation in terms of caste or clan could vary according to idioms and occasions specific to particular localities. Often it was a case of mutineers returning home to inspire their relatives living in that area to take up arms emulating the sepoys. This is how the soldier son of a Nadwasiya Gujar chief, 'who had mutinied and come from Meruth made resistance' in the Dadri region of Bulandshahr. Mutineers of local origin were the catalysts of the uprising in a part of Hamirpur too. 'The Zemindars of Romeree which forms part of Humeerpore are Thakoors', wrote the district officer in his narrative of the events of 1857, 'and many Sepoys, relatives of theirs, came in relating terrible tales of mutiny and bloodshed, which caused the Zemindars of the two *thokes*, Danda and Manjkhore, to band themselves together for plunder which they commenced early in June.' Further to the east, Ghazipur was the home of 'many Sepoys who had fled back to their hearths with halters round their necks', as a Jaunpur Magistrate put it. Since 'the sepoys themselves were residents of the district, wherever they went they found followers ready to their hand'. Indeed, more often than not, 'these men served as rallying points and leaders to their neighbours and clansmen'. There were about one hundred and fifty of them in Zamania where, it was said at the time, 'they formed nuclei round which large numbers of bad characters and disaffected zemindars rally whenever occasion offers'. Again in the Ballia and Rasra tahsildaris of Ghazipur where four to five hundred mutineers had returned to their villages, the local rebel force was recognized by the government as one 'consisting partly of sepoys of that neighbourhood and of their brotherhoods among the zemindars'. Altogether the uprising in that district was universally credited to the dual initiative of army deserters and their peasant kin, for, as it was put in an official narrative of events in the summer of 1858: 'The mutineers have almost everywhere in this district the sympathy of the population with whom most of them are connected by ties of kindred.'

A local insurrection, whatever its immediate cause, tended invariably to adapt itself to the existing pattern of ethnic solidarity in a given area. Allahabad provided a classic example. Here the Mewati response to the outbreak of the Mutiny was so instantaneous that it looked as if 'the Mewatis were the real contrivers of the rebellion of the sepoys and the Risala'. Known for their strong sense of communal identity, they used the customary authority of a panchayat to effect a massive mobilization of their close-knit exogamous villages fifty-one of these were specified by name in the rural belt around that city. Indeed, they had made the insurrection their own so quickly and so completely that it was not easy to distinguish between its military and civilian moments. It was caste fellowship again which secured the support of the Thakurs of Serowlee Buzurg and Khurd for the rebel zamindars of Romeree mentioned above, while in Badaun district the disturbances in tahsil Gunnaur was the work of 'the Aheer Zemindars of Neore Beora, Bheraothee and other adjacent villages of the same brotherhood'. In Bijnaur, too, the local uprising was considerably extended by ethnicity as 'the Gujars of the other side of the Ganges helped the Gujars of this side in the latter's activities'.

The sack of Sikandarabad was yet another demonstration of caste solidarity as a generalizing agent of the rebellion. The more militant of the Gujar villages prepared for this action by sending out their men to rally the others who were less forthcoming. 'The men of Khugooabas and Jhendoo, zemindar of Nugla Nyusookh, went to the Goojurs' villages, threw down their *pugries*, incited them all to disorder and assembled them in Punchayat at Tilbegumpoor.' The result was a spectacular and systematic act of pillage in which the entire community was involved. Primordial loyalty of this kind provided the insurgents not merely with bases for attack on the towns but also with asylum in nearby peasant homes when pursued by the enemy. A British officer was to recall later on how he and his men repulsed a party of raiders just about to charge into the sadar station of Bulandshahr, but found that 'the main body spread over the country and concealed themselves in the neighbouring villages'. The raiders as well as the villagers who offered them refuge were Gujars.

Caste ambitions which motivated some of these jacqueries also helped to emphasize their regionality and ethnicity. Such ambitions directly related to a sense of loss on the part of a rebel community loss of land, territory or prestige. It felt aggrieved because a substantial part of its lands had passed into the hands of moneylenders and auction purchasers; or because it had been ousted from what it considered its traditional homeland; or because a radical decline in the wealth or authority of its elite group had lowered its standing both in its own esteem and that of others. These were by no means mutually exclusive determinations, but coalesced to form the substance of almost any communal sense of deprivation. What brought them together was politics, for there was no loss, whatever its cause, that was not felt to be a loss of power. Even grievances arising from land alienations exceeded their purely economic character and were politicized. The ambiguity generated by such an overlap and its consequence for historiography may be seen in the difference between an administrator's interpretation of a local uprising and a scholar's. When the Rangars, a Muslim Rajput caste, broke out in revolt in Kunda Kalan, H. D. Robertson, the Assistant Magistrate of Saharanpur, could find no economic justification for it. 'Unlike the improvident Goojurs their villages are generally populous and wealthy', he wrote, 'so that plunder could hardly be their inducement to dissatisfaction.' He ascribed the rebellion to sectarian enthusiasm, to 'their bigoted daring' as he put it. Eric Stokes has found this explanation far too narrowly political. Robertson, 'like most British officials', he says, 'believed the revolt to be political in origin'. He puts his own emphasis primarily on economic motivation: ' in the Gangoh khadir the loss of nearly half the land to the mahajans must have affected sharply the attitude of the Kundra Rangars, however much Robertson might form an impression of their comparative prosperity'. Both interpretations contain a great deal of truth about this event but by trying to exclude each other demonstrate a failure to grasp its ambiguity. What apparently happened was that in an atmosphere charged with uncertainties about the very survival of the Raj an accumulation of economic discontent had caught fire and exploded as a formidable defiance of authority. The administrator on the spot registered his immediate response to its *éclat*; the historian, distanced by time, his reading of what triggered it. Neither came quite close to understanding its duplex character.

In some of the revolts involving these ethnic masses the political motivation could hardly be missed. They took up arms in order to recover what they believed to have been their ancestral domains. It was this which accounted for the power and extent of the Gujar uprising in Saharanpur for instance. Here the clan was so numerous that at one time the district was actually called Gujarat. A leader like Futtuah, therefore, found it possible to set himself up as a raja here with the object of 'regaining the consequence tradition has assigned them in this part of the country, once the principality of their ancestors'. Again, the Palwars, a Rajput sept, connected with Azamgarh by tradition and myth, muscled their way into the Mahul region of that district in June 1857 and 'claimed the villages of this pargana to be theirs'. In yet another eastern district, Mirzapur, the rebellion of both the Palwars and the Monas was said to have been inspired by their desire to make up for the decline in their former power. 'Both clans had, as they conceived, a long standing grievance and lost superiority to recover.' Of the two it was the latter who were particularly active in the Bhadohi pargana of that district. The *émeute* they caused offers a clear example of the territorial and political ambitions of a caste as the motor of a local peasant rebellion.

If legend may be said even remotely to approximate history, the Monas must have wanted Bhadohi very badly indeed for themselves. A party of their ancestors who had set out from their rude homeland in Rajputana on a pilgrimage to Banaras, were so greatly impressed by this fertile region of what is now Mirzapur district and coveted it so fiercely that they won their way into it after a long and bloody contest with its former settlers, the Bhars. The precise date of this conquest is difficult to ascertain but it is known that the pargana was ruled by a succession of Monas chiefs for over two centuries until 1746-7 when it passed into the hands of the rajas of Banaras. However, 'although the Raj had passed from the Monus clan yet the old reigning family was by no means extinct and was much looked up to in the pergunnah'. Indeed its standing was still high enough to enable it to involve the local population in its own dynastic strife when on the outbreak of the Mutiny the head of the clan, Udwant Singh, assumed his ancestral title of Raja of Bhadohi, and 'on the strength of this newly regained nobility' raised a private army of nearly two thousand of his caste fellows, took 'benevolences', organized pillage and felt bold enough to close the Grand Trunk Road.

The Monas had a reputation for turbulence going back at least to the seventeenth century. Peter Mundy travelling from Agra to Patna in the late summer of 1632 was much harassed by the 'Buddoyns' who in their utter defiance of authority were almost a law unto themselves: 'They neither regard the kinge nor his lawes verie much.' The same could be said of them with equal truth two hundred and twenty-five years later when in June 1857 they took up arms not only against the Raja of Banaras but also against the district administration regarded by them 'as more or less a partisan of the Rajah'. The insurrection of the sepoys and the civilian population in Allahabad, Jaunpur and Banaras which enclosed Mirzapur on three sides had already alerted the British authorities about the possibility of an outbreak in the most lawless pargana of the latter district. Already on 3 June 1857 the police officers of Bhadohi had been 'ordered to intimate to the zemindars and other respectable men that they might keep armed men if they chose for the defence of their lives and their properties and to be able to assist each other in case of a general rising among the people'. On 7 June the thanadar of Bhadohi reported a dacoity in a village within his jurisdiction. Three days later a party of rebels crossed over from Jaunpur 'to plunder some wealthy zemindars of the Bhudohey pergunnah' but retreated before the combined forces of the police and the local gentry. The same day the *sazawal* of the Raja of Banaras was attacked and severely wounded by the villagers of Bhinda. The district authorities, to leave no doubt on which side they stood, allowed Munshi Darshan Lal, the Banaras Raja's estate manager, to raise a force of two thousand men in order to meet the Monas threat. 'Anarchy became universal. Oodwunt Singh and his people plundered and burnt the villages of those to whom they owed grudges, and the homes of Oodwunt Singh and his friends were in turn burnt and plundered by the adherents of the Rajah.' The crunch came when Munshi Darshan Lal lured the Monas chief and two of his 'dewans' to come unarmed to a rendezvous where they were seized and made over to W. R. Moore, Joint Magistrate and Deputy Collector of Mirzapur, who promptly sent them to the gallows. This exemplary punishment produced a backlash for which the authorities were by no means prepared. Far from taming the Monas, it converted what was essentially a dynastic feud among the elite into a popular rebellion against the colonial power itself a classic instance of a vertical mobilization turned horizontal. For out of the ensuing turmoil there emerged a local leader of the insurgents, a Monas of no aristocratic pedigree 'his ancestors were only dependents of the old Monus Rajahs' a man called Jhuri Singh who not only avenged Udwant Singh by killing Moore and presenting his head to the widow of the Monas chief, but involved the,

> *The territoriality of a rebellion is not of course a matter of coincidence between its domain and a caste region in every case. A locality larger than a village, such as a pargana or a district, could also be the site of an uprising in which peasants of two or more castes joined forces. In Badaun district, for instance, Muslims and Thakurs worked together in the jacqueries that broke out in Bisauli pargana, and these two groups plus Ahirs in pargana Sahaswan. In Bijnor district 'the Mardhas and the butchers of Akbarabad after forming a big gang first looted the Patwaris of Akbarabad, then plundered the Jats of Sikandarpur, and then invaded Hajipur [and] looted Rampur'. The attack on Chandpur tahsil on 26 May 1857 was a joint operation by Mewatis and Pachandey Jats. The district of Bijnor as a whole was, according to its Magistrate, the scene of a collective violence of Banjaras, Gujars, Mewatis and Balochis all of whom had simultaneously taken to arms. In Saharanpur, too, 'the Rajpoots in most parts of the District and the Goojurs throughout the whole District took advantage of the times to plunder and to commit all kinds of atrocities'. Spankie reported 'a large assemblage of Goojurs and Rangurs' to the south and south-west of Saharanpur pargana on 21 May 1857 and the subsequent pillage of Mullypore village close to the sadar station and treasury. Even in Bulandshahr district where the Gujars constituted the main force of the insurrection, they had the Giroоas and the Gahlots as auxiliaries. All three groups were party to the sack of Sikandarabad and were represented at the panchayat at*

Tilbegampur which preceded and planned their combined onslaught. As one of the local raises *put it, 'there was no village of the Goojurs and Girooas in the neighbourhood which did not take part in this affair'. Indeed, Walidad Khan himself seems to have had such a plurality in mind when he wrote to Delhi about 'Gujars and other country-folk of this neighbourhood' having 'raised their heads'.*

For an example of a local rebellion which had its territoriality articulated as an intercaste mobilization involving many villages in several contiguous parganas cutting across three districts one could turn to the uprising headed by Meghar Singh in Ghazipur. In this the easternmost part of Uttar Pradesh bordering on Bihar the impact of the Mutiny did not register until about the middle of 1858. It took the incursion of Kunwar Singh's and Amar Singh's forces into this region to shatter its apparent calm. A police report of 30 May 1858 from the officer in charge of the thana at Dildarnagar in Zamania pargana is the first record we have of disturbances in eastern Ghazipur. It spoke of a raid on Rajpur in the Chausa pargana of Shahabad by a force of two platoons of Amar Singh's men '250 or 300 armed persons who appeared to be absconders' led by Meghar Singh, a Rajput zamindar of Gahmar in Zamania. The raiders killed a *barkandaz* and a *patwari* and were joined by a large number of sepoys who had returned home to their native villages in that pargana. They were said to have 'resolved to stay at Gahmar and Barah and to persuade the whole pargana to rebel against the Government'. For the next two days they camped in a grove at Dewal on the bank of the Karmanasa where the insurrection was publicly launched at an assembly of several thousand people from the neighbouring districts. Between 3 and 5 June they plundered and destroyed some factories and other buildings owned by an indigo planter at Gahmar and Bhadaura. The presence of Meghar Singh and four hundred 'rebel sipahis', that is, local peasants who had been in the army, was reported from the first of these two villages on 6 June. It was said that 'he went about from one village to the other to incite people to rebel', and apparently met with considerable success. For an informer's note dated 9 June mentioned 'supplies and other assistance' sent him by the villagers of Naoli, Bara, Gahmar, Karepa and Bhorai.

On 11 June Brigadier Douglas arrived at Gahmar and burnt it down. But such exemplary punishment inflicted on what was regarded as the most wicked of all insurgent villages in the area had apparently little immediate effect, for according to an official telegram of 14 June the Magistrate of Ghazipur still found his district entirely disorganized. In fact the burning of Gahmar appears to have helped in spreading the revolt rather than containing it. The local police and revenue officials whose authority was the subject of universal defiance were sensitive to it. 'Although the residents of Gahmar have left the place', wrote a tahsildar on 18 June, 'their zamindars are staying in the neighbouring villages at the distances of three, four or five *kos* and harbour evil intentions.' For already two days before that Meghar Singh had been seen at the head of a force of one hundred at Diwathia, a village in Zamania pargana. 'They had got together the rebels residing in the different villages' and stopped over at Kashni. On 19 June they attacked Niwalwan in Chainpur pargana of Shahabad district and threatened a planter's warehouse there. Throughout the rest of that summer the guerilla army went on adding to its size. Contingents of armed peasantry, many of them forced out of their villages by the increasingly vigorous counter-insurgency operations, and bands of army deserters with local ties poured into its ranks from all over the region. In August, for instance, one hundred sepoys crossed over from the other side of the Ganges to join Meghar Singh at Gahmar. Subsequently he was to recall how at one time he had as many as twelve thousand men at his command a genuinely popular army which, he emphasized, 'made no raids for plunder'. It was 'the people of the six parganas' ranged along the Ganges and the Karmanasa in the Ghazipur-Shahabad border area who, he claimed, 'met our expenses'.

In the event, Meghar Singh met the fate of all roving rebels. By December 1858 his army disintegrated under the impact of sustained military operations by the British. He retreated into Nepal with only about five hundred of his followers but was forced by the local raja to withdraw from there and re-enter Indian territory in the spring of 1860. He moved around for eight months as a pilgrim between various holy places a motif which recurs in the careers of many of our defeated rebels-and surrendered himself to the authorities at Banaras on 7 November 1860. The statement that he made three weeks later before the court of the Special Commissioner there offers some of the most detailed information we have of a local rebel mobilization in nineteenth-century India.

It is clear from Meghar Singh's recollection of the beginnings of the revolt in eastern Ghazipur that the mobilization there followed the classic pattern of parley and assembly common to peasant insurgency everywhere. The crucial meeting which decided on the insurrection was a conference of thirty-eight persons representing four castes from eighteen villages in three parganas one of Ghazipur and two of Shahabad linked by a river. Evidently, it was dominated by those who spoke for Zamania pargana which contributed as many as thirty, that is, nearly four-fifths of the total number of delegates. This was quite appropriate too. For it was the fear of a pre-emptive strike by the colonial army against some of its villages which had triggered off that uprising in the first place. Besides, the two sites to figure most prominently in its preparation, namely, Biranji on the Karmanasa where it was planned and Dewal where it was inaugurated at a public gathering, were both located there. Above all it was Gahmar within that pargana which was clearly the epicentre of the revolt. The inhabitants of this village were largely responsible for its organization. They formed the party of scouts who were sent to Ghazipur to verify rumours concerning the imminence of British attacks and whose report hastened the decision in favour of the uprising. They also led the group of ten emissaries chosen by the insurgents to negotiate with Amar Singh for aid in arms and men. And it was this village which provided the rebellion with its leader Meghar Singh himself. The fact that fifteen out of thirty-eight delegates at the Biranji conference came from Gahmar and that the destruction of the latter was intended by the army to serve as an object lesson for all the unruly masses of Ghazipur-Shahabad region is a measure of the importance attached to it both by the rebels and their enemies.

Insurgent mobilization in Zamania was a function of geographical as well as ethnic arrangements in that area that is, of both those sets of factors which combine to make up territoriality as we have defined it. The pargana derived much of its character from its separation on three sides from the rest of Ghazipur district by a broad bend of the Ganges and from being cut off from Shahabad by the Karmanasa on the remaining, eastern side. Within this arc the rivers with their deep beds and high banks, their floods and shallow backwaters and the alluvium deposited by them influenced not only the livelihood of the people as agriculturists but also their patterns

Table 2. Distribution of Rebel Delegates at Biranji Conference by Locality and Caste.

District	Pargana	Village	CASTE				Total
			Pathan	Brahman	Rajput	Bhumihar	
Ghazipur	Zamania	Bara	3	0	0	0	3
"	"	Baranpur	0	0	0	1	1
"	"	Basuka	0	0	0	1	1
"	"	Deoria	0	0	0	1	1
"	"	Gahmar	0	0	15	0	15
"	"	Hasanpara	0	0	0	1	1
"	"	Kahrna	0	0	1	0	1
"	"	Nauli	0	0	1	0	1
"	"	Reotipur	0	0	0	1	1
"	"	Sherpur	0	0	0	2	2
"	"	Sohwal	0	0	0	1	1
"	"	Utrawal	0	0	2	0	2
Shahabad	Chausa	Indore	0	0	1	0	1
"	"	Manikpur	0	1	0	0	1
"	"	Sopna	0	0	0	1	1
"	"	Sukran	0	0	0	1	1
"	Chainpur	Gura Sarai	0	0	3	0	3
"	"	Newhar	0	0	1	0	1
Totals			3	1	24	10	38

of residence and communal life. The alluvial tract of the pargana boasted some of the largest villages in the district in 1853 Reotipur had a population of 10,055, Gahmar 9,629, Sherpur 6,885 and so on with their locations 'determined solely by the configuration of the ground', according to the *District Gazetteer*, 'the houses being built on the most elevated spot so as to be beyond the reach of the floods'. A village under these conditions tended to develop as the focal point for a number of hamlets each of which was occupied by a distinctive caste while the site as a whole presided over dependent villages existing only in name but indistinguishable in fact from the surrounding fields excluded from residential use and given over entirely to agriculture.

Vicinage conditioned thus by river boundaries and village sites was emphasized further by the pattern of ethnicity in the pargana. It had been colonized like the greater part of the district by Rajputs and Bhumihars. The distinction between these two castes was often unclear. Some of their subdivisions bore identical names: Gautam, Kausik, Kinwar or Sikarwar could designate either a Rajput or a Bhumihar. Members of the two castes bearing the same clan name often referred to the same city or country as their original habitat, and at least in one case they claimed a common ancestry. It was therefore quite in order that all but one of the twelve villages represented at the Biranji conference should have sent men of one or the other caste to speak for them. The exception, Bara, described by the commander of a British gunboat as 'full of Badmashes' and shelled by him preceding an assault on its 'armed Mussulmans', delegated some Pathans. However, the plurality suggested by this fact is deceptive. For the Pathans of Zamania were mostly 'not Pathans at all, but the descendants of converted Rajputs and Bhumihars', as the *District Gazetteer* observes. To be more specific about it, the Musalmans of Bara were a branch of the Rajdhar Rai sept of Kinwar Bhumihars who had taken to Islam.

Thus the local mobilization inaugurated at Biranji was determined by two different kinds of proximity geographical and ethnic. The former was reinforced further by communication in the form of a network of unmetalled roads which crisscrossed the pargana and the latter by the networks of caste and sept. A look at some of the villages for which we have information on both counts may indicate how the location of particular communities and their linkages were arranged along these coordinates. Bara which constituted the eastern terminal point of the arc of the Ganges around the pargana was directly joined by road to Gahmar. Its village lands lay along the Karmanasa connecting the local community with the peasantry on the Shahabad side of the river. Within the district it had its historical ties with Birpur, a village on the other bank of the Ganges, an ancient seat of Kinwar Bhumihars who had turned to Islam and dominated the two eastern parganas of Dehma and Muhammadabad. As such its delegation of three Musalmans represented an element of mobilization with a pullreaching beyond its strictly local limits. Basuka adjoined Nauli on the east. Its owners were Bhumihar Sikarwars descended from Puran Mal whose progeny by several wives spread over a number of villages including Gahmar, Reotipur and Sherpur. Nauli itself was the headquarters of the Suklabansi Rajputs who had colonized a large tract of the country in this particular neighbourhood. They related in caste terms with Utrawal, a little to the north, which was the only other village on our list with a large Suklabansi settlement. Both, it should be noted, were represented by Rajputs. Both the villages lay on the road between Bhadaura and Reotipur. The latter was in 1853 one of the most populous of all the rural sites in Zamania pargana. Caste and propriety interests tied it historically to Sherpur on the opposite bank. Together these two villages formed a great taluqa held for many generations by the Sikarwar Bhumihars whose estate extended here over thirty-five villages along a seven-mile front on both sides of the river. The first Sikarwar to acquire these lands had by his three marriages and their issue planted the clan in several parts of the pargana. Its connections with Basuka have already been mentioned above. Yet other bonds with Gahmar and Usia added considerably to its ethnic range. At the former of these the Bhumihar Sikarwars shared some kind of a primordial affinity with the Rajput sept of the same name. The latter, Usia, was one of the six villages a threat to which was the immediate cause of the uprising. Here they related to Bhumihars who together with those of seven other settlements in the neighbourhood had abandoned the Hindu faith for Islam. An important link was forged in this way between the Sikarwars and the rest of the large mass of Muslim converts of Zamania. Thus the ethnic space of the twin villages of Reotipur and Sherpur, both represented appropriately enough by Bhumihars at the rebel conference, reached well beyond their geographical area into much of eastern and southern Zamania.

By caste as well as by the road that ran east towards the river from Ghazipur through Sohwal a largely Bhumihar settlement represented by a member of that caste at Biranji-Reotipur was directly linked with Gahmar. And both its caste composition and its physical location appear to have made the latter ideally suited to generate the kind of initiative that it did in the insurrection led by Meghar Singh. Colonized by Rajputs of the Sikarwar clan who still owned most of the taluqa there it had its ties not merely with settlements of the same caste elsewhere in that pargana but also with the Bhumihar Sikarwars of Reotipur-Sherpur and the Rajputs turned Muslim such as those of Bara and many other Zamania villages. Its ethnic range was thus nearly as wide as that of Reotipur. What however made Gahmar a place of relatively greater importance were two arterial roads the first of which situated it at a point equidistant between Ghazipur and Zamania, while the second, an older highway that bifurcated at the village, connected it with Banaras in one direction and Buxar at the other.

Communications such as these and the rivers whose junction a few miles further to the east below Birpur conferred on Gahmar a measure of strategic advantage, served as the practical instruments of rebel mobilization. They helped Meghar Singh, a Sikarwar Rajput zamindar and *lambardar*, to weld the primordial loyalties within the pargana into a fighting solidarity of all its principal ethnic communities, and what is equally important, to forge alliances beyond it. The roads carried his appeal westward to the raises of Mhanj and Narwan. The latter, in Banaras, was linked by tradition to Zamania pargana in so far as the Donwar Bhumihars of both places claimed common descent from ancestors who had once colonized the eastern part of Azamgarh district. The Karmanasa conveyed his message southwards to the principal men of Sassaram, and its ferries along the eastern border of Zamania helped him to negotiate for and secure the support of the two key parganas of Shahabad on the other bank, namely, Chausa and Chainpur, both of which were represented at Biranji, significantly enough, by seven Rajputs and Bhumihars out of a total of eight delegates from six villages. It was that river again which witnessed at Dewal, an ancient Bhumihar village and ferry ghat, the decisive meeting of the people of Zamania with ten to twelve thousand men who had assembled there from other parts of Ghazipur, Banaras and Shahabad districts to hail the proclamation of insurgency.

This description of events in eastern Ghazipur in 1858 provides us with yet another instance of territoriality as an intersection of ethnic space and physical space. It also shows that the domain of peasant insurgency need not be limited to single administrative units: it could indeed be as large as a pargana or even a number of parganas comprising many villages in a contiguous area extended over two or three neighbouring districts. And that takes us back to the question with which we began: how far does territoriality help or hinder the spread of a rebellion?

The answer provided by the evidence presented above is positive. Territoriality, in the conditions of nineteenth-century India, helped. The reason clearly lay in a *décalage*, that is, in the fact that the two kinds of space mentioned above did not quite coincide even when they converged. There were territorial units which were home to more than one ethnic group and there were ethnic regions which extended over more than one territorial unit. A peasant uprising tended, in either case, to fill in the gap by its own content and simulate a coincidence between community and habitat. An overlap of these two elements supplemented by the appropriation of one or the other by the act of rebellion was what constituted the latter's domain. This is how the domain of the hool came to include such non-Santal elements as lower-class Hindus and the Paharia Mal in the predominantly Santal territory of Damin-i-Koh, and that of the Hindu and Muslim peasants' revolt in the indigo districts of Bengal the adivasi labourers employed by the factories. [97] Conversely, the domain of the Kol insurrection of 1832 exceeded the limits of its geographical site in Chota Nagpur and drew in the Larka Kols who crossed over from Singhbhum to fight for their tribal brethren, while, to mention some non-tribal instances, the domain of Kunwar Singh's rebellion extended its ethnic range beyond Bihar to include his fellow Rajputs in the Ghazipur district of Uttar Pradesh and that of the Gujar uprising at Bijnor the members of that caste resident on the other side of the Ganges.

The role of territoriality in thus enlarging and defining the domain of insurgency is, of course, not a development unique to the colonial period of Indian history. Habib has identified this as a factor in the Jat revolt and 'the "lawless" activities' of Mewatis,

Wattus and Dogars in the late Mughal empire. Caste, he says, 'brought [the peasant] into contact with his peers in the most distant villages, through a thousand ties of blood and rites. If they took to arms, he could not stand aloof.' What, however, adds to the significance of territoriality in the peasant rebellions during the period under discussion is that it provided the anti-colonialist mass struggles of our people with some kind of an armature, however imperfect it must have been, at a time when organized nationalism (barring some small militant groups) was elitist and collaborationist, and the class organizations of the working people were either non-existent or ineffecttive.

Quite clearly the domain of rebellion still fell far short of the domain of the nation, and the two arms of territoriality, that is, co-residential solidarity and primordial loyalty, acted to no small extent in putting the brakes on resistance against the Raj. Narrow localism raised its head and impeded the progress of the insurgents at critical moments. Villagers would not allow a party of mutineers from other parts to cross the Ghaghra at Azamgarh. Caste would fight against caste Gujars against Rohs and Jats, for instance. The same caste would be at war with the British in one region and on their sidein another, as witness the contradictory careers of Gujar leaders like Futtuah and Sahib Singh. Even when solidaritybetween ethnic groups triumphed over separateness for a time, it weakened soon under pressure from their common enemy: the Mals and the Kumars ceased to co-operate with the Santals as counter-insurgency operations intensified. And the use made by the government of some sections of the non-tribal peasantry in order to supress the hool demonstrated how ethnicity was no substitute for class consciousness in uniting the peolpe against colonialism. In the event all resistance splintered into 'the hundred local revolutions as well as the hundred local reactions following them'. Yet all such limitations notwithstanding, where else except in this fragmented insurgent consciousness is one to situate the beginnings of those militant mass movements which surged across the subcontinent in 1919, and 1946? Territoriality was not indeed the stuff with which to build a revolutionary party, as Mao Tse-tung sadly observed at his base in the Chingkang mountains. But not to recognize in it the elements of what made the broader and more generalized struggles of the Indian people possible in the twentieth century would be to foreshorten history.

10

Modalities of Insurgency

Introduction

The wave of 'preliminary outrages' as it is called in official language. But insurgency soon extricates itself from the placenta of common crime in which it may be initially enmeshed and establishes its own identity as a violence which is *public, collective, destructive* and *total* in its modalities. Each of these constitutes a distinctive feature in the sense that it has its antithesis in crime, so that the opposition between the two types of violence may be represented as a series of binary contrasts thus public/secretive, collective/individualisti, destructive/appropriative and total/partial.

To turn to the first of these modalities, rebellion is by its very nature an open and public event. As such, it stands in clear opposition to crime which must rely on secrecy to be effective. It would perhaps not be untrue to say that a tendency towards an open and public affirmation is already evident in certain intermediate types of rural violence, such as the more advanced forms of social banditry, which fall just short of rebellion. The Robin Hoods of many countries have been known to express this tendency in terms of a nonchalance tinged often with a sort of black humour. This is illustrated by a hilarious and authentic anecdote in Jim Corbett's account of Sultana. A contractor who employed a large labour force to fell trees for logging in the jungles of the Terai was induced by the police to invite the dacoit chief and his band to an evening of festivities to begin with a nautch and end with a banquet. Sultana, whose 'intelligence staff numbered hundreds', knew that the invitation was a trap devised by the commander of the Special Dacoity Police Force, but accepted it. On arrival at the contractor's camp in the middle of the forest where the best nautch girls and musicians had been hired for the evening and much food and drink stocked up for the feast to follow, Sultana prevailed upon his host to reverse the scheduled order of merriment and start off with feasting, for, he said, 'his men would enjoy the dance more on full stomachs than on empty ones'. After they had eaten and drunk well, he gathered his band, thanked his host for his hospitality and left regretting that they could not stay for the rest of the entertainment as they had such a long way to go. By the time the drums struck up the signal simultaneously for the nautch to begin and the police party to close in on their quarry, Sultana and his men had slipped away in the darkness.

Not every public act of social banditry is however informed with such witticism. It can take a sombre, declamatory form, too, as it did with 'King John', the legendary chief of the Hampshire Blacks. Alarmed at being mistaken for a Jacobite, he made up his mind to define his position clearly and openly. He 'knew well what he was doing', observes Thompson, 'and took care to make it public'. He made it known that he intended publicly to answer the charge of Jacobitism at a specified date and place. On that day he rode up with a small armed escort to the appointed place, declared his allegiance to the Hanoverian succession before an audience of about three hundred people who had already gathered there, and made it clear at the same time 'that they [the Blacks] had no other design than to do justice, and to see that the rich did not insult or oppress the poor; that they were determined not to leave a deer on the Chase, being well assured it was originally designed to feed cattle, and not to fatten deer for the clergy, &c'.

An open affirmation of intent is of course even more characteristic of rebels than of social bandits. Unlike criminals they make no attempt to conceal violence by any pretence to conform to law and order. No criminal can possibly be so matterof-fact and explicit about the purpose of his visit to the site of his intended crime as were the Russian insurgents of 1905 during a raid on an estate as recalled by its landlord. 'Why have you come?' I asked them. 'To demand corn, to make you give us your corn', said several voices simultaneously. 'That is to say, you have come to plunder?' If you like, to plunder', said a young lad in the crowd.

These are not the voices of thieves operating under the cover of darkness. The Kols of Chota Nagpur too are known to have made a strident avowal when they finally gave up any hope of obtaining justice either form the colonial authorities or from the local chiefs and pledged themselves to annihilate all tax colllectors (*thikadars*), wreck all villages and townships including Govindpur itself and 'wash their weapons in the river (the Karroo) which flows past it'. The Santals involved in the hool made no secret either of their intention to slay the rajas of Pakur and Maheshpur as well as all other landlords, mahajans, policemen and white planters, railway engineers and officials they could lay their hands on. Every village they attacked was given an explicit warning well in advance, as the knowledgeable Captain Sherwill found out in the Colgong area. 'The burning of these villages', he wrote with reference to a number of these destroyed by the rebels on 19 and 21 July 2855, 'had been notified four days previously by the sonthals to the zemindars the very hour of the day being mentioned.' He also named seven other villages south of that station which 'had been in a similar manner warned for pillage and burning on or about 26th or 27th July', but were all except one saved by the timely arrival of the troops. The plan they had 'to advance by easy marches' towards Bhagalpur and Monghyr and sack these towns one after the other 'was also sent into Colgong by the sonthals for the information of the zemindars and Europeans'. Later on, in September that year, they were to send a bough with three leaves on it to Suri, the headquarters of the Collector of Birbhum, to indicate that they wished to raid that town in three days' time.

What testified even more to the open and public character of the hool was the *parwana* issued by Sido and Kanhu announcing their decision to take up arms. Described as 'The Thacoor's Perwannah', a sort of heavenly ultimatum communicated through the two inspired leaders of the uprising, it read in part:

> *The Sahibs and the white Soldiers will fight. Kanoo and Seedoo Manjee are not fighting. The Thacoor himself will fight. Therefore you Sahibs and Soldiers fight with the Thacoor himself. Mother Ganges will come*

to the Thacoor's (assistance). Fire will rain from Heaven. I will rain fire and all the Sahibs will be killed by the hand of God in person and Sahibs if you fight with muskets the Sonthal will not be hit by the bullets and the Thacoor will give your Elephants and horses of his own accord to the Sonthals and on seeing this perwannah you will understand all and you will send an answer, and if you fight with the Sonthals two days will be as one day and two nights as one night. This is the order of the Thacoor.

The leaders of the insurrection clearly felt authorized by God himself in declaring war on the Raj. As their adversaries were quick to recognize, it was from this spiritual justification that the hool derived much of its drive and fury. 'It is a war ordered by the gods, they say', observed the Magistrate of Bhagalpur. Some of the implications of such a belief will be discussed later in this work. Here it will suffice to say that in claiming to act on 'the order of the Thacoor' the Santals were merely affirming the public character of their rebellion.

Other rebels and social bandits too have been known to claim the support of higher authorities for themselves. The Bourbon brigands about whom Maffei wrote did not go so far as to invoke the authority of God, but came fairly close to it by invoking the authority of the Pope when they said, 'We were fighting for the faith and we were blessed by the Pope.' They also believed that they were acting for Francis II, thus staking a claim at a secular counter too for legitimization. In this they conformed to an even wider pattern of rebel activity. For it is very common indeed for a peasant revolt to articulate itself in the name of a secular public authority which in most cases happens to be that of the sovereign. The peasants of the Chernigor Guberniya in 1905 believed that pillage had been authorized by the Tsar. The Swing rebels acted on the conviction that they enjoyed the support of the King and Parliament. The jacqueries against the planters in the indigo districts of Bengal drew some of their considerable striking power from the belief then widespread among the rural masses that the Queen of England herself was on their side. The peasantry involved in the rent agitation in Pabna stretched the meaning of what was a relatively favourable official gesture in the form of the proclamation of 4 July 1873 to imply that 'the government was sympathetic to the resistance movement'. A belief in the alleged intervention of a superior and more just authority against the peasant's immediate oppressors was what fuelled the fury of the Deccan riots too in 1875. Both the versions of this belief as reported to the Commission investigating these disturbances agreed that the peasants acted on the certainty that 'orders had come from England' to force the Marwaris to part with their bonds.

The self-affirmation of a rebellion thus in the name of a public authority carried, appropriately enough, its own sanction in many cases. Armed as it was with a putative approval, blessing, inspiration or support of the highest public authority, insurgent violence assumed, in the eyes of its protagonists, the status of a public service. As such, it had to be paid for. Hence the levy of contributions in food, drink and money by the rebels on *their* public a feature common to many otherwise different national experiences. The French peasants who participated in the jacqueries of 1789' often demanded money because they were after all under the impression', says Lefebvre, 'that they were working for the king and they could not work for nothing or wear their shoes out for no return: you had to eat and, above all, you had to drink you couldn't live on air'.ft In much the same way the labourers of rural England involved in the Swing movement, especially those of Berkshire and Hampshire 'demanded a fixed monetary contribution, not so much to buy food and drink as a direct payment for services rendered'.

The dhing-kharcha (literally, the money to be raised to pay for the cost of the insurrection) imposed on the peasantry by the leaders of the uprising against Deby Sinha appears to have been a levy of the same order. However, the public character of this particular insurrection is even more clearly elucidated by an episode which glows with so much meaning and yet has failed to catch the historian's eye that it may be worth retrieving it from the musty narrative of *The Report of the Rungpore Commission on the Causes of the Insurrection in Rungpore in the Year 1189*. The peasants had elected Derjenarain as their chief 'Nawab' as they called him presented him with their nazar as the formal sign of fealty owing to an overlord, carried him in a palanquin to Balaganj where on the advice of Bara (Baru) Baxey, a local leader, they began to get ready for a march to Demlah. The kachari of Gaurmohan Chaudhuri, a big landlord 'who had three lakhs of rupees malguzari under him' and with whom the peasants had numerous scores to settle, was located here.

The insurgents determined to go to Demlah the next day when Bara Baxey told Derjenarain 'that there were horsemen and Barkandases stationed at Demlah who would attack them and therefore it was to little purpose to go there; however he proposed that the insurgents should go to Demlah, and if they obtained redress, it was very well, but if Gaurmohan should attack them, they would repel his attack'; telling Derjenarain that 'as he was Nabob, he must forgive them for what excesses (*loot mar*), plunder and murder were committed', that Derjenarain considered some time and replied 'that they did not go to fight, but were going for justice; that if Gaurmohan refused them justice and attacked them, they must do the best they could, and that he forgave all excesses (*loot mar*), plunder and murder'. On this the people all shouted and proceeded towards Demlah.

What we have in this episode is a rare record of the investiture of a rebellion with public authority. It tells us of the election of the rebel 'nawab' as an alternative source of authority and its formalization by the general body of the insurgents through the ritual presentation of *nazarana*. Even more important is the information it has to offer about the specific manner in which authorization issues from the putative nawab to 'forgive them [the insurgents turned subjects] for what excesses (*loot mar*), plunder and murder were committed'. The prayer for exoneration from guilt, the solemnity with which it was received and considered, and the advice so weightily pronounced granting the prayer to nobody's surprise but everybody's joy correspond to the classic three-step teleology of a Hindu *vrata* in which the uttered wish and its necessary fulfilment by divine grace must be mediated by a ritual worship of the granting deity. The ceremony described above is that of validation the validation, one could almost say sacralization, of rebel violence as a public service duly authorized by the head of a community and undertaken by its members for their own benefit.

The mass, communal aspect of rebel violence follows thus from its open and public character and differentiates it from the typically individualistic or small-group operation of crime. A rebellion (to borrow Lefebvre's term for the peasant revolts in France in 1789) is indeed a 'collective enterprises'. It uses communal processes and forms of mass mobilization, expresses mass violence in the idiom of communal labour and encourages communal appropriation of the fruits of pillage in many cases. The communal process of mobilization is best witnessed in the parleys and assemblies which inaugurate most agrarian uprisings everywhere. This is how the Peasant War in Germany began in 1525:

> *Then six or seven peasants met in a village near Ulm, called Baltringen, and they discussed many things while walking from one village to another, while meeting neighbours and while eating and drinking together as was peasant custom at that time. Those peasants [with whom they had eaten, etc.] went with them [to another village]. If anybody asked them what they wanted and what they were doing, they answered, 'We are collecting the Fastnacht cake'. In this way they travelled all Thursdays and their number increased day by day until they were 400 men. On the 8th day before the real Fastnacht they gathered together at Baltringen. When they saw how many they had become, they told each other: 'There are many of us'.*

We see a very similar process of consultations and gatherings building up into an insurgent mobilization by the rural masses in Rangpur on the eve of the dhing of 1783. To quote from the official narrative of events:

> *It appears that the ryots first met at Beedaltur in the perganah of Bamandangah and at Cornarmonah in Tepah. In consequence of a plan concerted then among themselves they assembled and from thence they proceeded to Kyneerry in Tepah where. Dirjinarain offered to head them. After this the insurgents sent 25 or 30 men to Dakallygange who released such people as were confined there for revenue. The Ryots of the neighbouring talooks assembled and came to them in great numbers. Dirjenarain mounted a palanquin and they proceeded to Balagange where by the advice of Baru Baxey it was proposed to go to Demlah. The insurgents then circulated letters to the various talooks ordering the ryots to assemble and join them.*

Confer, plan, assemble, attack the sequence occurs in many an Indian uprising. The initial meeting, often in the form of an extended panchayat of the leaders of the insurgent community, had an important role to play in formulating grievances, defining the course of action and generally preparing the mass of its members for the hostilities soon to ensue. Such a meeting was reported on the eve of Titu Mir's bidroha in which the Muslim weavers (jolas) played an active and militant role. The police at Basirhat received a report from a talukdar of Sarfrazpur (a village which was soon to earn much notoriety in the disturbances that followed) 'to this purport that 20 or 30 Persons had assembled in the House of one Bolaee julah and that he had sent 3 Persons to ascertain the cause of their

Congregation; his men, however, were maltreated and one Peadah severely beaten'. A number of such parleys are known to have preceded the Birsaite ulgulan. Some of these were reported by Rev. Hoffmann who appears to have been the voice of the true faith as well as the eyes and ears of the Raj in Munda country. 'I have been informed by a new adept of the village Simbua,' he wrote, 'that the attack was planned in the three panchayats on three Sundays before the event. In the two first of these panchayats, only Puranaks were present. There the date was fixed, and bands of three or sometimes four men were designated each to separate places to fire houses and send arrows among the Christian gatherings usually held on Christmas eve. In the last panchayat the nanaks or new adepts were informed of the attack.'

The Kol insurrection of 1831 too had begun with a consultative meeting of this kind. As Bindrai Manki, one of its leaders, was to recall later on: 'We returned home, invited all the Coles (our Brethren and Caste) to assemble at the village of Sankah in Tamar where we had a consultation. Our Lives we considered of no Value, and being of one Caste and Brethren it was agreed upon that we should commence to cut, plunder, murder and eat.' For the Santal rebellion we have the words of both Sido and Kanhu testifying to much preliminary cogitation before the actual outbreak. 'Then the Manjees & Purgunnaits assembled in my Verandah', said Sido after his capture, '& we consulted for 2 months.' The information occurs several times in the course of his statement: 'Ever since Chait two months before the Thacoor came, the Manjees had been consulting together to kill the Mahajans.' And again, 'The Manjee & pergunnaits consulted about this in Jait in my house.' It is as if by affirming this fact of frequent communal consultations that Sido was trying to establish what was to him the unquestionable legitimacy of the violence of the hool. Indeed, he came close to saying this in almost so many words: 'All the pergunnaits & manjees consulted & advised me to fight.'

Consultation and advice often figured among the very first steps in popular mobilization in UP too during the peasant revolts of 1857-8. The representatives of a community or a village would meet in a panchayat to decide what course of action the local masses should follow when they rose in arms. It was thus that in May 1857 'Panchayuts were held in the villages of Cheetee, Deotah,

Tilbegumpoor, Dadree, etc in order to loot Secundrabad so that the beams and rafters should not be left.' These were mainly a Gujar affair. But at the panchayat held at Tilbegampur they were joined by Girooas and Gahlot Rajputs to make the insurrection into a broad alliance of the vast majority of the peasants in that part of Bulandshahr district. Again, in Allahabad where 'the Mewatis were the real contrivers of the rebellion of the sepoys and the Risala', a panchayat of the leaders of that community was held on 5 June 1857 at Saif Khan's house in mauza Samadabad and 'all, excepting Saif Khan, decided to rebel the same day'. At about the same time when an émeute at Azamgarh acted as a signal for revolt for 'all the loafers and vagabonds of the villages'-official euphemism for the peasantry in Chiriakot, a pargana to the south of that town, 'the rebels counselled all the night on 4th June on the matter of robbing and that from June 5 they declared a general riot and mutiny'. And further to the east, in Ghazipur, as we shall see later, the rebellion of Meghar Singh of Gahmar was to be inaugurated the following year by a gathering of representatives of all sections of the local population at Biranji on the Karmanasa.

Yet another feature of the risings of 1857-8 was the vast assemblies of the local populations which preceded the actual outbreak of violence in most instances. It was as if the peasants, shaken out of their habitual docility and subservience, turned up in their thousands in response to some invisible, unspoken and yet universally understood signal to meet their enemy in an armed struggle. We know little of the actual mechanics of such autonomous mobilization the pull of the primordial ties of kinship, community and co-residence, the power of rumour, the compulsion of custom and religion all of which might have combined in various degrees to make up for the absence of any formal machinery of call-up standing outside and above the rural communities. No real understanding of insurgency in colonial India will ever be achieved without a proper study of this phenomenon. What, however, can be said with certainty at the present state of research is that most of the jacqueries of the period of the Mutiny witnessed large preliminary gatherings of the armed peasantry Gujars of the villages of Deotah and Til assembling at Cheetee for an attack on the jail at Bulandshahr in order to rescue the prisoners, the assembly of Gujars and others becoming more and more frequent as the revolt gathered momentum in Saharanpur district, massed crowds of Gujars and Rangurs converging on the southern and southwestern parts of Saharanpur pargana prior to the plunder of a village close to the district headquarters and the treasury, Gujars 'assembling in thousands under regular leaders' in Meerut district, large assemblies of 'rustics' in pargana Mandawar leading up to raids on the rich Roh villages in Bijnaur district, and so on, to quote examples chosen at random from western UP alone.

In the case of the Santal hool, too, the parleys among tribal chiefs led eventually to 'an assembly of sonthals at Bagnodee, at which there were many manjees, soobahs and Pergunnaits', as Kanhu was to confirm in his statement when captured. It is this assembly at Bhagnadihi which alarmed the mahajans and the police so much that they lost their nerve and triggered off the revolt by underestimating the peasants' militancy. How unnerving such mobilization often was for the authorities is perhaps best illustrated by a comic incident. The Barasat bidroha (which was itself an occasion for vast gatherings of the rural 'poor had just been suppressed when it was rumoured that he 'Moolavies' were assembling again in large numbers-six to seven hundred of them according to one report in the northern part of Jessore district. The Military Department of the government at Calcutta at once ordered 'a Department consisting of one Complete Battalion of the Native Infantry from Barrackpoor and two Six Pounder Horse Artillery Field Pieces manned with the necessary complement of Europeans from the troop of Dum Dum, with the usual supply of Service Ammunition, the whole under the Command of a Field Officer of Judgment and decision to March by the most direct practicable route towards Jessore'. At the same time the *India Gazette* published a letter from a correspondent 'stating that the Moolavies had broken out afresh at Buttai and Poorahattee'. The panic caught on. During a visit to the Kumarkhali station the Joint Magistrate of Pabna 'found all the Gentlemen there in great alarm the President had all his Muskets brought out to clean and his people were busily employed in bullet making'. However it soon became clear that the whole thing was a hoax invented by a local planter to amuse himself and induce a friend from a neighbouring station 'to come over and pay me a visit'!

The intervention of the custodians of law and order on such occasions is a measure of the fear they shared with their protégé, the rural elite, of any large body of peasants coming together to discuss and air their grievances, however peaceably. Even if no overt acts of violence such as plunder, arson or murder were committed, an assembly of discontented peasantry was often regarded, under the Raj, as a potential threat to the administration. The Pabna ryots' movement of 1873 illustrates this very well indeed. It was officially lauded as an agitation conducted with due respect for the law. Yet the colonial authorities who on the question of tenancy rights had their differences with the landlords, distrusted, as did the latter, any move on the part of the peasantry to mobilize for their rights, particularly when this assumed the form of large gatherings. The Indian Penal Code was used to forbid them from visiting villages in parties of more than ten in order to propagate the aims of the perfectly lawful association they had formed to resist extortion and rack-renting by the zamindars. On one occasion the local magistrate went so far as to override the police who had just released six men from custody for want of evidence and charged them with forming an 'illegal assembly'.

Indeed it would appear that any large and autonomous gathering of the peasantry brought about on their own initiative to air their grievances unaided by and often in defiance of the rural or administrative elite ran the risk of being regarded as 'illegal' by the colonial authorities for whom its suppression amounted to a veritable principle of government. This was made explicit in the course of the official discussions on this question following the anti-survey riots in Khandesh in 1852. The attempt made by the government in the winter of that year to introduce a revenue survey in Savda, Raver and Chopda ran into stiff and widespread resistance on the part of the Kunbi peasantry. This took the form of vast assemblies in which the peasants from both sides of the Tapti demonstrated their opposition to the survey. The gatherings assumed their most massive and menacing proportion at Yaval, Savda, Faizpur and Erandol. Peaceful at first they turned violent as more and more people collected at each of these places. Eventually the army was called up and the movement put down by the combined effort of several regiments of the Native Infantry and some companies of the Bhil Corps. Looking at this event in retrospect the authorities were convinced that it was not instigated by the local elite. 'The actors in the disturbances from first to last', wrote Mansfield, Collector of Khandesh and Wingate,

Revenue Survey Commissioner, in their joint report, 'were nearly confined to the Coonbee Caste, and among these the two tribes of Pajnee and Telolee Coonbees who form the great mass of the cultivators of the Sowda and Yawul Mahals, were most conspicuous.' Such mobilization, they pointed out, was indeed a part of the tradition of local peasant resistance and this was 'not the first instance of the Coonbees having assembled for the purpose of petitioning and with the object of carrying their point by a demonstration of their number and determination'. Apparently they had done the same thing and with much success on a previous occasion, in 1849, at Dharamgaon in protest of the erection of Boundary Marks to indicate the limits of their fields'. Did such a demonstration 'by collecting large numbers of ryots to petition against the survey' constitute a breach of the law? Not so, according to the Magistrate of Khandesh who wrote, 'I know of no law which prevents people from assembling in any numbers for the purpose of petition as long as they conduct themselves inoffensively.' But the view which prevailed at the top of the administration was sterner. As the Governor of Bombay formulated it in his minute of 14 June 1853, It may be necessary here to check the commission of such a crime by severer penalties than would be had recourse to in England and certainly the danger to the ruling power in this Country from a tumultuous assemblage of thousands *is greater* and the measures necessary to meet it involve far more expence and trouble than a corresponding movement by a mob would cause at home.

Nothing could be more explicit as an acknowledgement of the fear inspired by this particular form of autonomous peasant assemblies. It constituted a 'danger to the ruling power in this Country' in the eyes of those who were high enough in the bureaucracy to know which side to choose when consideration for petty legalities clashed with concern for the security of the colonial state. They were right from their point of view. For when a rebellion set out consciously to mobilize the rural masses for a war on the regime, such *rassemblements* could indeed be a most formidable challenge to the Raj. The Birsaite gatherings which preceded the Munda ulgulan of 1900 were, in this sense, the organs of a peasant war. Soon after his release from jail in November 1897 Birsa and his principal followers met for consultations at Bortodih and planned these rallies as a part of 'an organisation which was necessary to recover their lost rights and to drive out their enemies'. Suresh Singh's authoritative monograph on this subject mentions a very large number of these far in excess of the official estimate of sixteen spread over two years between the parley mentioned above and a meeting of about sixty Birsaite gurus in Singhbhum towards the end of December 1899, just a few days before the arrows began to fly. Many of these were addressed by the Munda chief himself. Long before the itinerant agitator was to emerge as a standard feature in the elite politics of the subcontinent, Birsa moved from village to village over an extensive area mobilizing his people. He did not have it all his own way on each of these occasions. Sometimes the Mundas would overrule their leader and impose their collective will on him. Thus at a famous meeting at Simbua hill in March 1898 they firmly and persistently resisted his advice in favour of a religious and reformist agitational procedure. In fact the cumulative upshot of these assemblies was 'the triumph of the neo-sardars' strategy of revolt over the peaceful means of struggle initially advocated by Birsa'. A genuine instrument of rebellion as a mass event, they mobilized the Munda peasantry for a war on the Raj.

Mobilization of this kind could often assume a religious form. It is well known that in pre-industrial Europe popular uprising tended to correspond to the Christian calendar of fasts and festivities. Wat Tyler's men entered London on 13 June 1381, the day of the feast of Corpus Christi. The Peasant War in Germany began with Fastnacht, 1525. 'The hour arrived for the fire to be raised', writes Johannes Kessler in his chronicle 'This was on Fastnacht when people tend to gather together.' Lefebvre has identified in this tendency of crowds to gather in feast days and start a riot a 'classic' pattern which repeated itself over and over again during the entire course of the French Revolution: 'Things would begin to stir on a Sunday: throughout the whole period, this day, like feast days in honour of local saints and *baladoires*, was almost a critical day; the peasants would go to mass, then, having nothing else to do, would drift along to the local café: there was nothing like this for starting a riot.' In India the calendar of pujas and *parabs* and the chronicle of rural disturbances did not correlate so directly, although the British authorities were constantly haunted by a fear of this happening during the Mutiny. 'The close of the "Roza" was approaching', wrote the Magistrate of Saharanpur, 'I looked for serious disturbances.'

Another officer in that area thought it probable that the local. Musalmans 'might take advantage of the Edd [Id] which occurred on the 26th [May 1857] to create a disturbance', Again, towards the end of July that year all European women and children were evacuated from Nainital in order to ensure to their safety in the event of an uprising to coincide with Bakr-Id at Rampur and its spread to that hill station. And at yet another hill station, Mussoorie, all seems to have benn well with the white community in those days except for 'an occasional alarm at the native feasts of Eeed, Buqr Eeed, etc.' The Mahommedan festivals passed off without violence at all these places. But there have been other occasions when religious and rebel gatherings are known to have intersected. Thus, on the eve of the hool the Santals of Bhagnadihi went in a large body to the bazaar at Panchkethia to worship the local deity there and seek her blessing for the ensuing enterprise. The communal visits to 'ancestral places' undertaken by Birsa's followers on his advice exceeded the limits of Sardar revivalism and developed into a series of carefully planned and (as soon as the government came to know of these) risky ceremonial marches to inspire the Mundas for the coming ulgulan. By the time the holy itinerary had been gone through over a period of two years and the 'ancestral possessions' recovered from hallowed sites the *tulsi* leaves from Chutia, the sandal paste from Jagarnathpur temple and the sanctified water and sacred thread from Naw Rattan-'the psychological preparation for the revolt was complete'. It was already November 1899 with just a few weeks to go before the critical Christmas eve when the uprising was due to begin.

However, it was only rarely that the mobilization of an insurgent peasantry adopted so explicit a religious form in colonial India. There was, of course, a pervasive undertone of religiosity in almost all that happened in village society. But beyond that level of generalization it would be perhaps more true to say that the rather secular idiom of communal festivity and corporate labour was what, more than anything else, characterized the agrarian uprisings of the period. In this respect again the Indian experience had a good deal in common with the European. Lefebvre mentions the 'very strong popular flavour' of some of the jacqueries of 1789. The peasants apparently enjoyed themselves. 'It is easy to see that they were delighted to down tools on the spot and go for a day's outing as though they were setting off to the market or the fair', he observes.

'The whole village would be on foot, the *syndic* leading the way in front of the most important inhabitants, sometimes with drums beating; there would be few guns, but a good number of farming implements and sticks instead of firearms; there were more young people than old. There were deafening shouts of "Long live the Third Estate!"' Rude, too, speaks of the ceremonial aspect of the Swing movement in England, which tended to be increasingly pronounced as the movement gained in strength: 'In the earlier (and later), days, when the militants were more inclined to fear detection raiding parties might blacken their faces and do their work at night; but as the movement developed, riots took place in open day, and were public performances and at times assumed a festive air.'

Ceremonialism thus emerged as a concomitant of the public and communal character of the Swing. This was true of some of the Indian rebellions too. In Pabna the peasants had started off by trying to mobilize support for their cause by word of mouth sent through individual emissaries, but this was soon given up for more forceful and public demonstrations as the movement acquired momentum and self-confidence. The method they then adopted was to call up large bands of men by sounding the horn, arm them with lathis (and with *polos* as we shall presently discuss), and take them round in imposing columns though the villages along a given route pleading with and if necessary, pressing the local population to join the agrarian league. Again, as Hunter observes, the rising of the Santals 'could not be distinguished at first from one of their great national processions headed by the customary drums and fifes'. The leaders of the hool, like those of the Swig movement, rode at the head of their raiding parties on conspicuous mount the subahs on horseback and the supreme commanders, Sido and Kanhu, on palanquins and elephants. The French and the English rebels of 1789 and 1830 respectively showed a distinct taste for dressing up for a raid. So did the Santals. We have Sido's own words testifying to the fact that during the attack on Maheshpur 'many of the Manjees were dressed in red clothes'. Other armed Santals were variously reported as wearing red *saloo* (a variety of cotton fabric used mostly for festive decoration), white *lungis*, white *dhotis* and *pagris*. The Birsaite march to Khunti for an assault on the police station there had all the marks of a ceremonial procession too: 'their bodies smeared with dust, their arms decorated with *chanwar*, wearing turbans and snow-white *dhoties'*, the insurgents arrived at Khunti 'dancing, jumping and brandishing their swords'.

The communal idiom most characteristic of rebel mobilization in India was that of corporate labour. It is often a figure of speech in rebel discourse which illustrates how for the insurgents a jacquerie was simply another way of working together. '*Khunti be rahar jaromakana, dolabu maea*' ('The rahar crop at Khunti is ripe, let's go and harvest it'), cried the Birsaites as they marched on the police station at Khunti. Or, as the formidable Gaya Munda exclaimed when he and his men sighted a posse of police constables, '*Samare hijulenako mar goekope*' ('The sambhar deer have arrived, kill them'). The displacement between the primary and secondary referents in these utterances generates that broad, black humour characteristic of peasants out on a raid: '*fricasser ce poulet*' is how the Mâconnais rebels on their way to Pollet's country house described their mission by a play on their victim's name. And the message in each of these Mundari sentences is a measure of the correspondence between its two poles collective violence against the enemy and co-operation in a task of communal labour such as harvesting or hunting. As we learn from the historian of the ulgulan, the Mundas themselves took their own rhetoric seriously enough to act up to its traditional implications. For when Gaya's party returned home after their successful encounter with the police at Etkedih in the incident mentioned above, 'their women turned out to greet them and wash their feet with water while the men sang hunting songs' all in the customary manner of concluding a good day's shikar.

Or take this circular issued by the Pabna ryots to mobilize support for their struggle against the zamindars in 1873:

> *So and so Projas! as soon as you see this circular, hasten over to the side of the insurgent party. If you fail to come within this day, rest assured that we go to fish in the beel, close by your village. We have already fished in the beels of so and so villages. Knows this order is peremptory.*

The imagery which is meant to mask and by masking drive home the dark message of this notice, relates to a mode of collective work which was as vital to the peasantry of Pabna as hunting was to the Mundas of Chota Nagpur. The *bils* are marshes and swamps which covered a large part of the district-an incomplete list in the *Pabna District Gazetteer* mentions nine of them spread over an area of 215 square miles and served as reservoirs of fresh water fish ample enough to provide a secondary source of livelihood for a predominantly ricegrowing population. A good deal of the corporate life of the villages related therefore to the exploitation of the bils, especially in the form of *polo* fishing, is an ctivity that involved all the peasants in a number of neighbouring hamlets and combinrd productive labour with much entertainment. 'Besides refular fishing, *polo* fishing is na old pastime indulged in by the villagers in the summer', writes O'Malley.

The villagers are called to the fishing by the blowing of a horn, and men and women children, sometimes numbering hundreds, troop with *polos* in hand to the nearest *bil*. The *polo* is a bell-shaped splitbamboo trap, with a small opening on the top and no bottom. The fisherman walks into the water, presses down the *polo* in front of him, and then stooping down, plunges his hands through the opening at the top and gropes on the mud for the fish that are trapped. All are busy catching fish in the shallow water, which is soon churned into liquid mud, and in a few hours the *bil* is despoiled of fish.

We have quoted this description *in extenso* in order to show how closely the idiom of this particular form of communal labour was replicated in the mobilization of the Pabna ryots for the bidroha of 1873. As in the case of bil fishing a few strident notes on a horn would summon the peasants of some neighbouring villages to an assembly. The time, more often than not, was a late hour of the night, the best time for an abundant catch, too, in the swamps. This nocturnal blowing of the horn was such a dreaded symbol of the movement that in some areas the district authorities issued orders under Section 518 of the Indian Penal Code 'forbidding the ryots to sound horns at night with a view to causing terror'. And just as the members of a party proceeding to a bil would carry polos as their most essential equipment, the peasant agitators, too, would arm themselves with lathis, each capped by a polo, as they marched from village to village agitating for their cause and terrorizing its enemies. The polo in its turn was regarded as a badge of insurgency. It gave to the movement and its participants their respective folk names 'Polo Bidroha' and 'Polowallahs'. To be told 'The Polowallahs are coming!' could indeed panic their opponents as much as did those midnight blasts on the buffalo horn. In this context no one who read the circular quoted above could mistake the peasants' intention 'to fish in the beel close by your village' for anything but the chilling euphemism it was meant to be that is, a warning to conform to the campaign or be pillaged. It is thus that a set of signs characteristic of mobilization for a mode of communal labour came to be associated with mobilization for an agrarian struggle: the *atideœa* that extended the signs from one domain to the other helped not merely to designate the peasant fishermen as rebels (*bidrohi*) they were literally known as such but also to integrate rebellion as a corporate enterprise of the rural masses.

Communal fishing was a part of the Santal tradition, too. But the operative idiom of the hool was that of another corporate activity shikar. It was a Santal custom for a *dihri*, a man who combined the functions of a master of the hunt with those of a priest, to summon all the able-bodied men within a circle of villages at a specified place, usually a jungle or a hill, on a particular day. According to Ranjit Parganait of Sarmi this was precisely how two Santal leaders, Munka Majhi of Chotbazar and Kowleah Majhi of Sindree, mobilized their community for the uprising during the spring of 1855. They 'called together a great number of Sonthals extensibly [sic] for the purposes of Shikar at Buro Koondee. Where [sic] they had assembled these two Manjees told the other Sonthals to assemble at Chotbazar from thence to go to Hazareebagh to consult the Soubah as to their grievances.' Ranjit himself was present at Barakundi. His testimony is confirmed by the somewhat mythified version of the event as recorded in *Mare Hapram Ko Reak Katha* where Jugia, the old Santal, remembers how the word had spread that all should gather for a shikar at Layogarh to celebrate the birth of a Soubah to a virgin girl. 'Layogarh is located in the hills of Hazaribagh. Some people did go there, saw the Soubah and joined him at a hunt in Kanchan forest too.' The Soubah apparently ordered another assembly for shikar to follow at Tirpahar near Deoghar, but this, says Jugia, was never held for reasons not known to him.

It is indeed appropriate that mobilization for a communal hunt should have merged thus with that for the hool. The Santals themselves made the association explicit by a homonymy: they used the word '*fauj*' (literally, 'troops') both for the mass of insurgents led by the Soubahs and the parties of armed men led by the dihri at shikar. For it was in either case a matter of arming the entire adult male population for a communal enterprise. After the dihri announced a chase, the villagers would start getting ready. 'They would string their bows, fit arrows with heads ground to a fine point, sharpen the blades of their axes (*tangis*) and fit them to handles, fasten spearheads to long staves and polish their swords to a shine.' And then, on the appointed day, a roll of drums at dawn would start calling them up to the assembly poixnt. This was also how the Santals prepared for war. When the time came, their enemies were quick to identify the hunting equipment by its other function and ban it as the insignia of rebellion. As an order issued at the height of the pacification campaign by MajorGeneral Lloyd commanding the Dinapore Division and Santal Field Force put it: 'All villages of the Tribe must be made to deliver up their arms, vizt. Bows and arrows, sword, battle axes & sacrificing knives as well as the Drum called Digdighee used for calling the sonthals together into bodies.' The order appears to have gone down well with the army, and many a gallant officer leading his men against a Santal village or a rebel camp in the jungle proudly reported the seizure of a few bows and arrows, axes, swords, drums, etc. as a part of the day's military achievement.

In one important respect, however, the communality of the hool exceeded that of a hunt. The latter was, among the Santals, an exclusively male undertaking, although it was customary for their women to prepare for them the provisions they took to the jungle and welcome them back home after shikar by ceremonially receiving them at the front door and washing their fect. But men and women would participate together in many other forms of labour essential for their livelihood, such as cutting timber, gathering leaves and harvesting a crop. On such occasions, says the Reak Katha, 'Santal men and women greatly enjoyed working together'. They worked together in the hool too. Out on a pillage, the men busied themselves with the rough and heavy job of wrecking enemy property while the women gathered the loot a replication, no doubt, of the standard division of labour between the sexes at harvest time.

Already in the first week of the rising the planter Maseyk had observed that a party of ten men who attacked and burnt down the village of Monkaparrah had 'a number of women with them to carry off the spoils'. The names of two women, Radha and Heera, both described as wounded, occur in a list of nineteen Santal prisoners produced before the Magistrate of Murshidabad on 20 July, a fortnight after the outbreak. And as the insurrection draws to a close in the autumn of 1855, women come up for mention a number of times in the official correspondence about the capture, incarceration and summary trial of the rebels. Thus, a party of four Santals was captured by a Sergeant Gillan near Mohammadbazar on 15 September 1855. The leader, Dhuna Majhi, charged with 'illegally and riotously assembling with offensive weapons for purpose of plunder and committing a breach of the peace' was sentenced to seven years' imprisonment 'with labour and irons'. His companions, all women, two of them girls of fourteen, 'accompanied the rebels with baskets and bags to carry off grain'. For this the older woman was given one year in jail plus a fine of fifty rupees, and the younger ones six months and a fine of twenty-five rupees each. Dhuna Majhi was transported to Chittagong jail at the other end of the province to serve his sentence while the three females were kept in detention in Birbhum. A rebel family of man, wife and daughters who had been in the hool together, was thus captured, punished and broken up.

Between October and November that year there were at least forty-five Santal women held in Birbhum jail. Some had their children with them. Quite a few of these still fed on the breast and were dying of dropsy and dysentery in the overcrowded and insanitary prison, which moved the Civil Surgeon with pity enough to urge for their immediate release but was regarded by the Officiating Magistrate 'only as the just retribution they have brought upon themselves'. When twenty of these women were brought to trial, thirteen were released. Of the seven others, one 'had accompanied a sonthal force which had gone forth to plunder the village of Deocha' in August and was shot twice in her left leg by the troops; captured and detained since then she had been far too ill to be produced in court and yet apparently regarded as far too dangerous to be released from custody. Five of the women sentenced by the Sessions Judge three to one year's imprisonment each and two to six months were 'all convicted on very clear evidence of having actively assisted the Insurgents in plundering and carrying off goods from different villages in this [Birbhum] district'. And one was detained on the order of the Magistrate himself, for she had failed to produce the security for good conduct demanded of her. 'The charge was established against her of having acted not only as a spy for the insurgents, but of having been the means frequently of supplying them, by purchases in this

Town [Suri] & elsewhere, with Tobacco, Salt, spirits and other necessaries and provisions.' She obviously was by no means unique, and the entire female population of the Santal districts in 1855 could have been accused of acting as the providers and as the eyes and ears of the rebel forces in precisely the same way.

The records of imprisonment and summary justice throw some light on yet another aspect of Santal collectivity the co-operation between people of the same village. Mutual aid and co-operative labour among fellow villagers were, according to the *Reak Katha,* an important part of their tradition. Such co-operation was needed and offered when a fairly wide range of skills had to be pooled together as in the construction of a house or when some of the more arduous agricultural operations like ploughing, transplanting and harvesting required more labour power than could be generated by single families working on their own. This apparently was common practice until the rebellion, and there is some evidence to suggest that it featured in the mobilization for the hool to some extent. I have examined three lists of Santal rebels for each of whom the records specify his residence. They were all produced before and found guilty by a Court Martial and a civilian court. Of the seventy-five men from nineteen villages there were only six who were on their own and not accompanied by at least one fellow villager. Four villages contributed two men each and another group of four villages three each. The number of participants from the six other villages varied between four and sixteen as shown on Table 10.1.

Two of these lists also specify the thana jurisdiction for each of the ten villages where thirty-seven of the rebels were said to have originated. Bunching them by thanas ten from the area of Afzalpur thana, twenty-three from Nalhati and four from Nungolia one can get some idea of local co-operation between groups of neighbouring hamlets within the jurisdiction of a police station. This is further confirmed by what we know about the residence of the participants in one characteristic act of the rebellion. The villages Katna in Birbhum was raided and pillaged by sixteen men five of them from three villages in Nalhati thana and ten from five villages in Afzalpur thana (not counting one from a village for which the thana is not given). And when under the pressure of Captain Peter's operations in that area the Santals were forced to fall back before Afzalpur, they regrouped at Jamjori fof an attack on the army unit posted at Jamtara a move the communal character of which was not lost upon their enemies. 'Almost every Sonthal village is furnishing its quota to Jamatarra', wrote the alarmed commander of the Birbhum and Bankura Field Force to his superiors in the Military Department.

Table 10.1. Distribution of Captive Rebels by Neighbourhood

Number of villages grouped according to size of participation	Number of participants per village in each group	Total number of participants per group
6	1	6
4	2	8
4	3	12
1	4	4
1	5	5
1	11	11
1	13	13
1	16	16
Total: 19	-	75

The fruits of corporate activity are communally shared. The portions are by no means equal, headmen, priests, drummers and other special functionaries being entitled to somewhat larger helpings before the remainder is equally divided. But as the Santal book of tradition makes it clear, there is nothing arbitrary about the distribution of reward. Whether it is a communal catch of fish or a communal kill at shikar, there are well defined and universally accepted rules as to who should get how much. The Santals appear to have carried this idiom into their conduct of the hool too. Travelling through the Rajmahal Hills in January 1851 Captain Sherwill had noticed a curious sign in a jungle near a village called Burwa. 'Observing a tuft of straw tied to a tree in the jungle', he wrote in his diary, 'I enquired of the manji the meaning or use of it; he informed me that wherever a Sonthal is desirous of protecting a patch of jungle from the axes of the villagers, or a patch of grass being grazed over, or a newly-sown field from being trespassed upon, he erects a bamboo in his patch of grass or field, to which is affixed a tuft of straw, or in the case of jungle some prominent and lofty tree has the same prohibitory mark attached, which mark is well understood and strictly observed by all parties interested.' Four years later the rebels were to use a variation of the same sign to indicate communal appropriation by pillage. They plundered thirty-four villages in Ooperbandah thana in Birbhum during the insurrection, and as Richardson, the Collector of the district, observed: 'In each plundered Village a bamboo has been fixed in the ground, with a piece of leather affixed, denoting that the Sonthals have obtained possession of the land.'

Since the villages were thus taken over in the name of the community, the loot had to be shared out among the raiders. 'When we attack villages', said Balai Santal after his arrest, 'the people run away and the plunderers take everything.' The cash would then be divided among the members of the party and all other property handed over to the Soubahs, some of which they were to keep for themselves and the rest for communal use. Kanhu, too, in his statement confirmed that 'the treasure plundered was shared amongst manjees and sonthals', and that he himself received a part of the booty. The portion made over to him as the supreme commander was of course far greater than anything an ordinary 'sipahi' like Balai could expect. 'The three Rupees that were (found) with me', said the tatter after his capture, 'I got at the plundering of a Rajah's near Agoonerjah'; whereas after the pillage of the princely estate of Pakur, said Kanhu, 'a manjhee brought me two Kulsies [brass pots] of rupees, 2 Elephants, 2 or 4 palkies [palanquins], 2 cloths'. There was nothing egalitarian about this any more than there was about the unequal apportioning of game and fish between the village leaders and the common Santals. What is important however is to note that by insisting on the principle of communal distribution of plunder the rebels placed the hool under the sign of a collective enterprise of the same order as shikar or fishing.

The function of this corporate violence is to undermine the authority of the peasant's enemies by destroying such of their resources as constitute the insignia and instruments of that authority. The means adopted by the rebels for this purpose often vary from event to event and from region to region. But with all its variety there are in this violence certain regularities of emphasis and pattern which have been noticed by some of the most discerning students of the subject. It was thus that Trotsky picked out of the welter of agrarian riots of 1905 in Russia four main 'types' or 'forms of struggle' which 'in different combinations, spread over the country, being adapted to the economic conditions of each region'. Mao Tse-tung, too, in his investigation of the conduct of the peasantry during the Hunan movement in 1927 made it a point to 'closely examine all their activities, one by one, to see what they have actually done' and in his famous report which 'classified and summed up' these activities he identified nine 'methods' governing the very large number of sanctions and coercive measures 'used by the peasants to hit the landlords politically'. The lesson to be learnt from such distinguished exercises is that to fail to investigate and identify these 'methods' and 'forms' of peasant violence is for a historian to be resigned to the point of view which sees in insurgency nothing but chaos, confusion and disorder 'a sort of blindness and madness', as a modern scholar has written of the Kol insurrection echoing the sentiments of the colonial officers who were sent out to suppress it. What this point of view misses out is that there is much order in this apparent 'madness', a great deal of discipline in what looks like pure spontaneity. To quote Lefebvre's memorable words precisely on this question: 'These are not acts of collective madness, as has so often been suggested. The people always has its own way of dealing with things.'

If one examines carefully enough the record of peasant activities during the great rural disturbances under the Raj and combs through the debris of undigested detail stacked in the primary sources, making up an inventory, so to say, of the means and objects of violence, one will probably have no difficulty in concluding that there were *four methods or forms of struggle* which stood out as the most conspicuous and the most prevalent. These were *wrecking, burning, eating* and *looting*. It is not that each of these figured to the same extent in all the events. On the contrary, it was the want of uniformity in their combinations and the uneven distribution of their relative weightage which helped to distinguish one uprising from another and lent to each its individuality. However, taken together it was these forms which made insurgency so distinctively *destructive* and *political* in its character and put it in a class apart from crime.

To turn first to wrecking, it is well known that the demolition of the symbols of enemy authority was common to all peasant insurrections. In early and modern Europe nothing seemed to the rural poor to express more blatantly the difference between the material conditions of their own life and those of the life of the upper classes than the grandeur and inaccessibility of the residential houses of the latter. The elimination of this measure of their subalternity was therefore an obvious first step for the insurgents to take towards turning things upside down. Jean de Venette, one of the chroniclers of the Jacquerie of 1358, has observed how eager the peasants were to destroy manor houses; and Trotsky on his account of the jacqueries of 1995 in Russia mentions this particular form of violence to have been so widespread that 'in certain districts the landowners' houses that were left standing could be counted on one's fingers'. Some of the other peasant revolts in Europe during the five centuries between these two dates witnessed the same type od violence as the many references to the destruction of abbeys and castles in Germany in 1525 and of priories and chateaux in France in 1789 testify respectively in Zimmermann's and Lefebvre's histories of those times. Insurgency operated by similar methods in India as well. The wrecking of Deby Sinha's mansion in Rangpur during the dhing was celebrated thus as a mass event in a popular ballad:

> *Thousands of peasants marched together. They took with them their staves, picks, sickles and choppers. There was no one who woudn't join. They took on their shoulders heavy carrying poles and yokes used for ploughing. The paupers made their way over fields lying fallow. Indeed the peasants of Rangpur came from all the four directions, while the gentry [*bhadragula*] gathered there smply to witness the fun. They [the peasants] hurled a lot of stones and brickbats which came down thudding on all sides. Some people had their bones broken by the missiles. And Deby Sinha's mansion was reduced to a heap of bricks.*

In some of the uprisings the insurgents used wrecking as a weapon to carry out the war into enemy territory. The Kols of Chota Nagpur launched their insurrection by announcing 'that they would destroy every village of the Sonepore Pergunnah', and were almost as good as their word. And in the course of the fituris of 1899 the Saora in a taluk of the Ganjam Agency attacked and razed to the ground 'in the most deliberate manner' the houses of their hated exploiters, the Doms, in some fifteen villages. The more spectacular acts of demolition in the period under survey had the familiar symbols of British presence in the subcontinent as their targets. The revolt against the tyrannical system of indigo plantation culminated in some instances in the destruction of the factories. Titu Mir's men, for instance, spent a morning demolishing the Burgurreah factory on the Ichamati and did so thorough a job of it that the Magistrate of Nadia had to confess having 'never witnessed a more complete ransack and wanton destruction of property than the empty Bungalow on the shore'. Again in a wellknown case the Farazis of Faridpur destroyed a factory at Panch Char belonging to the planter Dunlop in December 1846. During the period of the Mutiny, too, the planters came under attack. As one aggrieved member of this fraternity was to recollect later on, his factories in a part of Ghazipur district of eastern UP were raided jointly by mutineers and the local villagers and destroyed in the course of two nights' work. The Santals wrecked railways and the railroad engineers' bungalows wherever they happened to come across these during the hool. And that unmistakable emblem of colonial authority in rural India, the sadar station, with its bungalows and administrative buildings, met with the same fate when peasants marched into towns as they often did during the disturbances of 1857-8. The destruction of Bulandshahr by the Gujar insurgents provides us with a fairly typical experience in this respect:

> *As the Goojurs had entered the station they fired each house, commencing with the Dak Bungalow; and during the four days we were absent the station was completely destroyed, and all property private and public, was carried off and burnt, the city people and those of the neighbouring villages taking a very active part in the work of demolition.*

This description taken from an official narrative matches well with Mark Thornhill's account of the sack of Mathura. 'The plunder of the [revenue) office', he wrote, 'was followed by that of the English houses. In this amusement the villagers spent what remained of the day. The houses contained little that they valued; that little they carried off, the rest they broke to pieces. In the morning they returned and continued the work of destruction. They concluded it by setting fire to the houses.'

The use of fire as a principal instrument of demolition was also by no means exceptional. On the contrary, wrecking and burning almost invariably went together in all great peasant revolts in India as well as abroad. Trotsky noticed the power of this combination in the course of the uprisings in the Russian countryside in 1905. He quoted from a contemporary newspaper to show how a torch set to a landowner's estate it night would often announce the beginning of a jacquerie. The incidence of arson in attacks on farms, stacks and barns in the course of the Swing movement in England in 1830 was so high that Rudé felt justified in characterizing some of the most affected areas as 'incendiary counties'. Lefebvre thought that there was a logic to all this burning. There are instances to show that the peasants often 'proceeded to destroy and burn in a very methodical way'. And according to him, a historian hardly given to generalizing too much, 'All the peasant revolts followed this pattern'. It was, he suggests, as if the rebels exercised a sort of 'right of arson' like what the bourgeois of Flanders enjoyed till the very end of the Middle Ages 'to punish anyone who had injured them or attacked their privileges by burning down his house'.

In rural India it wits not so much a sense of right but tradition supported by faith which people living close to nature had in the destructive power of fire that made them adopt arson is a major instrument of rebellion. Its use was frequent to the print of being almost universal in the Kol insurrection. In the most recent and detailed account that we have of it there is hardly a case of pillage mentioned without arson. Figures available for four divisions of Chota Nagpur (and those not amongst the most. built-up regions) speak of a total of 4,086 houses burnt down.

These included not only police thanas and mahajans' gadis, but entire residential wards in diku villages and townships as well. The scale of fire-raising by the Kol on this occasion was on a par with that by the Santals in Damin-i-Koh in 1855. They too burned down mahajans' and zamindars' houses everywhere. They reduced to ashes the indigo factory at Balbadda and the railway bungalows at Sreekund and Pakur in fact, all railway bungalows north of the river Brahmani. Pakur burned particularly high and the blaze could be seen a long way off. Indeed the hool appears never to have stopped burning. It was hardly a week old when an official marching at the head of some troops from Baharampur to Aurangabad found nearly thirty villages burnt down along his route. And 'we could see, as we were marching along, the smoke from 7 or 8 villages distant some 8 or 10 miles from us', he wrote from Kadamsar the following day reporting on what he saw of insurgent activities since leaving Aurangabad. Again, in a memorandum written on 21 July 1855 precisely at the end of the second week of the insurrection Captain Sherwill noted down his observations made during journeys to and from Rajmahal thus: 'Villages all round Colgong have been told off for loot and burning by the Santals. Major Burroughs says he will move out this afternoon (21 July) to try and endeavour to stop burning. The villages on fire seem to the East and South-cast and are visible more as I write." And nine weeks later on 24 September 1855 the Magistrate of Birbhum mentions the burning of over thirty villages in Nangulia and Ooperbandah including the police station at the latter place during the previous fortnight.

Arson played an important role in inaugurating and extending the rebellion of 1857-8. Carey saw a sign of the things to come in a series of fires which destroyed a cantonment, an army officer's bungalow and a telegraph office at Raniganj and Barrackpore in the last week of January 1857. 'And thus', he wrote in retrospect, 'the Fire King began to demonstrate an inkling of what was in store for almost every station in the North Western Provinces ' The Fire King was indeed much in evidence later on that summer. At Aligarh, for instance, the burning down of a bungalow was the obvious and instantaneous index of the tension generated by the news of the outbreak at Meerut, and when within a week the sepoys of the local garrison themselves mutinied, the Collector's kachari and the post office, too, went up in flames.At Etawah at about the same time a similar set of buildings, all of them the visible symbols of the Raj-the kachari, the sessions court house, the post office and two bungalows-met the same fate at the hands of incendiaries. Later on, in June, when the mutineers from Jhansi arrived there, the Mewatis felt bold enough to destroy the rest of the bungalows by fire. In Hamirpur, the zamindars of mauza Gohand burnt down the tahsil, its building and its records. It was the same story everywhere with the insurgents setting fire to all administrative buildings and European residential bungalows in district after district throughout Uttar Pradesh.

The same means of destruction was used by the peasants in their struggles in other parts of the country as well-e.g. by the Kunbi as they made bonfires of the Marwari moneylenders' bonds, shops, houses, fodder stacks, etc. during the riots of 1875 in Poona and Ahmadnagar; by the Moplah as they burnt down the landlords' houses and temples again and again in the course of their numerous uprisings in Malabar during the nineteenth century. The last great rebellion of the century, the Birsaite ulgulan too was marked by an 'epidemic of burning and arrowshooting', particularly in its initial phase. The official statistics of 33 cases in Chakradharpur, 45 in Tamar, 39 in Khunti and 4 in Basia-a total of 121-do not obviously include many unreported incidents, and their value for our study of arson is diminished in any case by their being lumped together with arrow-shooting. But since the two forms of violence often occurred at the same time, these figures may perhaps still serve to give some idea of the fairly high incidence of burning. On one of these occasions after a successful attack on a police station the raiders set fire to a few sheds and thatched houses belonging to the police and some of the local moneylenders and danced around the blaze to celebrate their victory. The impact that this relatively minor incident had on a Belgian missionary who witnessed it is a measure of the fear generated by arson. 'It was a terrible night', he wrote, 'to see in the brilliant blaze of this conflagration these hundreds of savage and infuriated Mundas dancing and jumping about with loud shouts and yells and brandishing their terrible battle axe (s).' What made the Munda insurgent dance with joy made T. van der Schueren, S.J., of the Belgian mission shudder.

It should be emphasized here that destruction by wrecking and burning was by no means limited in any of these cases to 'useless' objects of luxury and conspicuous consumption alone. For if that were the case one would have found it difficult to explain why on so many occasions the rebels chose to demolish things and resources of obviously great economic value to themselves. Take, for instance, the classic case of the destruction of railway works by the Santals during their hool. There can be no doubt about the fact that the introduction of railways added considerably to income and employment in the Santal country. 'High embankments, heavy cuttings, many-arched bridges, created a demand for workmen such as had never been known in the history of India.' For the Santals this provided an opportunity to extricate themselves from the state of landlessness, low wages and bonded labour into which they had fallen thanks to the combination of an administratively engineered rise in the local population by as much as thirty times in less than fifteen years, according to one authority and cynical exploitation by mahajans and zamindars under the protection of the Raj.

The economic prospect was indeed so radically improved for them that Hunter was persuaded to put the relevant parts of his account in *The Annals of Rural Bengal* under the ecstatic caption:

'The Railway Abolishes Slavery'. Yet when violence actually broke out in July 1855 the beneficiaries seem to have had no hesitation about slaying the goose that laid the golden eggs for them.

The records are quite clear on this point: indeed, railway works were among the very first and most frequently destroyed objects mentioned in the reports received from the disturbed areas within the first week of the uprising. In one of these key reports Richardson identified this particular orientation of the hool and explained this in terms found convincing enough by his superiors as well. 'The object of the Hillmen', he wrote from Suri on 14 July, 'appears to be to destroy everything connected with the Railway works, and their anger has been roused, I have no doubt, by the Railway Officers carrying on intrigues with their women as well as bullying the laborers.' This was corroborated by the Officiating Commissioner of the Burdwan Division who forwarded this report to the authorities in Calcutta saying 'that the Sonthal women have been disgraced and this injury calls amongst them for vengeance'. Quite clearly the Santals had decided that it was not worth their while coming back home to their villages with all the money earned on the rail roads 'with their girdles full of coin and their women covered with silver jewellery, "just like Hindus"', as Hunter put it if they could not defend the honour of those women and their own dignity as workers against the raping, bullying railway sahibs. In other words, in one of those unpredictable leaps of consciousness prestige suddenly assumed for them an importance exceeding that of money and politics transcended economics.

This was by no means the only instance one could cite. On yet another occasion later on the Santals destroyed all the green crops belonging to Bengali villagers hostile to them in the neighborhood of Jamjorie in Birbhum district indicating once again that they regarded the uprising as a war in which political considerations had to be given a priority over strictly economic ones, the need to destroy the enemy over that of safeguarding economic resources from destruction. The Kols are known to have 'plundered and burned' a little over 29,859 metric tons of gram in four divisions of Chota Nagpur in the course of their insurrection in 1831-2. And to turn to the experience of the year of the Mutiny, the damage done by the rebels to the coal mines at Kotah and their not so successful attempt to wreck those in Rewah, the destruction of canal locks by the peasants in order to prevent Major Reid's battalion from reaching Bulandshahr by boat, the numerous attacks on railways and factories by the rural poor dependent for their livelihood on them in many parts of Uttar Pradesh in those days were all witness to the primacy of politics in Indian peasant rebellions of our period.

There was nothing of course about all this which may be said to have been peculiarly Indian. Parallels abound. During the Peasant War in Germany in 1525 the rebels were known to have damaged crops in fields and barns, destroyed the entire stock of fish in some lakes, burned down a forest and cut down a vineyard ignoring the proprietor's offer of wine, meat, bread and money as inducement to leave him alone. The French jacqueries of 1789 duplicated the pattern: game was killed, woods laid waste, abbey lands ruined, pigeons and dovecotes destroyed, salt pans damaged, and mills, forges and sawmills broken up. On the eve of the Maji Maji rebellion the peasants of Tanganyika defied their leader's advice to continue cultivating cotton for the German colonialists and asked themselves, 'How do we start the war? How do we make the Germans angry? Let us go and uproot their cotton so that war may rise.' They uprooted cotton and thereby inaugurated the revolt. In China in 1927 the Hunan peasantry sought 'outlets for their feelings against those who oppressed them' by slaughtering the pigs and sheep of 'the local tyrants and the evil gentry'. It is indeed not possible to explain solely or even primarily in terms of economic interests the destruction of so much of productive resources so often by insurgents operating under such widely different circumstances in so many countries.

We thought it fit to insist on this destructive aspect of rebel activities in order to avoid the error of reading purely economic motives in them. For that might tend to blur the distinction between two qualitatively different types of violence rebel violence which expresses itself in what are essentially political acts intended to turn things upside down and criminal violence against property aimed at transferring economic resources from its victims to its protagonists. This is a functional difference not to emphasize which could lead to a narrowly economistic interpretation of peasant insurgency. Labry's account of the disturbances in the Russian countryside in 1905 provides us with an instructive specimen of precisely such an interpretation. Describing the sacking of the country-houses in the Chernigov Guberniya he writes:

A very large number of those who took part in these attacks refused to regard their actions as in the least *criminal*, since, as they put it, they had been granted *rights*. They even believed that in acting as they did, they were helping to transfer the lands of the landlords into their own hands, which was the natural consequence of the *rights* they had been granted. Only this explains why on the estates they destroyed orangeries and flower-gardens which were *useless* to them with particular fury, and in the houses, pictures and furniture, in a word all that they regarded not as a *necessity of life*, but as a *sign of comfort and luxury*. On the other hand they spared the cattle and took care not to destroy stocks of corn.

Quite clearly it is the author's intention to read in this violence *both* a political and an economic meaning. He starts off by emphasizing the former. The peasants, he says, acted from a consciousness of their own rights, that is, from a political consciousness which, if true, must have had its oh objects predicated as political. It is thus that they came to regard themselves as involved not in crime but in political action aimed at demolishing the insignia of the landlords' authority. To regard this pillage then as a merely selective attack directed '*par calcul*' against 'useless' and economically unproductive luxuries and suggest, as Hobsbawm does on the basis of this account, that 'destruction is never indiscriminate, what is useful for poor men is spared', is to depoliticize this violence, make it into an economism and consequently render it impossible for us to understand why 'those who took part in these attacks refused to regard their actions as in the least criminal'.

Indeed the correct reading of this experience should be that destruction is 'never indiscriminate' only in the sense that the peasant discriminated between what stands for landlord authority and what does not, and not between what is 'useful' and what is 'useless' in the narrowly economic sense of these words. One can perhaps even go so far as to generalize that the more a violence of this type shifts away from crime towards rebellion the more it comes to be dominated by politics rather than economics, and vice versa. This is why it is often difficult to assign any clear-cut economic motive even to some of the more radical forms of social banditry which come fairly close to rebellion but fall just short of it on the spectrum of rural violence. Blacking, for instance, in most parts of eighteenth-century England could hardly be explained in terms of the poachers' involvement in the illicit venison trade. 'Other motives were *dominant*', says E. P. Thompson. 'The deer killed were often either eaten by the hunters, or their carcasses were left in the parks. Whereas there were distinct venison seasons, with the culling of bucks in midsummer and of hinds in mid-winter, the attacks of the Blacks were at all seasons, at times when the meat would not only be poor, but its attempted sale would attract notice. Above all, the whole pattern of Black actions the threatening letters, felling of young trees, blackmail of forest officers disallows a simple economic explanation.' The dominant motive here is clearly political that of undermining the authority of the gentry by the demolition of its symbols. This inversive function of popular violence is raised to its highest power by insurgency, and destruction becomes in that context the signifier of a consciousness which is as negative in orientation as it is political in content.

No narrowly economic interpretation can explain some of the other forms of rebel activities either, such as eating and looting. There was nothing of the calculus of saving and investment in these. Taken together they acted as a foil to the other pair-wrecking and burning, and complemented by expropriation what the latter achieved by demolition, the function of both being to assist insurgency to destroy.

Eating, in this context, must be understood as an integral part of a political process. Neither the gargantuan scale on which it is often organized by the peasants to celebrate a successful jacquerie nor the enormous waste involved makes any sense at all of this as simply a measure of satisfying hunger. On the contrary, its use by the rebels as an instrument of inversion and/or as a penalty imposed on their foes in order to remunerate themselves for 'public services' rendered in the cause of insurgency bears testimony to its political character. It is precisely this meaning that is emphasized by Mao 'Tse-tung when he identifies this as one of 'the methods used by the peasants to hit the landlords politically' during the Hunan movement and characterizes it as a political demonstration thus:

Major demonstrations. A big crowd is rallied to demonstrate against a local tyrant or one of the evil gentry who is an enemy of the [peasant] association. The demonstrators eat at the offender's house, slaughtering his pigs and consuming his grain as a matter of course. Quite a few such cases have occurred. There was a case recently at

Machiaho, Hsiangtan County, where a crowd of fifteen thousand peasants went to the houses of six of the evil gentry and demonstrated; the whole affair lasted four days during which more than 130 pigs were killed and eaten. After such demonstrations, the peasants usually, impose fines.

Demonstrations of this kind occurred frequently in Germany in 1525, in France in 1789, in England in 1830. However, the Indian parallels I have come across are rather less numerous. There is a reference in Sajon Gazi's ballad to Titu Mir's men feasting on the eve of the battle of Laughati. Again, Bindrai, the Kol leader, mentions that 'it was agreed upon that we should commence to cut, plunder, murder and eat'. Cut, plunder and murder they certainly did, but there is little evidence of the last of those resolutions being acted upon as a 'major demonstration'. Kanhu too says in one of his recorded statements that at Pulsa he and his men 'looted & burnt the Sahib's bungalow & took lots of wine'. We also know that on one occasion, at Umurpore, they were surprised by the troops in the midst of what was obviously a banquet in progress after a successful raid on two neighbouring villages. The Santals escaped leaving behind them 'the remains of an ample feast, a bullock half devoured, quantities of grain, cooking pots and numberless fires where they had just been cooking'. And to go by Krishnadas Ray's near-contemporary verses, they stopped at the house of one Gayaram in another village and 'held a sumptuous feast there'. Elwin in his account of the fituris in Ganjam mentions a case when in the course of a raid on a Pano village the Saora 'took pigs and goats which they killed and ate on the spot a characteristic touch'.

It should be evident even from these few instances that in India as elsewhere it sometimes happened that the peasants involved in a jacquerie would consume large quantities of edibles seized from their enemies as a method of destroying some of those resources which made the latter so rich and powerful-and indeed so different from themselves. However, it is difficult to decide at the present state of research how widespread this was and whether our want of information on this point is due simply to a gap in the records, or to a failure on the part of historians in extracting this detail from the primary sources if only because they have not grasped its significance, or to the fact that its emergence as a common and popular form of struggle was genuinely inhibited by the fear of ritual pollution through eating even among the non-Hindu peasantry like the Kol and the Santal who had long been influenced by Hindu caste customs.

No such doubt however can occur in the case of the other major type of such destructive activity, viz. looting. Truly ubiquitous, it appears to have made its presence felt in almost all uprisings in every land. In India it featured prominently even in the most 'peaceful' of peasant struggles such as those of Pabna in 1873 where looting occurred in as many as thirty out of the fifty-three (not counting five dismissed as false) recorded cases in the sadar sub-division. In yet another series-the Deccan riots of 1875-noted officially for its moderation the houses, shops and granaries of the Marwari and Gujar sahukars were looted in a number of districts. In the more violent jacqueries plunder and demolition went together in most cases. The ryots who rose against Deby Sinha in northern Bengal in 1783 plundered and burnt down the kacharis in several parganas and on one occasion looted the East India Company's grain stores at the flourishing centre of trade at Bhabaniganj.

Looting supported by wrecking and burning-pillage, to call this complex of rebel activities by its composite name-occurred on a massive scale during the Kol insurrection as well. A quick run through its chronology should make this clear. It started with four villages in the Sonepur pargana of Chota Nagpur being raided, plundered and burnt down by a body of seven hundred insurgents on 20 December 1831. This was followed up by the plunder of two other villages on 25 December by three hundred rebels and the sack of three villages on 2-3 January 1832 by a thousand men. On 12 January the entire pargana of Belkudra was looted and set to fire, and so were all villages within the jurisdiction of Govindpur thana as well as Barkagarh pargana and thana by 13 January. Several hundred villages under Jhikuchatti thana ended up in the same way during the next three days and the whole area was abandoned to the rebels by 16 January. All of Armai thana was overrun and pillaged by 24 January aand the entire Barwa pargana by the 26th-the date by which the Kols were officially recognized as having taken 'complete possession of the whole of [Chota] Nagpore' excluding some inconsiderable tracts in the southern and north-eastern corners of the region. The value of the property and goods plundered in the four divisions of Tori, Lohardagag, Sonepur and Palkote, for which alone we have complete figures, was estimated at 203,722 rupees not counting 32,494 rupees looted in cash.

Pillage, again, emerged as the central modality of the revolt of the Santals in 1855. To Balai Majhi wounded and captured on the seventh day of the hool during a raid by several thousand peasants on Charles Maseyk's indigo factory rebellion was pillage. 'I came to plunder', he said simply and succinctly to his interrogator, and then proceeded to fill in the details thus:After plundering Kudumsha, we looted the residence of the Maheshpore Rajah; then turned back, & went north & plundered all the villages along the back of the river, and we had settled to go as far as Bhaugulpore. I was present at the looting of many villages and the three Rupees that were (found) with me I got at the plundering of a Rajah's near Agoonerjah and we divided all the Rupees. All the other property has been taken to Takoor Sidoo & Kaloor's house and when we attack villages, the people run away and the plunderers take everything. The above named Sidoo and Kaloo declared themselves Rajas & [said] they would plunder the whole country and take possession of it they said also, no one can stop us; for it is the order of Takoor. On this account we have all come with them. This insurgent view of the hool as one massive plundering expedition was shared by all the local officials too. For them no less than for ' Buliye Sonthal, Manjee, son of Bushye occupation cultivator, caste Sonthal, inhabitant of Bahoo or Barah Masseeal, Perghò Zilleagur' the rebellion *was* pillage. 'They go and loot villages daily 4 or 5. They say this is at the order of a God', wrote the sub-divisional administrator of Aurangabad in his first breathless 'demi-official' report two days after the outbreak. And from that point onwards official correspondence on the subject never looks back. There is hardly a despatch from the area that does not mention pillage. It recurs frequently in a diary kept by the Collector of Birbhum at the height of the rising. Thus,

> *19 September 1855. The Reports from Saruth & Opurbandah are most unsatisfactory-The Sontals are evidently steadily advancing, looting every village en route.*
>
> *20 September 1855. Birchunder, a village about 8 miles West of Nugger, has been looted*
>
> *21 September 1855. The Sontals are looting to their hearts' content in the Saruth & Opurbandah jurisdictions. A report has just come in that the Sontals in very great numbers are at Bindabone & that they have looted Bilkandu.*

Within a fortnight, according to this collector, 'upwards of thirty villages have been plundered and burned by the insurgents in Thannah Operbundha and Nangoolea'. This account of the progress of pillage agrees with despatches from the Commissioner on Special Duty. 'The Sonthals are assembled in large numbers marching & plundering without discrimination All along the South of the Bhaugulpore District N and NW of Beerbhoom and along the foot of the hills', he writes. The insurgents had apparently done so thorough a job Already in that part of the country that he had 'no apprehension of any plunder being attempted between this [i.e. Suri] and Rampore Haut for the best of reasons, that the whole of the country to the North of a line drawn between this and that post has been plundered and there is nothing the Sonthals can gain by invading it now'.

It was indeed this sweep and power of pillage which the peasants' enemies feared most. The description of a panic in Burdwan within a fortonight of the Santal uprising was a measure of the extent and intensity of the alarm it had caused. The local correspondent of the *Somprakash* wrote:

> *The rich as well as the poor residents of Burdwan have all been seized with panic here. The rich have heard of the depredations of the Santal rebels of the hills and are contemplating various means by which to save their wealth, honour and lives. Thus, some of them have increased the strength of their house-guards by ten times. Some others have hidden all the cash they have in pits dug into ground and are crying out over again, 'O Lord! Save us!' 'O Lord! Save us!' Somes others have their eyes glued to the newspapers. And still others are busy gathering news at the railway station about the number of troops sent up by the Company's government. Altogether thus a big furore is being made.*

There is clearly a recognation here of the threat to property Sense by those who had most to lose from rebel violence. But

> ____________________*note how very similar their response was to that of affluent villagers threatened by brigandage burying cash and jewellery underground was a traditional measure of security against robbery in rural India and how little this related to the actual practice of looting in the hool. For it was* not *money that was plundered most. 'Grain was our chief plunder and cattle', said Kanhu after his capture; 'many seizures have been made by the Troops, and the remainder are in the jungles'. This is corroborated fully by the records of the anti-insurgency campaign. Officers would return from their pursuit of the rebels with tales about forest hide-outs stacked with grain and herds of cattle. A Captain Phillips reports on 30 October 1855 from Camp*

Kurwun that in the course of that day's dour *he came upon an 'encampment which was in the midst of very heavy jungle' and destroyed the large quantities of grain and other stores he found there 'all by setting fire to the encampment'. A Captain Pester reports on the following day from Camp Jamtarah how his detachment destroyed 'two large encampments and a great quantity of grain'. A Major Hampton reports from Kandra on the same day that he found the two hills near Luckunpore, a large Santal village, 'filled with grain, a great quantity of which was carried off by some 3 or 400 men who crossed the Burrakur and followed my detachment; the remainder was as far as possible destroyed'. The amounts mentioned are impressive. Four to five thousand maunds of grain were destroyed or carried off and 650 heads of cattle seized by the Bengalis (who systematically scavenged on the trail of the army with the latter's encouragement and connivance) from the 1950 huts burnt down by the forces in twenty-three Santal villages of Birbhum. And at Suburpoor, west of Jamtarah, the troops confiscated 5,000 heads of cattle and destroyed a 'large quantity of grains reported by Captain Nicholls as sufficient to supply a large force [for] at least 2 years'. Looting in the Kol in-surrection, twenty-four years before the hool, had followed the same pattern. It had started off with cattle-lifting, and grain and cattle were the objects pillaged most, as the campaign against the rebels was to demonstrate on that occasion too. Russell, the Jungle Mahal Magistrate, recovered 1,200 heads of cattle and 6,000 maunds of grain in the course of his military operations in one sector alone.*

The pattern of plunder thus did not quite correspond to what the men of property had feared it would turn out to be. Their initial response to a *levée en masse* in the countryside clung far too closely to the stereotype of the peasant as a dacoit a failure on their part to recognize (as we have seen above) that a codeswitching had occurred. For the peasant, as a rebel, was out not to rob but to destroy the authority of his enemies by expropriating them. Lefebvre's emphasis on this important distinction has a validity far beyond the particular experience to which it refers. Commenting on the character of insurgent activities in rural France in 1789 he writes:

These peasants did not band together to go stealing: they, came to destroy and they gave this one basic aim their best attention.

Crime had, in his view, very little to do with the jacqueries which broke out in such large numbers in those days. Even brigandage was rare. A certain amount of petty and rather innocuous pilfering would of course occur almost inevitably during a raid on a chateau, and some would help themselves 'to something they fancied and which was often quite. valueless'. But by and large the French rebels were positively *not* criminals.

This could be said of their opposite numbers in India too. The storming of the police station at Khunti was a major event of the Birsaite revolt, but the Larakas 'did not touch the money received in the thana the same day' nor did they rob the houses in that town. The evidence that we have of the nature and amount of fortune acquired by some of the Santals during the hool shows how little ralation the scale of that vast and violent enterprise bore to the size of individual gains. Balai Majhi's share of plunder amounted to 3 rupees; Jata's to some 'silver ornaments and green tin Box he plundered from a Mohajun's house in one of the villages'; and Kanhu Subah's to:

No. 1 A looking glass in a brass case

No. 2 A Wai[s]t plate belonging to the late Lieutt. Toulmin

No. 3 Some silver ornaments

No. 4 Three Pocket Books, and an old Book on locomotive, a few visiting cards of Mr Burn, Engineer, with some torn leaves and envelopes and bits of thin English paper

No. 5 & 6 Two purses containing 12 Rupees and 1 Gold Mohur in the first, and 17 Rupees in the second, and some pice

No. 7 Pieces of silk and Native dresses, Chudders, etc

all described graphically as 'the property on the table' that is, as. objects spread out for quick inspection on the top of a desk in Brigadier L. S. Bird's headquarters at Camp Raniganj. Not counting the twenty rupees in that list which represented Kanhu's own savings 'brought from home and mine', as he said during the interrogation, the remainder was not much indeed to show for the supreme commander of a rebel army that had wiped out the Raj in ten weeks from an area exceeding one thousand square miles in three districts.

No, 'these peasants did not band together to go stealing', as Lefebvre rightly observes. It was not their purpose to appropriate resources by petty crime. Their 'basic aim' was 'to destroy' their enemy's resources and with these his authority by means of a special form of activity of the masses. They distinguished this activity from other types of violence in name by calling it 'ulgulan' in Mundari, 'hool' in Santali, 'dhing' in a dialect of northern Bengal and so on, as well as in practice by imposing on it a rhetoric of war in the form of pillage. In India pillage was not systematized according to the conventions of medieval warfare in the same way as it was done in Germany in 1525. But its war-like figure was never less than obvious.

Major Sutherland, the first official to investigate the uprising of the Kols, remarked that 'they had enriched themselves with the *spoils* of their enemies for such they considered all foreigners'. In the perception of the insurgents plunder was thus identified as spoils rather than as criminal acquisition.

Looting as art extension of war was explicit in the operations of the Santals, too. They used this as a direct instrument of attack, reprisal and self-defence, depending on the occasion that called for it. Major-General Lloyd commanding the Dinapur Division and the Sonthal Field Force emphasized this when he asked the government carefully to consider the pros and cons of the counter-insurgency tactics. 'For every village or store of plunder we destroy, they burn and plunder at least five', he reported. Subsequently, after the hool had passed its peak by the autumn of 1855 looting came to be used by rebels increasingly as the means of self-defence. Burnt out of their villages by the Company's troops and forced to retreat further and further into the jungle, they plundered in order to stockpile provisions for what they obviously expected to be a protracted war. 'It is reported that the depredations now committed by the rebels are mainly for the purpose of plunder in order to supply themselves with the necessaries of lift', wrote the Secretary to the Bengal Government, 'for though possessed of money they are unable to purchase supplies owing to the Bengallees flying at their approach. This state of things has produced a new featurte in the insurrection the rebels being now stated to come in force at night & carry away the crops which are just ripening'. This is flow the troops came upon and in their own turn, plundered and destroyed vast granaries and large herds of cattle in the course of their *dours* in the jungle. It was also during this period when the Santals came under heavy enemy pressure that they used plunder as a form of punishment against collaborators. After the capture of Kewala, the bandit who had turned into a leader of the hool, Kanhu with about one thousand of his men raided Londeeha, the village where this happened, and looted it as a punitive measure.

It is precisely because of this quasi-military, hence political, character of plunder that cash and other objects of conspicuous consumption which fell into the hands of the insurgents tended to be treated not as articles of theft but as booty to be shared out amongst all or centralized for use by the leadership in their work for the uprising. The statements of Balai, a rank-and-file insurgent captured at the very beginning of the hool and of Kanhu, its supreme commander captured towards its end, both testify to the fact that all the looted cash was 'shared amongst the manjees and sonthals'. The means of transport seized from the enemy were handed over to the commanders for their use horses for the middle-ranking darogas and palanquins for the Subahs. And objects which were not immediately distributed or could not be broken up into divisible units for that purpose, were evidently gathered into a sort of communal store and placed under the custody of the supreme command Sido and Kanhu. It was one such collection of booty 'consisting of Palkees, a Buggy, Brass and Copper utensils, silks, cloths and miscellaneous property' worth four thousand rupees as well as cash amounting to over seven thousand rupees which the rebels looted at Maheshpur but had not yet had the time to share out, that fell into the hands of the troops after they routed the Santals at that village in one of the most critical encounters of the insurrection.

It should be evident from this survey that in its power to destroy, its mass character and its nearly universal use as a form of struggle looting taken in its wider sense as pillage was a quintessential aspect of insurgency. It derived its strength from the collective will of large rural populations acting together to settle accounts with sarkar, sahukar and zamindar. Each plundering expedition of the Kols and the Santals was the work of thousands of people. Even in the relatively less explosive Pabna movement as many as 22,130 ryots were involved in the twentyfive cases of plunder for which figures are given an average of 885. In eleven out of these twenty-five cases the number of peasants involved ranged between 100 and 500 in ten between 1,000 and 7,000. And pillage, as we have shown above, move fast. The cutting edge of the Kol and Santal insurrections, it spread rebel power, however thinly, over the whole of Chota Nagpur in about five weeks and over Damin-iKoh in ten. There was nothing in the character, mass or velocity of this violence that did not distinguish it clearly from crime.

To conclude this discussion of the distinctive features of insurgency it is perphaps necessary to emphasize that these forms of struggle constitute *a total and integrated violence*. Taken separately each of these would stand for a particular form of crime. In rebellion, however, these four types of destrcuctive activity lose their separate indentities and funtion as mutually connected elements of one single complex. At this level, the distinction between crime and insurgency corresponds to that between two types of violence-partial and total, the former as the expression of the will of a single individual or a small group in any society and the latter as that of the will of the Many.

This distinction is represented clearly in their respective patterns Crime, as discussed above, expresses itself in two diffferent ways. It is either a singular violence addressed to one particular object or, as it often happens under conditions of acute social conflict, one particular type of violence directed againts a variety of objects and conversely, many different kinds of violence againts one particular class objects. The violence of rebellion, however, is conspicuous by its plurality in both respect in the forms it assumes as well the objects it chooses. It is the combination of this vertical and horizontal plurality which makes an insurrection so comprehensive in its scope and its articulation so very powerful indeed as ultimately to overcome any ambiguity that it may have at an initial stage. This totality is too obvious to be missed out by any serious student of a rural uprising. Rudé Has commented on this aspect of the Swing thus: 'A remarkble feature of the labourers' movement of 1830, distinguishing it from many others of its kind, was its multiformity arson, threatening letters, "inflammatory" handbills and posters, "robbery", wages meetings, assaults on overseers, parsons and landlords, and the destruction of different types of machinery all played their part."

This 'multiformity' is clearly another name for 'totality' as defined above that is, the coming together of many different forms of insurgent activity and its multifarious objects. Even the most casual account of an Indian rebellion, with all its differences of detail indicates a very close similarity, if not identity, of pattern. A comparison of the experiences of three peasant insurrections ranging from the least to the most organized and spanning almost the entire period of colonial rule at fairly even intervals should make this clear. The rising against Deby Sinha in Rangpur and Dinajpur in 1783 had among its targets the persons and properties of landlords and their officials, the East India Company's troops, its granaries, kachari buildings and money and papers found by the insurgents there; the means of violence used by the rebels were arson, killing, armed assault, plunder, physical and ritual humiliation of the enemies, robbery, arrest and forcible detention, rescue of prisoners and looting of grain stores. Again, the violence of the highly disciplined movement of the Pabna peasantry in 1873 counted among its objects landlords' kacharis and estates, houses of zamindari officials and the rural gentry, groceries, police officers, and the person and houses of those who collaborated with the zamindars against the peasant union; the acts of violence ranged from raids on houses and police stations, rescue of prisoners, plunder and extortion of money to rioting, unlawful assembly, intimidation by blowing horns, abuse, theft, trespass and so on in fact offences covering as many as twenty different sections of the Indian Penal Code in just one subdivision alone. And the violence of the peasant revolt led by the communists in Telengana at the end of the Raj was directed against the landlords, their private armies, the armed forces of the state, moneylenders and collaborators; and it articulated itself in the destruction of landlords' orchards and agricultural tools, social boycott, murder of zamindars, sahukars and des*mukhs*, plunder and destruction of their houses, seizure of their grain stores, standing crops and other articles of consumption, destruction of usurers' bonds, etc.

In the case of the most massive and powerful of such uprisings such as those of the Kols, the Santals and Birsaites which bordered on peasant wars, the range of the rebel attack was so wide, its form so varied and its targets so numerous the horizontal and vertical pluralities were indeed so well integrated that in the perception of the colonial authorities the acts of violence often lost their separate identities and merge into a blur to which the law would then assign a name as one undifferentiatedcrime and deal with it according to the rules of summary justice. This is how all but one of a group of forty-two participants in the hool who were pruduced before the Sessions Judge of Birbhum and tried in the course of one week in November 1855 came to be convicted of crimes described in almost identical phrases. Twenty insurgents sentenced on 9 November were each convicted of 'illegally and riotously assembling with offensive weapons for the purpose of murder and to commit a breach of peace';

each of the two on 12 November 1855 of 'illegally & riotously assembling with weapons for the purpose of plunder to commit a breach of the peace'; three on 14 November of 'illegally - riotuosly assembling with weapons for plunder [of] property of parties unknown'; and each of the sixteen on 17 November of 'illegally & riotuosly assembling with weapons and plundering the village of Katna in Zlò Beerbhoom'.

Such want of discrimination was no doubt a sympton of that infimity of the official mind on some aspects of which Hunter has left us some wry comments in his accounr of the Santal insurrection. But there was more to this blurred and stereotyped jargon than the inertia of administrative perception. It also stood for a groping and hesitant acknowledgement on the part of the court that the offence it was given to adjudicateConstituted a totality greater than the sum of the charges. Indeed there were many among the colonial authorities, especially those entrusted to deal with an uprising on a scale larger than that of a single locality, who made no mistake about its comprehensive character. The mutually interacting processes of its collective violence, its mass and velocity, gave it, in their eyes, the semblance of a 'system'. It was thus that Neave and Russell, two of the principal officers involved in the suppression of the Kol rebellion in 1832, came, respectively, to speak of it as a *'system of burning, plundering and killing'* and a *'system of plunder and outrages'*, just as in England at about the same time, their opposite numbers operating against the Swing movement were accusing the peasantry as having established a *'system of pillage'*. Nothing testifies more to the distinction between rural crime and insurgency than such recognition of the systematic, total character of the latter on the part of those to whom it was addressed. It shows that violence, confined no longer to that grey zone where the peasant met his enemy in single combat, had emerged into the open as a war between the classes.

In insisting on this omission we have paid heed to the many references to blood and sword in our evidence and convinced ourselves that these testify less to any considerable loss of life than to the terror which grips the peasants' enemies on the outbreak of an uprising. For the sudden and inversive character of the latter tends to elicit an exaggerated and often hysterical response from those most seriously threatened by it. In so far as the primary sources of our information are made up to a large extent of precisely this kind of response, it is useful perhaps to start by differentiating within this genre of violence between two modes which are often merged in a gory mess in elite perception and hence in elite discourse.

The first of these is the death of members of the armed forces of the Raj or those of its non-official protégés such as white civilians and rural gentry (e.g. those who fought on the side of the government during the Mutiny and the Santal rebellion respectively) caused by peasants in the course of war-like encounters such as those at Mandalghat and Patgong during the Rangpur dhing, at Narkelberia during the Barasat revolt, at Maheshpur and Pakur during the hool in 1855, at Sail Rakab during the Birsaite insurrection and at many places throughout Uttar Pradesh in the year of the Mutiny. Most of these battles were fought by the rebels as defensive engagements and decided in favour of the regime by the sheer force of its superior fire power, but not before a few soldiers had been brought down on some occasions by arrows or by the rare volley from a rebel's musket. Yet the very fact that the usually passive and peaceable peasant had, against all expectation, resisted the sarkari troops and even drawn a little blood was blown u into tales of massacre by flustered officers, frightened sepoys and correspondents scared out of their wits as they wrote to the vernacular and English-language press. If anything, it was counterinsurgency rather than insurgency that made of killing a principal modality in such cases, as witness the indiscriminate slaughter of Munda women at Sail Rakab which moved even a brazen Government of India to record a mild regret.

However, the attribution of killing as a characteristic feature of insurgency does not rest primarily on such war-like situations where a peasant mass is driven to defend itself by arms against the troops or some other armed formations acting on behalf of the colonial state. What is at issue here is the notion of violence leading to the annihilation of individuals among the groups or classes hostile to the rebels. The evidence we have on this point is indeed as striking as it is negative. Contrary to the polarized myths of peasant savagery and rebel heroism estimated, in both cases, in terms of the magnitude of killing, the incidence of the latter appears to have been so low indeed as to be negligible. This is true even of the most violent and widespread of Indian peasant revolts. 'Murder has not been *general*', wrote the Collector of Birbhum in his diary recording, at the very height of the hool, the impact of a raid by the Bhagalpur Santals in the course of which 'the Thannah & Village of Operbundah were plundered & burnt'.

This pattern of violence articulated in its most destructive form in plunder and arson but stopping just short of murder, holds for the Kol insurrection too. To quote from an official report on the havoc it caused in a small township inhabited by a large number of those whom the rebels hated most, namely moneylenders:

Boondoonugger was on the 18th January 1832 taken possession of by the Insurgents. The town being extensive and peopled by wealthy Mohajuns occupied them four days in plundering it and then it was burned to the ground the houses of all the respectable men of the Pergunnah not of the class of Coles were in a few days also destroyed, but the only murders that were committed took place in the Town of Boondoo where 3 Pattons and 2 others were put to death.

Five killings in a town that took four days to sack is perhaps a fair approximation of the incidence of murder as compared to that of the other forms of struggle. This is borne out also by the statistics we have of non-tribal persons (specified as Hindu and Muslim men and women) killed during the entire course of this insurrection in five divisions of Chota Nagpur 3 in Tori, 244 in Lohardagga, 47 in Sonepur, 12 in Palkote and 9 in Tamar and the Five Parganas. A total of 315 this is not much to show in terms of bloodshed for one of the most violent of all rural disturbances which had wiped off the Raj from Chota Nagpur in a matter of weeks. The relative paucity of this phenomenon is further demonstrated by the fact that the total number of houses (presumably belonging to the same groups) burnt down during this period in the first four of the divisions mentioned above was 4,086 that is, one killing for less than fourteen acts of arson.

One wonders if the Indian experience is altogether unique in this respect. Not so, judging by what we know of the French peasant uprisings of the period of the Great Fear in 1789. Lefebvre examined with his customary scruple the charge of atrocities alleged to have been committed during the jacqueries in the Franche-Comté where 'violence was in general more pronounced and was directed mostly at people rather than objects' and concluded that even in this apparently extreme instance 'all in all, though attacks and harassments were many, there were no murders'. And Rudé estimates the number of people murdered by the peasants in all the regions taken together at a total of three. 'Only three landlords are known to have been killed', he writes in his introduction to Lefebvre's great work.

Mao Tse-tung, too, indicates the somewhat exceptional character of this violence when he describes it as 'confined to the worst local tyrants and evil gentry' during the Hunan movement. There is a suggestion here not only of the limited use made of it but also of its logic a logic of punishment and vengeance. Most of the murders committed by Indian rebels also appear to have been discriminatory. From the cases on record one can see two governing principles at work, one punitive and the other retributive a distinction which is merely notional and useful for analytic purposes alone, for in real life there was of course a good deal of overlap between the two.

Punitive killing derived its rationale from the exigencies of an ongoing insurrection and its victims were those who resisted it either indirectly by collaboration with the peasants' enemies or directly by arms. Hence the execution of informers was a feature common to many of the events included in our survey. Even a natural ally would not be spared if he worked for the other side, as did that *gwala* whom the Kol would have normally done nothing to harm but ended up by killing because he had betrayed to his master a plan they had to attack him. For much the same reason, again, traitors were singled out for assassination a question to which we shall return in the next chapter. The taking of life was also the rebels' way of dealing with those who met their force by force either as individuals or as members of official or private armies. 'I ordered', said Kanhu, the Santal leader, 'that all men who fought were to be killed and all who did not fight to be spared.' It was as if he looked upon this particular type of violence as an extension of the peasant war itself and as a measure vital to the defence of the rebellion against efforts to undermine it by counter-violence.

By contrast retributive killing did not derive its rationale from the actuality of a rebellion but from its context. It had its referent in no current project of turning the rural world upside down but only in the insurgent's past, his prehistory as the subaltern for whom no oppression had been too much to put up with. Murder was thus charged with the memory of wrongs suffered. More often than not the killers and the killed were related as polar elements in the power structure of rural society, as its upper and nether millstones so to say as landlord and tenant, usurer and debtor, upper-caste and untouchable, and so on. The servant killing the master epitomized the reversal indexed by this violence. The motif occurred again and again. A bondman beheaded his master when the latter was found in his hiding place by a party of Kols during a raid on his village. Jagannath Sirdar joined the hool to slay his former master, the notorious Dindayal Ray of Pakur, and so on. The excessive cruelty of many of these executions was a measure of the bitterness which inspired them. A veritable settling of accounts, the violence was almost codified in some instances each offending limb of a landlord or moneylender being chopped off by the Santals as punishment for a particular offence of which it was an instrument ('With those offending fingers you counted your interest and ill-begotten wealth!') and each of the seven cuts inflicted by the Kols on any oppressive sud standing for 'the dissatisfaction with some particular tax or duty imposed on them'.

If oppression was what made the peasants wreak vengeance by murder and there was indeed a great deal of oppression around, why were they so sparing in their use of this type of violence? The answer must be sought in two aspects of rebel consciousness namely, its inertia and its negativity. It was not a liberated consciousness. On the contrary, with all its attempt to reverse the old relations of power it was still trapped in the old culture. That culture imbued the peasant with a sense of reverence for the body of anyone ranked as his superior. For the form of the human body is a symbol, as Hegel said, and its symbolism in the highly semioticized world of traditional India was very potent indeed. What was it there that 'ultimately and firmly' distinguished one person from others, we could ask taking a cue from Marx and answer with him, 'The *body*'. There, like in all semi-feudal societies, 'certain dignities, and indeed the highest social dignities' were, as he put it, 'the *dignities of certain bodies predestined by birth*'. Hence in all relationships between the *uttara* (superior) and the *adhara* (inferior) an acknowledgement of the dignity, amounting almost to sanctity, of the former's person was a condition of the latter's subalternity.

This was formalized at Akbar's court by His Majesty's 'mode of showing himself' in the daily ritual of *darsan* 'when', according to

*Ain*73, 'people of all classes can satisfy their eyes and hearts, with the light of his countenance'. This was formalized, too, in his own way by the landlord and headman (Gauda) of a small Andhra village where his infant son's 'mode of showing himself' was a part of his grooming for succession to his father's authority as well as an affirmation of the latter. 'The Gauda's son is eighteen months old', wrote a visiting anthropologist: 'Every morning, a boy employed by the Gauda carries the Gauda's son through the streets of Gopalpur. When the boy is not available to perform this service, a poor relation brought to Gopalpur for that purpose, carries the child. When he is carried along the street, the old women stop their ceaseless grinding and pounding of grain and gather around. The Carpenter puts down his tools.' For the Gauda's son, no less than for the Grand Mughal, 'his *body* is his *social* right'. This body was still sacrosanct to the peasant even when he was angry and armed. To raise his hands against it was a sin a notion he shared with his oppressors. As a Chamar beaten up by his Thakur told Cohn, 'How could I have struck him back? He is my Thakur and a Thakur is respected like a father'. Thus an illiterate and untouchable villager spoke in the authentic voice of the sacred texts of the Hindus to assimilate his landlord's authority to his father's after that paradigm by which all superordinate authority was assimilated, in the Dharma to that of the King, the Brahman, the father, the guru and so on. It was the voice of the ruling culture and even an insurgent was not ready to defy it. His violence stopped short of killing not out of compassion but because of his failure to overcome fully the spiritual conditions of his subalternity.

But this was not entirely a matter of the inertia of the old culture putting the brakes on murder. It did not figure as a principal modality of struggle also because insurgency did not need it to achieve its general aim. It was not yet equipped with a mature and positive concept of power, hence of an alternative state and a set of laws and codes of punishment to go with it. This is not to deny of course that some of the more radical of the rural revolts of our period did in fact anticipate power at least to a degree and expressed it, albeit feebly and crudely, in terms of a rough justice and punitive violence laced with vengeance. Beyond that however the project in which the rebels had involved themselves was predominantly negative in orientation. Its purpose was not so much to reconstitute the world as to reverse it. This could be done quite effectively indeed by destroying and defying any of that entire range of objects and norms which represented the authority of the elite no less than did their bodies. In a land where the peasant could wreck his superordinate enemy's prestige simply by walking past his house with an umbrella on his head or by substituting *tu* for *vous* in an argument with him, why should insurgency need killing to make its point except in battle?

11

NEGATION IN INSURGENCY

Introduction

It was they who made him aware of his place in society as a measure of his distance from themselves a distance expressed in differentials of wealth, status and culture. His identity amounted to the sum of his subalternity. In other words, he learnt to recognize himself not by the properties and attributes of his own social being but by a diminution, if not negation, of those of his superiors.

All the force of the ruling ideologies, especially that of religion, imbued the peasant with this negative consciousness and pandered to it by extolling the virtues of loyalty and devotion, so that he could be induced to look upon his subservience not only as tolerable but almost covetable. There were ancient cults which fostered *bhakti* 'the basic need in feudal ideology', according to Kosambi to make total dedication to one's superiors. divine as well as human, a matter of spiritual commitment. There were the consecrated memories of legendary low-born servants who had died for their high-caste masters. In Bengal, Kalu the Dom was immortalized in a cycle of late medieval ballads composed in honour of the deity, Dharma. Born to one of the most 'unclean' of Hindu castes, he was slain in battle while trying to help his lord recover some lands usurped by a rival magnate. Then there was the Poleya who, according to a legend of the Coorgs, was so grieved at his master's death that he committed suicide by throwing himself into the latter's funeral pyre and earned his reward posthumously in the form of an offering of food and drink in a ritual of ancestor worship. And in many of the Nayar taravads of Malabar propitiatory rites of the same kind were addressed to the spirit of faithful serfs who had died similarly broken-hearted at the loss of their patrons or in the course of heroic ventures to defend the prestige and properties of their owners as did the Tiyyar servant in Kottayam who, so goes the story, first killed his master at his bidding and then courted death fighting rather than be captured and converted to Islam by raiders who had come with Tipu Sultan's army in the 1780s.

Thus the power of ideas and the circumstances corresponding to them made the peasant sensitive to the distance which separated him from the pillars of that society, a distance regarded by him as ;almost the natural condition of his existence. Indeed, the authority of all superordinate classes and groups was secure only so far and as long as he was reconciled to that condition. However, paradoxically enough, his revolt against that authority, when the hour struck, derived much of its strength from the same awareness. Taken by itself this did not of course constitute a mature and fully evolved class consciousness. Yet it would be wrong not to regard this as the very beginning of that consciousness. Gramsci helps us to grasp its precise moment in characterizing this 'merely as the first glimmer of such consciousness, in other words, merely as the basic negative, polemical attitude'. Indeed, with all his warning against overestimating. it, he acknowledges its importance as a necessary; beginning. 'The lower classes, historically on the defensive,' he writes, '*can only achieve self-awareness via a series of negations*, via their consciousness of the identity and class limits of their enemy.'

This consciousness has a historical tendency to 'come to the surface' locally among some of the more radical sections of the rural masses long before being generalized on a national scale in any country. This can be seen from Hilton's study of the peasant movements in late medieval Europe. In spite of all dissimilarities in other respects, 'there was one prominent feature which they had in common', he says: 'the emergence, among some of the participants, of a consciousness of class. It was, however, a negative class consciousness in that the definition of class which was involved was that of their enemies rather than of themselves: in other words, the nobility.'

Our study of peasant insurgency in colonial India too must take such negation as its point of departure. This is not only because of the precedence due to it as that form of rebel consciousness which anticipated others but also because it provides us with an insight into some of the more important principles governing the practice of rebellion. These principles have not always received the attention they merit. The bustle and panic caused by agrarian violence has often been responsible for highlighting its drama rather than its logic and consistency. However, once the glare of burning mansions died down and the eye got used to the facts of an uprising, one could see how far from haphazard it had been.

The negations characteristic of insurgency in our period were worked out in terms of two sets of principles. The first, which we shall call discrimination, was realized in its most explicit form in the violence selectively directed by the peasants at particular targets. The frequency and regularity with which this occurred make no sense except as symptoms of wilful commission. The pattern shows up most obviously of course in those cases where the rebels had only one or two clearly specified foes to deal with, such as the notorious Deby Sinha of Rangpur or the indigo planters of lower Bengal, so that the uprisings of 1783 and 1860 could be clearly seen as having their edge turned respectively against the kacharis and the factories. However, even in the course of violence that was more comprehensive in scope, its protagonists often made their emphasis speak for itself. It was this which enabled some of the local administrators in Uttar Pradesh to discern an element common to all the many-sided disturbances in that province in 1857. 'Here as in other parts of the country', wrote the magistrate of Muzaffarnagar, 'the Buneahs and Mahajuns were in the majority of cases the victims', an observation echoed by his opposite number in Hamirpur for his own district when he said that 'the great feature' of the *émeute* there had been 'the universal ousting of all bankers, Buniyas, Marwarees, etc. from landed property by whatever means they acquired it, whether at auction, by private sale or otherwise'.

Concentration such as this was all the more remarkable for the care with which it chose its object and demonstrated how clearly the peasants distinguished between enemies and allies. The definition of friend and foe could of course vary from one insurrection to another and occasionally between groups of protagonists within the same event depending on the conditions in which they operated and the levels of their consciousness. However, the fact that a discrimination of this order entered into insurgent practice at all, must be understood as indicative of its rationale. Hilton brings out this element of 'conscious hostility' in his observations on the Jacquerie of 1358. 'Without any declaration of aims', he says, 'its existence could be concluded from the fact that the objects of the peasants' attacks were *exclusively* knights, squires and ladies along with the castles in which they lived.' Emphasis added. The Peasant War in Germany, too, witnessed much selective violence of this kind. During the sack of Weinsberg in April 1525 Metzler and Hipler made their men limit plunder strictly and exclusively to the properties of the clergy and to those of the Keeper of the Wine-cellar, the Bailiff, the City Clerk and the Mayor among the burghers. All others of the latter category were spared on the condition that they provided the victors with food and drink and looked after their wounded so long as they were there. To Engels this phenomenon was important enough to be picked out of the tangled history of that great revolt. The insurgents, he observed, had won over the burghers of Heilbronn to their side, so that when the town capitulated to them, it was '*only* the possessions of the clergy and the Teutonic Order' which were singled out for the customary pillage. 'They *only* wanted the clergy, their *enemies*', according to Zimmermann on whose documentation Engels based his account. Lefebvre, too, made it a point to emphasize how in the course of the jacqueries of the French Revolution the peasants used all possible means to wreck the properties of those opposed to the Third Estate, but often stopped short of arson, although that would have been simpler and more effective. They were 'reluctant to use it [i.e. fire] because they naturally feared that it might get out of control and spread to the village'. He cites an occasion when a crowd proceeded to destroy and burn a seigneur's farms and residence 'in a very methodical way carefully evacuating anything belonging to the farmers and the servants'. According to him, 'all the peasant revolts followed this pattern'.

The Indian experience agrees with this pattern to some extent. In the course of the popular disturbances following the Mutiny in Aligarh, for instance, the crowds plundered European properties with much thoroughness but did relatively less damage to those of the natives. Again, nothing illuminates more the character of the Kol and Santal uprisings of 1832 and 1855 respectively than the well-known fact that in both instances the peasants spared the tribal population and concentrated their attack on the non-tribal 'outsiders' *suds* and *dikus*, as they called them. 'Throughout the whole of this devastation', wrote one administrator to another about the first of these events, 'not a single Cole's life was sacrificed nor a home belonging to them destroyed except by accident, and self-interested motives induced the Insurgents to exempt Blacksmiths Gwalas and occasionally the manufacturers of earthen vessels (who were not Coles) from their indiscriminate slaughter.' Indeed, as grudgingly acknowledged in these words, the limits of solidarity and antagonism were specified by the distinctions made between those elements of the non-tribal population to whom the rebels were positively hostile, e.g. landlords and moneylenders, and those subaltern classes and castes who lived and worked with them in the same rural communities and were treated as loyal allies. Such discrimination about which official notice was taken to the effect that 'in many villages the houses of Mahajuns were burnt & those of ryots spared' by the Santals, showed where ethnicity stopped and an incipient form of class consciousness began. Conversely, the selective violence of the Kunbi peasantry in Poona and Ahmadnagar districts in 1875 testified to a modification of class consciousness by localism. 'The Marwari and Gujur sowkars were almost *exclusively* the victims of the riots', wrote the Commissioners appointed to inquire into those disturbances, 'and in villages where sowkars of the Brahmin and other castes shared the money lending business with Marwaris it was usual to find that *the latter only* were molested.'

Negative consciousness of this type had a tendency to extend its domain by a process of analogy and transference, which we shall call its *atideœa* function (following the usage in Sanskrit grammar and linguistics). A detail of the Swing movement in England may help to illustrate this. The violence of the rural proletariat on this occasion had only threshing machines as its initial object. However, this was soon generalized in two ways-first, as an attack on all farming implements including iron ploughs, harvesters, chaff-cutters, hay-makers and seed and winnowing machines, and then, as an attack on industrial machines of all kinds such as those used in foundries, sawmills, woollen manufactories and so on. The rioters themselves made the point quite clearly when in order to justify the destruction of a winnowing machine 'they said it must go, as it was a machine, and it was broke to pieces',20 or as one of their leaders declared, after his men had wrecked all the machinery in two neighbouring mills one that made threshing-machines and the other sacking 'they had come from miles above London and were going as far down the country as there was any machinery, to destroy it'. Violence extended thus by *atideœa* from one particular implement to all other implements in the same class and from one class of machinery to another.

The logic of this extension applies to people as much as to things. It is indeed usual for a rebellion to broaden its thrust as it develops and include among its targets groups and individuals who may have no part at all in causing the outbreak. This implies, first, that under such circumstances peasant violence may tend to direct itself against all members of a given class of enemies without pausing to sort out the 'good' individuals among them from the 'bad', and secondly, that it may tend to hit out against all classes and sections of the population hostile to the peasantry, irrespective of whichever of these might have been the rebels' initial object of attack. This is why in 1830 the incendiary's torch did not spare the barns and outhouses of a Surrey farmer although (as *The Times* ruefully observed after the event) he 'neither used a thrashing machine nor even employed strangers to work in his employment' two practices the labourers were known most to hate. For, by the time this act of arson was committed in the autumn of that year the battle lines had been drawn far too clearly to induce any leniency among the village poor towards even the least oppressive of their enemies in south-eastern England. The same tendency, the negative character of which was emphasized by Trotsky when he described it as a 'wave of class hatred', was conspicuous in the peasant riots of the Russian Revolution of 1905 too. 'Estates were sacked almost regardless of the existing relations between peasants and individual landowners', he wrote: 'if the estates of reactionary landlords were wrecked, so were those of liberals.' The jacqueries triggered off by the revolt of the sepoys in 1857 provided a good many Indian parallels of this phenomenon. When, for instance, the villagers in Allahabad district responded to the mutiny at the *sadar* station by their own uprising, they made little distinction in their attack between official and non-official institutions. 'The very asylums built from charitable funds provided by the Christian population for the relief of the people were burnt down and demolished with as much ill-will as our public offices', wrote a bewildered and somewhat pained British magistrate reporting the holocaust to his superior.

The same official report also testified to the other and even more significant, because radical, aspect of the *atideœa* function, that is, to the manner in which rebel violence tended to spread analogically developing its initial attack on any particular element among the peasants' enemies into a general attack on all or most of them, a process by which insurgency came to permeate an entire domain constituted by such authorities, institutions and groups as were hostile to the subaltern population. Thus the rebellion of 1857 in Allahabad extended soon beyond the barracks where it had originated and hurtled against everything which, like the army, represented the authority of the Raj. A prison, a *chowkidar*'s post, a factory, a railway station, 'every house or factory belonging to Europeans and every building however large or however insignificant', in fact everything '*with which we are connected*', became, according to the local magistrate, an object of pillage, destruction and arson in the city and the surrounding countryside. The pattern occurs again and again in the course of all the major uprisings during our period. Whatever might have been the immediate cause of any particular outbreak, the rebels almost invariably enlarged the scope of their operations to include all British 'connections' all white military and civilian officials as well as non-official whites such as planters, missionaries, railwaymen, etc.; all seats of official power such as courts, jails, police stations, treasuries and so on as well as non-official building, (e.g. factories, bungalows, churches, etc.) symbolizing British presence. The evidence on this point is far too abundant and accessible to require citing here in detail. One has only to recall the threat to the East India Company's headquarters at Rangpur and its granaries at Bhowaniganj during the dhing of 1783, the attacks on churches and clergymen during the Birsaite ulgulan, the Santal hostilities towards railway engineers and planters during the hool, and the numerous raids on *thanas*, jails and public offices in all these instances and at the time of the Mutiny to realize the almost universal tendency of the more militant peasant uprisings to take on the entire range of British authority in both its official and non-official sectors.

Generalized violence of this kind was not necessarily delimited by ethnicity. The whites were not alone in being subjected to it. On the contrary, it was not unusual for attacks on government property and personnel and Europeans directly associated with these to develop into attacks on the principal native collaborators of the Raj as well. For, no matter which one of their three main oppressors sarkar, sahukar or zamindar-was the first to bear the initial brunt of a jacquerie in any particular instance, the peasants often showed a remarkable propensity to extend their operations widely enough to include among their targets the local representatives of one or both of the other groups too. Many of the more powerful events of our period testify to this. Titu Mir's bidroha in Barasat and the series of Moplah rebellions in nineteenth-century Malabar started off as anti-landlord struggles but culminated as campaigns against the Raj itself. Conversely, the movements of the Farazis and the indigo ryots against European planters often developed into resistance to rack-renting and other forms of zamindari despotism. The Kol insurrection of 1832 in Chota Nagpur had landlords and moneylenders among the suds as its initial objects of hostility but ended up as a war against the Company's government itself. And, conversely again, the Birsaite ulgulan launched with the declared aim of liberating the Mundas from British rule made no secret of its hatred for banias and mahajans as it progressed.

Transference of this kind was most conspicuous in the course of the peasant uprisings of the period of the Mutiny. Inspired by and foil to a revolt in the armed forces threatening the very foundation of the regime, these jacqueries were directed as much against the government as against moneylenders. Indeed, the expression of anti-bania hatred was widespread enough to be regarded by many contemporaries as the principal aspect of these disturbances. Yet as Stokes has shown by a careful investigation of this phenomenon in Uttar Pradesh, there was little in the incidence of usurious transactions to justify the extent and intensity of the aggression against their protagonists in the regions where this occurred most in 1857-8. The attacks on mahajans and auction-purchasers, he concludes, were motivated less by economic than political considerations. The importance of this finding can hardly be exaggerated. For the symbiosis of sarkar, sahukar and zamindar was a political fact rooted in the very nature of British power in the subcontinent. By directing his violence against all three members of this trinity irrespective of which one of them provoked him to revolt in the first place, the peasant displayed a certain understanding of the mutuality of their interests and the power on which this was predicated. However feeble and incipient, this represented the emergenece of a political consciousness, even if no more than its very, 'first glimmer'.

An *atidæœa* function of the Santal rebellion of 1855 may be recalled here to illuminate further this particular type of rebel perception. As is well known, violence spread in this case with the utmost speed from targets identified with the colonial administration and the whites to those representing the authority of landlords and moneylenders, though by no means in the same sequence in all regions. The Santals made it obvious that they intended to spare no person or property associated with sarkar, sahukar or zamindar, and thus established within a matter of days a well-defined domain of insurgency in which their operations had a free play between all three categories of their foes and were permuted in all possible ways. That this was not just the work of some kind of 'instinct' characteristic of primitive rebels' but followed from the logic of a certain understanding anti will, is easily documented. For it conforms fully to the view that Sido and Kanhu, the leaders of the insurrection, had of their enemies and which they had recorded in their historic parwana sent out long before the outbreak of the insurrection. 'The Mahajuns have committed a great sin', it declared. 'The Sahibs and the amlah have made everything bad, in this the Sahibs have sinned greatly. Those who tell things to the Magistrate and those who investigate cases for him, take 70 or 80 Rs. with great oppression in this the Sahibs have sinned. On this account the Thacoor has ordered me saying that the country is not the Sahibs.' There is some evidence here of a grasp, however weak and crudely stated, of the linkage between the indigenous exploiters and the colonial authorities with the emphasis weighted slightly albeit very slightly in favour of the suggestion that the transactions of the former were contingent on the power of the latter.

It will be wrong not to see in all this the imprint of a consciousness trying to identify some of the basic elements of economic exploitation and the political superstructure which legitimized these. However, to overestimate its lucidity or depth will be equally ill-advised. For it is still a rather hesitant, inchoate and disjointed perception, not unlike the discourse which registered it. It describes empirically some aspects of the peasant's conditions of existence, but falls far short of conceptualizing the structure of authority which made such conditions possible. 'The only form in which the State is perceived', one could say after Gramsci, is in terms of officialdom of the sahibs. This characteristic expression of a negative consciousness on the insurgent's part matched its other symptom, that is, his self-alienation. He was still committed to envisaging the coming war on the Raj as the project of a will independent of himself and his own role in it as no more than instrumental. 'Kanoo and Seedu Manjee are not fighting. The Thacoor himself will fight', stated the parwana in which the authors did not recognize even their own voice, but heard only that of God: 'This is the order of the Thacoor.'

The other modality of negation characteristic of insurgency consists of the peasants' attempt to destroy or appropriate for themselves the signs of the authority of those who dominate them. The inversion which is necessarily brought about by such a process has been frequent and widespread enough to constitute a stereotyped figure of speech in many languages. 'Those who used to rank lowest now rank above everybody else; and declared. 'The Sahibs and the amlah have made everything bad, in this the Sahibs have sinned greatly. Those who tell things to the Magistrate and those who investigate cases for him, take 70 or 80 Rs. with great oppression in this the Sahibs have sinned. On this account the Thacoor has ordered me saying that the country is not the Sahibs.' There is some evidence here of a grasp, however weak and crudely stated, of the linkage between the indigenous exploiters and the colonial authorities with the emphasis weighted slightly albeit very slightly in favour of the suggestion that the transactions of the former were contingent on the power of the latter.

It will be wrong not to see in all this the imprint of a consciousness trying to identify some of the basic elements of economic exploitation and the political superstructure which legitimized these. However, to overestimate its lucidity or depth will be equally ill-advised. For it is still a rather hesitant, inchoate and disjointed perception, not unlike the discourse which registered it. It describes empirically some aspects of the peasant's conditions of existence, but falls far short of conceptualizing the structure of authority which made such conditions possible. 'The only form in which the State is perceived', one could say after Gramsci, is in terms of officialdom of the sahibs. This characteristic expression of a negative consciousness on the insurgent's part matched its other symptom, that is, his self-alienation. He was still committed to envisaging the coming war on the Raj as the project of a will independent of himself and his own role in it as no more than instrumental. ' Kanoo and Seedu Manjee are not fighting. The Thacoor himself will fight', stated the parwana in which the authors did not recognize even their own voice, but heard only that of God: 'This is the order of the Thacoor.'

The other modality of negation characteristic of insurgency consists of the peasants' attempt to destroy or appropriate for themselves the signs of the authority of those who dominate them. The inversion which is necessarily brought about by such a process has been frequent and widespread enough to constitute a stereotyped figure of speech in many languages. 'Those who used to rank lowest now rank above everybody else; and dread of the inversive process was to be systematized later into a chiliastic image of total cataclysm in the *Vâyupurânòam*. It envisaged a great upheaval (*samkshovah*) with the advent of Kali at the epoch's end (*yugânta*). Among the many reversals characteristic of that topsy-turvy age, Brahmans, it was predicted, would behave like Sudras and Sudras like Brahmans, kings would take to the vocation of thieves and thieves to that of kings, women would be faithless to their husbands and servants to their masters.

It is precisely in order to prevent such inversions from occurring in real life that the dominant culture in all traditional societies allows these to be simulated at regular calendric intervals, and in so far as such a culture is almost invariably mediated by religion, the reversals condoned, in fact enjoined, by it, are acted out as sacred rituals. Hence the religiosity associated with such prescriptive inversions everywhere no matter whether the protagonists are Europeans involved in Shrove Tuesday carnivals or Zulu women in ceremonies meant to propitiate the goddess Nomkubulwana. The vast literature on the subject shows how on such privileged occasions the 'structural inferiors' in the given societies enjoy the licence to indulge in rites of status reversal with respect to their superordinates. Servants act like masters, women like men, children like grown-ups, juniors like seniors, and so on. 'Degree, priority and place' are not observed so long as these festivals of contraries continue and most of the visual and verbal signs of authority and obedience which represent social morality are mutually substituted for the time being. Yet, as all observers agree, the outcome of such prescriptive inversion is not to destroy or even weaken a social order, but to buttress it. It is of course possible that on some of these occasions the liminality of the participants and their particular circumstances might bring about a sudden switching of codes turning what is intended as a mock rebellion into a real one, a festival into an insurrection.

For the liminal, as Turner has emphasized, is 'necessarily ambiguous' and tends to 'elude or slip through the network of classifications that normally locate states and positions in cultural space'. Hence the not too rare correspondence between sacred days and insurgency as witnessed, for instance, by the incursion of Wat Tyler's men into London on the morning of Corpus Christi, 13 June 1381, the beginning of the great series of peasant revolts in Germany during Fastnacht 1525, the conversion of a carnival featuring Mère Folle and her Infanterie into a riot in masquerade against the royal tax officials in Dijon in 1630, the coincidence of some of the jacqueries of 1789 in France with Sundays, feast days, etc. as mentioned by Lefebvre and the threat of a massive uprising in Bombay during Muharram and Diwali in the year of the Mutiny. However, it is important to remember that such cases, numerous as they are, occur in spite of prescriptive inversion and represent the failure of what is meant and indeed has generally proved to be a safety-valve device. For the purpose of such rituals is clearly to empty rebellion of its content and reduce it into a routine of gestures in order to reinforce authority by feigning defiance. Gluckman's observation about the Zulu ceremony mentioned above could indeed apply to the entire genre. 'This particular ritual', he wrote, 'by allowing people to behave in normally prohibited ways, gave expression, in a reversed form, to the normal rightness of a particular kind of social order.' Some of the more permissive Hindu festivals may be said fully to bear this out.

Take, for instance, the Teyyam festival as celebrated in parts of Malabar. This centres around the shrines of the female deity

Bhagavadi, which are attached to the landowning and politically as well as economically dominant Nayar taravads. The propitiatory rituals are, for each taravad, officiated by one of its lower-caste servants who puts on a mask at a particular point of the ceremonial process and is possessed by a malevolent ghost of the *teyyam* (derived from the Sanskrit word *deva*, 'god' type. While in this state, the servant can and often does adopt an aggressive or authoritative attitude towards his superiors, demands gifts and voices threats and blessings all as an instrument of the spirit of the dead working through him. And when at the end of the ceremony the oracle takes off his mask and reverts to his menial status, he receives a fee for the ritual service rendered and gets on with his other customary duties. Kathleen Gough, to whom we owe this account, has stated the importance of such prescriptive reversal in emphasizing the traditional authority of the Nayar landed gentry over the subaltern groups in their villages. 'For the low caste officiant', she writes, 'these festivals permit a limited, stylized expression of aggression and a temporary assumption of authority towards their high caste masters. At the same time, the festivals underline both the interdependence between the castes, and ultimately, the lower castes' permanent, secular role as submissive servants.'

A very similar dialectic of ritual inversion and reinforcement of authority has been observed by Srinivas in his study of the Coorgs. Among them the Banna constitute an inferior caste whose traditional duty has been to serve aristocratic *okkas* as priests and oracles on certain ritual occasions. They are a polluting caste, so polluting indeed that at the annual festival of the deity Kakkot Achchayya a Brahman priest carrying the idol risks defiling it as well as himself even by catching a glimpse of the Banna oracle. Normally the latter is regarded as too unclean to have access to the central hall of any uppercaste Coorg ancestral house, which must be kept in the highest state of ritual purity. Yet it is precisely in that central hall that he is made to preside over the prestigious ceremony of ancestor worship as its chief officiant. And when in the course of performing the propitiatory rites he is possessed by each of the ancestral spirits in turn, he feels free not merely to press sumptuous demands for food and drink on his landlord hosts but even to admonish the head of the okka for neglecting the paddy, for not looking after his inheritance assiduously enough and generally for failing in his duties. 'As the temporary vehicle of the spirit of an ancestor he is entitled to say and do things which he normally would not dream of saying or doing.' But the licence is short-lived. Srinivas insists on the purely temporary character of such role reversal which does little to diminish, far less end, the structural cleavages in Coorg society. The same could be said also of the ritual elevation of the Poleya, one of the most impure and exploited of all castes in this region traditionally a caste of agrestic slaves who are required 'to exercise power over people belonging to the higher castes' during certain festivals, thereby 'compensating them for the low position they normally occupy in the caste structure'. In the event, however, it is not their inclusion in some festivals and its 'compensation-aspect' but their exclusion from most of these as indicative of their real, ineradicable state of degradation which emerges as the central fact of their existence. As at the end of the splendid oracular drama the Banna returns to his role as the musty repository of landlord family tradition, so after his exposure to a modicum of simulated authority in short sacred seasons the Poleya sinks back to his place at the bottom of Coorg society as its most disenfranchised member. The only purpose which the process of ritual inversion may be said to serve in either case is to affirm and make explicit at regular intervals the distance separating each of these subaltern groups from those who rule the villages.

What emerges clearly from these instances is the part played by religion in sacralizing the authority of the rural elites. But more than in any other festival this is made explicit in the celebration of Holi in the course of which these reversals are acted out with a vigour and on a scale as at no other occasion of the same kind. One of the most ancient of popular ceremonies in this ancient land, its origins go back to prehistoric times-to the late Stone Age according to some scholars long before the beginnings of feudalism. Yet when the latter came to be established in the subcontinent, brahmanical Hinduism, often so hostile to vestiges of the autochthonous culture, bent backwards to confer on it full shastric status. Having made a début in some of the later medieval Puranas it was already enfranchised as a sacred event in the sixteenth-century law-books of Raghunandana and Govindananda. And by the time British officials and American anthropologists had come to write about it, spanning roughly a century and a half between BuchananHamilton and McKim Marriott, it had settled down comfortably in its role as a *vrata* complete with fasting, bathing, puja and other concomitants of the Hindu ritual process. Hence nothing happens at this festival to upset society in spite of the seemingly radical *bouleversement* of the Holi schedule. The saturnalia, the systematic violation of structural distances between castes and classes, the defiance of rules governing interpersonal relationships between members of the family and community, the blatant undermining of private and public morality all of which feature in this ceremony, add up not to a disruption of the political and social order in the village but to its reinforcement. A great deal of verbal and physical violence, inflicted respectively by abusive speech and actual belabouring by cudgels, takes place on this occasion as all observers agree. But there is no punishment for it and yet the world is not turned upside down in spite of Manu's fear to the contrary. The impunity is, of course, deceptive. If the exercise of *danòdòa* is suspended, it is only because none of these stylized reversals constitutes a real transgression. Just as in Sanskrit grammar the injunction against any breach of rules is emphasized by the licence allowed to deviant usage in the holiest of all texts the Vedas *chandasi*, as Panini would put it ever so often turning aside from the rigour of his own great discourse so too does the ritual of inversion at Holi affirm the general legitimacy of spiritual and social sanctions against nonconformity by condoning the latter on one prescribed occasion. Its overall effect is 'the stressing, not the overthrowing of the principle of hierarchy through reversal, a process whereby it *remains* the structural vertebra of village life'.

But it is not the collusion between religion and authority which alone makes Holi, like other ceremonies of this type, so innocuous. Predictability which goes with tradition, has also a part to play in this. For all such festivals based on prescriptive inversion are necessarily *anticipated* by their protagonists and the local communities where they belong. They are a part of the cyclical rhythm of life in any society based on a stagnant economy, primitive technology and pre-capitalist culture. Such 'calendrical rites', as Turner calls this genre, 'are performed at well-delineated points in the annual productive cycle, and attest to the passage from scarcity to plenty (as at first fruits or harvest festivals) or from plenty to scarcity (as when the hardships of winter are anticipated and magically warded against)'. The Indian villager recognizes them as a fixture in the annual schedule of public celebrations. Co-ordinated closely with the farm calendar and the seasons they make up an established and irrevocable sequence. They are indeed almost as 'natural' to him as, for instance, is the order of transplanting in monsoon and harvesting in winter to the rice-growing peasant of Bengal. Religion helps to promote this 'natural' look of most folk festivals and intercalate them with the seasonal routines of work on the land. It does so by, among other devices, inserting in their ritual procedure such markers as refer directly to agricultural products, many of them grown in the festival seasons. Hence the association that is there between the popular rituals of this type in each region and some of its principal crops of grain and fruit rice and coconut in the south and the east, wheat and barley in western Uttar Pradesh (UP) and Punjab, sugarcane in Bihar and eastern UP, mangoes in UP again, and so forth. It is this mediation by religion of the natural conditions of the peasant's labour and its products which makes the villager look upon these festivals as pre-ordained as the coming of the rains and the hoar-frost and agricultural operations dependent on them. This is why he is not taken by surprise at Holi or any other 'calendrical ritual' of prescriptive inversion. On the contrary, he anticipates it in every detail, if only because its conventions are all too familiar to him. Marriott's dramatic account of the beginning of the 'Feast of Love' as he witnessed it in a north Indian village should lead no one to believe that the natives, too, shared his sense of alarm and astonishment on that fateful night. For they had been coolly preparing for this sacred rumpus for some time, as the author himself indicates. As a matter of fact, organization for this particular event begins at least a month in advance, as another anthropologist reports from the same cultural region. In other words, ritual inversion stands for a continuity turned into sacred tradition by long recursive use under the aegis and inspiration of religion. As such, it represents the very antithesis of peasant insurgency.

For if the function of prescriptive reversal is to ensure the *continuity* of the political and moral order of society and *sacralize* it, that of peasant insurgency is to *disrupt* and *desecrate* it. In conditions governed by the norm of unquestioning obedience to authority, a revolt of the subaltern shocks by its relative entropy. Hence the suddenness so often attributed to peasant uprisings and the verbal imageries of eruption, explosion and conflagration used to describe it. What is intended by such usage in many languages and cultures is to communicate the sense of an unforeseen break, a sharp discontinuity. For while ritual inversions help to ensure the continuity of village society by allowing its upper and nether elements to change places at regular intervals and for strictly limited periods, the aim of peasant insurgency is to take it by surprise, put the existing power relation on its head and do so for good. As Christopher Hill has pointed out, the traditional foolery of Shrove Tuesday and the Feast of Fools used to serve as a safety-valve for medieval European society releasing tension and making the social order 'perhaps that much more tolerable', but 'what was new in the seventeenth century was the idea that the world might be *permanently* turned upside down'. It is this threat, real or imaginary, that it carries of a permanent subversion of the local hierarchies of power which distinguishes a peasant rebellion from the simulated upheavals discussed above.

Such radical subversion, this *real* turning of things upside down, which is only another name for rebellion, constitutes a semiotic break: it violates that basic code by which the relations of dominance and subordination are historically governed in any particular society. Indeed, there is no society where politics, like every other department of the superstructure, is not regulated by such a code. For, to paraphrase Barthes, man is busy everywhere all the time charging reality with meaning and setting up semiological systems by converting things into signs and attributing signification to what is perceived by the senses. However, the degree of semioticity varies according to whether the dominant culture of a society is more or less feudal in character. Juri Lotman's comments on the 'medieval type' (as against the 'enlightenment type') of Russian culture can help us to grasp this distinction:

> *The 'medieval' type is distinguished by its high semioticity. It not only tends to impart the character of a cultural sign to everything that has meaning in natural language, but proceeds from the assumption that everything is significant. For this type of code, meaning is the index of existence: nothing is culturally meaningless.*

This could be said of the medieval type of culture in all other countries too. Huizinga has shown how the authority of the sign permeated every aspect of Western thought during the Middle Ages. It is not only that icons and images figured prominently in religious expression, but politics, too, was highly semioticized. Liveries, colours, badges and party cries were conspicuously displayed in the course of public disputes, and notions of power and subalternity worked out in elaborates, and of symbols: for, 'feudal or hierarchic thought expresses the idea of grandeur by visible signs, lending to it a symbolic shape of homage paid kneeling, of ceremonial reverence'.

Feudal culture in the Indian subcontinent also waxed fat on signs systematized into codes of authority and deferential response. Two contrasting and yet complementary processes, one popular and the other elitist, went into the making of such codes. First, it was through centuries of recursive practice at the grassroot level that these signs congealed into a naive tradition. Secondly, the literati, especially the sacerdotal class, conceptualized and formalized these into a set of influential, indeed decisive, prescriptions constituting the vast shastric literature of the Smròtis. This priestly intervention went a long way to add a touch of sanctity to these codes. Even more importantly, perhaps, this helped to perpetuate and generalize them. For as Indian feudalism came of age, some of the more important sets of power relations, e.g. those between parents and sibling, guru and *œishya* (spiritual disciple), god and man, etc., emerged as paradigmatic in the sense that others were derived from or modelled on them, and it was the function of the Smròtis to record and confirm this development.The first of two devices generally employed for this purpose was grammatical, that is, to insert the Sanskrit equivalent of a sign of predication between a derivative and its paradigm. The copulae italicized in the following selection of sentences from the *Laws of Manu* offer a fair sample of such use:

- between [a ten-year old Brâhmanòa and a hundred-year-old Kshatriya] the BrâhmaG7a *is* the father.
- he [an infant king] *is* a great deity in human form.
- the wife of an elder brother *is* for his young (brother) the wife of a Guru.
- A maternal aunt, the wife of a maternal uncle, a mother-in-law, and a paternal aunt *are equal* to the wife of one's teacher.
- the (pupil) *shall consider* [his Vedic instructor] as his father and mother.
- Towards a sister of one's father and of one's mother, and towards one's own elder sister, one *must behave as towards* one's mother.
- a husband *must* be constantly *worshipped* as a god by a faithful wife.

The other device was structural and this operated in two ways. For one thing, it was as a matter of convention that each of these sacred texts reproduced the more important hierarchical prescriptions already laid down by its predecessors. This was true even of the most celebrated of all such compilations-the one quoted above, and it is clear from Bühler's edition of this work that large chunks from it had found their way into the later Smròtis.

Intertextuality helped thus to sustain tradition. However, the law-givers did not stop at that: they innovated too and went on adding to the range of some of the older paradigms with almost each recension. Thus, the paradigm guru/œishya which, according to Manu, subsumed no more than two other dyads represented by the guru's wife (if of the same caste) as the first term in one pair and by his son (if also a teacher) as that in the other, came to serve, some centuries later, for as many as sixty other relations in the *Vi?nòusmròti*. The outcome of such accretion was, in the long run, vastly to extend the scope of feudal authority by distributing its signs among the constituent paradigms. For as the latter had more and more relations stacked into them, their boundaries overlapped and they tended to merge into a generalized system signifying dominance and subordination in the society as a whole. By the time that colonialism came to establish itself firmly in the subcontinent, it had already at its disposal a well-developed semiotic apparatus which was partly inherited and partly its own invention. This was comprehensive enough to express its authority and that of the collaborating native elites. The subaltern masses too were familiar with this apparatus if only as those whose deference it was primarily designed to enforce and it is by throwing a spanner or two into the works from time to time that they learnt the rudiments of rebellion. Indeed, it would be quite in order to say that insurgency was a massive and systematic violation of those words, gestures and symbols which had the relations of power in colonial society as their significata.

This was perceived as such both by its protagonists and their foes. The latter were often quick to register their premonition of an uprising as a noise in the transmission of some of the more familiar signals of deference. A resident at Saharanpur on the eve of the Mutiny wrote thus of the anxieties of the white community there in those days: 'Early in the month of May, it became a subject of general remark with us, that the sepoys on duty at this station had thrown off their customary quiet and respectful behaviour, and had become forward, if not insolent; they paraded the public roads in parties, scarcely deigning to move to one side for a passing carriage, and singing at the highest pitch of their unmelodious voices, heedless of who heard them.' Later on, when the violence of that 'Red Year' had already reached its height, an army doctor on the run through the Gwalior countryside was to notice how 'every villager was uncivil, and the smile of respectful submission with which the European officer was to be greeted, was displaced by an angry scowl and haughty air towards the despicable Feringhee whose raj was at an end'. Quite clearly the British expected Indians to show their subservience to the governing race by a series of abject gestures and self-imposed restraints in their public behaviour. To make room for a sahib's landau on the road, to refrain from raising one's voice within his earshot, to smile submissively in his presence had all come to be regarded as 'customary', that is, as part of an established code signifying the power of the rulers over the ruled. Crowded streets, noisy singing, 'angry scowls and haughty air' were therefore suspect in the eyes of those who had the most to benefit from deference. They saw in these reversals not only an absence of the highly cherished collaboration between master and servant but, indeed, its replacement by hostility on the latter's part. There was no room for neutrality in this binary relationship: nonantagonism could turn only into antagonism.

Evidence of this kind is by no means rare, although it has not often been read as an index of a clash between rival consciousnesses. The signs of elite authority were so ubiquitous, so completely did they pervade the whole of our life under the Raj and so common indeed was their violation in the course of any popular disturbance that the historian's sensitivity to his *matériel* has been numbed with redundancy. Yet the character of the subaltern movements in India can hardly be grasped without specifying how dominance and subordination were represented in the ruling culture and their subjects forced to change places by the activity of the masses.

The class of signs most often and most instinctively reversed by insurgents and hence the least noticed in studies of insurgency is what constitutes, according to Bourdieu, an 'official language'. One of its functions, he writes, is to service 'the system of concepts by means of which the members of a given group provide themselves with a representation of their social relations (e.g. the lineage model or the vocabulary of honour)' and in this way it 'sanctions and imposes what it states, tacitly laying down the dividing line between the thinkable and the unthinkable, thereby contributing towards the maintenance of the symbolic order from which it draws its authority'. This was precisely how verbal deference functioned in colonial India, upholding semi-feudal relationships between old and young, male and female, high caste and low caste. For as Durkheim has observed, 'the word is [a] way of entering into relations with persons'. It was therefore essential that in a society which enjoined formal respect for senior kin on the part of their juniors theres should be some rules of speech strictly to govern such behaviour. The latter are forbidden from mentioning any of the elders by their proper names in many communities. 'This is because calling a person by name', says Srinivas with reference to the Coorgs, 'is not consistent with putting him in a position of respect.' With the Kamar of Chhatisgarh the range of interdiction included a man's father, mother ,grandparents, uncles, aunts, father-in-law and elder brothers. The ban was even more severe when applied to a woman. Particularly excluded were the names of her husband and some of his relatives. Transgression in the former respect could lead her to being put out of caste at least for some time, as was the custom among the Dhanwar of Madhya Pradesh even until a few decades ago.

If deference in speech mattered so much in demarcating kinship and sexual status, it did so to a still greater extent in the domain of caste and class relationship where feudal authority prevailed in its most explicit and effective form. Here again one can go far back into the past and find the elements of a linguistic discrimination between castes entrenched in some of the most ancient Sanskirt texts. Thus, a well-known Paninian rule was interpreted in such a way as to make the words standing for the four varnas replicate the varna hierarchy itself in a compound of the *dvandvasamâsa* class and put them together in their ascriptive order descending from Brahman to Sudra.

Again, Manu prescribed a series of syntactic variations on a string of words to make beggars identify themselves by their respective castes while calling for alms:

An initiated Brâhmana should beg, beginning (his request with the word) lady (*bhavati*); a Kshatriya, placing (the word) lady in the middle, but a Vaiœya, placing it at the end (of the formula).

This meant in effect that if ABC could be said to represent the sequence of the three words in the sentence *'Bhabati bhikshâm dehi'* as uttered by a Brahman beggar, a Kshatriya's call was to be construed as BAC and a Vaisya's BCA. Vocabulary, too, could serve for caste markers. Among acquaintances, for instance, phatic statements about each other's health had to include the word *kuœala* if addressed to a Brahman, *anâmaya* to a Kshatriya, *kshema* to a Vaisya and *anârogva* to a Sudra.

This tradition of using language as a register of caste status was still very much alive when Logan came across it in late nineteenth-century Malabar. A man's deference towards those ranked higher than himself was demonstrated in explicit verbal acknowledgements of his own inferiority. In any conversation he had to debase himself by stigmatizing whatever he had. Convention required him to refer to his own food not simply as rice, but as 'stony or gritty rice', his money as nothing more than 'copper cash', his house as a 'dungheap'. The indigenous perception of the structural cleavages in Malabar society of a century ago was recorded in a list of words for houses, as given by Logan. He wrote:

> *The* house *itself is called by different* names *according to the occupant's caste. The house of a Pariah is a* cheri, *while the agrestic slave the Cheraman lives in a* chala. *The blacksmith, the goldsmith, the carpenter, the weaver, etc., and the toddy-drawer (*Tiyan*) inhabit houses styled* pura *or* kudi; *the temple servant resides in a* variyan *or* pisharam *or* pumatham, *the ordinary Nayar in a* vidu *or* bhavanam, *while the man in authority of this caste dwells in an* idam; *the Raja lives in a* kovilakam *or* kottaram, *the indigenous Brahman (Nambutiri) in an* illam, *while his fellow of higher rank calls his house a* mana *or* manakkal.

This imprint of hierarchical divisions within a speech community is perhaps most clearly witnessed in diglossia. Ferguson (to whom we owe the initial use of this term in English) had noticed this phenomenon in the coexistence of 'high' and 'low' varieties of dialects in Arabic, Modern Greek, Swiss German and Haitian Creole. The first and more prestigious of the two was used for religious sermons, academic or political lectures, personal correspondence, newspaper editorials, etc., and the second for instructions to servants, waiters, workmen and clerks, for conversation among friends, colleagues and members of one's family, for use in folk literature, and so on. The same could be said of the native speakers of Java where, as Geertz has observed, the entire etiquette system is perhaps best summed up and symbolized in the way [they] used their language'. He goes so far as to say that 'in Javanese it is nearly impossible to say anything without indicating the social relationship between the speaker and the listener in terms of status and familiarity'.

Diglossia of this kind, if not quite on the same scale, has been a traditional feature of many of the linguistic communities in India. For instance, the well-entrenched caste division between Brahman and non-Brahman in parts of southern India has benn found to correspond to dialectal differences between Brahman and non-Brahman speech in Tamil and Kannada both with regard to vocabulary and to salient aspects of phonology and morphology. Class characteristics, too, are often branded on speech. Thus, in a Hindi-speaking village of northern India, Gumperz noticed how the distinction between *moti boli* (coarse speech) and *saf boli* (refined speech) stood for the social distance separating the 'poorer Rajputs and members of the lower castes who spend their days in physical labour' from the 'wealthier Rajputs, merchants and artisans, those who held clerical positions, and especially political leaders'. The speech of the untouchable sweeper, ranked lowest both in class and caste, diverged significantly from that of his high-caste master although he spent much of his time every day on chores around the latter's household.

There is yet another aspect to differences of this kind. The same speaker would often vary his speech between the 'high' and the 'low' dialectal modes depending on the solemnity of an occasion or the importance of the person addressed. Even a person of high status could use the moti boli in speaking to his servants or his junior kin, while he would almost invariably adopt the saf boli as a vehicle of discourse on elevated political or religious topics. Such switching between a formal and an informal style, corresponding by and large to a literary and a colloquial style, is common to speakers of many Indian languages including the two Dravidian varieties mentioned above. However, the freedom of switching from one to the other, especially from low to high, is far from absolute. Whether this is permitted at all, and if so to what extent, depends on the speaker's standing relative to the addressee's: this is all right when a person is speaking to his subordinates or equals, but anathema if the addressee happens to be of superior status. For the formal or high style is often closely associated with education, and in a land where most people are illiterate and far too poor to pay for schooling of any kind, this appears, by contrast, as an unmistakable sign of elite culture and authority. To adopt that mode of speech is therefore to claim an elite standing which is, of course, denied to the subaltern. This is why in a UP village the Chamar may not imitate Rajput speech 'for fear of incurring the displeasure of the higher castes' nor a Bengali peasant utter *sadhubhasha*, the characteristic speech of the bhadralok elite, as an indigo planter's dewan drives it home to an erring ryot in Dinabandhu Mitra *Neel-Darpan*.

Nothing demonstrates the involvement of language with authority more forcefully than the fact that usages such as these should be regarded as deviant, hence reprehensible. And it is precisely in order to prevent transgressions of this kind from occuring in real life that societies allow a degree of licensed violation of linguistic etiquette to be ritually acted out at calendrical intervals just as they provide for prescriptive rebellions as an insurance against real ones. This is why verbal aggression figured so prominently in carnivals which, as we have noticed above, functioned as a safety-valve for popular discontent in early modern Europe. Similarly, the ritual exchange of 'cathartic abuse' (*les insultes cathartiques*) by means of 'shameless ditties' (*chants qui point pas la honte*) sung by rival groups of men and women in the course of harvesting and mowing was regarded as a positively 'liberating' influence on the Dogon of western Africa. To the south of that continent the chanting of lewd songs was a customary part of a certain Zulu agricultural operations as well as of the ceremonial shifting of a Tsonga village site. 'The village is broken to pieces', it was said in justification of the latter, 'so are the ordinary laws. The insults which are taboo are now allowed.' In southern India much the same kind of indulgence was shown towards low-caste officiants at Nayar and Coorg propitiatory festivals: they could, on such occasions, utter the unspeakable in voicing pent-up grievances against their high-caste masters or even reprimanding them. And in the northern parts of the country the profusion of verbal abuse has always been a well-established feature of that most radical of all mock rebellions Holi.

However, indulgence such as this stopped as soon as a breach of verbal etiquette strayed beyond the previleged domain of ritual inversion. It amounted then to what Narada, an ancient Hindu law-giver, had defined as a form of *sâhasa,* that is, a crime of violence. The scale of penalties is revealing too. Though the precise amount of fines imposed on the offender is not quite the same in all the texts, they concur on one basic principle: that is, the lower the status of the speaker relative to that of the object of his insult the higher the penalty, which, as readers familiar with the Sm?tis will recognize, is the very reverse of what was prescribed in the case of 'crimes' of pollution. One could hardly improve on that as an instance of the correspondence between language and social hierarchy. Thus, as Manu says, the penalty for speaking ill of a Brahman increased with the hierarchical distance between him and the speaker: 100 *panòas* for a Kshatriya offender, 150-200 for a Vaisya, and corporal punishment (*vadham*) for a Sudra. The latter could be imposed in one of three ways depending on the precise character of the Sudra's crime; he could 'have his tongue cut out', or get 'an iron nail, ten fingers long thrust red-hot into his mouth', or have 'hot oil poured into his mouth and into his ears'.

This ancient recipe (by no means uniquely Indian) for dealing with verbal delinquency by destroying the organs of speech offers some idea of linguistic control in an authoritarian society. And what was sought to be controlled was not the spoken word alone, but also the zero sign of utterance that is, silence used formally and yet eloquently enough as 'a significant absence' of speech. It was as if language was made to operate in a state of Paninian *lopa* and was known only by virtue of its elision so that the ban imposed by custom on various kinds of discourse could announce and display the subordination of junior kin to senior, of wife to husband, of low caste to high caste and generally of the underdog to the elite. In Gujarat a Patidar youth was not to initiate conversation in the company of his elders, and as Beals found out in an Andhra village a young mail would be sharply rebuked if he tried to put in a word edgeways 'when big people are talking'. In the same village nuptial songs would insist that to 'keep silent in your husband's house' was a part of a young bride's novitiate. And silence was a sign of subordination to authority in other spheres too. In Orissa, a Bauri untouchable was not to speak to a high caste person until spoken to, while in a UP village 'one frequently finds it lower-caste individual sitting or standing at a slight distance from a higher group engaged in discussion, listening to what is said, but not participating'. In parts of southern India a servant would cover his mouth while receiving his master's command in a sort of metalinguistic acknowledgement of the latter's power over himself. In Bengal a landlord would it an affront if a peasant were to speak up to him. When Abu Molla, the hapless tenant-cultivator in Mir Mosharraf Hosein's play, Jamidar-Darpan, pleads his inability to pay a fine arbitrarily imposed by the wicked zamindar, the latter has a fit of temper not so much because of what is said but because it is a subordinate talking back. 'Shut up, you son of a pig', he shouts; 'How dare you open your mouth and utter anything in my presence! Take him away at once. Take him away'.

In that play the poor ryot'sverbal protest is not followed up by any militant act of resistance to his oppressor. But when a real uprising takes place and turns things upside down, the norms of verbal deference too are demolished together with the authority structures corresponding to them. There has never been an occasion of this kind when the peasant did not desecrate language either by direct abuse addressed to his superiors or by adopting the latter's mode of speech and thereby breaking into the hallowed precincts of elite culture. 'Violent, even ferocious, language used by rioting groups' was a prominent feature of the agricultural labourers' revolt in England in 1830. And it was all a part of the rebellious self-assertion of the Hunan peasantry in 1927 that, as Mao Tse-tung reported at the time, 'not a day passes but they drum some harsh, pitiless words of denunciation into these [evil] gentry's ears'.

There is hardly an instance of open and violent conflict between Indian villagers of different castes or classes that does not lower and often cross the threshold of verbal etiquette. The terms of an altercation as recorded by Freeman in an Oriya village bring this out. The exchange of insults here between an untouchable farm hand of the Bauri caste and his landowning, Brahman master reaches a climax making the latter scream, 'This wife's-brother Bauri boy speaks like a king. Has your face gone up, as if proud, or what?' Clearly, the unspeakable has been spoken and a social distance measured out in words or denoted by their absence, violated. This however was merely a quarrel between two individuals involving no physical assault at all. A great deal more can and does happen when violent disputes involving large masses of the local population break out in any particular village or region. The abuses, insults and, generally speaking, breaches in the norm of social discourse are often far too numerous and figure far too integrally in such cases to be noticed and reported on their own. Indulgence in 'bad' language is taken for granted on these occasions. Indeed the violence against person and property dominates events of this kind to such an extent as to make verbal violence relatively unimportant for purposes of administrative or judicial intervention. Since official records constitute the principal source of our information about such conflicts, it is easily understood why the Kautilyan category of vâkpârushyam (verbal violence) had so little to do with the historical evidence on rural crimes under the Raj. Yet one can perhaps make up for this lacuna to some extent by recalling some of the idealized accounts of peasant violence in nineteenth-century literature. Take, for peasant Act III, Scene 3 of *Neel-Darpan* where Torap, the rebel peasant, confronts the white planter and beats him up to the accompaniment of a shower of abuse describing the latter variously as wife's-brother, as a dog and a thief insults which under conditions other than insurgency would be addressed, the other way round, by planter to peasant. This linguistic inversion was homologous to the reversal brought about by the 'blue mutiny' in the relationship which had existed until then between the indigo factories and the rural masses in the Bengal districts dominated by them.

A conspicuous aspect of this verbal inversion, as anyone familiar with the text of this play would notice, is Torap's use of the intimate, hence in this case derogatory, pronoun *tui* and its derivatives rather than the reverential *apni*, in addressing his superordinate foe. These Bengali words correspond respectively to the French *tu* (*T*) and *vous* (*V*), and stand for what has been described as the 'nonreciprocal power semantic'. According to this notion the more powerful of any two interlocutors says *T* and receives *V*, all relations such as 'older than', 'parent of', 'employer of', 'stronger than', 'nobler than' and other hierarchical expression which can be assimilated to these being subsumed for the purpose of this generalization under the term 'more powerful than'. Brown and Gilman who have done much to investigate the *T-V* index of authority in many cultures, past and present, have observed that it is 'associated with a relatively static society in which power is distributed by birthright and is not subject to much redistribution'. They have situated it historically in the feudal and manorial systems of medieval Europe and identified it as a marker of 'caste difference' between the black native and the white colonialist in French Africa. In post-colonial India they found 'this truly feudal pronominal pattern', part of a long-standing tradition. still largely operative in the *T* - *V* expressions used in the Gujarati and Hindi languages nonreciprocally between elder brother and younger brother as well as between husband and wife. The series could of course be extended to the entire range of power relations including those of caste and class in many of the other Indian speech communities too.

When the feudal or semi-feudal authority structure of a society like any of these is overturned or seriously challenged by insurgency, the conventional use of *T* - *V* as a particularly sensitive register of existing power relations comes under attack at the same time. The French Revolution has provided us with a classic instance of such verbal' *bouleversement*. A speaker at a session of the new parliament in 1793 condemned the asymmetric deployment of these pronouns as an expression of '*l'csprit de fanatisme, d'orgueil. et de féodalité*' and the Committee for the Public Safety 'ordered a universal reciprocal *T*'. For some time the mutual *tu* became a sort of linguistic badge of revolutionary citizenship and when Robespierre addressed the president of l'Assemblée Nationale by this pronoun, it was clear that the old order had indeed come to an end. But here, as in some other respects, the innovations of a victorious bourgeois democracy were anticipated by its uncouth and naive precursor peasant insurgency. The substitution, albeit spontaneous, of *V* by *T* was a well established feature of the German Peasant War of 1525 and we have it on Zimmermann's authority that the rebels often used the more familiar *du* instead of the honorific *Sie* in denouncing and mocking the nobility overpowered by them. In colonial India the Bengali ryot's violation of the rules of pronominal deference in the course of disturbances like those of 1860 had its parallel in Malayali usage during the Moplah risings of the 1850s. It was a sign of these Malabar peasants' subalternity that the powerful Nayar landlords addressed them in terms of T while they responded by *V*. In 1852, however, in a series of instructions aimed at stimulating Moplah resistance the Thangal of Thirurangadi called upon his followers to drop the customary *V* and return *T* for *T* in verbal exchanges with the *jenmi* as an open demonstration of their will to challenge the latter's overlordship.

The inversion of verbal authority brought about by rebellion was not limited to spoken utterance alone but extended to its graphic form as well. There was hardly a peasant uprising on any significant scale in colonial India that did not cause the destruction of large quantities of written or printed material including rent rolls, deeds and bonds, and public records of all kinds. When in the course of the dhing against Deby Sinha the ryots of Dinajpur attacked his kachari at Dihi Jumtah, they made it a point to take away the papers they found there, and this was the fate common to landlords' estate offices wherever these lay in the path of a jacquerie. Again, popular violence was often astutely selective about all written evidence of peasant debts. Even the semi-official*Calcutta Gazette* noticed how during the Barasat insurrection led by Titu Mir a raid on an indigo factory in the neighbourhood did not lead to 'mere wanton destruction', for apart from a little damage done to some furniture only its 'papers were destroyed [and done so] most probably by the villagers for the purpose of destroying the record of their own debts'. In much the same way, the revolt of the Kunbi peasantry in Poona and Ahmadnagar districts in 1875 was distinguished by its singular concentration on the instruments of usury. 'The object of the rioters was in every case to obtain and destroy the bonds, decrees etc in their creditors' possession', according to the Commission set up to inquire into these disturbances. Indeed it was led to believe that this 'was not so much [a] rebellion against the oppressor as an attempt to accomplish a definite and practical object, namely, the disarming of the enemy by taking his weapons (bonds and accounts)'. Large deposits of official documentation too were often wrecked by insurgent crowds. The *levée en masse* triggered off by the Mutiny ended up by destroying 'all records of every kind' in Hamirpur district of Uttar Pradesh, as its magistrate was ruefully to observe soon after the event. In Muzaffarnagar, again, the records of the Civil, Criminal and Collectorate Duftars were burnt by the local population on the night of 14 May 1857, an incident regarded by the irate local officer as by no means 'a solitary instance' but as part of a pattern seen 'throughout this rebellion' of the burning of government offices by 'budmashes'.

Regarded from a less hostile perspective, however, one could see in all this a rather different pattern that of the objectification of the peasants' hatred for the written word. He had learnt, at his own cost, that the rent roll could deceive; that the bond could keep him and his family in almost perpetual servitude; that official papers could be used by clerks, judges, lawyers and landlords to rob him of his land and livelihood. Writing was thus, to him, the sign of his enemy, and 'favoured the exploitation of human beings rather than their enlightenment'. The sense of these words was dyed into his soul by his everyday experience. On Lévi-Strauss, to whom we owe this formulation, its truth dawned in a flash as he witnessed the very first attempts at a crude mimicry of writing (inspired unintentionally by the anthropologist himself) and the uses made of it by a Nambikwara chief fraudulently to retain his authority over his illiterate people living in conditions of a Stone Age culture in the Brazilian jungles.

The reaction of the Nambikwara to writing was as forthright as it was negative. Having 'felt in some obscure way that writing and deceit had penetrated simultaneously into their midst' they deserted their chief and their village and retreated to a remote area of the bush. In an equally negative gesture the Indian peasant who had nowhere to hide when driven to desperation, burnt down the graphic instruments of zamindari, sahukari and sarkari dominance the deeds, bonds, *khatas* and files, and their repositories the kachari, the gadi and the government office. This by itself contributed significantly enough to turning things upside down in the countryside and conformed, as such, to a tradition of insurgency as old as Jack Cade. But the process was taken a step further in some instances by the rebel trying, positively, to appropriate the sign of writing for himself.

Ideally such appropriation should have been no problem at all. The peasant could avail himself of the institutional means which were there precisely for this purpose. He could go to school, at least to its lowest denomination, at the village *pathsala* and acquire the three Rs. Unfortunately, however, he lived in no ideal world. The colonial government, keen on educating the middle classes in order to ensure manpower for its administration, was hardly interested in bringing literacy to the tillers of the soil. Primary education for the latter was left to the mercy and munificence of local landlords who took pride in setting up schools on their estates but were careful not to encourage too much literacy among the ryots. When Govinda Samanta, the hero of *Lal Behari Day's* well-known story about rural Bengal, pleads his inability to pay an arbitrary feudal levy (mathot), this is immediately seen as insolence bred by primary education. For he had indeed attended the village pathsala for some years when he was a child. 'So you have become a *pandita* [man of learning]', shouts the zamindar at him, 'and your eyes have got opened, therefore you refuse to pay the mathot. I must forbid Rama Rupa to teach any peasants' sons.' This was fairly representative of the attitude of the rural elite towards education for the peasantry under the Raj. Teach the *chasha* the three Rs and he will 'have his eyes opened' and learn to resist!

In no way therefore was the peasant in a position to appropriate writing as it really was, that is, as the graphic representation of a natural language. Want of literacy barred him access to it as a secular, intellectual aid to remembering, learning, understanding. In order therefore to use it for insurgency, for purposes of reversing the world, he appropriated it symbolically. He had been conditioned by his own subalternity and the elite monopoly of culture to look upon writing as a symbol of dominance. Lévi-Strauss noticed how in some of the villages of what is now Bangladesh the moneylender also functioned as the local scribe and this combination gave him a 'hold over others'. Indeed all who had a hold over the peasant, whether as rentiers, usurers or officials, used writing as a direct instrument of authority in one form or another. He regarded this, as he did many other expressions of power in a semi-feudal society, not as a social, empirical phenomenon, but as something that was quasi-religious and magical: to write was not a matter of skill but of inspiration. The written word was endowed with the same sort of mediatory, occult quality as he customarily attributed to the spoken utterances of an oracle possessed by the spirit of the dead during a propitiatory ceremony. The popular Hindu association of writing with priesthood on the one hand and with deities like Ganesa and Saraswati on the other enhanced this sense of sanctity about it. It was this sacred and magical power of writing which Sido and Kanhu appropriated for themselves as they declared war on the sahib and the diku.

Writing figures so prominently indeed in the Santal leaders' own perception of the hool that it is not possible for the historian to ignore it. What concerns us here is the authority they derived from it in the conduct of the hostilities. Both the Subahs acknowledged, in retrospect, that their decision to launch the insurrection had been directly prompted by writing. But this was writing seen as divine intervention. As Sido explained at the interrogation following his arrest, half a piece of paper fell on my head before the Thacoor came & half fell afterwards. I could not read but Chand & Seheree & a Dhome read it, they said 'The Thacoor has *written* to you to fight the Mahajens & then you will have justice'.

This, he said, was 'the Thacoor's order' an order given in *writing*. Kanhu was to confirm this later on when he, in his turn, was captured and related the circumstances leading to the revolt. Asked, 'What was the Thacoor like?' he replied:

> *Ishwar [God] was a white man with only a dootee & chudder he sat on the ground like a Sahib he wrote on this bit of paper. He gave me 4 papers but afterwards presented 16 more.*

Thus the authority of the graphic form was further reinforced by fusing together the images of a supernatural being, a white official and a native scribe sitting cross-legged on the floor and scribbling away. In what was clearly a case of overdetermination, the power of the colonialist sahib and that of the penpushing dhoti-clad babu were telescoped here in a composite vision and raised to divine power. The apotheosis of writing could not be more explicit nor indeed its use by the insurgents to justify turning the world upside down in the Thakur's name.

Of the non-verbal expressions of authority which come under attack in all uprisings, there are those which are paralinguistic in character and operate as kinesic and proxemic systems under the sign respectively of gestures and body movements and that of distances in space and time. Every society treats the body as a memory in which to store the basic principles of its culture 'in abbreviated and practical, i.e. mnemonic form', as Bourdieu has observed. This is particularly true of pre-literate societies 'which lack any other recording and objectifying instrument' so that 'inherited knowledge can survive only in its embodied state'. It is quite in order therefore that gestures of obeisance should figure so prominently in the Hindu Dharmaúâstras as the key to a better life. Why, for instance, must a youth leave his seat and greet an older man? 'For', says Manu, 'the vital airs of a young man mount upwards to leave his body when an elder approaches; but by rising to meet him and saluting he recovers them.' There are many other verses in that text devoted to the virtues of rising, prostrating, clasping of feet, etc. as indicative of subordinate status. And the authority of this language of the body derived not only from sacerdotal prescriptions but also from the power of the state. Thus according to Abû-l Fazl, kings 'made regulations for the manner in which people are to show their obedience'. This was meant to promote 'true humility'. For instance, *kornish,* an approved mode of salutation at the Mughal court, signified that the saluter 'placed his head (the seat of the senses and the mind) into the hand of humility, giving it to the royal assembly as a present', and another, known as *taslim,* that he was 'ready to give himself as an offering'.

The substitution of Mughal royalty by the British made little difference to such feudal kinesics. They continued to operate as status markers in colonial India too. 'When a Coorg meets an elder on a ritual occasion', wrote Srinivas, 'he has to salute the latter by bending the upper half of his body and touching the elder's feet thrice with both hands. After each touch the younger man takes his hands to his forehead, where he folds them together.' This, he remarked, was not very different from the form of salutation one adopted towards a deity. In fact, variations of 'bodily automatism' of this kind featured in all homologous relations between father and son, husband and wife, landlord and tenant, high caste and low caste. In Madhya Pradesh, for instance, it was customary for the wife to demonstrate her fidelity by bending down before her husband at a distance and touching the earth with her fingers. A Balahi, ranked as one of the lowliest in rural society in this region, would replicate this movement on meeting a Brahman, bending forward to touch the ground and lifting his hands, palms folded to his forehead. Elsewhere, in Orissa, a Bauri untouchable had to adopt much the same self-debasing posture under similar circumstances. 'When we passed by higher-caste people', said Muli to the visiting anthropologist, 'we crouched so that one hand touched the ground; we walked by in that position, so that our faces were toward the ground.'

It was not the rise and fall of empires but the violence of the masses which alone interrupted from time to time this age-old avowal of subservience by gestures. Yet another index of the world turned upside down, this might have been the reversal feared by the dominant brahmanical culture when among the many topsy-turvy features of the mythical 'epoch's end' (*yugânta*) it counted Sudras who were 'controlled in the movement of their eyes' (*jitâkshah*), not unlike, presumably, their superiors in the varna hierarchy! Less fantastically, however, and indeed in our own epoch there have been occasions in the course of agrarian disturbances when insulting gestures appeared to have hurt the peasants' enemies no less than acts of physical assault. A detail of the Birsaite ulgulan should make this clear. On 16 August 1895 the villagers of Chalkad drove out a police party which had camped out there for about a week in an attempt to seize the Munda chief but had failed to do so. As the posse began to withdraw in the face of superior insurgent forces, this was how it felt to the Head Constable of Tamar to be, for once, at the receiving end:

> We then moved off by the Birbanki road towards Tamar followed by some 800 to 900 men who were having [sic] winnowing fans, beating toms and waving bows as insults to us. They were also carrying the three bedsteads (*khatia*) on which we had lain. These latter they flung into the river which we reached about one mile from Chalkad. In throwing the *khatias* in the river the crowd exclaimed, 'The Sarkar's Raj is at an end and their servants are dead, hence we throw their beds into the river.' They were beating the toms and the fans not only as insulting signs but as a very inauspicious thing, as they consider Birsa was preaching to the people not to attend to the *bhooth* or make sacrifice but to obey him.

There are references in this account to physical violence, too-to the guardians of the law being pushed and hustled and pricked with spears by the pursuing Mundas. What however sticks out in the Head Constable's memory of this ordeal is the rebels' use of the 'insulting signs'. Far from being treated as the august representatives of the sarkar to the accompaniment of obsequious body movements they were treated as *bhut*, dead souls fit only to be exorcised by the whiff of winnowing fans and the noise of drums. Far from being regarded as distinguished guests who brought prestige to a village by visiting it, they were unceremoniously rejected as polluting agents so that even the beds they had slept in had to be thrown away in a simulation of funerary rites. Far from being feared as the strong arm of the state they were mocked and defied by the Mundas flaunting their bows at them. In other words, what shocked the Head Constable was that these downtrodden and docile people had 'now audaciously *lifted up their heads'* (as Mao was to say of the Hunan peasantry) a figure of speech signifying the very opposite of what bending and prostrating stood for.

There is yet another class of paralinguistic signs which represents social rank and grade in terms of distances. Thus temporal distances indicating degrees of authority were often expressed as rights of precedence. In nineteenth-century Calcutta clan leaders used to fight over precedence during the ceremonial distribution of sandal paste and flowers at sacred recitals and funeral banquets. Again in Malwa, according to Mayer, a wife's standing in her husband's family varied according to whether she was allowed to have her meal at the same time as the other women of the household or afterwards. Among the Coorgs the headman was traditionally called the *mûpayanda,* which means 'having precedence', and as Srinivas observes, 'the sense of precedence is ubiquitous'. It was the headman who took the first shot at target-shooting contests on ritual occasions, it was he who led the village dance at harvest festivals, and it was his pack-bullocks which had the right to lead a caravan. Precedence such as this governed relations between castes as well. In Nimar district a high-caste villager's bullock-cart had the right of way over a Balahi's, and in agricultural operations high-caste farmers had the right to help themselves first to the local supplies of labour: 'Only after they are satisfied will field servants go to work on the fields of their Balahi creditors.'

Foil to these were distances in space used both laterally and vertically as status markers. 'The regulation of the difference among men in rank' at Akbar's court was quite clearly a matter of seating and standing arrangements: the nearer a royal prince or nobleman was to the throne, the more important he was supposed to be. Centuries later distance was still very much in evidence as an index of seniority in age and caste in rural society. It was a part of Coorg etiquette that a youth did not walk with an elder side by side but a few respectful paces behind him. Informal gatherings around a cot in a UP village often conformed to the same pattern. 'If all are members of one caste, the oldest person sits at the head of the cot others sit next in order of prestige ranking. If a Brahman is present he will be offered the head seat. Lower caste persons and sometimes also poor Rajputs will sit on the floor and untouchables at a slight distance from the group.' Notice how the inferiority of the poorer Rajputs and untouchables is indicated by the fact of their having to squat on the floor while the Brahman has his seat on the cot. This constitutes yet another aspect of proxemics, that is, the expression of hierarchical differences in terms of levels of seating. The subordinate must not be seated above the superordinate. An unmistakably feudal notion, this too has an ancestry stretching back to the Smrȯtis. 'When his teacher is nigh', said Manu, a pupil must 'let his bed or seat be low'. The principle worked with the followers of Islam as well. When the Pir Pagaro was taken out in a ceremonial procession, a devout Hur, we are told, left her perch on the roof of a nearby house so that she would not be situated higher than her spiritual leader when the latter passed along that road. Secular authority also operated by the same sign. Beals observed that in Gopalpur even the more important men of the village would, when they called on the landlord, sit on the ground beneath the platform occupied by the latter.

Distance thus was a measure of prestige. No wonder that the followers of Birsa remembered this when in explaining to their people how they 'had lost their honour and were biting dust', they mentioned that the Mundas were, among other humiliations, barred by the Raja and the zamindars from using chairs and high seats. Indeed their revolt, like all others of its kind, was made up of the peasant's urge to recover his self-respect by eliminating or turning against his oppressors the apparently innocuous, because traditionally tolerated, signs of subalternity, such as those of prescribed distances, which had been imposed on them. Inversions of this order occur frequently and on a large scale in the course of all such massive explosions of violence. The rule of differential heights is broken whenever the peasants ride past a landlord's or an upper-caste man's house on horseback during a riot in defiance of customary prohibitions. The calculated and otherwise inviolable margins of avoidance in a caste-ridden society sensitive to pollution are necessarily infringed whenever they raid a zamindar's or a bania's residence, or lay their hands on the person of anyone in authority. Violations of this kind are indeed so numerous that these are almost taken for granted in reporting or commenting on rural disturbances, so that what catches the observer's eye and survives the levelling influence of redundancy in his narrative is the destruction by the rebel of the more obvious symbols of his enemy's power.

Such symbols constitute the staple of peasant grievances. The rural masses everywhere use these both as a measure of their own deprivation and as objectives worth fighting for when roused to do so. These figure therefore conspicuously in all rebel discourse in that ancestral voice of insurgency, John Ball's Sunday exhortations, as well as in the Birsaite propaganda on the eve of the ulgulan. 'They are clad in velvet and camlet lined with squirrel and ermine, while we go dressed in coarse cloth', said the 'crack-brained priest of Kent', contrasting the lords' way of life with the serfs': 'They have the wines, the spices and the good bread: we have the rye, the husks and the straw, and we drink water. They have shelter and ease in their fine manors, and we have hardship and toil, the wind and the rain in the fields. And from us must come, from our labour, the things which keep them in luxury.' Dress, food, mansions-these and other 'things which keep them in luxury', crowd into all *cahiers de doléances* wherever they originate. Adapted to Indian conditions, hence with some variation of detail, the same sort of contrast is implied in the Munda *pracharaks'* enumeration of the wrongs (some elements of which have been noticed above) suffered by their tribe.

The Raja and zamindars exploited them and reduced them to a position of carriers (forced and unpaid labourers) and dependants, deprived them 'of their clothes, their *dhoti* and garments, turban and footwear'; they could not use even an umbrella. They were not allowed to sit on chairs and high seat, to enter a temple or to eat from golden or silver or brass plates.

The list of course could be longer. For the authority the elite had over the peasantry was nearly all-pervasive and symbolized by many objects and attitudes. Indeed the struggle for any significant change in existing power relations in the countryside often appears as a contest between those who are determined to retain their traditional monopoly of such status symbols and others who are keen on appropriating them that is, as a cultural conflict. This is why all dominant cultures are particularly sensitive to anything which even remotely looks like usurpation and quick to discipline offenders.

Take, for instance, the set of symbols which related directly to the body either as its parts or as ornament and garment. Physical characteristics were often regarded as indicative of rank both by peasants and their enemies. The leaders of the rebel Tuchin movement of central France in the fourteenth century suspected courtliness or elegance in all who had smooth uncalloused hands, and rather than recruiting them to their bands, marked them out for killing. Conversely, the brahmanical nightmare of a cataclysmic upheaval, as evoked by the *Vâyupurâam*, had in it the image of Sudras with teeth as white as those of members of the higher varnas. Even under less mythical circumstances the rural elite have been known for their aversion to sharing any of their own distinctive physical styles with their social inferiors. The curled, up-turned moustache represents one such style for upper-caste upper-class males in many parts of India. When a member of the triditionally labouring community of Bareias was found sporting such a moustache in a Gujarat village dominated by rich and politically powerful Patidars, he was forcibly shaved, beaten up and driven out beyond its boundaries. This anecdote was recorded by an anthropologist as evidence of 'greater concern with caste order in the past', presumably in colonial times and before. However, in the light of the facts published by the Elayaperumal Committee's report, it seems that the ban on the up-turned moustache continues to be a feature of the outcaste's subalternity even in India today.

Objects of wear too were seen as status markers. It was 'out of respect to the higher castes' that no woman of the Bharia caste of farm-servants and agricultural labourers in Madhya Pradesh would wear a nose-ring, as Russell and Lal had noticed. Many decades later social inferiority still continued to be denoted in much the same way in Uttar Pradesh by means of sanctions against the use of jewellery by outcastes: 'Shoemaker women, for example, report having been prevented by Rajputs from wearing ornaments and clothes similar to those of the Rajput women.' Umbrellas and shoes too have been jealously guarded symbols. A part of the insignia of feudal monarchies the umbrella retained some of its importance as an exclusive 'sign of noble rank not permitted to the commonalty', even after it had ceased to be an appanage of kings. Throughout the colonial period it continued to operate as a general index of dominance and subordination, sorting out, especially in the rural areas, the rulers and the ruled, high caste and low caste, and so on: in Champaran no Indian 'whatever his status' could hold an umbrella on his head in the presence of a white planter, nor could a Bania do so while passing by a Bundela Rajput's house in Saugor. Shoes, too, could offend if worn in the presence of one's superiors.

Members of the lower castes, particularly if they were women, had to take these off on meeting a high-caste man and in some villages even while going past an upper-caste residence or through caste Hindu wards. Indeed, umbrellas or shoes could be so suggestive of power that often under conditions of growing antagonism between the peasant and his enemies both sides regarded these as symbolic sites of conflict. The ban imposed on their use by the diku landlords was felt to be an unbearable tyranny by the Mundas as they became increasingly politicized. Conversely, the Tamil Nadu landlord who identified shod feet as the symptom of rebelliousness among agricultural labourers at the time of the Kilvenmani massacre, spoke up against what was, to his class, a real affront: 'Things used to be very peaceful here some years ago. The labourers were very hard-working and respectful. But now the fellow who used to stand in the backyard of my house to talk to me comes straight to the verandah wearing slippers and all. These fellows have become lazy and arrogant, thanks to the Communists. They have no fear in them any more.'

However, of all things worn on the person it is clothes which are the most semioticized. For the body 'as purely sensuous, is without significance', and it is clothing, writes Barthes following this Hegelian dictum, which 'ensures the passage from the sensuous to the meaningful: it is, one could say, the signified par excellence'. Nowhere is this more explicit than in the countryside where the distinction between peasants and others-townsmen, officials, gentry, etc. is often perceived as one of dress in the first instance. 'Dress is a fundamental element of distinction', said Gramsci about Italy. Indeed, this was true of most societies, especially of those vegetating for long under colonial and semi-feudal conditions. It is known, for instance, that in Bolivia under Spanish rule dress was 'a means of publicly manifesting the status of the *persona*' and of 'social control in favour of the estamental order'. In India too castes, classes and ethnic groups were often differentiated by the clothes their members wore and the manner of wearing them. The Bengali bhadralok was utterly self-conscious about his dress, for 'no self-respecting person could go about his business in society wrapping himself up in a dirty knee-length *gamcha*', wrote the *Sadhana* in a clear reference to typically lower-class garment.

In south India it was obligatory for a low-caste man to approach anyone of the upper castes or indeed for a servant his master by first stripping himself to the waist as a mark of respect. In Gujarat, the so-called impure Mahars 'were not allowed to tuck up their loin-cloth but had to trail it along the ground', while in central India among the Kurmi the difference in length between the peasant's jacket, *bandi*, covering the trunk only up to the hips and the landlord's long coat, *angrakha*, reaching down to the knees, was indicative of the difference in their social standing. And among the Santals the word *deko* referred not only to alien Hindu landlords, but also, according to Bödding, 'any Indian in good clothing'.

It is not surprising therefore that in societies so sensitive to dress differentials any serious crisis of authority should be expressed in sartorial terms as well. Dress has indeed a way of insinuating itself into the history of all of the more widespread and militant agrarian movements. It is at such times that distinctions of this order tend to generate the utmost animosity and many of the reversals characteristic of these conflicts are acted out symbolically by the reallocation of garments and styles of wear between peasants and their enemies. Zimmermann recorded a number of such incidents in his account of the German Peasant War of 1525 an insurgent snatching away a nobleman's hat and putting it on himself, some of the counts forced to take off their gloves by the peasants while the latter keep theirs on in defiance of all rules of etiquette, and so on. During the Bolivian peasants' revolt of 1899 all who wore trousers (*pantalones*) or rather were not clad in coarse rustic homespuns, were marked out by the rebels as their enemies. Willka, their leader, had it as one of his aims to try and abolish distinctions of dress between the estaments by introducing the use of homespun for all; and following a tradition of insurgency going back to the eighteenth century they forced homespun peasant clothes on townsfolk in some instances. And in Tanzania during the Maji Maji rebellion the Christian missionaries feared that the Ngoni would kill all who wore European clothes.

In rural India, too, dress which discriminated so clearly between the elite and the subaltern as a matter of course, acquired an added significance in the eyes of both the parties in periods of serious confrontation between them. The Rangpur dhing of 1783, for instance, broke out at a time when widespread disturbances were not uncommon in that part of Bengal, thanks to gang robberies and incursions of fakirs, sannyasis and predatory soldiers of the East India Company's army. When, therefore, a large gathering was reported from Kadagaon and Magurrah, its character as a mass of rebel peasantry was identified, among other things, by the dress worn by the members of the crowd. 'Each of these peasants has a stick or bamboo in his hand', reported an official witness, 'their dress is like that of the ryots or villagers, they are neither sepahis, fakirs or night robbers.' In yet another historic struggle, that of the tenant cultivators of Pabna in 1873, the manner of dress was recognized by all concerned landlords, their *proja* and the administration as an index of class divisions made explicit by antagonism over the rent question. The officer in charge of the sub-division most affected by the bidroha put it in unmistakable terms in a report to the higher authorities:

> *This class feeling was so universal that the opinion of any native on the agrarian question may be told to a certainty by looking at his dress. If he wore a light chadar on his shoulder, used shoes on his feet and carried an umbrella, one could make sure that he was a zamindar's man. If merely clad in the dhoti and gamcha he was at heart an unionist.*

Dress had a place in the Santal hool, too, as an element of the idiom of that revolt. At the battle of Maheshpur, said Sido after his capture, 'many of the Manjees were dressed in red clothes'. Neither he nor his brothers had taken to wearing red until then. However, it appears that after his death, when the insurrection was at its peak, Kanhu, Chand and Bhairab adopted this rather conspicuous garment as an assertion of authority, as indeed a gesture of turning things upside down, just as ' Giuliano's solitaire ring, the bunches of chains and decorations with which the anti-French bandits of the 1790s festooned themselves in Southern Italy, would be regarded by the peasants', according to Hobsbawm, 'as symbols of triumph over the rich and powerful'. There was yet another striking instance of the use of dress the turban (*pagri*), to be precise as a means of reversal during this rebellion. This form of headgear carries much weight in many regions of rural India. With some local communities, such as the Balahi, it is only the headmen who have the right to wear this. In Gujarat this used to be an exclusive privilege of the dominant caste of Patidars, so that anyone of a lower caste risked being severely punished if he was tempted publicly to try it on. The Mundas, as noticed above, held it against the dikus that the latter denied them the right to put on a turban. And if it was a matter of prestige to wear a pagri, to confer it was all the more so. This is precisely what Kanhu, the supreme commander of the Santals, did at the very height of the insurrection. As stated in a report from Major-General Lloyd on 19 November 1855, ' Kanoo Manjhee with his Brothers and Followers had visited on Bechoo Raout a gwallah the head of the village of Sooria Haut. Kanoo had created him a Soobah and as a Symbol of the rank conferred, had bound a turban on his head.' The turban came thus to stand for a historic inversion, for nothing turns the world upside down more radically than when the subaltern feel bold enough to delegate power seized in an act of rebellion.

There were of course other objects, apart from those worn on one's person, which also acted as status symbols and had a part to play in the negative articulation of rebel consciousness. Some of these were means of transport identified with rank in many feudal societies and subject, like the latter, to the shocks and tremors of agrarian disturbances. In a well-known incident of the Peasant War in Germany the rebels used this symbolism for a particularly dramatic act of reversal: forcing a wicked countess to sit in a dungcart they mocked her, 'In a golden carriage camest thou to Weinsberg, in a dungcart must thou depart! The Hunan movement, reported by Mao Tse-tung, saw a good deal of smashing of sedan-chairs. And in the period of the civil war in England fraught with so many threats to the status quo, 'the wisest of men saw it to be a great evil that servants should ride on horses: an evil now both seen and felt in this unhappy kingdom'.

The use of horses by low-born villagers was unacceptable to the Indian elite as well. No Balahi was to ride on his horse past an upper-caste person or village, no Bania past a Bundela Rajput's house, no subordinate past his superior officer. The equestrian figure was embedded in the traditions of the meek and much harassed Santals as an image of pure force. 'Kings and rich people move about on horseback as conquerors', according to the Mare Hapram Ko Reak Katha. The other privileged form of transport in India was the palanquin. Some of the foreign powers who had acquired territorial bases in the subcontinent used this to indicate their superior standing as rulers: in Bombay under Portuguese occupation no native was ever allowed to ride in a palanquin except with the

Viceroy's permission, a practice which the British kept in force in their turn at least until 1788. In rural India the native elite, especially the big landlords, continued for a long time to treat the palanquin as a part of the insignia of their authority and no one of inferior standing was allowed to ride in it through their residential villages. If a zamindar was really powerful, even some junior white officials could risk being thrown out of his village for violating this code. It was therefore symptomatic of a radical inversion in rural society that the peasants should publicly appropriate such vehicles. They did so when during the Rangpur insurrection they carried around their leader, Dirjenarain, in a palanquin. Nothing could have been more topsyturvy than that. For as we know from Ratiram's ballad on this event, no one could pass through the hated Deby Sinha's estate in that district in any form of transport whatsoever without being beaten up by his paiks and that too in the most defiling manner that is, with shoes. And palanquins as well as horses were used by the leaders of the Santal forces during the hool. 'There were five or six Palkees [palanquins] with us', said a rebel taken captive soon after the outbreak. ' Sidoo and Kanoo ride in them. Whatever horses we found at Putgutteeah were mounted by the Sonthal Darogahs (Sirdars).' Kanhu himself was to state later on that he 'was on horseback' leading his men in some of the more dramatic actions such as the sack of the Pakur Raj a neat inversion by which a symbol of the authority of rajas and the rich was transformed into an instrument of their destruction by the poor.

The power of the rural elite in all pre-industrial societies is perhaps most conspicuously displayed by the size and elegance of their residence. In periods of sharpening antagonism in the countryside this can provoke much hostility among the peasant masses. John Ball's bitter contrast between the living conditions of lords and serfs was to be echoed five centuries later in the complaint of a peasant woman of Palermo during the uprising of 1893: 'I have five small children and only one little room, where we have to eat and sleep and do everything, while so many lords (*signori*) have ten to twelve rooms, entire palaces.' It is not to be wondered therefore that stately homes have often been the object of violence in many of the major peasant revolts in Europe manor houses during the Jacquerie, castles and abbeys in the German Peasant War, chateaux in the French Revolution.

All over the Indian subcontinent difference in types of residence was and still continues to be a fairly accurate indication of difference in status. In colonial times this was true of distinctions between the rulers and the ruled as well as of those between the indigenous castes and classes themselves. As Anthony D. King has demonstrated so well by his researches, what he calls 'the bungalow-compound complex' functioned throughout this period as 'the basic residential unit of the colonial community'. Originating from a traditional housetype known in Bengal the bungalow was adapted to the urge of the governing elite to use residence as a space to demarcate itself politically and culturally from the natives without involving the actual loss of that direct physical contact so essential for purposes of administration. The result was of course that by the middle of the nineteenth century the bungalow, 'the most usual class of house occupied by Europeans in India', came to be regarded as a symbol of the authority of the whites and the Raj. In all hostile demonstrations against the government or its European associates such as planters and railway officials, it featured almost inevitably as a target of popular wrath. The Santal rebellion, for instance, was only eight days old when the Magistrate of Murshidabad arrived at Pulsa, a principal station, to find the bungalows built by the railroad engineers there 'entirely destroyed'. His was by no means a unique experience. For as one of his fellow officers was to report three days later, 'the whole of the Bungalows along the line from Rajmehal to Pulsa have been burnt down and sacked'.

The size and character of the residence were also regarded as a clear indication of status differences among the Indians themselves. As noticed above, this was integral enough to the culture of Malabar to show up in the regional language by way of a direct correspondence between caste names and hierarchically ordered names for caste dwellings. In general, a brick-built house was a decisive sign of affluence and high standing in the rural areas, as James Forlong, the planter, said about Bengal in his evidence before the Indigo Commission in 1860. This seems to have been the case in the Madhya Pradesh region too where by the end of the century a pucca building had come to be recognized as evidence of the malguzars' prosperity and power raising them distinctively above the level of the mass of the tenantry: 'They have almost without exception good pucca houses built with an elaborate main entrance (*darwaza*) which is easily distinguishable from the houses of the tenants, and around which cluster their cattle sheds and granaries.' Further up the scale, a big landlord's house was often very conspicuous indeed both in size and in elegance. Day wrote of one of these in his *Bengal Peasant Life* as 'the largest and best building in the village', with its solid masonry outer gate, imposing wooden door, the complex of inner compounds, halls and suites of rooms constituting the *kachari-badi*, the *dalan-badi* and the *andar-mahal*. Fairly true to life, such structures testified to the disparity between the bigger zamindars and the rest of the rural population both in terms of material resources and of power.

The chagrin felt by the peasant on this score would also occasionally find its way into the otherwise placid prose of our primary sources to accuse his oppressors.

The Wani uses the large house now. We can't get houses for hire. I would be willing to give up everything and be free, but I should like a bit of a hut somewhere in the village.

In testifying thus before the Deccan Riots Commission a potter, Tatya Saloo, convicted of rioting against a Wani in his own village Supa, gave voice to that bitterness and desperation which drove the rural poor so often to vent their anger on such conspicuous symbols of the power of local landlords and moneylenders. Far too numerous and well documented to need recounting, here, the attacks on the kacharis at Boda, Saal Ullah, Allanchurry, Dhee Hat, Baragang, Jamta and Dimla as well as on Deby Sinha's palace during the dhing of 1783, on the mansion of Krishnadeb Ray, zamindar of Punrah by Titu Mir's men during the Barasat rebellion of 1830, on 'all the respectable looking houses in the villages' within the area of the Kol insurrection of 1832, on the kachari of the zamindar of Ambar pargana at Jhikarhati and the house of the Raja of Maheshpur by the Santals in 1855, on the kacharis at Mirpur, Pasuria Bari, Chitturlia and Woodhunia and the house of the Majumdars of Gopalnagar during the Pabna bidroha of 1873, and on the residence and gadis of banias and mahajans throughout Uttar Pradesh in 1857-8 and in the Poona and Ahmadnagar districts of Maharashtra in 1875 are among some of the instances which come readily to one's mind.

It was not only by attacking the material symbols of governmental and landlord authority that the insurgents upset the established order. They did so by undermining its dominant semi-feudal culture as well. In so far as religion constituted the most expressive sign of this culture in many of its essential aspects, the peasants' defiance of the rural elite often involved an attempt to appropriate the dominant religion or to destroy it. To those who were high up in society the emulation of their culture by the lower strata seemed always fraught with danger. There have been occasions when, thanks to the stimulus given to casteism by British colonial policy, sanskritizing movements among the lower castes to upgrade themselves by adopting the rituals and religious idioms of their superiors were resisted by the latter and generated much social tension and even some actual violence. If this could happen in conditions of social peace, the subaltern's urge to assert his identity not in terms of his own culture but his enemy's a characteristic index of negative consciousness was boosted, understandably enough, when the existing structure of authority in rural areas began to crumble under the impact of a mass uprising.

The Santal hool of 1855 was a clear demonstration of this phenomenon. Involved in a bitter and bloody war against Hindu landlords and moneylenders, the rebels took to Hindu religious practice with a vengeance. Certain forms of ritual worship (*puja*) regarded as conducive to spiritual merit by the Hindus were adopted by the insurgents too. Indeed the very first intelligence report about their movements which we have on record, speaks of' their 'intention' to march to Baniagram 'where they are to do Poojah and bathe in the Ganges' before proceeding to Rajmahal. This Hindu idiom showed up emphatically and with a certain amount of consistency in the conduct of their leaders whom the crisis had invested with a degree of spiritual authority too. Thus, a headman called Ram, a local leader, was taken prisoner while 'engaged in performing Poojah', for he 'could not . . . be disturbed or warned by his followers' as the counter-insurgency forces closed in on his village and surrounded it. Kanhu himself is on record as having said that he 'made poojah' at a difficult moment during the battle of Maheshpur in an attempt, presumably, to influence its outcome in favour of his fauj. His brother Sido, the coleader of the hool, had, we are told, his own plans to celebrate Durga Puja in the grand manner of the Hindu gentry of Bengal for whom the pomp and scale of this autumn festival served as a customary affirmation of religiosity as well as of social authority. And to leave no one in doubt about the genuinely Hindu character of this ceremony the insurgents abducted two Brahmans to make them perform the prescribed rituals correctly and in accordance with the highest standards of purity. As the Magistrate of Birbhum wrote to his superior officer: 'The gang of from 5 to 7,000 Sonthals under Seeroo Manghee whom they term *Soobha Thacoor* at *Telabonee* have strengthened their position by earthen works and dug Tanks there they have also made preparations for celebrating the Doorgapooja, for which purpose they have carried off and detained two Brahmins from one of the villages plundered by them in Thanna Nagoolea.' Such an open and energetic avowal of Hinduism on the part of a lowly, 'unclean' tribal peasantry could not have been regarded by the Hindu elite as anything but subversive. For it was indeed an integral aspect of their dominance that they should consider it threatened by any unauthorized affiliation to the ruling culture. This is why the prospect of Sudras practising dharma in the manner of the upper varnas was envisaged in Puranic literature as a sign of the cataclysmic advent of Kali, and the slaying of Úambûka was instigated by the Brahmans and applauded by the gods as a great deed on the part of its eponymous hero in the Ramayana.

The insurgents undermined the dominant culture in its most important, that is, religious aspect not only by emulating it, but more directly and dramatically by acts of desecration. The Peasant War in Germany has provided us with some classic instances of this particular form of reversal. There in the first quarter of the sixteenth century the Catholic church was still a major feudal power in its own right and commanded wealth and political authority on a vast scale through its abbeys and monasteries. To the peasants it was as much of an enemy as any of the secular lords of the land, and consequently when they rose up in arms in the spring of 1525 there was little to restrain them from defying conventions and defiling objects sanctified by the church. It was Lent and time for fasting, yet they behaved as if they were Protestants and fasting did not concern them. They ate and drank freely. At Roggenburg drunken peasants broke up the church organ, battered the tabernacle with it rod, took away the chalices and other sacred vessels and shredded the vestments and flags for use as trouser belts. At Kempten armed contingents of them paraded past the church during the hour of high mass laughing and mocking. They brought down the pictures of the saints, sawed off the head of a beautiful statue of the Virgin

Mary and smashed up the figure of the child in her arms. Indeed they made a mess of 'everything considered holy' (*übten den grössten Unfug an allem aus, was man für heilig hielt*).

In India the temple was an outstanding symbol of Hindu religion and often of the prestige of a local Hindu landlord if it happened to be patronized by his family or situated within his residential precincts. As such it often figured as a focus of conflict between Hindu landlords and non-Hindu peasantry. Being denied the right to enter a temple was among the grievances the Birsaite pracharaks made much of in their propaganda against zamindars, and it was as a decisive step towards the ulgulan that the Munda chief led his men into the forbidden Chutia temple, held a nautch there, threw down and defiled the images, and altogether desecrated this place of worship held sacred by the dikus. The violence of this sacrilege was not lost on the authorities who promptly issued a warrant for Birsa's arrest and put up a reward for his capture.

Attacks of this kind acquired a very special significance when the peasantry concerned happened to be Muslims. For apart from affecting power relations in the countryside even to the point of reversing them in some cases, these often led to the overdetermination of class struggle by sectarian conflict in a manner which was a commonplace of Indian politics under the Raj. Instances abound. In Malabar where the authority of the jenmi landlords derived not merely from their near monopoly of landed property but also, as Logan observed, from their function as trustees of village temples, attacks on and defilement of the latter featured in almost each of the numerous Moplah risings throughout the nineteenth century. Again in some parts of eastern Bengal where the Farazi movement launched by Shariatullah converged with militant resistance to Hindu zamindars' tyranny on the part of predominantly Muslim tenant populations, the latter were accused of defiling private shrines in landlords' houses by slaughtering cows, by forcing their entry there in clothes fastened by strips of cow-hide and at least in one case, by demolishing a set of lingas, a traditional surrogate for the image of the deity Siva. The correspondent who reported these outrages in a mufassil periodical in 1837 voicing the alarm that spread among the Hindu gentry of Dacca and Faridpur districts at the time, recalled the not very dissimilar pattern of violence witnessed during the Barasat insurrection only a few years ago. Places of worship sacred to both the faiths had come under attack during that historic struggle. In order to terrorize the mass of the peasantry inspired by Titu's Islamic revivalism and roused and organized by him to resist zamindari oppressions, Krishnadeb Ray, a powerful Hindu landlord, had raided a Muslim hamlet and burnt down some houses and a mosque. The insurgents returned the compliment by invading Ray's own residential village, Punrah. 'The Zemindars had put a slight on their religious feeling', reads the official report on this event, 'and they retaliated by seizing a cow which they killed in the public market place of the village, scattered the blood over the walls of a Hindu temple and hung up the four quarters of the animal in derision before it.' And as if to emphasize the purely symbolic character of this act 'on this occasion they committed no plunder beyond carrying of what articles they found lying immediately exposed in the shops in the market place'. Desecration was used thus by both the parties to undermine each other's prestige by the Hindu zamindar the prestige of the rebellion and the new faith which fuelled it; by the Muslim peasantry the prestige of the landlords and its emblem, the old established religion.

It was this fight for prestige which was at the very heart of insurgency. Inversion was its principal modality. It was a political struggle in which the rebel appropriated and/or destroyed the insignia of his enemy's power and hoped thus to abolish the marks of his own subalternity. Inevitably, therefore, by rising in revolt the peasant involved himself in a project which was, by its very nature, negatively constituted. The 'names, battle-cries and costumes' he assumed in order to carry this out were all taken over from his adversaries. It was no doubt a project predicated on power, but its terms were derived from the very structure of authority against which he had been driven to revolt. He spoke thus in a 'borrowed language' that of his enemy, for he knew none other. 'In like manner', wrote Marx as he framed the paradoxes of the first bourgeoisdemocratic revolutions of modern Europe in a linguistic analogy, 'a beginner who has learnt a new language always translated it back into his mother tongue." The peasant rebel of colonial India, the infantile, blundering and alas, invariably frustrated, precursor of a democratic revolution in the subcontinent had set out to learn his very first lesson in power, but in this earlier period prior to the emergence of a modern bourgeoisie, an industrial proletariat and advanced ideas of democracy he could do so only by translating it backwards into the semi-feudal language of politics to which he was born. A historically necessary exercise in negative consciousness, this was demonstrated in its general form as a process of inversion turning, as Manu had warned, the lower (*adhara*) into the higher (*uttara*).

12

Analysis and Results of Asian Insurgencies

Introduction

The United States and Great Britain found themselves immersed in tensions throughout Asia. Always related to the overt actions of cold war politics, both nations also found themselves involved in suppressing separate insurgencies as part of extending their individual foreign policy objectives. The United States was caught in the middle of helping to establish a friendly government in the Philippines, one sympathetic to U.S. security concerns after 1946. Even with the eventual loss of the naval facilities at Subic Bay and the volcanic destruction of Clark Air Force Base, the Philippines remain critical to U.S. global security interests.

Great Britain, in its own right, was attempting to quell a rebellion turned insurgency over its holdings on the Malayan peninsula. Partly due to U.S. pressure seeking a colonial-free postwar world, and due in large part to the faltering British economy, an initial step to make a clean but gradual break from its colonial holdings was in process. These affairs are important to this study for three critical reasons: First, they represent a wide variety of nationalist problems needing resolution after the Second World War and illustrate the kind of warfare both allies believed lay ahead for them in attempting to thwart the increasing tide of communism in a Third World wrought with cold war tensions. Second, they are the earliest of the large, modern insurgencies that took place in Asia in the post-1945 period and provided successful examples that would have direct impact on the conduct of American political and military operations in Vietnam. And, third, these events bring forth a new cast of characters who would have direct influence over American policies on insurgency warfare to be formulated and implemented in the future.

The Philippines, 1946-1953

American involvement in the Philippines after 1945 took on an almost historical quality. Not only had the United States been involved in trade with the Filipinos for almost a century, it had been militarily involved in the region for nearly fifty years. The desire to maintain certain strategic control and security in the Philippine region seemed to be uncontestable, even natural, to many Americans by the time General Douglas MacArthur and the U.S. Sixth Army returned in October 1944. But the Philippines were in a desperate situation economically and politically following Japanese occupation, and the United States had pledged to grant them independence a year after the war ended. Thus, when the repatriated Philippine President Sergio Osmena asked President Harry S. Truman for economic help in 1945, he did not have to wait long.

While economic and financial needs were paramount, the weak political infrastructure in devastated Manila could not be ignored. Here, successive Philippine governments had wrestled with the problem of eliminating the most volatile of the competing political factions. The Hukbo ng Bayan Laban Sa Hapon, or Hukbalahap, a contraction meaning People's Anti-Japanese Army, was indeed the most serious threat to a stable Filipino government sympathetic to U.S. interests. The Huks, as they were commonly called, controlled a large part of the rice and cane growing areas of central Luzon. They carried out political and military operations throughout the archipelago, eventually bringing nearly 150,000 Filipinos in this region under their control. From the development of sound military training and operational experience in fighting the Japanese, the Huks were able to hone guerrilla war techniques. As a military arm of the Communist Party in the Philippines, however, Huk ambitions always exceeded mere anti-Japanese activities.

In spite of their initial base of band of rebel thugs, this Huk organization, under the military leadership of Taruc, had developed into a competent insurgent political and military organization. Although inclusion appeared attractive in the beginning, the Huks decided that their strength and growing numbers warranted procession down a noninclusive track, a track that appeared to capture the common passions of the Philippine people. The bitter circumstances surrounding this newly established phase one insurgency ran deep. As Asprey states:

> Taruc and his associates represented a distinct challenge to the hegemony exercised by immensely powerful landowners and industrialists spawned during four decades of American overlordship. This group, which included substantial American interests, had usurped the old landowning role of the Church, which had made itself hated by peasants.

With farmers only owning 10 percent of the land they tilled and paying to the government some 50 percent of its cash crop, a small plot of farmland was never destined to pay for itself. Farmers and their families were in a perpetual state of financial hardship, and in some cases, starvation. But this financial system was over four centuries old. It explained generations of "poverty punctuated by uprisings, and, in 1946, it explained a Communist popularity that a reactionary government was too greedy and frightened to admit or accept." Communist Huks preyed upon the fragile nature of this peasantry, who themselves probably believed less in the virtues of communism than in the fight against a perverted democracy. Discarding any future intentions of provoking change through legislation, Taruc and his followers fled to the hills to provoke change through open revolt.

The prospect of just such an eventuality had not gone unrecognized by Taruc and the Huks, nor was it a surprise to government officials. Taruc had already been arrested, released, rearrested, and released again by the Philippine government for inciting rebellion even before he was elected to office. That Taruc and many of his followers were prepared to go beyond peaceful reform and would now attempt the violent overthrow of the government was quite evident. Due to sound organization and thorough planning after the war with the Japanese, it was also quite possible that they might succeed.

Although the communist character of the Huks was not clear on the surface to some, roots ran extensively through the political organization. Huk legend speaks of a political and military training school established as early as 1942 on the slopes of Mount Arayat, a peak which looms above Huklandia, the nickname for the Huk controlled area in central Luzon. Here a competent Chinese officer corps helped to train personnel in guerrilla tactics and politically indoctrinate the future communist leaders of the Philippines. Although somewhat suspicious, the Armed Forces of the Philippine (AFP) handbook records that a "colonel, " a member of the Red Chinese Eighth Route Army, instructed Huks in the art of guerrilla warfare. Works about guerrilla warfare by Mao Tse-tung and Chu-teh were used as fundamental textbooks. Even Edgar Snow's *Red Star over China* was said to have provided inspirational reading.

A village network of Communist Party leaders was established called the Barrio United Defense Corps (BUDC). These farmer-by-day, guerrilla-by-night peasants would take on anti-Japanese operations based out of their own villages. The network helped provide the necessary intelligence information for exposing various targets of opportunity, assisting and providing reinforcements when needed, and simply helping to dominate the local citizenry. But a growing mistrust of the Huks came out of this period, particularly after many villagers witnessed murders, vendetta killings against other Huks, and the brutal techniques often used by Huk policing units. While there was a menacing side to the Huks, there was also the side that protected and nurtured the poor and established hope through sound organization. Still, the power over life and death in the barrio remained in the hands of the BUDC.

With this vast infrastructure in place, it did not take Taruc and his followers long to begin operations against government forces. The period between 1946 and 1950 proved nearly disastrous for the struggling Filipino government. After elections in 1946 brought Manuel Roxas to the presidency, the government pledged to end the Huk insurgency within sixty days. This only led to a greater fiasco put on by the Philippine government and further angered the peasantry of central Luzon, where the Huks already enjoyed their largest support. Incidents such as off-handed killings by government troops and the shelling of barrios only fueled antigovernment sentiment. Soldiers were placed in towns, and garrisons were established in villages and hamlets. Checkpoints were often used by the soldiers patrolling them as a way to line their pockets with "incentive monies" from villagers simply wishing to pass through. If a villager was too poor to make payment, the usual beatings ensued. Rampant abuse was permeating the otherwise confused intentions of the Roxas government. This "mailed fist" approach was widely viewed as inappropriate, reversing the trends that the United States had hoped from afar would take place.

However, two events occurred during the Roxas administration that particularly favored U.S. interests. One was the Military Base Agreement signed in March 1947. This effectively established an American military presence in the Philippines at both Subic Naval Station and Clark Air Field, a presence which would continue for nearly forty-five years. Most important, however, and particularly significant as related to the government conflict with the Huks, was Roxas's signing of the Military Assistance Pact with the United States which created the Joint United States Military Advisory Group (JUSMAG). Now the United States would be able to intervene directly by modernizing the Filipino military, teaching them current strategy and tactical concepts, and providing welcome supplies and equipment to beleaguered government forces.

When Roxas suddenly died in June 1948, his successor, Elpidio Quirino, offered the Huks "accommodation rather than confrontation." An attempt was made to appease the Huks through an amnesty program that brought Luis Taruc back to Manila. Taruc made several public appearances, collected back pay as a duly elected official, and then returned to the hills. He accused the government of wrong-doing and declared that the Huks would not surrender until reforms were attained.

The promising overtures of compromise came to no avail. In 1950, Quirino maintained his political power in what seemed to many Filipinos to be a fixed election. The outrage that ignited in Manila did nothing to mend existing discontent throughout the barrios. Taruc and the Huks felt more convinced daily that victory lay around the corner.

Fortunately for the future of the Philippines, a thoughtful, honest, and charismatic leader emerged in 1950 and took the political scene in Manila by storm. This was the dynamic Ramon Magsaysay, whom Quirino appointed as Minister of National Defense. The forty-three-year-old congressman from Zambalas possessed a guerrilla background but had no formal military training. What he did have was the ability to attract "bright, young technocrats to his service and inspire the loyalty of his men." Above all else, what Magsaysay had was a plan, the first part of which necessitated a trip to the United States to ask for more money. What he got when he arrived in Washington, D.C., was not the check for which he had hoped, but rather an introduction to a man that would eventually bring the most decisive changes to postwar politics in the Philippines yet seen, as well as an end to the Huk insurgency.

When Edward Lansdale was a lieutenant colonel, he was one of those officers that believed that a transfer from the army to the air force meant more "cutting edge" assignments for the future. But after his transfer in 1948, Lansdale was bored with his work. He was stationed in Denver, Colorado, as a teacher at Lowry Air Force Base and was quite unsettled with his situation.

Lansdale yearned for a more active life. After all, he had just returned from the Philippines where he had finished the war as public information officer for Armed Forces Western Pacific (later changed to the Philippines/Ryukyus Command). During the period following the Japanese surrender, Lansdale had made repeated trips into Huklandia in an attempt to uncover the true essence of the guerrilla movement. What fascinated him was the overwhelming support given to the Huks from the many barrios dotting the central Luzon plain. Villager support appeared resolute. Lansdale was not opposed to mixing in with the Huks to satisfy his curiosity further. On several occasions he could be witnessed camping on a Huk trail, often to the surprise of the guerrilla patrol that stumbled upon him. After the offer of cigarettes and a smile, there were brief opportunities to stop and speak to Huk patrol leaders about their philosophies, problems, and even tactics. Notes that Lansdale made after such meetings would prove invaluable to his future mission.

During his early tenure, as his biographer Cecil B. Currey states, Lansdale also learned to walk the "labyrinthine corridors of Philippine politics." His acquaintance with political leaders from Manila, as well as newspapermen, journalists, and businessmen from the region, taught Lansdale what he considered to be the most important lessons of the time: that U.S. policy needed to take a close look at what it was attempting to accomplish in the Philippines and recognize the Filipino people as possessing ideals similar to those that once moved Americans toward independence. He believed that Filipinos and Americans shared the same ethics, principles, and dreams for democracy.

His efforts paid off in that Filipinos gave Lansdale their lifelong admiration and friendship. What is more, they gave Lansdale an incurable desire to return one day and help the cause against Huk insurgency, which he wholly believed to be a misguided communist affair. That the Huks appeared to be gaining a stranglehold on the government by the late 1940s possessed Lansdale's thoughts almost daily.

Lansdale came to occupy a position as an intelligence analyst in Washington by 1949, where he was involved in the rather grey area of psychological warfare, or PSYWAR. His area of specialization was intended to be Eastern Europe, but out of habit, many discourses that he presented to senior military leaders at the Pentagon illustrated circumstances in the Philippines. By 1950, Lansdale was involved directly in preparing recommendations for the Philippine government when a friend and Filipino advisor, Major Mamerto Montemayor, introduced Lansdale to the Philippine defense minister. Magsaysay and Lansdale quickly became close friends, forming a relationship that would endure through the difficult times that lay ahead.

When Montemayor told Lansdale that Magsaysay had good ideas about changing the government's approach in dealing with the Huks, Lansdale's interest was piqued. Not only did the two discuss problems which beset the Quirino government, as well as problems with Filipino military strategy and its general officer corps, but they also found that they concurred on nearly every policy issue. By the end of Magsaysay's visit to Washington, the two men had convinced policymakers that they understood the key to stabilizing the ongoing and problematic Filipino situation, and that there was little time left. The Huk insurgency was about to reach its largest gains in terrorist activity, guerrilla force numbers, and sympathetic support of the population. Shortly after Magsaysay left for home, Lansdale was packing his own bags for an extended tour in the Philippines.

When Lansdale arrived in Manila in early September 1950, he quickly took up his position with the Office of Policy Coordination

(OPC) under the JUSMAG command. After some maneuvering, he managed to be essentially left alone, or at least to his own devices, and was able to report directly to JUSMAG command. Because the U.S. Central Intelligence Agency (CIA) would not absorb OPC into its ranks until the late 1950s, Lansdale had no direct affiliation with the intelligence community outside of his military links. In fact, as a means to extend his cover through OPC, Lansdale had his title changed in Washington from intelligence officer to psychological warfare officer.

His official mission was a difficult one. In just three months time, Lansdale was expected to protect American interests in the Philippines and consolidate a power base for Ramon Magsaysay. In addition, he was to provide counsel and support for the new defense minister, encourage positive change in the Philippine military, and help the government make progress in its war with the Huks, specifically by way of devising political reform that would be appealing to the people and feasible in the given time frame.

The complete success of this mission brought about the demise of a serious Huk threat to the government's authority, the holding of "free" elections, and the cementing of U.S.-Philippine relations. While the end result is easy to see, what is important to this study is the path that was followed to reach such a positive outcome, or more specifically, the way in which an insurgent movement with the apparent upper hand was eventually derailed.

Success did not come easy, nor as quickly as some in Washington had hoped. But by 1953, the Huk rebellion was thwarted, Filipino corruption curtailed, and free elections held. The Huks exist to this day as guerrilla fighters, but the power base they enjoyed in the late 1940s exists no more. How did Lansdale and Magsaysay achieve this? While observers try to give credit to one man or the other, it is difficult not to view Lansdale as the true mastermind behind the success in the Philippines. Some state that Lansdale went on to groom Magsaysay for the presidency, a literal kingmaker. Still others state simply that Magsaysay was Lansdale's personal creation. Perhaps a more accurate summation might be that neither had the power to change circumstances without the other. Magsaysay came along at an opportune moment in Philippine politics and at a time when Lansdale was able to advise him. Lansdale was quick to note that he intended only a background role for himself, and it was the

Philippine people who should receive the credit. Much truth was perceived by Lansdale. While he possessed the concepts for success, it took the Filipinos to realize and implement those concepts. For Lansdale to see his ideas come to fruition, he knew that Ramon Magsaysay, and those following him, would have to supply the necessary leadership.

Magsaysay's talent therefore lay in an ability to understand the primary mission, the provision of effective government. Although the principal difficulties stemmed from the single popular grievance of land reform, Lansdale had always maintained that such problems were politically solvable. Heavy-handed authority and militarism was not the way to bring about a peaceful and equitable solution. Magsaysay could ensure that the government's actions were clearly defined within the parameters of furthering the primary mission: that government respect the wishes of the governed. He could also see to it that the government earnestly sought an effective, timely conclusion to the internal social strife, as well as the political turmoil, something which only discouraged democratic growth. "The blunt fact is," state two veterans of the Philippine insurgency, "that because it failed to do these things, the government of the Philippines from 1946 to 1950 failed to suppress the Huk movement." Hardened discontent had led to the employment of force in order to effect a satisfactory peace. Clausewitz was correct when he implied that war is the final means by which to reach a political decision. And that war had still to be won.

Lansdale's ideas for defeating the Huk guerrillas stemmed first from the need to effectively organize. Not only was he a brilliant and imaginative man, but he was a theorist as well, and "steeped himself in the doctrines of warfare from Sun Tzu to Vo Nguyen Giap." Lansdale was also a student of Mao Tse-tung's writings. He well understood Mao's three general rules: All actions are subject to command, do not steal from the people, and be neither selfish nor unjust. Mao expanded on these rules with eight remarks:

Replace the door when you leave the house. (A frequent custom among Chinese in the countryside was to remove the doors of a house to use as a bed.) Roll up the bedding on which you slept. Be courteous. Be honest in your transactions. Return what you borrow. Replace what you break. Do not bathe in the presence of women. Do not without authority search the pocketbooks of those you arrest.

These were indeed virtues on which the Filipino troops and constabulary during the preceding four years had fallen miserably short. It was also something about which Lansdale did not have to convince Magsaysay. Not long after the two men reestablished their connection in Manila, positive actions were being implemented. Magsaysay was noted for leaving in the middle of the night from his quarters, often with Lansdale at his shoulder, to spring any number of visits on an unsuspecting army field headquarters. Officers were typically not quite certain who Magsaysay was until Lansdale, usually in uniform himself, entered and explained the official nature of their visit. After the formality of salutes were exchanged, Magsaysay began tearing into file drawers, checking balance sheets, duty rosters, and whatever else came to mind. Discovering inefficiency usually did not take long, and once a thorough berating had been handed out, the commanders were given notice that no more would be tolerated. Magsaysay came from honest stock and expected the same honesty from fellow Filipinos especially those charged with leadership in a military already in bad straits with the people. An immediate relief of command was also not beyond Magsaysay. Needless to say, Magsaysay's tactics were creating positive changes in the way officers were treating their responsibilities.

One particular problem Magsaysay tackled was the continual promotion of officers who did nothing but run a desk in the safety of the rear area. There were certainly competent officers performing in necessary rear-area jobs, but Magsaysay uncovered a majority of officers who had accepted these positions as a way to get ahead. To Magsaysay, the way to get ahead in the Philippine army of 1950 was to kill Huks! And as far as he was concerned, little of that was being accomplished.

At one point, while reviewing a promotion roster, he asked about the first officer on the list and how many Huks he had killed. The answer was none. While board members extolled the virtues of the officer's noncombat performance, "Magsaysay tossed the recommendation back, refusing to consider him for promotion at that time. The remaining recommendations were reviewed in the same manner. All were turned down." If an officer needed any clarification on how one was to be promoted under the current regime, he need only check the statistics regarding Huk battle casualties to see under who's sector of control the most kills were recorded. During the nine-month period from April to December 1950, AFP reports indicated that more than twelve hundred Huks had been killed, nearly two thousand for the entire year. By 1951, Huks were being killed at the astounding rate of forty to fifty a week.

Lansdale and Magsaysay spent many hours conversing on such tactics. Killing for the sake of killing was not the purpose. In fact, it might likely be interpreted that body count was the essential ingredient to success. This posed obvious dangers, the least of which was the prospect of unconfirmed or inflated field reports. Magsaysay himself preferred, and eventually supported, a massive placement of Huk guerrillas on combined citizenry farms, giving each Huk family land to cultivate. Although such opportunities were not offered in central Luzon, the prospect of owning land by merely surrendering to the authorities seemed preferable to death. Magsaysay convinced the government of the viability of the plan by holding true to his word, making the appeal more attractive than fighting for disillusioned Huks. But before such promising avenues could be traveled, government units needed to become a force to be reckoned with for the Huk guerrillas, and a force to be trusted and relied upon for the tenant farmers. Otherwise, no Filipino was going to take the government seriously.

One critical change that Magsaysay saw to was the suspension of the writ of habeas corpus, a law which did more to protect the Huks than it did to guarantee justice. Under the old system, it was not uncommon for a suspect Huk guerrilla to be detained only to be released within a seventy-two-hour period if definite evidence on the charges could not be produced. This meant that the most carefully laid plans by the constabulary to capture Huk guerrillas were generally a waste of time, not to mention demoralizing. With the change, Huks that were captured remained captured, and were treated like the outlaws that they were. Magsaysay was pulling the government into accepting the principle of all out war, which was, he believed, the only way the government could save itself and his country from communist rule.

The Philippine army and constabulary forces were now being reworked by efficient officers into competent fighting units. One particular change for the army was the establishment of the Battalion Combat Team (BCT), a more lightly armed force that proved its efficiency in the jungles, where previous conventional units could not effectively work. Huk guerrillas found themselves being chased, cornered, and ambushed all over what was once friendly Huklandia. Though not all BCT operations were a success, the advent of such a diverse and aggressive force, one that could quickly react to sound battlefield intelligence, eventually devastated Huk guerrilla operations.

Great reward also came from the way food and supplies were being denied to the guerrillas. Routes that were at one time unchallenged by government forces became critical ambush points to trap unsuspecting Huks. The sources for these Huk supplies, predominantly sympathizers in the larger towns and villages, were uncovered and broken up.

While all of these factors at one time or another were addressed or even suggested by Lansdale, perhaps his most important contribution lay within the field he embraced so wholeheartedly psychological warfare, a discipline in which he believed his own country sadly lacked any great competency. Moreover, Lansdale possessed what was probably the perfect background to engage in a psychological warfare campaign against the Huks. Before he entered active service with the government in 1941, he ran a lucrative advertising firm in California. Perhaps it is true, that the two professions, advertising and psychological warfare, do share common ground. Lansdale spent much of his time thinking up ways to implement PSYWAR and intelligence operations, and encouraged Magsaysay to create a PSYWAR division as part of his own personal staff. Thus was born the Civil Affairs Office (CAO), for which Lansdale envisioned two distinct missions: the performance of psychological combat operations, and an improvement in the attitude and behavior of troops toward civilians "those masses whose loyalty is the imperative stake in a people's war as waged by the Communists." Thus, CAO set out to make the soldiers behave as the "brothers and protectors of the people." Lansdale reflected that one of the main problems was getting troop commanders in the field to view such actions as greater than mere "politics," something outside the military realm. "If a commander were to practice civic action honestly and thoroughly," Lansdale guaranteed, "it would increase his unit's raw take of tactical intelligence by 100 percent in a week. It often took less time than that."

The combat operations side of the house was where the real imagination of Lansdale took over. If one expected his PSYWAR proposals to consist of leaflets and broadcasts appealing to the enemy to surrender, as such things traditionally were, then one seriously underestimated Lansdale's view of PSYWAR as an art. Though certain proposals never made it off the drawing board, and others did not quite accomplish what was intended, most of the ideas worked splendidly. Some of these ideas deserve explanation.

One such operation included the direct work of the famed 7th BCT, under the steadfast Colonel Napoleon Valeriano. In 1947, Valeriano established a unit of soldiers who were pulled out of the conventional army and trained in unconventional methods. Although not too novel an idea on the surface, what this so-called Force X did was to pose as Huk guerrilla bands, with the entire purpose of drawing unsuspecting Huks into firefights and ambushes in which they would be at certain disadvantage. In 1950, as part of the CAO's PSYWAR program, Valeriano and the 7th BCT were called on again to form Charlie Company out of Force X veterans who volunteered. Taking the Force X principle one step further (perhaps two steps), Lansdale helped to create a unit whose sole purpose was the gathering of intelligence information. This represented serious danger for Charlie Company soldiers, as they were to eat, sleep, and breath among the Huks in the jungle while sending regular intelligence reports out to nearby BCT couriers. The success of Charlie Company was part of the reason why the Huks were being chased, cornered, and ambushed with such effectiveness by BCT units.

One psychological warfare operation which Lansdale conceived had, as his biographer states, "a touch of the macabre." The story is well recounted by Lansdale himself, and crosses the border of PSYWAR into the realm of terrorism. In one particular area, Huk raids were becoming a regular occurrence, and BCT efforts to station more troops in the troubled areas were not working. The Huks felt so secure in certain towns that they openly took over after sunset. The night belonged to the enemy, so Lansdale went to work.

Stage one: He ordered PSYWAR teams to spread rumors, presumably believable, throughout public places in villages and towns, about an *asuang*, literally translated, a vampire. The stories were told in disjointed pieces and were based on the reputed soothsaying of a noted local prophet. In short, they predicted that men with evil in their hearts would be preyed upon by vampires.

Stage two: They hunted for victims. PSYWAR ambush teams waited along a trail for a Huk patrol to make its way by. Letting the patrol pass, they silently snatched the last man, their move unseen in the dark night. They punctured his neck with two holes, vampire-fashion, held the body up by the heels, drained it of blood, and put the corpse back on the trail. When the Huks returned to look for the missing man and found their bloodless comrade, every member of the patrol believed that the "asuang" had got him and that one of them would be next if they remained.

As the story goes, the patrol became so terrified that they cautiously but quickly made their way back to base camp, packed all their belongings, and abandoned their entire operation before dawn.

Lansdale was shrewd enough to use local customs and superstitions to effect very real battle losses on the enemy. In these and other ways, CAO and its collection of PSYWAR teams built an impressive record of successful operations against the Huks. But in the end, it was the sum total of events that Lansdale was aiming for. Each isolated event was unimportant by itself. What mattered was the collective toll that his intelligence gathering BCT units, along with his PSYWAR infiltration teams, could level on the large population of Huk guerrilla bands Lansdale's "total force" concept would eventually pay dividends.

Due in part to Huk miscalculation, but in much larger part to the intelligence-gathering system Lansdale had devised, the roof came crashing down on the Huk *intelligencia.* One early October morning in 1950, a Military Intelligence Service (MIS) team, waving search warrants, stormed a house in the suburbs of Manila. The raid accomplished nothing less than the capturing of the Huk politburo secretly meeting in what was thought to be a communist safe house. MIS teams were trained to carry out just such an operation and did so with perfection. Weapons, radios, code books, and the like were taken with the booty. Captured documents revealed that the Huks believed they were capable of somehow seizing power from the government relatively soon. Magsaysay and his people could never have been more grateful, for the MIS action paralyzed Huk political planning. While some of the communist infrastructure remained in the hills, the Huks could never replace what they lost on that morning.

As a result, Huk guerrillas began acting in less consort after the politburo capture. Reckless and less organized terrorist actions were taking place more frequently. The result was that peasant allies were turning into government informants. Eventually, key Huk leaders remaining at large would either surrender or be hunted down and liquidated. In the end, Huk political organization lacked dominant and imaginative control over its terrorist and guerrilla arm, never acquired sufficient economic support to sustain its indigenous threat, and could not ultimately sway enough of the population to support its cause. With pressure from a decisive and unyielding government insurgent force, the Huks were clearly forced to make desperate moves at a time they could ill afford to do so. The critical lesson is that subversive organizations must be discovered during phase one of their insurgency, and pushed by the government insurgent apparatus into a defensive posture, one where the subversive organization is forced into countering government momentum. Under such circumstances, it might even be said that the Magsaysay government successfully usurped the insurgents' own agenda on land reform. When this was done the subversive insurgent force had little credibility with the people. Consequently, the legitimate Filipino government further "legitimized" itself by ridding the people of a potentially dangerous subversive group that appeared to be fighting only for its own self-aggrandizement.

Before Lansdale left the Philippines in 1953, Magsaysay gained the presidency. It was the crowning achievement for two men who had worked so diligently to restore the integrity of a people and its national sovereignty. Though some terrorist activity persists today at extremely low levels, the challenge of the Huk insurgency, vintage 1950, exists no more.

Malayan Emergency, 1948-1960

Differences, as well as similarities, between the insurgency in the Philippines and the circumstances in Malaya are plentiful. The time period, postwar tensions, desires for national sovereignty, the challenge in political leadership, and the potential communist threat are all familiar ingredients. But while the conflict in the Philippines remained essentially an indigenous insurgency, a struggle between two separate internal political factions, the Malayan threat existed between two non-indigenous political factions the British colonial rulers on the one hand and a Chinese population base linked to mainland China on the other. The opportunity for the Malayan Chinese to join the Malayan Communist Party (MCP), as well as their desire to separate themselves from the already diverse population mix, placed their interests and those of communist China in direct conflict with British designs for national unification and eventual independence for the Malayan people.

As with the Filipino Huks, the MCP was able to build a strong political base during Japanese occupation. The Malayan People's Anti-Japanese Army (MPAJA) was formed by Malayan Communist leaders in February 1942, and with British consent and support, it developed a guerrilla force to continue the struggle. The British were well aware of the MPAJA and its roots within the Malayan Communist Party, as well as its ultimate designs to manage a controlling political interest in Malaya after the war. But because the British also knew that the MCP was the only organization in Malaya capable of conducting guerrilla operations against the Japanese, they took a "calculated risk and supported the [MPAJA] with supplies, training, and direction."

Subsequently, the MPAJA was reinforced in December 1943 when British Special Operations Executive (SOE) landed an advance element of Force 136, a special combat intelligence team that trained specifically for just such a guerrilla mission. But with the end of war in sight, the MPAJA increasingly turned its attention toward the task of planning the eventual seizure of power. The only action which curtailed that early attempt was the establishment of an effective British military administration immediately following the Japanese surrender. When the war ended however, some four thousand of the original ten thousand MPAJA guerrillas remained in hiding. The coming struggle was readily apparent.

Three major ethnic groups exist on the peninsula: Malays, Chinese, and Indians. Immediate postwar attempts by the British to unify some 5.5 million people with such ethnic diversity, fell well short of the mark. The Union of Malaya, the first British plan, only created more problems for an already stumbling colonial bureaucracy. A political hiatus was thus caused by misguided planning, which suited the intentions of Malayan Communist leaders who were looking for time to develop further political support. This support came with the formation of the Min Yuen, a civilian-controlled organization which augmented the party hierarchy and broadened the support for the guerrillas in the field.

In early 1947, Ch'en P'ing replaced the ousted Loi Tak, an exposed British double agent, as the MCP secretary general. Loi Tak had suddenly disappeared, taking MCP funds with him, as well as a vast knowledge of the MCP infrastructure. Things were not all going the way of the Malayan Communists following the war, and this grand disaster did everything to slow them down. Nearly a year later the Communists were still engaged in solving their internal problems, and in some quarters the Loi Tak affair was believed to hold the potential disintegration of the party. Ch'en P'ing eventually rebounded from the loss, consolidated the party under the vast operations of the Chinese Central Committee, and was ready to begin a communist takeover of the government. This took place not more than three weeks after the issuing of the Loi Tak paper, which called for the greater scrutiny of future party leaders. Although the British government had received much information from Loi Tak, they failed to react quickly when he defected and therefore missed a chance to arrest several of the top party leaders before they too went into hiding to avoid capture.

A major part of the MCP guerrilla force were the Min Yuen fighters, which effectively represented much of what Filipino Huks (the BUDC) were to their own brand of insurgency – the farmer-by-day, guerrilla-by-night communist soldier. In addition, there was the so-called Blood and Steel Corps, Ch'en P'ing's personal band of terrorists. This primitive organization was responsible for a growing number of strikes, bombings, extortions, robberies, sabotage operations, and murders by early 1949, but they were spread too thin and terrorist activity dropped sharply by the summer.

While both the Min Yuen and the terrorists operated in the hills and in the jungle, it was the terrorists who proved most effective in the inner cities. In late 1949, Ch'en P'ing shifted many of his terrorist units from the rural arena in order to consolidate a ring of terror along the fringe of the jungle. The intent was to form communist "liberated areas." Now in phase one, terrorist activity quickly increased. Although Chinese Kuomintang leaders were the original targets of terrorist bombings and murder, uncooperative Malayans also found themselves on the wrong list. During all of 1949, some 723 people were killed, of which 494 were civilians. MCP hit-squads stepped up their activity the following year, committing some 534 acts by May alone. The initiation of such widespread terrorist acts led quickly to an erosion of whatever base of support the Communist Malays had hoped for. A better understanding of why the MCP insurgency failed rests with this inability to follow perhaps the clearest of all Maoist principles, the winning over of the "hearts and minds" of the people.

In his superb analysis of the Malayan communist movement during this period, Lucian Pye indicates several reasons for the "cool reception" given the MCP by many Malays. The Malays were much more secure with social and cultural development than were the Chinese of the peninsula. Malayans were always able to turn to the country's industry, while maintaining closer ties with their traditional communities. They generally had cordial relations with the British, who were considered protectors and advisors. Thus, Malays "have been able to recognize the authority and the sternness of the British as those of a teacher and not a political foe." The appeal of communism was therefore minimal among Malayans from the outset, and the hatred by the MCP of those Malays noncompliant with their own party doctrine increased.

Going further, Pye states that the "MCP was too foreign in nature to even offer a sense of security," especially to those Malays who showed the slightest bit of wavering. It also lacked the advantage of representing well-known institutions in the homeland. What the Communists did was to concentrate on infiltrating the leadership of existing groups, exploiting those concerns as if they were their own until their particular agenda became dominant. With a few select killings here and there, the time frame for achieving that agenda seemed to shrink.

In direct relation to this Communist desire to do away with noncompliant Malays, especially those who stood intentionally in the way of MCP prerogatives, was a peculiar desire to keep Malays out of the political picture altogether. Though MCP objectives still centered upon ruling the country, its immediate purposes were served by "maximizing all desires for neutrality and non-involvement among the population. Only in very selective situations did the party require positive cooperation." Participation in any form of political activity was made to seem excessively perilous. Terrorism as a tool encouraged precisely this outcome. "Thus the Emergency progressively took the form of a political struggle in which the MCP desperately sought to create a political vacuum among the Malayan Chinese." Thus, the "hearts and minds" approach was not dropped in the eyes of the MCP, merely reestablished among a selective group.

Because the MCP was placing a greater reliance on terrorism as the approved method for achieving its political objectives, guerrilla units were placed under the auspices of the Malayan Races' Liberation Army (MRLA). The objective then became for the MCP to use its two elements, terrorism and the MRLA, to divide British troops in the field and the constabulary forces in the cities. The MCP was betting on certain limitations which they felt were inherent to British forces in Malaya. One was the fact that Britain, having other global commitments due to cold war tensions, would be forced to place a cap on the number of reinforcements they could send to the peninsula.

Another limitation had to do with the fact that the British were pledged to protect the Malayan population from harm. Since the MCP was directly targeting certain elements of the population through a seemingly unrestrained terrorist campaign, the British were believed to be in a no-win situation. Early on in the emergency, both limitations restricted the government's field forces from concentrating on guerrilla activities. But as police, guard, and special constabulary units were expanded, the army was released from its policing activities.

To the MCP leadership, this strategy stemmed from their own interpretation of Maoist doctrine. And because of this interpretation, Gene Z. Hanrahan points out, they had no intention of relegating themselves to guerrilla warfare only. The terrorist actions were perceived as a means to effectively wage total war against the economy of a superior force, a force which the MCP believed was unwilling to suffer the kind of damage and humiliation it was felt could be leveled against it. When terrorists perceived their actions as successful, the operational use of terrorism increased. This MCP model for an insurgent strategy of terror, which appeared to succeed in the early stages, from 1948 to 1950, began turning sour for the Communists by 1950, when the British introduced new emergency military measures. From 1952 to 1954 these measures bred success and the military defeat of the insurgents. After a brief foray at the bargaining table, Ch'en P'ing was turned away by a government that needed no compromise and demanded total surrender. It took five more years to complete the mopping up operations of the Communists. However, as in the Philippines, communist insurgent activities remain today at a low rumble, bombing and murder a favorite tool.

In looking at the outcome of the Malayan Emergency over a twelve-year period, one wonders whether the Communist defeat was attributable more to government success or to the failure of Malayan Communist strategy? Pye again provides the most in-depth account of Communist strategic imperfections. He cites three specific reasons for MCP failure. First, the MRLA faced tremendous logistical problems which impacted on their ability to organize large enough forces that could, at the very least, fight British troops to a stalemate. The Min Yuen also hampered MRLA organization and reduced its maneuverability in the field. Thus, by 1950, MCP security forces rather than MRLA units were engaged in the bulk of military field ambushes.

Second, Pye finds that Maoist theory supplies and munitions. Since this was the very reason for establishing base camps, as Mao stated, the strategy executed by the MCP contained inherent faults which finally became irreversible.

Third, the MCP was never able to solve communication problems. Crude methods of communication, which included couriers and prearranged jungle meetings, further crippled guerrilla strategy and meant that separate MRLA units could never coordinate and maneuver in a fluid manner under a centralized command. This in turn fed the demise of guerrilla operations and boosted indiscriminate terrorism.

As inept as MCP actions may have been, the potential for ineptitude was equally great for a government which initially believed that it was on the defensive, and needed merely to react to insurgent tendencies. The MCP maintained the notion that terrorism alone was the primary impetus of their overall strategy. They believed the British did not possess the will to stay the course under such terrorist pressures. It is likely that most nations do not have the mettle to stay such a course, particularly when that course may be ill defined, the time frame for success unknown, and the cost too great in resources and manpower. Thus the MCP pushed hostilities in that direction for the express purpose of achieving British withdrawal.

Pye concluded that the primary reason why the MRLA did not succeed against British forces was because it could not raise an army of its own that was competent and large enough to defeat the conventional British military force. However, this conclusion does not fit with the principal objective of the MCP, which was British withdrawal, not the defeat of the British military in the field. It may be difficult to understand, but the one is not equivalent to the other. It was highly possible for the Malayan Communists to have succeeded in obtaining British withdrawal, given their original strategy and the likely British reaction. But the British, much to their credit, changed their strategic philosophy from one which created reactive defenses, to one which created offensive opportunities within an insurgency framework. The outcome saw the Malayan Communists logistically too weak to then sustain a protracted struggle. All that was needed was the proper implementation.

To redefine its problem, the British Malayan government brought in the necessary planners and developed a clear course of action. The important aspect of revised British planning, much like that of Lansdale's and Magsaysay's in the Philippines, was that it was not based on futile, "counterinsurgent-type" objectives. As a result, the British were able to exploit obvious MCP inadequacies quicker and with greater precision. What the British Malayan government achieved was nothing short of stealing the initiative away from the Malayan Communists during the transition from phase one to phase two of their insurgency.

During the height of the emergency, from 1950 to 1952, the British employed a strategy which consisted of three key factors: an increase in able intelligence gathering and psychological warfare operations; small unit force structures that emphasized mobility and concentrated on specific targets; and the initiation of a "new village" program which would effectively remove the rural population base from Communist control. The first two elements, which Lansdale knew to be critical in seeking victory over the Huks, were perfected and employed by the British with clear intent. Intelligence operations became more compartmentalized, and thus, developed into a more focused government apparatus. An example of this is the development of Special Branch, an intelligence group which courted MCP suspects, encouraging surrender in exchange for amnesty. These so-called "surrendered enemy prisoners," were interrogated thoroughly, yielding much significant information about MCP planning and MRLA activities, and providing an opportunity to dispense government misinformation. This misinformation campaign helped to strengthen psychological warfare operations in a way that effectively spread government propaganda into the rural areas.

The use of light military units was also something that aided the government. Much like the battalion combat teams utilized in the Philippines, British small-unit engagements were centered on closing with the enemy and destroying both him and his potential to exist. This strategy finally led to the implementation of a plan devised by a young Special Branch officer, Captain H.S. Latimer. Conducted in two phases, Latimer's plan called for operations that first made a thorough reconnaissance of enemy guerrilla activities and base camps, and recorded MRLA movements and habits. Along with a thorough topographical study came an intense personality profile of MRLA leaders and supporters. Second, a curfew and a supply denial campaign were initiated with the main purpose of keeping the guerrillas from stores of food and supplies. A follow-on tactic was to bait the guerrillas into other areas which were misrepresented by Special Branch agents to be "safe areas" where food and supplies could be found. Unknowingly, the guerrillas would walk into "killing grounds," designated ambush and capture points. Because the plan eventually worked so well, guerrillas began surrendering in wholesale lots by 1954.

Third was the concept of the "new village," unique to British planning and based upon earlier British operations during the Boer War. Now centered on a scheme by General Sir Harold Briggs, the new operational chief in April 1950, it addressed the continuing problem of winning the population over to the government so as to deny the guerrillas necessary bases of support. Because the guerrillas controlled large segments of the Chinese squatter population, constabulary and security forces had a difficult time moving about existing villages and gathering intelligence information. Conversely, the guerrillas had no difficulty learning new information about government forces and intensions.

Like earlier segregation schemes, the Briggs Plan was an ingenious resettlement operation, designed to move some five hundred thousand people into four hundred newly constructed villages, maintained and guarded heavily by the government. In effect, this is what would later be referred to in Vietnam as the strategic hamlet. As such, the "new villages" of the Briggs Plan allowed the successful implementation of Latimer's food denial program, a selective pacification strategy used against the MRLA. How much the MRLA was forced to channel their own supply routes to avoid government security forces was in direct relation to the number of new villages established and the number of people removed from rural areas. By 1954, the new village program reached its height when a large free zone, or "white area," was established, allowing inhabitants to go about their lives without the "irritations and hindrances of food controls, curfews, police identity checks or searches." Its success allowed the proliferation of "white areas" to continue and bolstered confidence among the population when a new constitution was formed and free elections established in 1955. Eventually, "after 1959," Pye states, "it was the Security Forces rather than the MRLA who were laying most of the ambushes."

Therefore, one can see that the three elements of British strategy were indeed three sequential steps, each following on the success of the previous element. The food-denial and search-and-destroy operations were successful because the new village resettlement plan effectively removed the population base of support from the guerrillas. This in turn was possible only after a thorough improvement of intelligence gathering techniques and psychological warfare operations. Because of such sweeping successes on the part of the British Malayan government, one can more easily recognize that it was the Malayan Communists who were eventually reacting to a British Malayan government offensive. The problems experienced by the MCP as outlined by Pye only sharpened in the face of certain defeat after 1954. As an insurgent movement reaches a declining state, desperate acts become even more desperate.

Several fine military and political minds surfaced for the British during this period. Officers like Briggs and Latimer helped to set the correct operational tone, while General Sir Gerald Templer, who arrived in early 1952 in the role of high commissioner, provided the necessary political outlook. But none who were involved understood the trappings of insurgency warfare better than Sir Robert

Thompson. During the Second World War, Wing Commander "Bobbie" Thompson as he was affectionately known to his then boss, and commander of the famed Bush Warfare School, Brigadier Michael Calvert, made the best of an opportunity to learn the crucial techniques of guerrilla warfare how guerrilla units interfaced with conventional force units, how they operated effectively in dense jungle terrain, and how they wielded their truly destructive capabilities on larger regular forces this from one of the modern masters of guerrilla strategy, General Orde Wingate. Thompson and Calvert were two of a select handful of British officers who worked closely with Wingate during those early days of the Burma campaign, playing a key role in planning and carrying out operations for what would become some of he most intense and exhausting guerrilla fighting of the war. Becoming a veteran of both Chindit campaigns against the Japanese, Thompson was asked to apply his expertise after the war to the situation in Malaya, a land he was quite familiar with since joining the Malayan Civil Service in 1938.

Serving in Malaya as a civilian for the better part of a decade, the nature of his "special" assignments often making him appear a shadowy and elusive character, Thompson at first helped direct operational matters against the MCP. He soon moved to develop sound intelligence-gathering measures and combined them effectively with small combat teams in fighting the guerrillas of the Min Yuen. Finally, in 1957, he became secretary of defense for Malaya and coordinated the mop-up period to 1960. While Thompson spent time in later years deflecting attention from himself, giving credit to others for much of what he himself accomplished, his legacy of written works and future counsel to U.S. presidents remains as testimony to his strong convictions and experience in dealing with subversive insurgencies. Unfortunately, Thompson's nearly twenty-seven years of service in Southeast Asia has largely been ignored by historians.

Given the very nature of the established colonial government and the diversity of the Malayan population, Thompson never had the free rein that Lansdale experienced in the Philippines. However, Thompson's reasoning and knowledge about communist insurgencies and the success he helped to attain in Malaya won the admiration of several foreign governments. Consequently, Thompson would have a future role as head of the British mission to Saigon in the early 1960s, advising the South Vietnamese government as well as the American military assistance command. It would prove to be a far less rewarding assignment than anticipated, one fraught with jealousy, antagonism, and grave danger. And then there was the enemy.

13

Benazir Bhutto: A Profile

Introduction

Benazir Bhutto (1953-2007), Pakistani political leader, who served as first female prime minister of a Muslim country, she served for Pakistan from 1988 to 1990 and from 1993 to 1996. Born into a wealthy landholding family with a tradition of political activism in southeastern Sindh province, Bhutto enjoyed a privileged childhood.

Bhutto was educated at Harvard's Radcliffe College in the United States and at the University of Oxford in England, where she excelled in studies as well as other activities including debating competitions, she was the first Asian woman to be elected president of the Oxford Union. The daughter of a intelligent and Charismatic Prime Minister Zulfikar Ali Bhutto (1971-1977), she returned to Pakistan in june 1977, planning on a career in the foreign service. But only two weeks later, however, military officers led by General Muhammad Zia-ul-Haq, capitalizing on public protests of disputed parliamentary elections overthrew Prime Minister Zulfikar Ali Bhutto in a bloodless coup. Benazir Bhutto spent the next eighteen months in and out of house arrest as she struggled to rally political support to force Zia to drop fallacious murder charges against her father. The military dictator ignored worldwide appeals for clemency and had Zulfikar Bhutto hanged in April of 1979.

Bhutto's persecution began in earnest after the dismissal of her father's government in 1977 and his execution in 1979 as she intensified her denunciations of Zia and sought to organize a political movement against him. Repeatedly put under house arrest, she was finally imprisoned under solitary confinement in a desert cell in Sindh province during the summer of 1981. Bhutto described the hellish conditions in her wall less cage in "Daughter of Destiny":

> *"The summer heat turned my cell into an oven. My skin split and peeled, coming off my hands in sheets. Boils erupted on my face. My hair, which had always been thick, began to come out by the handful. Insects crept into the cell like invading armies. Grasshoppers, mosquitoes, stinging flies, bees and bugs came up through the cracks in the floor and through the open bars from the courtyard. Big black ants, cockroaches, seething clumps of little red ants and spiders. I tried pulling the sheet over my head at night to hide from their bites, pushing it back when it got too hot to breathe."*

Released in 1984, she went into exile in Britain until 1986, when martial law was lifted in Pakistan. She returned with a huge crowd numbering in the hundreds of thousands turned out on the streets to greet her, by then the leading symbol of the anti-Zia movement, when she returned to Lahore in April of 1986. Formally elected chair in the following month, Bhutto lost no time in organising mass protests and civil disobedience campaigns to pressure Zia to relinquish office and call national elections. Bhutto's stirring oratory, familiar name, and striking appearance helped give her a strong mass appeal, but she had to struggle to wrest real power from the PPP's old-guard leadership, members of which were wary of her gender, youth, and political wisdom. Supported by tumultuous crowds, Bhutto again called for fresh elections, resulting in another short prison term that same year. She also had to contend with internal dissension among the anti-Zia forces.

In 1988 Zia was killed in an airplane crash, less than three months after announcing that elections would take place. In the November elections the PPP gained a huge popularity in the National Assembly, and in December 1988 Bhutto, 35 only became prime minister of Pakistan, the first woman to hold this office in any modern Islamic state. During her first term, Her objective was to return Pakistan to civilian rule and oust the men who executed her father, she also started Peoples Program for economic uplift of the masses. Benazir Bhutto lifted a ban on student and trade unions. Government hosted the fourth S. A. A. R. C. Summit held in Islamabad, in December 1988.

In August 1990, however, President Ghulam Ishaq Khan dismissed her, charging her with incompetence and corruption. The President and the Caretaker Prime Minister filed a series of references against Mohtarma Benazir Bhutto. Her husband, Mr. Asif Ali Zardari was arrested and imprisoned for over two years on a number of up charges.

Her party was soundly defeated in the elections that followed in November 1990, and Bhutto became an opposition leader in the parliament. Subsequent attempts to oust the ruling party resulted in Bhutto's deportation to the city of Karachi in 1992, and she was temporarily banned from entering Islamabad, the capital of Pakistan.

In July 1993, the President of Pakistan dismissed the Government of Prime Minister Mian Nawaz Sharif on corruption charges and called for fresh elections. The Pakistan Peoples Party went to the people in October, 1993 with a new "Agenda for Change". The programme envisaged government at the door-step of the people and priority to the social sectors. Mohtarma Benazir Bhutto was again elected Prime Minister with a broad mandate after achieving strong popular support in all the four provinces of Pakistan.

Bhutto's platform has been leftist, including food for the hungry, health care, jobs, slum clearance and a monthly minimum wage.

She has been opposed by Islamic fundamentalists who have been suspicious of the PPP because of its alleged leftist. Due to Benazir 's Personal world popularity, during her term Pakistan's relation with other countries improved ,her moderate foreign policy had been credited for improving the wrong image of Pakistan around the world ,however domestically she and her party have been widely blamed for excessive corruption.

Benazir again faced trouble from the opposition. In the autumn of 1994, Nawaz Sharif led a "train march" from Karachi to Peshawar. This was followed by general strike on September 20. Two weeks later Nawaz Sharif called a "wheel jam" strike on October 11.

Bhutto was dismissed from office for the second time in late 1996. In October, large street demonstrations shut down the capital, and Bhutto aroused criticism when she had arrested several rival party leaders who had participated in the demonstrations.

Bhutto came under pressure from the press and public, who charged her government with corruption and mismanagement. On November 5, 1996, President of Pakistan Farooq Leghari dismissed Prime Minister Bhutto and dissolved the National Assembly. Bhutto's husband, Zardari, was the focus of much of the criticism. She had appointed him to the cabinet post of investment minister. He was accused of taking bribes and pocketing money from government contracts. President Leghari also charged that Zardari was responsible for "extrajudicial killings" in Karachi, where Bhutto rivals had been killed by police. She denounced all charges as politically motivated, and went into self-imposed exile. In 2001 the Supreme Court of Pakistan suspended a high court's 1999 conviction of Bhutto, ordering a retrial, but in a separate trial Bhutto was sentenced in absentia to three years in prison. She is currently still in self-exile in London and faces charges if she returns back.

She has been mentioned as "The world's most popular politician" in the New Guinness Book of Record 1996. The "Times" and the "Australian Magazine" (May 4, 1996) have drawn up a list of 100 most powerful women and have included Benazir Bhutto as one of them. She has received many honoury degrees and awards from several countries. She also lectures and takes part in several major world events.

A week of turmoil has gripped that nation, as nearly 60 people have died, fuelled in large part by the utter disbelief expressed over the official explanation now being given in the death of former prime minister, Benazir Bhutto.

On Dec. 27, a suicide bomber attacked a rally for Pakistani opposition leader Bhutto and at least 20 people died including the popular former prime minister, who had returned from exile on Oct 19. In all, 135 people died that day in various bombings across the region.

Bhutto had only recently returned from exile and was being supported by Washington in a plan aimed at forming a political partnership with Musharraf. Since her death, many U.S. intelligence officials have joined the fray in expressing reservations over the validity of the government's official statement into the matter. Initial news reports said Bhutto had been shot in the chest and neck, on Dec. 27, then there was a report saying she had died from shrapnel from the bomb. Later still, the government reported that she hit her head on a lever on the sunroof of her bullet proof vehicle. There was no official autopsy; and she was buried the following day. The Pakistani government has also hinted they know who was responsible. Authorities contend they overheard militant leader Baitullah Meshud praising the killers in a subsequent cell phone conversation.

Pentagon sources say U.S. intelligence is now also examining whether there could have been any other enemies of Bhutto, such as Pakistani Taliban types, who could have pulled off the killing. News sources say the U.S. is even looking at elements of Pakistan's own intelligence service in relation to the killing of Bhutto. Meshud is prominently in Musharraf's crosshairs because of recent attacks on government, military and intelligence targets. Some 400 people have been killed in the last few months due to a string of bombings.

The news agency Adnkronos International was quoted in the Clarin, Argentina as saying a leader of Al-Qaeda in Afghanistan, Mustafa Abu al Yazid, has claimed responsibility for the assassination of Bhutto.

No matter how she was killed, or by whom; most analysts agree that the world's most unstable nuclear-armed nation is plunging deeper into crisis. An editorialist in the Financial Times wrote that Bhutto's death "leaves a hole" in Pakistani national politics and adds a "vicious dimension" of "disintegration".

Parliamentary elections, which were scheduled for Jan. 8, have been postponed until Feb. 18. Bhutto was campaigning for her Pakistan Peoples Party (PPP) when she was killed. The PPP is now led by Bhutto's 19-year-old son, Bilawal Bhutto Zardari, an Oxford University student and her husband, Asif Ali Zardari, 51, a party power broker who served in his wife's second administration as its environment minister. With the appointment of Bhutto's son to head the party, it marks the extension of Pakistan's famous political dynasty to a third generation.

Observers say the February date would probably be accepted by the Bush administration.

Her untimely death has many wondering just who Benazir Bhutto was? She was born into the powerful Bhutto family in 1953, in Karachi, Pakistan, earning degrees from Radcliffe College in 1973 and Oxford in 1976. In 1988 and at the age of 35, Benazir Bhutto became prime minister and thus the first female leader of a Muslim nation. She served a second term from 1993 to 1996. Her father, Zulfikar Ali Bhutto, served as prime minister from 1973 to 1977. He was deposed and executed in late 1977 after a military coup. Benazir was forced into exile in 1999 after charges of corruption surfaced.

Just how powerful a politician was she? Well, after her assassination, U.S. stocks dropped over fears of global unrest. Many say she was a world spokesperson for female equality. Then there is the outpouring of sentiment around the world. Here in New York City, Mayor Michael Bloomberg issued a statement:

> *"Today all New Yorkers, including the more than 100,000 who can trace their heritage to Pakistan, are saddened to learn of the assassination. Hers was a voice for democracy, and the silencing of it by such brutal means – is a shock to all of us."*
>
> *"I am shocked and outraged by the assassination of Mrs. Benazir Bhutto. This represents an assault on stability in Pakistan and its democratic processes," stated UN Secretary-General Ban Ki Moon. British Prime Minister Gordon Brown: "Benazir Bhutto was a woman of immense personal courage and bravery."*
>
> *Qin Gang, Chinese foreign ministry spokeman, said "China's shocked and strongly condemns the terrorist attack."*

Publications

Benazir Bhutto is the author of two books "Foreign Policy in Perspective" (1978) and her autobiography, "Daughter of the East" (1989). Several collections of her speeches and works have been compiled which include "The Way Out", Pakistan Foreign Policy, Challenges and Responses in the Post-Cold War era in "After the Cold War" by Keith Philip Lepor and Male Domination of Women offends her Islamic religion in "Lend Me Your ears: Great Speeches in History" by William Saffire. "The Way Out" (1980). She has also contributed to many periodicals and to the books, "Predictions for the Next Millennium" by Kristof and Nickerson and "Book of Hopes and Dreams" published by Bookmaster Inc.

Awards and Honorary Drgrees

- Bruno Kreisky Award of Merit in human Rights, 1988.

- Honorary Phi Beta Kappa Award (1989), presented by Radcliffe College.
- Highest Moroccan Award "Grand Cordon de Wissam Alaoui"
- Highest French Award "Grand-croix de la Legion Honneur" (1989)
- The Noel Foundation Award, 1990 (UNIFEM).
- The Gakushuin Honorary Award, Tokyo (1996)
- Award by the Turkish Independent Industries and Businessmen Association (MUSAID) on account of providing assistance to the people of Bosnia.
- Golden medal Dragon of Bosnia awarded by President of Bosnia (1996)
- Key to the city of Los Angeles, presented by the Mayor of Los Angeles (1995)
- Presidential Medal, Paul Nitze School of Advanced International Science (1995)
- Medal by University of California at Los Angeles (1995)
- Honorary Doctorate of Law, L.L.D Harvard University (1989)
- Honorary Doctorate of Law (Honoris Causa), University of Sindh (1994)
- Honorary Doctorate from Mendanao State University, Philippines (1995)
- Honorary Doctorate of Law (Honoris Causa), Peshawar University (1995)
- Honorary Doctorate of Economics, Gakushuin University, Tokyo (1996)
- Honorary Fellowship by Lady Margaret Hall, University Oxford, (1989)
- Honorary Fellowship by St. Catherine College, University of Oxford, (1989)
- Honorary Professor of the Kyrghyz State National University (1995) Kyrghyzstan.
- Honorary Professor of Yassavi Kazakh Turkish University, Kazakh-Turkish International Language University, Kazakhstan, 1995.

- Honorable Member of OHYUKAI, Alumni Association of Gakushuin, conferred by OHYUKAI Tokyo (1996).
- Awarded the 2000 Millennium Medal of Honor by American Biographical Institute, Inc. in November 1998.
- Awarded American Academy Award of Achievement in London, October 28, 2000.

14

Victims of Insurgencies in India and Pakistan

Introduction

Mohandas Karamchand Gandhi

Mohandas Karamchand Gandhi (October 2, 1869–January 30, 1948) was a major political and spiritual leader of India and the Indian independence movement. He was the pioneer of *Satyagraha* resistance to tyranny through mass civil disobedience, firmly founded upon *ahimsa* or total non-violence which led India to independence and inspired movements for civil rights and freedom across the world. Gandhi is commonly known in India and across the world as Mahatma Gandhi and as *Bapu*. In India, he is officially accorded the honour of *Father of the Nation* and October 2, his birthday, is commemorated each year as *Gandhi Jayanti*, a national holiday. On 15 June 2007, the United Nations General Assembly unanimously adopted a resolution declaring October 2 to be the "International Day of Non-Violence."

As a British-educated lawyer, Gandhi first employed his ideas of peaçeful civil disobedience in the Indian community's struggle for civil rights in South Africa. Upon his return to India, he organized poor farmers and labourers to protest against oppressive taxation and widespread discrimination. Assuming leadership of the Indian

National Congress, Gandhi led nationwide campaigns for the alleviation of poverty, for the liberation of women, for brotherhood amongst differing religions and ethnicities, for an end to untouchability and caste discrimination, and for the economic self-sufficiency of the nation, but above all for *Swaraj* – the independence of India from foreign domination. Gandhi famously led Indians in the disobedience of the salt tax on the 400 kilometre (248 miles) Dandi Salt March in 1930, and in an open call for the British to *Quit India* in 1942. He was imprisoned for many years on numerous occasions in both South Africa and India.

Gandhi practised and advocated non-violence and truth, even in the most extreme situations. A student of Hindu philosophy, he lived simply, organizing an ashram that was self-sufficient in its needs. Making his own clothes the traditional Indian dhoti and shawl woven with a charkha he lived on a simple vegetarian diet. He used rigorous fasts, for long periods, for both self-purification and protest.

Struggle for Indian Independence (1916–1945)

In 1915, Gandhi returned from South Africa to live in India. He spoke at the conventions of the Indian National Congress, but was primarily introduced to Indian issues, politics and the Indian people by Gopal Krishna Gokhale, a respected leader of the Congress Party at the time.

Champaran and Kheda

Gandhi's first major achievements came in 1918 with the Champaran agitation and *Kheda Sqtyagraha*, although in the latter it was indigo and other cash crops instead of the food crops necessary for their survival. Suppressed by the militias of the landlords (mostly British), they were given measly compensation, leaving them mired in extreme poverty. The villages were kept extremely dirty and unhygienic; and alcoholism, untouchability and purdah were rampant. Now in the throes of a devastating famine, the British levied an oppressive tax which they insisted on increasing. The situation was desperate. In Kheda in Gujarat, the problem was the same. Gandhi established an ashram there, organizing scores of his veteran supporters and fresh volunteers from the region. He organized a detailed study and survey of the villages, accounting for the atrocities and terrible episodes of suffering, including the general state of degenerate living. Building on the confidence of villagers, he began leading the clean-up of villages, building of schools and hospitals and encouraging the village leadership to undo and condemn many social evils, as accounted above.

But his main impact came when he was arrested by police on the charge of creating unrest and was ordered to leave the province. Hundreds of thousands of people protested and rallied outside the jail, police stations and courts demanding his release, which the court reluctantly granted. Gandhi led organized protests and strikes against the landlords, who with the guidance of the British government, signed an agreement granting the poor farmers of the region more compensation and control over farming, and cancellation of revenue hikes and its collection until the famine ended. It was during this agitation, that Gandhi was addressed by the people as *Bapu* (Father) and *Mahatma* (Great Soul). In Kheda, Sardar Patel represented the farmers in negotiations with the British, who suspended revenue collection and released all the prisoners. As a result, Gandhi's fame spread all over the nation.

Swaraj and the Salt Satyagraha (Salt March)

Gandhi stayed out of the limelight for most of the 1920s, preferring to resolve the wedge between the Swaraj Party and the Indian National Congress, and expanding initiatives against untouchability, alcoholism, ignorance and poverty. He returned to the fore in 1928. The year before, the British government had appointed a new constitutional reform commission under Sir John Simon, with not a single Indian in its ranks. The result was a boycott of the commission by Indian political parties. Gandhi pushed through a resolution at the Calcutta Congress in December 1928 calling on the British government to grant India dominion status or face a new campaign of non-violence with complete independence for the country as its goal. Gandhi had not only moderated the views of younger men like Subhas Chandra Bose and Jawaharlal Nehru, who sought a demand for immediate independence, but also modified his own call to a one year wait, instead of two. The British did not respond. On December 31, 1929, the flag of India was unfurled in Lahore. January 26, 1930 was celebrated by the Indian National Congress, meeting in Lahore, as India's Independence Day. This day was commemorated by almost every other Indian organization. Making good on his word, he launched a new satyagraha against the tax on salt in March 1930, highlighted by the famous Salt March to Dandi from March 12 to April 6, marching 400 kilometres (248 miles) from Ahmedabad to Dandi, Gujarat to make salt himself. Thousands of Indians joined him on this march to the sea. This campaign was one of his most successful at upsetting British rule; Britain responded by imprisoning over 60,000 people.

The government, represented by Lord Edward Irwin, decided to negotiate with Gandhi. The Gandhi–Irwin Pact was signed in March 1931. The British Government agreed to set all political prisoners free in return for the suspension of the civil disobedience movement. Furthermore, Gandhi was invited to attend the Round Table Conference in London as the sole representative of the Indian National Congress. The conference was a disappointment to Gandhi and the nationalists, as it focused on the Indian princes and Indian minorities rather than the transfer of power. Furthermore, Lord Irwin's successor, Lord Willingdon, embarked on a new campaign of repression against the nationalists. Gandhi was again arrested, and the government attempted to destroy his influence by completely isolating him from his followers. This tactic was not successful. In 1932, through the campaigning of the Dalit leader B. R. Ambedkar, the government granted untouchables separate electorates under the new constitution. In protest, Gandhi embarked on a six-day fast in September 1932, successfully forcing the government to adopt a more equitable arrangement via negotiations mediated by the Dalit cricketer turned political leader Palwankar Baloo. This was the start of a new campaign by Gandhi to improve the lives of the untouchables, whom he named Harijans, the children of God. On May 8, 1933 Gandhi began a 21-day fast of self-purification to help the Harijan movement.

In the summer of 1934, three unsuccessful attempts were made on his life. When the Congress Party chose to contest elections and accept power under the Federation scheme, Gandhi decided to resign from party membership. He did not disagree with the party's move, but felt that if he resigned, his popularity with Indians would cease to stifle the party's membership, that actually varied from communists, socialists, trade unionists, students, religious conservatives, to those with pro-business convictions. Gandhi also did not want to prove a target for Raj propaganda by leading a party that had temporarily accepted political accommodation with the Raj.

Gandhi returned to the head in 1936, with the Nehru presidency and the Lucknow session of the Congress. Although Gandhi desired a total focus on the task of winning independence and not speculation about India's future, he did not restrain the Congress from adopting socialism as its goal. Gandhi had a clash with Subhas Bose, who had been elected to the presidency in 1938. Gandhi's main points of contention with Bose were his lack of commitment to democracy, and lack of faith in non-violence. Bose won his second term despite Gandhi's criticism, but left the Congress when the All-India leaders resigned en masse in protest against his abandonment of the principles introduced by Gandhi.

Freedom and Partition of India

Gandhi advised the Congress to reject the proposals the British Cabinet Mission offered in 1946, as he was deeply suspicious of the *grouping* proposed for Muslim-majority states Gandhi viewed this as a precursor to partition. However, this became one of the few times the Congress broke from Gandhi's advice (though not his leadership), as Nehru and Patel knew that if the Congress did not approve the plan, the control of government would pass to the Muslim League. Between 1946 and 1948, over 5,000 people were killed in violence. Gandhi was vehemently opposed to any plan that partitioned India into two separate countries. An overwhelming majority of Muslims living in India, side by side with Hindus and Sikhs, were in favour of Partition. Additionally Muhammad Ali Jinnah, the leader of the Muslim League, commanded widespread support in West Punjab, Sindh, NWFP and East Bengal. The partition plan was approved by the Congress leadership as the only way to prevent a wide-scale Hindu-Muslim civil war. Congress leaders knew that Gandhi would viscerally oppose partition, and it was impossible for the Congress to go ahead without his agreement, for Gandhi's support in the party and throughout India was strong. Gandhi's closest colleagues had accepted partition as the best way out, and Sardar Patel endeavoured to convince Gandhi that it was the only way to avoid civil war. A devastated Gandhi gave his assent.

He conducted extensive dialogue with Muslim and Hindu community leaders, working to cool passions in northern India, as well as in Bengal. Despite the Indo-Pakistani War of 1947, he was troubled when the Government decided to deny Pakistan the Rs. 55 crores due as per agreements made by the Partition Council. Leaders like Sardar Patel feared that Pakistan would use the money to bankroll the war against India. Gandhi was also devastated when demands resurged for all Muslims to be deported to Pakistan, and when Muslim and Hindu leaders expressed frustration and an inability to come to terms with one another. He launched his last fast-unto-death in Delhi, asking that all communal violence be ended once and for all, and that the payment of Rs. 55 crores be made to Pakistan. Gandhi feared that instability and insecurity in Pakistan would increase their anger against India, and violence would spread across the borders. He further feared that Hindus and Muslims would renew their enmity and precipitate into an open civil war. After emotional debates with his life-long colleagues, Gandhi refused to budge, and the Government rescinded its policy and made the payment to Pakistan. Hindu, Muslim and Sikh community leaders, including the Rashtriya Swayamsevak Sangh and Hindu Mahasabha assured him that they would renounce violence and call for peace. Gandhi thus broke his fast by sipping orange juice.

Assassination of Mahatma Gandhi

Mahatma Gandhi was assassinated on January 30, 1948, shot at point-blank range by Nathuram Godse, an activist of the Hindu nationalist Hindu Mahasabha. Since 1934, there had been five preceding unsuccessful attempts to kill Gandhi.

Assassination

After the failed attempt at Birla House, Nathuram Godse and Narayan Apte returned to Pune via Bombay. With the help of Dr. Dattatraya Parchure and Gangadhar Dandavate they purchased a Beretta automatic and eleven rounds of ammunition at Gwalior and reached Delhi on January 29, 1948. On January 30, 1948, at around 5:10 p.m., Nathuram Godse got close enough to Mahatma Gandhi and shot him three times in his chest at point-blank range. Gandhi died the following day. Many have also said that sweets were distributed in Pune and other places of India, when the news of Gandhi's assassination reached them through the supporters of Hindu Mahasabha. Shri Dharam Jit Jigyasu gave an account of that tragic day in world history to Muni Jaitly, his grandson, in 2000.

Previous Failed Attempts

First attempt

On June 25, 1934, Mahatma Gandhi was in Pune along with Kasturba to deliver a speech at "Corporation Auditorium". They were travelling in a motorcade of two cars. En route, they came across a railway level crossing. The car in which the couple was travelling was left behind and the first car reached the auditorium. Just when the first car arrived at the auditorium, a huge bomb was thrown, which exploded near the car. This caused grievous injury to the Chief Officer of the Pune Municipal Corporation, two policemen and seven others. Nevertheless, no account or records of the investigation nor arrests made can be found. Gandhi's secretary, Pyarelal Nayyar believes that the attempt failed due to lack of planning and co-ordination. Many have alleged that Nathuram Godse and Narayan Apte were involved in the attack.

Second Attempt

The second attempt on the life of Mahatma Gandhi may not have been an attempt to assassinate as much as a demonstration of anger by an angry young man. In May 1944, Gandhi was released from Agha Khan Palace prison and soon after he contracted malaria. On the advice of doctors, he took a vacation to Panchgani, a hill station near Pune. During his stay at Panchgani, Gandhi was staying at Dilkush Bungalow. A group of 15-20 young men came to Panchgani after realizing that Gandhi was staying there. This young crowd, led by Nathuram Godse, came through a chartered bus. These youth held a day long protest demonstration, but declined to talk with Gandhi when invited. However, by evening, during the prayer meeting, Nathuram Godse rushed towards Gandhi with a dagger shouting anti-Gandhi slogans. He was unable to reach Gandhi as he was overpowered by Mani Shankar Purohit (proprietor of Surti

Lodge, Pune) and D. Billare Guruji of Satara (who later became a Congress legislator from Mahabaleshwar).

The documentary evidence of this attack can be found in the depositions made by Mani Shankar Purohit and D.Billare Guruji before the Kapoor Commission set up to investigate the assassination of Gandhi. However, the Kapoor Commission rejected this theory as many of the close associates of Gandhi were not present during that time.

Third Attempt

The third attempt was also a demonstration. However, people who testified before the Kapoor Commission referred it as an attempt to murder. Mahatma Gandhi began his talks with Mohammad Ali Jinnah on 9 September 1944 which lasted for 14 days. While leaving for Bombay from Sevagram Ashram, a group of Hindu activists stopped him. They did not want him to go to Bombay to hold talks with Jinnah. However, these protesters were stopped by volunteers of the ashram.

The leader of this group, Nathuram Godse, was again found in possession of a dagger. The policeman who found the dagger then looked up to him and joked, "Why do you want to kill Gandhi? Let's leave it to the leaders themselves... perhaps (Veer) Savarkar will finish off the job!" At which Godse retorted, "Gandhi does not require such an honour. Even the jamadar (sweeper) is enough for that!"

Dr. Sushila Nayyar testified to this effect before the Kapoor Commission and she considered this an attempt at assassination. This incident has also been portrayed in the film *Gandhi* by Sir Richard Attenborough. However, it is not portrayed as an attempt to murder but as a peaceful demonstration in which the demonstrators were waving black flags.

Fourth Attempt

June 29, 1946, the train carrying Mahatma Gandhi called *Gandhi Special* derailed between Neral and Karjat stations of Bombay Section. The report submitted by the motorman or driver of the train claimed that boulders were placed on the tracks of the train, with the intention to derail it. The train had crashed into the boulders. The Pune police claimed that the boulders were placed by looters to stop trains carrying goods. The police have not disclaimed sabotage. Since the Gandhi Special was the only train on that route at that time, and there were no goods trains on the section, either before or after, it is highly plausible that Gandhi must have been the target.

Fifth Attempt

On January 14, 1948, Madanlal Pahwa, Shankar Kistaiya, Digambar Badge, Vishnu Karkare, Gopal Godse , Nathuram Godse (An RSS: Swayam Seva Sangh Volunteer), and Narayan Apte came to Birla Bhavan (aka Birla House) in Delhi to carry out an attack on Mahatma Gandhi. Except for Madanlal Pahwa and Vishnu Karkare, everyone else reached the venue through the rear entrance in a cab. Surjeet Singh was the cab driver. Madanlal Pahwa tried to bribe the driver at Birla Bhavan, named Choturam, to let him go behind the podium to take pictures of Gandhi. However, Choturam became suspicious and asked Madanlal Pahwa, why he needed photographs from behind, and inquired about the absence of a camera. Madanlal Pahwa just left, having Choturam think he was going back to the taxi; however, he placed a cotton ball enclosing a bomb on the wall behind the podium and ignited it. The bomb went off without creating any panic. The team had left after abandoning Madanlal Pahwa.

On interrogation, Madanlal Pahwa admitted that he was part of a seven member gang who wanted to kill him. The plan was that Madanlal Pahwa would explode the bomb as close to the podium as possible while Digambar Bagde or Shankar Kishtaiyya would shoot Gandhi in the head, ensuing panic and stampede, using the chaotic situation to effect their escape. Vishnu Karkare was to compound the chaos by hurling hand grenades. However, faced with Choturam's suspicious attitude, Digambar Bagde decided not to act at the last minute, and also instructed Shankar Kishtaiyya (who was his servant) to do the same.

Later, Madanlal Phawa led the police to the Marina Hotel where Nathuram Godse and Narayan Apte were staying and also to Sharief Hotel where all other gang members were staying. Everyone had left by that time and the police was only able to recover some letters and clothes which had the initials "NVG" on it. By this time they were able to ascertain that the members of that team were from Maharashtra; however they were not able to establish the identity and the involvement of Nathuram Godse.

During the Mahatma Gandhi murder trial, Madanlal Pahwa was identified by Mrs. Sulochana Devi, who had come to Birla

Bhavan in search of her three year old son (who used to play in the servant quarters). She was the fifteenth witness in the trial, and Surjeet Singh, the driver was the fourteenth witness.

Liaquat Ali Khan

Nawabzada Liaquat Ali Khan (October 2, 1896 – October 16, 1951) was a Pakistani politician who became the first Prime Minister of Pakistan. Liaquat rose to political prominence as a member of the All India Muslim League. He played an influential role in the partition of India and the creation of Pakistan. In 1947, he became the prime minister of Pakistan, a position that he held until his assassination in October 1951. In Pakistan, he is regarded as the right-hand man of Muhammad Ali Jinnah, the leader of the Muslim League and first governor-general of Pakistan. Liaquat was given the titles of Quaid-e-Millat (Leader of the Nation), and posthumously Shaheed-e-Millat (Martyr of the Nation).

Liaquat was a graduate of Aligarh University and of Oxford University. He rose into prominence within the Muslim League during the 1930s. Significantly, he is credited with persuading Jinnah to return to India, an event which marked the beginning of the Muslim League's ascendance and paved the way for the Pakistan movement. Following the passage of the Pakistan Resolution in 1940, Liaquat assisted Jinnah in campaigning for the creation of a separate state for Indian Muslims. In 1947, British Raj was partitioned into the modern-day states of India and Pakistan.

As Prime Minister of Pakistan, Liaquat was responsible for guiding the new nation through its early years. Following partition, India and Pakistan came into conflict over the fate of Kashmir. Liaquat negotiated extensively with India's Prime Minister, Jawaharlal Nehru, and pushed for the referral of the problem to the United Nations. During his tenure, Pakistan pursued close ties with Britain and the United States of America. The aftermath of Pakistan's independence also saw internal political unrest and even a foiled military coup against his government. After Jinnah's death, Liaquat assumed a more influential role in the government and passed the Objectives Resolution, a precursor to the constitution of Pakistan.

Political Career.

On his return from Britain in 1923, Liaquat entered politics, determined to eradicate what he saw as the injustices and ill treatment meted out to the Indian Muslims under the British. In his early life, Liaquat believed in Indian Nationalism. His views gradually changed. The Congress leaders asked him to join their party, but he refused and joined the Muslim League in 1923. Under the leadership of Muhammad Ali Jinnah, the Muslim League held its annual session in May 1924 in Lahore. The aim of this session was to revive the League. Liaquat was among those who attended this conference.

Liaquat began his parliamentary career as an elected member of the United Provinces Legislative Council from the rural Muslim constituency of Muzzafarnagar in 1926. In 1932, he was unanimously elected Deputy President of UP Legislative Council. He remained a member of the UP Legislative Council until 1940, when he was elected to the Central Legislative Assembly.

Liaquat took active part in legislative affairs. He was one of the members of the Muslim League delegation that attended the National Convention held at Calcutta to discuss the Nehru Report in December 1928.

Liaquat's second marriage took place in December 1932. His wife Begum Ra'ana was a prominent economist and an educator. She, too, was an influential figure in the Pakistan movement.

Following the failure of the Round Table Conferences, Muhammad Ali Jinnah had settled in London and was practicing law before the Privy Council. Liaquat and his wife had a number of meetings with Jinnah and convinced him to come back to India to take up the leadership of the Muslims of the region .

Liaquat Ali Khan as Prime Minister

After independence, Liaquat Ali Khan was appointed the first Prime Minister of Pakistan. Pakistan faced a number of difficulties in its early days. Liaquat and Jinnah were determined to stop the riots and refugee problems and to set up an effective administrative system for the country. Liaquat established the groundwork for Pakistan's foreign policy. He also took steps towards the formulation of the constitution. He presented The Objectives Resolution, a prelude to future constitutions, in the Legislative Assembly. The house passed it on March 12, 1949. It has been described as the "Magna Carta" of Pakistan's constitutional history. Liaquat called it "the most important occasion in the life of this country, next in importance, only to the achievement of independence". Under his leadership a team also drafted the first report of the Basic Principle Committee and work began on the second report.

During his tenure, India and Pakistan agreed to resolve the dispute of Kashmir in a peaceful manner through the efforts of the United Nations. According to this agreement a ceasefire was effected in Kashmir on January 1, 1949. It was decided that a free and impartial plebiscite would be held under the supervision of the UN.

After the death of Muhammad Ali Jinnah, the problem of religious minorities flared during late 1949 and early 1950, and observers feared that India and Pakistan were about to fight their second war in the first three years of their independence. At this time, Liaquat met Indian Prime Minister Jawaharlal Nehru to sign the Liaquat-Nehru Pact in 1950. The pact was an effort to improve relations and reduce tension between India and Pakistan, and to protect the religious minorities on both sides of the border. In May 1951, Liaquat visited the United States and set the course of Pakistan's foreign policy towards closer ties with the West. An important event during his premiership was the establishment of National Bank of Pakistan in November 1949, and the installation of a paper currency mill in Karachi.

In January 1951, Liaquat appointed Ayub Khan as the first Pakistani commander-in-chief of the army with the retirement of the British commander, Douglas Gracey. In the same year, an attempted coup was launched against the government by senior military leaders and prominent socialist. Akbar Khan, chief of general staff, was arrested along with 14 other army officers for plotting the coup. This Rawalpindi Conspiracy, as it became known, was the first attempted military coup in Pakistan's history. The arrested conspirators were tried in secret and given lengthy jail sentences.

Death

On October 16, 1951, Liaquat had been scheduled to make an important announcement in a public meeting of the Muslim City

League at Municipal Park, Rawalpindi. Liaquat was shot twice in the chest during that meeting by a man sitting in the audience only fifteen yards away. It was reported that the police immediately killed the assassin, who was later identified as Saad Akbar Babrak, an Afghan from the same Zadran tribe as Pacha Khan Zadran. Liaquat was rushed to a hospital where he was given a blood transfusion, but he succumbed to his injuries. The exact motive behind the assassination has never been fully revealed. However, Liaquat was an ardent supporter of partition, which involved absorbing Pushtun land into Pakistan. He did not believe Pushtun land east of the Durand Line deserved to be reunited with Afghanistan after its illegal annexation into British India in 1893. Afghans, as well as the Pushtuns living in the disputed territory, including those of the Zadran tribe, held political animosity toward Liaquat Ali Khan because of this, and Saad Akbar Zadran is believed to have killed the Prime Minister after he made inflammatory statements about Afghanistan and Pushtuns during his speech.

Upon his death, Liaquat Ali Khan was given the honorific title of "Shaheed-e-Millat", or "Martyr of the Nation".

His last words are said to have been, "May God keep Pakistan safe."

Municipal Park, where he was assassinated, was renamed Liaquat Bagh Park in his honor.

Former Pakistani Prime Minister Benazir Bhutto was assassinated just outside the same park on December 27, 2007 and was attended to without success by Dr Mussadiq Khan whose father Dr Sadiq Khan had tried, in like manner, to save the life of Liaquat Ali Khan in 1951.

Indira Gandhi

Indira Priyadarshini Gandhi (19 November, 1917 - October 31, 1984) She was the Prime Minister of India for three consecutive terms from 1966 to 1977 and for a fourth term from 1980 until her assassination in 1984. She was India's first and to date only female prime minister. She is noted for creating a dictatorship by declaring Emergency after a court struck down her election in 1975, and also for her handling of the Operation Blue Star against Sikh militants, which eventually resulted in her assassination.

Born in the politically influential Nehru dynasty, she grew up in an intensely political atmosphere. Her grandfather Motilal Nehru was a prominent Indian nationalist leader. Returning to India from Oxford in 1941, she became involved in the Indian Independence movement.

In the 1950s, she served her father unofficially as a personal assistant during his tenure as India's first Prime Minister. After her father's death in 1964, she was appointed as a member of the Rajya Sabha by the President of India and became a member of Lal Bahadur Shastri's cabinet as Minister of Information and Broadcasting.

Chosen to become Prime Minister by Congress Party insiders after Shastri 's death, Gandhi soon showed an ability to win elections and outmanoeuvre opponents through populism. She introduced more left-wing economic policies and promoted agricultural productivity. A crushing victory in the 1971 war with Pakistan was followed by a period of instability that led her to impose a state of Emergency in 1975; she paid for the authoritarian excesses of the period with three years in opposition.

President of the Indian National Congress

During 1959 and 1960, Gandhi ran for and was elected the President of the Indian National Congress. Her term of office was uneventful. She also acted as her father's chief of staff. Nehru was known as a vocal opponent of nepotism, and she did not contest a seat in the 1962 elections.

Nehru died on May 27, 1964, and Gandhi, at the urgings of the new Prime Minister Lal Bahadur Shastri, contested elections and joined the Government, being immediately appointed Minister for Information and Broadcasting. She went to Madras when the riots over Hindi becoming the national language broke out in non-Hindi speaking states of the south. There she spoke to government officials, soothed the anger of community leaders and supervised reconstruction efforts for the affected areas. Shastri and senior Ministers were embarrassed, owing to their lack of such initiative. Minister Gandhi's actions were probably not directly aimed at Shastri or her own political elevation. She reportedly lacked interest in the day-to-day functioning of her Ministry, but was media-savvy and adept at the art of politics and image-making.

"During the succession struggles after 1965 between Mrs. Gandhi and her rivals, the central Congress party leadership in several states moved to displace upper caste leaders from state Congress party organizations and replace them with backward caste persons and to mobilize the votes of the latter castes to defeat its rivals in the state Congress [party] and in the opposition. The consequences of these interventions, some of which may justly be perceived as socially progressive, have nevertheless often had the consequences of intensifying inter-ethnic regional conflicts.

When the Indo-Pakistani War of 1965 broke out, Gandhi was vacationing in the border region of Srinagar. Although warned by the Army that Pakistani insurgents had penetrated very close to the city, she refused to relocate to Jammu or Delhi. She rallied local government and welcomed media attention, in effect reassuring the nation. Shastri died in Tashkent, hours after signing the peace agreement with Pakistan's Ayub Khan, mediated by the Soviets.

Shastri had been a candidate of consensus, bridging the left-right gap and staving off the popular conservative Morarji Desai. Gandhi was the candidate of the 'Syndicate', regional power brokers of immense influence, who thought that she would be easily led.

Searching for explanations for this disastrous miscalculation many years later, the then Congress President K. Kamaraj made the strange claim that he had made a personal vow to Nehru to make Gandhi Prime Minister 'at any cost'. With the backing of the Syndicate, in a vote of the Congress Parliamentary Party, Gandhi beat Morarji Desai by 355 votes to 169 to become the fifth Prime Minister of India and the first woman to hold that position.

Operation Blue Star and assassination

Gandhi's later years were bedevilled with problems in Punjab. In September 1981, Jarnail Singh Bhindranwale, the leader of a separatist Sikh religious group and his well-armed followers took up positions within the precincts of the Golden Temple, Sikhism's holiest shrine. Gandhi and president Zail Singh ordered the Army, led by Kuldeep Singh Brar, to the Golden Temple to remove Bhindranwale and his followers on June 3, 1984.

On October 31, 1984, two of Indira Gandhi's own bodyguards, Satwant Singh and Beant Singh, assassinated her with machine guns in the garden of the Prime Minister's Residence at No. 1, Safdarjung Road in New Delhi. As she was walking to be interviewed by the British actor Peter Ustinov filming a documentary for Irish television, she passed a wicket gate, guarded by Satwant Singh and Beant Singh, where they opened fire with machine pistols before being shot themselves by other bodyguards. One bodyguard was killed and the other wounded.

Gandhi died on her way to the hospital, in her official car, but she was not declared dead until many hours later. She was taken to the All India Institute of Medical Sciences, where doctors operated on her and reportedly removed 31 bullets from her body. She was cremated on November 3, near Raj Ghat and the place was called Shakti Sthal.

After her death, sectarian unrest engulfed New Delhi and several other cities in India, including Kanpur, Asansol and Indore, leading to the death of thousands of Sikhs and leaving many homeless. At that time many Gurudwaras were burnt. Some members of the Delhi Pradesh Congress Committee, long accused by human rights activists of a hand in the violence, were tried for incitement to murder and arson many years later; the cases were all dismissed for lack of evidence.

Rajiv Gandhi

Rajiv Gandhi, born in Mumbai, (August 20, 1944 - May 21, 1991), the eldest son of Indira and Feroze Gandhi, was the 7th Prime Minister of India (and the 3rd from the Nehru-Gandhi family) from his mother's death on 31 October 1984 until his resignation on December 2, 1989 following a general election defeat. Becoming the Prime Minister of India at the age of 40, he is the youngest person to date to hold that office.

Rajiv Gandhi worked as a professional pilot for Indian Airlines before coming into politics. While at Cambridge, he met and subsequently married Italian-born Sonia Maino. He remained aloof from politics despite his mother being the Indian Prime Minister, and it was only following the death of his younger brother Sanjay Gandhi in 1980 that Rajiv was convinced to enter politics. Upon the assassination of his mother in 1984 after Operation Blue Star, Indian National Congress party leaders convinced him to become the new Prime Minister.

Rajiv Gandhi led the Congress to a major election victory in 1984 soon after, amassing the largest majority in Parliament. He began dismantling the *License Raj* - government quotas, tariffs and permit regulations on economic activity - modernized the telecommunications industry, the education system, expanded science and technology initiatives and improved relations with the United States. He also was responsible for sending Indian troops for peace efforts in Sri Lanka, which soon ended in open conflict with the Liberation Tigers of Tamil Eelam (LTTE). The Bofors scandal broke his honest, corruption-free image and resulted in a major defeat for his party in the 1989 elections.

Rajiv Gandhi remained Congress President till the elections in 1991. He was assassinated while campaigning, by a female LTTE suicide bomber Thenmuli Rajaratnam. His Italian-born widow Sonia Gandhi became the leader of the Congress party in 1998, and led the party to victory in the 2004 elections. His son Rahul Gandhi is a member of parliament. He was awarded the Bharat Ratna posthumously in 1991.

Entry into Politics

It was following his younger brother's death in 1980 that Rajiv was pressured by Indian National Congress party politicians and his mother to enter politics. Rajiv and his wife were both opposed to the idea, and Rajiv even publicly stated that he would not contest for his brother's seat, but he finally accepted his mother's urging and announced his candidacy for Parliament. His entry was criticized by many in the press, public and opposition political parties, who saw the role of Nehru's dynasty intensifying in Indian politics.

Elected for Sanjay's Lok Sabha (parliamentary) constituency of Amethi in Uttar Pradesh state in February 1981, Rajiv became an important political advisor to his mother. It was widely perceived that Indira Gandhi was grooming Rajiv for the prime minister's job, and Rajiv soon became the president of the Youth Congress - the Congress party's youth wing.

Prime Minister

Rajiv was in West Bengal when Indira Gandhi was assassinated on October 31, 1984. Top Congress leaders, as well as President Zail

Singh pressed Rajiv to become India's Prime Minister, within hours of his mother's assassination by two of her Sikh bodyguards. He has been accused of taking anti-Sikh stand and not doing enough, in his capacity as the country's Prime Minister, to stop the anti-Sikh riots which ensued, killing more than 3,000 Sikhs. Commenting on the violence in national capital Delhi, Rajiv Gandhi said, "' When a giant tree falls, the earth below shakes"; a statement for which he was widely criticised. Many Congress politicians were accused of orchestrating the violence. Soon after assuming office, Rajiv asked President Zail Singh to dissolve Parliament and hold fresh elections, as Lokh Sabha completed its five year term. Rajiv Gandhi also officially became the President of the Congress party.

Owing largely to the feelings of sympathy in wake of Indira's murder, the Congress party won a landslide victory - with largest majority in history of Indian Parliament, giving Rajiv absolute control of government. Rajiv Gandhi also benefited from his youth and a general perception of being *Mr. Clean*, or free of a background in corrupt politics. Rajiv thus revived hopes and enthusiasm amongst the Indian public for the Congress.

Prime Minister Rajiv Gandhi began leading in a direction significantly different from Indira Gandhi's socialism. He improved bilateral relations with the United States - long strained owing to Indira's socialism and close friendship with the USSR - and expanded economic and scientific cooperation. He increased government support for science and technology and associated industries, and reduced import quotas, taxes and tariffs on technology-based industries, especially computers, airlines, defence and telecommunications. He introduced measures significantly reducing the *License Raj* - allowing businesses and individuals to purchase capital, consumer goods and import without red-tape and bureaucratic restrictions. In 1986, Rajiv announced a national education policy to modernize and expand higher education programs across India. Rajiv Gandhi was the founder of Jawahar Navodaya Vidyalaya System in the year 1986. Rajiv Gandhi can be called the father of telecom revolution. His efforts created MTNL in 1986 and the public call offices, better known as PCOs, helped spread telephones in the rural areas. The work that he did then laid the foundation for a telecom boom in 1990s.

Rajiv authorized an extensive police and Army campaign to contain terrorism in Punjab. A state of martial law existed in the Punjab state, and civil liberties, commerce and tourism were greatly disrupted. There are many accusations of human rights violations by police officials as well as by the militants during this period. It is alleged that even as the situation in Punjab came under control, the Indian government was offering arms and training to the LTTE rebels fighting the Government of Sri Lanka. The Indo-Sri Lanka Peace Accord was signed by Rajiv Gandhi and the Sri Lankan President J.R.Jayewardene, in Colombo on July 29, 1987. The very next day, on July 30, 1987, Rajiv Gandhi was assaulted by a Sinhalese naval cadet named Vijayamunige Rohana de Silva, while receiving honor guard. Though the embarrassed Sri Lankan President J.R. Jayewardene initially attempted to pass off the bizarre assault as "Rajiv tripped a little and slightly lost his balance", Rajiv Gandhi while enroute to New Delhi asserted to J.N. Dixit who was in charge of arranging that disastrous visit, "What is all this nonsensical speculation. Of course, I was hit." Rajiv's government suffered a major setback when its efforts to arbitrate between the Government of Sri Lanka and the LTTE rebels backfired

Rajiv Gandhi Assassination

The assassination of Rajiv Gandhi, the seventh Prime Minister of India, took place in Sriperumbudur in Tamil Nadu, India on the 21st of May, 1991. It was one of the first uses of suicide bombing for the purposes of political terror.

The assassination was carried out by Thenmuli Rajaratnam, a female member of the Liberation Tigers of Tamil Eelam. At the time India was embroiled in a complicated civil war in Sri Lanka.

Subsequent accusations of conspiracy have been addressed by two commissions of inquiry, and have brought down at least one national government. The LTTE itself has said of the assassination that it was "great tragedy, a monumental historical tragedy which we deeply regret."

The Assassination

Rajiv Gandhi's last public meeting was at on 21 May 1991, in a village approximately 30-miles from Chennai, where he was assassinated while campaigning for the Sriperumbudur Lok Sabha Congress candidate Mrs Maragatham Chandrasekhar in Tamil Nadu. The assassination was carried out by the LTTE suicide bomber Thenmuli Rajaratnam also known as Dhanu. Later, the real name of the suicide bomber came to be known as Gayatri.

Rajiv Gandhi had arrived at Chennai about two hours earlier and then was driven by motorcade in a white Ambassador car to Sriperumbudur, stopping along the way at a few other election campaigning venues. During the drive to Sriperumbudur, he was accompanied by a foreign journalist who interviewed him in the car. When he reached the venue at Sriperumbudur, he got out of his car and began to walk inside towards the dais where he would deliver his speech. Along the way, he was garlanded by many well wishers, Congress party workers and school children. At 10:10 p.m., the assassin Dhanu approached him and greeted the former Prime Minister. She then bent down to touch his feet and detonated an RDX explosive laden belt tucked below her dress. The former Prime Minister along with many others were killed in the explosion that followed. The assassination was caught on film through the lens of a local photographer, whose camera and film was found from the site. The cameraman himself also died in the blast. The Rajiv Gandhi Memorial was built at the site and is one of the major tourist attractions to the small industrial town.

Benazir Bhutto

Benazir Bhutto (June 21, 1953 - December 27, 2007) was a Pakistani politician who chaired the Pakistan Peoples Party (PPP), a centre-left political party in Pakistan. Bhutto was the first woman elected to lead a Muslim state, having twice been Prime Minister of Pakistan (1988–1990; 1993–1996).

Bhutto was the eldest child of former prime minister Zulfikar Ali Bhutto, a Pakistani of Sindhi descent and Shia Muslim by faith, and Begum Nusrat Bhutto, a Pakistani of Iranian-Kurdish descent, of similarly Shia Muslim by faith. Her paternal grandfather was Sir Shah Nawaz Bhutto, who came to Larkana Sindh before partition from his native town of Bhatto Kalan, which was situated in the Indian state of Haryana.

Bhutto was sworn in for the first time in 1988 at the age of 35, but was removed from office 20 months later under the order of then-president Ghulam Ishaq Khan on grounds of alleged corruption. In 1993 Bhutto was re-elected but was again removed in 1996 on similar charges, this time by President Farooq Leghari. Bhutto went into self-imposed exile in Dubai in 1998.

Bhutto returned to Pakistan on October 18, 2007, after reaching an understanding with President Pervez Musharraf by which she was granted amnesty and all corruption charges were withdrawn. She was assassinated on December 27, 2007, after departing a PPP rally in the Pakistani city of Rawalpindi, two weeks before the scheduled Pakistani general election of 2008 where she was a leading opposition candidate.

Assassination

On December 27, 2007, Bhutto was killed while leaving a campaign rally for the PPP at Liaquat National Bagh, where she had given a spirited address to party supporters in the run-up to the January 2008 parliamentary elections. After entering her bulletproof vehicle, Bhutto stood up through its sunroof to wave to the crowds. At this point, a gunman standing behind and to the left of the vehicle fired three shots at her with a pistol (still photographs exist which show a man in dark glasses holding up a handgun, and film footage has also been shown in which a pistol is seen firing a number of shots whose muzzle-flashes are clearly visible). Immediately afterwards, someone in the area (perhaps the white-robed individual visible in several still photographs standing close to the gunman) detonated explosives stored about their person, killing approximately 20 people. Bhutto was critically wounded and was rushed to Rawalpindi General Hospital. She was taken into surgery at 17:35 local time, and pronounced dead at 18:16.

Bhutto's body was flown to her hometown of of Garhi Khuda Bakhsh in Larkana District, Sindh, and was buried next to her father in the family mausoleum at a ceremony attended by hundreds of thousands of mourners.

There was some disagreement about the exact cause of death. Bhutto's husband refused to permit an autopsy or post-mortem examination to be carried out. On December 28, 2007, the Interior Ministry of Pakistan stated that "Bhutto was killed when she tried to duck back into the vehicle, and the shock waves from the blast knocked her head into a lever attached to the sunroof, fracturing her skull". However, a hospital spokesman stated earlier that she had suffered shrapnel wounds to the head and that this was the cause of her death. Bhutto's aides have also disputed the Interior Ministry's account.

Al-Qaeda commander Mustafa Abu al-Yazid claimed responsibility for the attack, describing Bhutto as "the most precious American asset." The Pakistani government also stated that it had proof that al-Qaeda was behind the assassination. A report for CNN stated: "the Interior Ministry also earlier told Pakistan's GEO-TV that the suicide bomber belonged to Lashkar i Jhangvi an al-Qaeda-linked militant group that the government has blamed for hundreds of killings" The government of Pakistan claimed Baitullah Mehsud was the mastermind behind the assassination. Lashkar i Jhangvi, a Wahabi Muslim extremist organization affiliated with al-Qaeda that also attempted in 1999 to assassinate former Prime Minister Nawaz Sharif, is alleged to have been responsible for the killing of the 54-year-old Bhutto along with approximately 20 bystanders, however this is vigorously disputed by the Bhutto family, by the PPP that Bhutto had headed and by Baitullah Mehsud. On January 3, 2008, President Musharraf officially denied participating in the assassination of Benazir Bhutto as well as failing to provide her proper security.

BIBLIOGRAPHY

Ahmed, Samina, 'The Military and Ethnic Politics', in Kennedy, Charles and Rais, Rasul (eds), Pakistan 1995. Boulder: Westview, 1995, pp. 103-31.

Alavi, Hamza, 'The Army and the Bureaucracy in Pakistan', International Socialist Journal (Vol. 3, No. 14, March- April 1966), pp. 149-88.

Alavi, Seema, The Sepoys and the Company: Tradition and Transition in Northern India 1770-1830. Delhi: Oxford University Press, 1995.

Ali, Chaudhri Muhammad, The Emergence of Pakistan. New York: Columbia University Press, 1967.

Ali, Imran, The Punjab Under Imperialism 1885-1947. Princeton: Princeton University Press, 1988.

American Society for Political and Legal Philosophy. Revolution: Nomos VIII. Edited by Carl J. Friedrich. New York: Atherton Press, 1966.

Amin, Mohammed, et al., Defenders of Pakistan. Lahore: Ferozsons, 1988.

Arif, Khalid Mahmud (General), Working with Zia: Pakistan's Power Politics 1977-1988. Karachi: Oxford University Press, 1995.

Asghar Mohammad Khan (Air Marshal), Generals in Politics: Pakistan: 1958-1982. New Delhi: Vikas Publishing House, 1983.

Ayub Mohammad Khan (Field Marshal), Friends Not Masters: A Political Biography. London: Oxford University Press, 1967.

Beaumont, Roger, Sword of the Raj: The British Army in India, 1747-1947. New York: The Bobbs-Merrill Co., 1977.

Black Cyril E., and Thornton Thomas P., eds. Communism and Revolution. Princeton: Princeton University Press, 1964.

Bordewich, Fergus M., ' "The Pakistan Army: Sword of Islam"', Asia (New York), September- October 1982, pp. 16-23, 48-53.

Brinton Crane. The Anatomy of Revolution. Rev. ed. New York: Prentice-Hall, 1952.

Callahan, Raymond A., The East India Company and Army Reforms, 1783-1798. Cambridge, Mass: Harvard University Press, 1972.

Campbell Arthur. Guerrillas: A History and Analysis. New York: The John May Company, 1968.

Chang, D. W., ' "The Military and Nation-building in Korea, Burma and Pakistan"', Asian Survey (Vol. 9, No. 11, November 1969), pp. 818-30.

Chishti, Faiz Ali (Lt.-General), Betrayals of Another Kind: Islam, Democracy and the Army in Pakistan. London: Asia Publishing House, 1989.

Chorley Katherine C. Armies and the Art of Revolution. London: Faber and Faber Ltd., 1943.

Clissold Stephen. Whirlwind: An Account of Marshal Tito's Rise to Power. London: The Cresset Press, 1949.

Cloughley, Brian, A History of the Pakistan Army: Wars and Insurrections (Karachi: Oxford University Press, 1999).

Cohen, Stephen P., 'State Building in Pakistan', in Banuazizi, A., and Weiner, Myron (eds), The State, Relgiion and Ethnic Politics. Lahore: Vanguard Books, 1987, pp. 299-332.

Cohen, Stephen P., The Pakistan Army. New Delhi: Oxford University Press, 1998. (First edition, 1984, by University of California Press, Berkeley.)

Condit D. M. Case Study in Guerrilla War: Greece During World War II. Washington: Special Operations Research Office, 1961.

Connell, John, Auchinleck. London: Cassell, 1959.

Coser Lewis A. Continuities in the Study of Social Conflict. New York: Free Press, 1967.

Cross James Eliot. Conflict in the Shadows: The Nature and Politics of Guerrilla War. New York: Doubleday, 1963.

Crozier Brian. The Rebels: A Study of Post-War Insurrections. Boston: Beacon Press, 1960.

Dar, E. H. (Major General), ' "The Pakistan Army in the Eighties"', The Army Quarterly and Defence Journal (Vol. 114, No. 3, July 1984), pp. 287-94; and (Vol. 114, No. 4, October 1984), pp. 412-15.

Das, S. T., Indian Military: Its History and Development. New Delhi: Sagar, 1969.

Davies James C. "Political Stability and Instability: Some Manifestations and Causes." Journal of Conflict Resolution 13 (March 1969): 1-18.

Debray Regis. Revolution in the Revolution? Translated by Bobbye Ortiz. New York: Grove Press, 1967.

Deitchman Seymour J. Limited War and American Defense Policy. Cambridge, Mass.: M.I.T. Press, 1964.

Denton Frank H., and Phillips Warren. "Some Patterns in the History of Violence." Journal of Conflict Resolution 12 (March 1968): 182-95.

Dewey, Clive, 'The Rural Roots of Pakistani Militarism', in Low, D. A. (ed.), The Political Inheritance of Pakistan. New York: St. Martin's, 1991.

Dinerstein Herbert S. Intervention Against Communism. Baltimore: Johns Hopkins Press, 1967.

Effendi, Muhammad Yahya, ' "Pakistan Army Officer Corps: Values in Transition or the Erosion of a Value System"', Pakistan Army Journal (Vol. 34, No. 1, March 1993), pp. 45-58.

Farewell, Byron, Armies of the Raj: From the Mutiny to Independence, 1858-1947. New York: W.W. Norton, 1989.

Feierabend Ivo K., and Feierabend Rosaline L. " Aggressive Bebaviors Within Polities, 1948-1962: A Cross-National Study." Journal of Conflict Resolution 10 (1966): 249-71.

Galula David. Counterinsurgency Warfare: Theory and Practice. New York: Praeger, 1964.

Gauhar, Altaf, Ayub Khan: Pakistan's First Military Ruler. Lahore: Sang-e-Meel, 1994.

Giap Vo-nguyen. People's War, People's Army: The Viet Cong Insurrection Manual for Underdeveloped Countries. New York: Praeger, 1962.

Gill, Azam, Army Reforms. Lahore: People's Publishing House,

Greene T. N., ed. The Guerrilla – And How to Fight Him: Selections from the "Marine Corps Gazette." New York: Praeger, 1962.

Guevara Ernesto (Che). Guerrilla Warfare. New York: Random House, 1968.

Gurr Ted. "A Causal Model of Civil Strife: A Comparative Analysis Using New Indices". American Political Science Review 62 (December 1968): 1104-25.

Halperin Morton H. Limited War in the Nuclear Age. New York: John Wiley and Sons, 1963.

Hashmi, Bilal, 'Dragon Seed: Military in the State', in Gardezi, H. and Rashid, J. (eds), Pakistan: The Roots of Dictatorship: The Political Economy of Praetorian State. London: Zed Press, 1983.

Heathcote, T. A., The Indian Army: The Garrison of British Imperial India, 1822-1922. New York: Hippocrene Books, 1974.

Heeger, Gerald A., ' "Politics in the Post-military State: Some Reflections on the Pakistani Experience"', World Politics (Vol. 29, No. 2, January 1977), pp. 242-62.

Heilbrunn Otto. Partisan Warfare. New York: Praeger, 1962.

Huntington Samuel P. "Political Development and Political Decay." World Politics 17 (April 1965): 386-430.

Husain, Noor A. (Brigadier), ' "Pakistan's Growing Defence Industries"', Strategic Studies (Vol. VII, No. 1, Autumn 1983), pp. 38-53.

Hussain, Asaf, ' "Ethnicity, National Identity and Praetorianism: The Case of Pakistan"', Asian Survey (Vol. 16, No. 10, October 1976), pp. 918-30.

Jalal, Ayesha, The State of Martial Rule: The Origins of Pakistan's Political Economy of Defence. Cambridge: Cambridge University Press, 1990.

Johnson Chalmers A. Peasant Nationalism and Communist Power: The Emergence of Revolutionary China, 1939-1945. Stanford, Calif.: Stanford University Press, 1962.

Jureidini Paul A.; LaCharite Norman A.; Cooper Bert H.; and Lybrand William A. Casebook on Insurgency and Revolutionary Warfare: XXIII Summary Accounts. Washington: American University Special Operations Research Office, 1962.

Khan, Gul Hasan, Memoirs of Lt.-General Gul Hasan Khan. Karachi: Oxford University Press, 1993.

Khan, Mohammad Akbar (Major General), ' Phali Jang-i-Kashmir ki Fire-bandi aur Pindi Sazish Case, (Urdu), Hikayat (Lahore) (Vol. 5 No. 1, September 1972).

Khan, Mohammad Nawaz, The Guardians of the Frontier: The Frontier Corps. Peshawar: Frontier Corps, 1994.

Kukreja, Veena, Civil-Military Relations in South Asia. New Delhi: SAGE, 1991.

Lasswell Harold D., and Lerner Daniel. World Revolutionary Elites. Cambridge, Mass.: M.I.T. Press, 1968.

Latif, Rahat (Major General), ... Plus Bhutto's Episode: An Autobiography. Lahore: Jang Publishers, 1993.

Lawrence T. E. Seven Pillars of Wisdom. New York: Doubleday, 1935.

Leiden Carl, and Schmitt Karl M. The Politics of Violence: Revolution in the Modern World. Englewood Cliffs: Prentice-Hall, 1968.

Lieuwen Edwin. Arms and Politics in Latin America. New York: Published for the Council on Foreign Relations by Praeger, 1960.

Looney, Robert E., ' "Budgetary Dilemmas in Pakistan: Costs and Benefits of Sustained Defense Expenditures"', Asian Survey (Vol. 34, No. 5, May 1994), pp. 417-29.

MacMunn, George F., The Armies of India. London: Adam & Charles Black, 1911.

Magnus, Philip, Kitchener: Portrait of an Imperialist. London: John Murray, 1958.

Malik, Iftikhar Haider, State and Civil Society in Pakistan. New York: St Martin's, 1997.

Malik, S. K. (Brigadier), The Quranic Concept of War. Lahore: Wajidalis, 1979.

Malik, Tajammal Hussain (Major General), The Story of My Struggle. Lahore: Jang Publishers, 1991.

Malik, Zafar Mehmood, ' "Pakistan Ordnance Factories: A Force Behind the Forces"', Asian Defence Journal (July 1998), pp. 40-1.

Mao Tse-Tung. Selected Military Writings. Peking: Foreign Language Press, 1963.

Martz John D. Central America: The Crisis and the Challenge. Chapel Hill: U.N.C. Press, 1959.

Mazari, Shireen M., 'Militarism and Militarization of Pakistan', in Rupesinghe, K., and Mumtaz, Khawar (eds), Internal Conflicts in South Asia. London: SAGE, 1996. .

Miksche Ferdinand Otto. Secret Forces: The Technique of Underground Movements. London: Faber, 1950.

Mitchell Edward J. "Inequality and Insurgency: A Statistical Study of South Vietnam." World Politics 20 (April 1968): 42138.

Modelski George. The International Relations of Internal War. Research Monograph no. 11. Center of International Studies. Princeton, N.J.: Princeton University Press, 1961.

Molnar Andrew R. Undergrounds in Insurgent, Revolutionary, and Resistance Warfare. Washington: Special Operations Research Office, 1963.

Moore, Raymond A., ' "The Army as a Vehicle for Social Change in Pakistan"', The Journal of Developing Areas (Vol. 2, No. 1, October 1967), pp. 57-74.

Moore, Raymond A., Nation Building and the Pakistan Army, 1947-69. Lahore: Aziz Publishers, 1979.

Musa, Mohammad (General), Jawan to General. Karachi: East & West Publishing Co., 1984.

Nasution Abdul Haris. Fundamentals of Guerrilla Warfare. New York: Praeger, 1965.

Ney Virgil. Notes on Guerrilla War: Principles and Practices. Washington: Command Publication, 1961.

O'Ballance Edgar. The Algerian Insurrection, 1954-62. Hamden, Conn.: Archon Books, 1967.

Omissi, David, The Sepoy and the Raj: The Indian Army, 1860-1940. London: Macmillan, 1994.

Osanka Franklin M., ed. Modern Guerrilla Warfare—Fighting Communist Guerrilla Movements, 1941-1961. New York: The Free Press of Glencoe, 1962.

Parimoo, J. N., ' "Night of the Generals"', The Illustrated Weekly of India, 23 October 1988, pp. 20-3.

Pasha, Mustafa Kamal, Colonial Political Economy: Recruitment and Under-development in the Punjab. forthcoming.

Pataudi, Nawabzada Sher Ali Khan (Major General), The Story of Soldiering and Politics in India and Pakistan. Lahore: Wajidalis, 1978.

Peers, Douglas M., Between Mars and Mammon: Colonial Armies and the Garrison State in India, 1819-1835. London: I.B. Tauris, 1995.

Poshni, Z. (Captain), Zindigi Zinda Dili Ka Nam Hai (Urdu), Karachi: the author, 1976).

Qureshi, M. I. (Major), The First Punjab Regiment. Aldershot: Gale & Polden, 1958.

Rahman, M. Attiqur (Lt.-General), The Wardens of the Marches: A History of the Piffers, 1947-71. Lahore: Wajidalis, 1980.

Richter, William L., ' "Persistent Praetorianism: Pakistan's Third Military Regime"', Pacific Affairs (Vol. 51, No. 3, Fall 1978), pp. 406-26.

Rizvi, Gowhar, 'Riding the Tiger: Institutionalizing the Military Regimes in Pakistan and Bangladesh', in Clapham, Christopher and Philip, George (eds), The Political Dilemmas of Military Regimes. London: Croom Helm, 1985.

Rizvi, Hasan-Askari, ' "Civil-Military Relations in Contemporary Pakistan"', Survival (Vol. 40, No. 2, Summer 1998), pp. 96-113.

Rizvi, Hasan-Askari, The Military and Politics in Pakistan. Lahore: Progressive Publishers, 1st edition: 1974, latest edition: 1986.

Rizvi, S. Haider Abbas (Brigadier), Veteran Campaigners: A History of the Punjab Regiment, 1759-1981. Lahore: Wajidalis, 1984.

Robert, Andrew, Eminent Churchillians. London: Weidenfeld & Nicolson, 1994.

Rosen, Stephen P., Societies and Military Power: India and its Armies. Ithaca: Cornell University Press, 1996.

Salik, Siddiq (Brigadier), Witness to Surrender. Karachi: Oxford University Press, 1979.

Saxena, K. M.L., The Military System of India, 1850-1900. New Delhi: Sterling, 1974.

Sayeed, Khalid B., 'The Role of the Military in Pakistan', in Doom, J. V. (ed.), Armed Forces and Society. The Hague: Mouton, 1968, pp. 274-9.

Shafqat, Saeed, Civil-Military Relations in Pakistan: From Zulfikar Ali Bhutto to Benazir Bhutto. Boulder: Westview, 1997.

Siddiqi, A. R. (Brigadier), ' "Of Pakistan's First War and Coup"', (The Rawalpindi Conspiracy including an interview with Major General Akbar Khan), Defence Journal (Vol. 11, Nos. 6 & 7, June- July 1985), pp. 1-32.

Siddiqi, A. R. (Brigadier), The Military in Pakistan: Image and Reality. Lahore: Vanguard Books, 1996.

Sieveking, O., ' "Pakistan and Her Armed Forces"', Military Review (Vol. 43, No. 6, June 1963), pp. 91-7.

Singh, Jasjit, ' "The Army in the Power Structure of Pakistan"', Strategic Analysis (New Delhi), (Vol. 18, No. 7, October 1995), pp. 855-80.

Singh, Madan Paul, Indian Army under the East India Company. New Delhi: Sterling Publishers, 1976.

Sinha, N. C. and Khera, P. N., India's War Economy: Supply, Industry and Finance (Official history of the Indian Armed Forces in the Second World War). New Delhi: Orient Longmans, 1962

Tahir-Kheli, Shirin, ' "The Military in Contemporary Pakistan"', Armed Forces and Society (Vol. 6, No. 4, Summer 1980), pp. 639-53.

Tirmazi, S. A.I. (Brigadier), Profiles of Intelligence. Lahore: Room 30, Faletti Hotel & Fiction House, 1995.

Venkateswaran, A. L., Defence Organisation in India. New Delhi: Publication Division, Ministry of Information and Broadcasting, Government of India, 1967.

Wilcox, Wayne A., ' "The Pakistan Coup d'État of 1958"', Pacific Affairs (Vol. 38, No. 2, Summer 1965), pp. 142-63.

Zaheer, Hasan, The Times and Trial of the Rawalpindi Conspiracy, 1951: The First Coup Attempt in Pakistan. Karachi: Oxford University Press, 1998.

Ziring, Lawrence, The Ayub Khan Era: Politics in Pakistan, 1958-69. Syracuse: Syracuse University Press, 1971.

INDEX

M

N

O

P